THE CONSTITUTION
AND THE STATES

THE CONSTITUTION AND THE STATES

The Role of the Original Thirteen in the Framing and Adoption of the Federal Constitution

EDITED BY
PATRICK T. CONLEY AND JOHN P. KAMINSKI

Sponsored by the
U.S. Constitution Council of the Thirteen Original States and
The Center for the Study of the American Constitution

MADISON HOUSE

Madison, Wisconsin 1988

Conley and Kaminski, eds.
THE CONSTITUTION AND THE STATES:
The Role of the Original Thirteen in the
Framing and Adoption of the Federal Constitution

LIBRARY OF CONGRESS CATALOGING IN PUBLICATION DATA

The Constitution and the states.

   Bibliography: p.
   Includes index.
   1. United States—Constitutional history.
2. United States—Politics and government—1783–1809.
I. Conley, Patrick T.   II. Kaminski, John P.
III. U.S. Constitution Council of the Thirteen
Original States.   IV. University of Wisconsin–
Madison. The Center for the Study of the American
Constitution.

| KF4541.C585 1988 | 342.73'029 | 88-9028 |
| ISBN 0-945612-02-8 | 347.30229 | |

Designed by William Kasdorf

Typeset in Janson by Impressions, Inc.
Produced for Madison House by
Impressions, Inc., P.O. Box 3304, Madison, WI 53704

Sponsored by the
U.S. Constitution Council of the Thirteen Original States and
The Center for the Study of the American Constitution

Published by
MADISON HOUSE PUBLISHERS, INC.
P.O. Box 3100
Madison, Wisconsin 53704

SECOND PRINTING—FEBRUARY 1992

CONTENTS

FOREWORD

DISCUSSIONS ABOUT the history of our Constitution and its creation often focus on the debates at the Philadelphia Convention during the summer of 1787. Although the debates are both fascinating and of great historical significance, they are all the more fascinating and significant when viewed in light of the events that went before and that came after. This book treats the events leading up to the convention, the convention itself, and its aftermath from an interesting perspective—that of the individual states.

After the English colonies formally declared their independence in 1776, the locus of power became the individual state—each one was an independent, sovereign nation; each had separate taxing powers; each could independently maintain armies and navies and regulate trade. The states did share a common language and some common experiences, and they had formed a "firm league of friendship" to fight the war. But after the war, that alliance's unifying spirit dissipated and was replaced by discord and contention growing out of regional and ideological conflicts and commercial rivalries between the states. The story of the creation of the Constitution is largely the story of how these thirteen separate nations compromised their differing interests, and how they agreed to give up part of their sovereignty after overcoming their fears of a strong central government.

The reaction of the states to the proposed Constitution also has a significance that is often overlooked. The United States, as a true nation, was conceived in Philadelphia in the summer of 1787, but it was not yet born until the document was ratified. The Constitution was a compact between the ratifying states, and the people of those states. To accurately interpret the Constitution—to fully understand its meaning—one must have some idea of what the document meant to those who participated in its ratification. The debates at the Philadelphia Convention also provide useful guidance to constitutional interpretation—indeed, many of the delegates to Philadelphia were also instrumental in the state ratification conventions. But the original meaning of the Constitution from the perspective of the states that ratified it deserves further study.

These essays will prove valuable to the citizens of the first thirteen states as they celebrate the 200th anniversaries of their state ratifications. Indeed, all those interested in the institutions which secure our liberty will profit from this volume. As George Mason, one of the Founding Fathers from Virginia, wrote, "No free government, nor the blessings of liberty, can be preserved to any people, but . . . by frequent recurrence to fundamental principles."

WARREN E. BURGER
Chairman, Commission on the Bicentennial of the Constitution
Chief Justice of the United States, 1969–1986

PREFACE

IN THE TWO HUNDRED YEARS since the ratification of our Constitution, much has been written—and justifiably so—about this enduring and enormously influential document. Surprisingly, however, no single volume has systematically analyzed, in depth, the overall contribution made to the framing and adoption of the Constitution by each of the original thirteen states (although Forrest McDonald's *We the People* and Robert A. Rutland's *The Ordeal of the Constitution* took important strides in that direction).

This gap in our constitutional literature becomes more perplexing when certain facts associated with the founding are recalled. It was the states that dispatched delegates to Philadelphia, where the framers voted not as individuals but as members of their state delegations. For example, when two of New York's three representatives—Robert Yates and John Lansing, Jr.— departed early from the convention, New York was left without a quorum, and Alexander Hamilton was left without the power to register his state's approval of the final draft. With Rhode Island absent, the unanimous declaration had only eleven, rather than thirteen, affirmative votes. And when the thirty-nine signers affixed their names to the famous document, they did not sign randomly, but by state delegation in a north-to-south succession— New Hampshire to Georgia. The clause introducing those signatures reads, "Done in Convention by the Unanimous Consent of the States present."

Despite the famous phrase "We the People," the Constitution was not ratified by national plebiscite or local referenda but by state-called ratifying conventions. And the document itself became operative, according to the provisions of Article VII, only when nine states had given their approval.

In the state ratifying conventions, the major concerns of opponents were the threats that the new basic law posed to existing state sovereignty and its failure to include a bill of rights. When amendments were drafted to deal with these alleged defects, the changes required approval by two-thirds of the House of Representatives and passage by a similar margin in a Senate where the state legislatures chose the membership. That upper chamber, apportioned on the basis of state equality, represented not the people but the states. Then, when the proposed revisions cleared the congressional hurdles, they needed ratification by three-fourths of the states to become part of the basic law of the land.

Not only was the role of the states central in framing, ratifying, and revising the Constitution, but the new federal Constitution was permeated with the influence of state constitutions and local precedents. No fewer than eighteen different state constitutions preceded the national document (some states having experimented with more than one basic law by 1787). According to the calculations of historian Donald Lutz, "The states are mentioned explicitly or by direct implication 50 times in 42 separate sections of the U.S. Constitution." Further, Lutz observes, "anyone attempting to do a close textual analysis of the document is driven time and again to the state constitutions to determine what is meant or implied by the national constitution."

The point of this recitation is to show the importance of state action in creating the Constitution and the Bill of Rights. In this era of national supremacy, the key role played by the states is a fact often forgotten by those of us who witnessed the passing of dual federalism. In its title and its contents, this book reminds us of federalism's historic reality and suggests why the first century of American constitutionalism was dominated by the struggle between the states and the national government over their relative powers.

When reading the thirteen state essays contained herein, one immediately recognizes the theme of diversity and realizes the inadequacy of simplistic generalizations in explaining the Constitution's origins. Delaware wanted a strong central government to establish order and command respect abroad; Georgia sought security through union; New Jersey and Connecticut desired relief from interstate tariff levies; and Pennsylvania, led by its business interests, sought economic stability and commercial growth. Conversely, prosperous New York was content with the existing system; North Carolina desired to maintain states' rights; and obstinate Rhode Island fought to preserve its liberty and autonomy. Factions, issues, and motives differed from state to state, so when ratification was finally achieved, the new Union could truly be characterized as "one out of many." Such pluralism is still a salient feature of American life.

This book tries to fill a void in existing scholarship. It deals with a major constitutional theme and distills its contributors' long years of research and specialization into a readable, jargon-free narrative. *The Constitution and the States* is the authors' contribution to our bicentennial observance. We hope it will prove illuminating to laymen and scholars alike.

PATRICK T. CONLEY
JOHN P. KAMINSKI

ACKNOWLEDGMENTS

THIS BOOK, like most others, is the product of many hands and minds. All of the authors generously volunteered their time and expertise to produce a volume unique in the historiography of the Constitution. Like the editors, they were amazed that such an obvious book had never been written (though we understand that one with a similar format is now underway).

The U.S. Constitution Council (originally the Bicentennial Council of the Thirteen Original States), chaired by Edna Flanagan of New Hampshire, sponsored the project and provided a substantial grant to ensure its publication. Council trustees were also instrumental in securing authors to write the various state essays. Especially helpful in this task were Russell Chase (N.H.), Fred Biebel (Conn.), Stephen Schechter (N.Y.), Larry Tise (Pa.), Tim O'Rourke (Va.), and Carroll Hart (Ga.). Four council trustees—Paul Scudiere, Greg Stiverson, Albert Saye, and Patrick Conley—contributed chapters to the book.

In the administration of the project, which involved contact and coordination among fifteen different and scattered authors, Phyllis Cardullo of Providence College was indispensable. She also performed all of the preliminary typing chores. The Rhode Island Publications Society, chaired by Patrick T. Conley, furnished operating capital, office facilities, and the services of its talented editor, Dr. Hilliard Beller.

The Center for the Study of the American Constitution, directed by John P. Kaminski, reviewed all essays for accuracy, completeness, and consistency and provided a wide range of editorial assistance to prepare the volume for the printer. Margaret C. Leeds typed the final manuscripts sent to the publisher, Charles D. Hagermann served as the computer liaison with the printer, and Charles H. Schoenleber assisted in the preparation of the index.

PATRICK T. CONLEY
JOHN P. KAMINSKI

CHRONOLOGY
Ratification of the Constitution

State (in order of ratification)	Date of Ratification	Vote in State Convention	Rank in Pop.	1790 Population	Reps. in 1st Cong.
1. DELAWARE	Dec. 7, 1787	30 to 0	13	59,096 (8,887 slaves)	1
2. PENNSYLVANIA	Dec. 12, 1787	46 to 23	3	434,373 (3,737 slaves)	8
3. NEW JERSEY	Dec. 18, 1787	38 to 0	9	184,139 (11,423 slaves)	4
4. GEORGIA	Jan. 2, 1788	26 to 0	11	82,548 (29,264 slaves)	3
5. CONNECTICUT	Jan. 9, 1788	128 to 40	8	237,946 (2,764 slaves)	5
6. MASSACHUSETTS (incl. Maine)	Feb. 6, 1788	187 to 168	2	475,327 (no slaves)	8
7. MARYLAND	Apr. 28, 1788	63 to 11	6	319,728 (103,036 slaves)	6
8. SOUTH CAROLINA	May 23, 1788	149 to 73	7	249,073 (107,094 slaves)	5
9. NEW HAMPSHIRE	June 21, 1788	57 to 47	10	141,885 (158 slaves)	3
10. VIRGINIA (incl. Kentucky)	June 25, 1788	89 to 79	1	821,287 (292,627 slaves)	10
11. NEW YORK	July 26, 1788	30 to 27	5	340,120 (21,324 slaves)	6
12. NORTH CAROLINA (incl. Tennesee)	Nov. 21, 1789	195 to 77	4	429,442 (100,572 slaves)	5
13. RHODE ISLAND	May 29, 1790	34 to 32	12	68,825 (948 slaves)	1

THE CONSTITUTION
AND THE STATES

INTRODUCTION

"In Order to Form a More Perfect Union"

The United States, 1774–1791

PAUL J. SCUDIERE

State Historian of New York

I N SEPTEMBER 1774 twelve rebellious English colonies organized in Philadelphia as the First Continental Congress, an ad hoc gathering of seven weeks' duration called to protest the perceived misrule by the mother country. When this first fateful step toward national union failed to secure colonial demands, a second Continental Congress was organized in May 1775. Called in response to the outbreak of hostilities at Lexington and Concord, this thirteen-member union continued in operation as the impasse between England and its colonies grew irreconcilable. Finally, on June 7, 1776, after nearly fourteen months of intermittent military skirmishing, Richard Henry Lee of Virginia offered a motion to his fellow delegates that "these united colonies are, and of right ought to be, free and independent states"; that they ought to obtain assistance and sign treaties with foreign countries; and that a form of confederation ought to be drafted.

After three days of debate on this proposal, Congress appointed a five-man committee consisting of Thomas Jefferson (Va.), John Adams (Mass.), Benjamin Franklin (Pa.), Robert R. Livingston (N.Y.), and Roger Sherman (Conn.) to write a declaration justifying Lee's motion. The committee completed its draft on June 28. Although Adams and Franklin helped to improve it, the paper was chiefly the work of thirty-three-year-old Jefferson, a Virginia lawyer. On July 2, 1776, representatives from the thirteen dissenting colonies voted for independence and two days later they approved the final text of the Declaration of Independence. Eventually fifty-six courageous rebels affixed their signatures to this document.

Drafting the Articles of Confederation

While it took seven years of war to make freedom from British rule a reality, constructing a new and permanent form of government to replace the monarchy would take twice as long. When George Washington was officially sworn in as the first president of the United States in April 1789, he promised "to preserve, protect and defend the Constitution of the United States." This pledge, made by every president since Washington, marked the successful culmination of a long and painful effort to establish a secure and independent nation.

When Congress appointed a committee to draft the Declaration of Independence, it also appointed a committee to prepare a formal plan of confederation for the thirteen newly proclaimed states. The committee, headed by John Dickinson of Pennsylvania and Delaware, developed a plan and reported on July 12, 1776.

The Dickinson proposal called for the creation of a central legislature in which each state would have one vote, regardless of its size and population. Dickinson's arrangement further provided that the expenses of the national legislature would be apportioned among the states according to the value of all land within their borders, and that the acquisition of western lands by any colony would not be restricted.

The Dickinson report was debated intermittently for a year and a half, and, after some substantial amendments, the Articles of Confederation were approved by Congress on November 15, 1777. This first national constitution began by declaring that "the style of this Confederacy shall be 'The United States of America.' " Under it, each of the thirteen former colonies was designated a state, and each retained "sovereignty, freedom and independence, and every power, jurisdiction, and right, which is not . . . expressly delegated to the United States, in Congress assembled." The thirteen states agreed to what was termed "a firm league of friendship."

The central government under the Articles consisted of a one-house Congress, with each state represented by not less than two nor more than seven delegates. However, in accordance with the Dickinson report, each state delegation had one vote, with a majority of nine needed to make major decisions and a unanimous vote of the state legislatures necessary to amend the Articles.

This new national Congress had the sole right to declare war and make peace, to name ambassadors to and receive them from foreign governments, and to negotiate treaties and alliances. It was empowered to determine the value of United States coins and those issued by the states, to fix the standards of weights and measures, to establish and regulate post offices, to appoint all United States military and naval officers, and to supervise Indian affairs.

The closest the Articles came to an executive branch was a Committee of the States, consisting of one delegate from each, to act only during congressional recesses. There was no supreme court. The highest tribunal consisted of judges appointed by states involved in disputes with one another or chosen from a panel of three jurists from each of the thirteen states.

The Articles of Confederation, which were accepted by Congress while war with Britain was still raging, demonstrated deep distrust of central authority. One indication of this suspicion was the absence of a separate executive branch. Another was the weak Congress, lacking in coercive power over individual citizens or states. Fear of central legislatures like the British Parliament made the revolutionaries reluctant to endow Congress with strength. So did their concern for the independence of the states, which retained control over their own commerce, the right to coin money, and the power to levy taxes. Despite the need for a coordinated central government, it took almost four years to secure formal approval of the Articles from all the states. This delay was due, in part, to the unwillingness of some states to assign their western land claims to the national government, and to Maryland's refusal to ratify until such cessions were acknowledged. Eventually it was the struggle to win the war, coupled with Virginia's statement in principle that its western lands would be ceded to Congress, that secured Maryland's ratification of the Articles, thus putting the new central government into operation.

Shortcomings of the Articles of Confederation

Even before the Articles of Confederation became effective on March 1, 1781, the voices of critics could be heard. One of the most outspoken was New York's Alexander Hamilton, who lamented the absence of a strong central government, declaring that "an uncontrollable sovereignty in each state will make our nation feeble and precarious." As the critics pointed out, Congress' inability to regulate commerce and its powerlessness to enforce the collection of taxes and the raising of troops were major deficiencies in the Articles. Yet, in spite of these concerns, fear of government too far removed from local control and strong states' rights sentiments worked against any effort to strengthen the central government.

Aggressive commercial competition between Virginia and Maryland finally led both of these states to agree that something needed to be done to correct the weaknesses of the Articles with respect to interstate commerce. Delegates from these rival sovereignties met at the Mount Vernon home of George Washington in March 1785 to resolve differences over the navigation of the Potomac River and Chesapeake Bay.

The legislature of Maryland believed that the cooperation of Pennsylvania and Delaware was also necessary to ensure the smooth flow of interstate commerce in the mid-Atlantic region. Virginia went even further in January 1786 by inviting all the states to a convention in Annapolis, Maryland, to examine the trade relations of the states. Only five states participated in this brief September conclave: Delaware, New Jersey, New York, Pennsylvania, and Virginia. Four other states—Massachusetts, New Hampshire, North Carolina, and Rhode Island—appointed delegates, but they delayed attending, so the five states already in Annapolis met without them. Georgia, South Carolina, Connecticut, and Maryland believed a convention of all the states was either unnecessary or dangerous and did not send delegates.

Mount Vernon, the Virginia home of George Washington, seen from the east side of the mansion that looks across the Potomac to the Maryland shore. Courtesy of Mount Vernon Ladies Association.

The Need for a Constitutional Convention

Although there was much discussion at Annapolis about the weaknesses of the Articles of Confederation, it was clear, with only five states present, that the convention could not speak with real authority. At this point Alexander Hamilton proposed that a nationwide meeting be held in Philadelphia in May 1787 to improve the Articles of Confederation. The proposal was sent to the Confederation Congress and the governors of every state. After several months, Congress agreed in mid-February 1787 to call a convention of the states to meet in Philadelphia to revise the Articles of Confederation.

Five states—Virginia, Delaware, New Jersey, North Carolina, and Pennsylvania—responded to the Annapolis Convention's call for a general convention by naming delegates before Congress officially sanctioned such a meeting. These states were then joined by Georgia, Maryland, Massachusetts, New York, South Carolina, and Connecticut. New Hampshire ap-

Mann's Tavern, site of the Annapolis Convention. Sketch from original sources by Polli Rodriguez, courtesy of the Maryland State Archives.

pointed its delegates one month after the convention's scheduled May 14 opening, and they failed to arrive until July 23. Contrary Rhode Island, "home of the otherwise-minded," refused on three separate occasions to participate.

In all, fifty-five delegates attended at least some of the convention sessions. These so-called Founding Fathers ranged in age from twenty-six (Jonathan Dayton of New Jersey) to eighty-one (Benjamin Franklin), with an average age of forty-five. More than half the delegates had some college education. Lawyers were in the majority, followed by merchants and planters.

George Washington and multitalented Benjamin Franklin were the best-known delegates. Because of his great prestige and proven leadership ability, Washington was chosen president of the convention. Prominent roles in the debates were also played by such notables as James Madison, Edmund Randolph, and George Mason of Virginia; Gouverneur Morris and James Wilson of Pennsylvania; Roger Sherman and Oliver Ellsworth of Connecticut; Elbridge Gerry and Rufus King of Massachusetts; William Paterson of New Jersey; Charles Pinckney of South Carolina; and John Dickinson of Delaware. William Jackson of Pennsylvania was appointed secretary of the convention, which met in secret sessions closed to the public and the press.

Conspicuous by their absence were lawyers Thomas Jefferson and John Adams, both of whom were on diplomatic assignments in Europe, and Revolutionary leaders Thomas Paine of Pennsylvania, Abraham Clark of New Jersey, Samuel Adams of Massachusetts, and Patrick Henry and Richard Henry Lee of Virginia.

The Debates in the Constitutional Convention

On May 29 Governor Edmund Randolph of Virginia introduced a proposal, drafted primarily by Madison, which directed the course of the convention by becoming the blueprint for the Constitution. Randolph claimed that because the Articles of Confederation were ineffective they must be thoroughly revised in order to promote "the common defense, security of liberty, and general welfare" of the country. Randolph believed that these objectives could be accomplished only by strengthening the central government and making it national rather than federal in character.

The so-called Virginia Plan proposed a bicameral, or two-house, Congress. Members of the lower house would be elected by the qualified voters in each state. The number of representatives from each state would be determined either by the amount which that state contributed to support the national government or by its total number of free inhabitants. Delegates in the upper house, apportioned like those in the lower house, would be nominated by their respective state legislatures and elected by the lower house for unspecified terms. Each member of Congress was to have one vote. No member would be eligible for immediate reelection.

According to the Virginia Plan, each house of this national Congress could originate bills and enact laws in all cases in which the separate states were not permitted to act. The proposal gave Congress the power to invalidate state laws which were in conflict with the national interest and provided for the use of national force against states that acted contrary to the national welfare. The plan proposed an executive elected for one term by Congress and possessing the administrative powers that the Congress exercised under the Articles of Confederation. It also called for a national judiciary consisting of a supreme court selected by Congress, the judges to hold office during "good behavior." The executive and a number of judges could serve as a council of revision to veto acts of Congress.

Despite some opposition to the Virginia Plan, many Convention delegates were convinced that the Articles of Confederation did not provide the necessary national security, and a resolution in support of the plan was finally approved. The only states that did not endorse the resolution were New York, which was divided; New Jersey, which lacked a quorum; New Hampshire, which was unrepresented until July 23; and Connecticut, which was definitely opposed.

Independence Hall in Philadelphia, designed by lawyer Andrew Hamilton, was built as the state house for the province of Pennsylvania. Begun in 1732, the structure was not completed until 1756. In 1775 the Second Continental Congress met in the east room of the ground floor. Here, on July 4, 1776, it adopted the Declaration of Independence. Eleven years later the Constitutional Convention assembled in the same room to draft a new basic law for the United States of America. Photo by Jack E. Boucher, 1974, courtesy of the National Park Service.

The Virginia (or large state) Plan prompted a number of counter-proposals. The small states were convinced that they would lose much of their power under the Virginia formula if it were allowed to stand. They were against using population or wealth as a basis for representation in Congress because such an arrangement gave too much influence to the three large states of Virginia, Massachusetts, and Pennsylvania. Primarily because of this concern, William Paterson of New Jersey offered nine resolutions to modify the Articles of Confederation. Paterson's proposals, which collectively became known as the New Jersey (or small state) Plan, called for continuation of a one-house legislature with expanded, though limited, authority and equal representation for each state. It also provided for an executive consisting of a small committee which could be removed by a majority of the states. However, the New Jersey proposal included a supreme court and a provision making federal laws and treaties the "supreme law" and binding upon the states. This provision became the basis of the national supremacy clause in the final document.

Alexander Hamilton saw weaknesses in both the Virginia and New Jersey plans. He advanced his own prescription for a strong national government by recommending a two-house legislature, with the members of one house elected by the people for three-year terms and the members of the other

This is an interior view of Independence Hall showing the restored assembly room where both the Declaration of Independence and the Constitution were debated and signed. Restored Assembly Room, photo by Jack E. Boucher, 1974, courtesy of the National Park Service.

house selected by electors chosen by the people. In Hamilton's scheme, there would be a strong executive who had the power to veto acts of Congress and who would serve as commander in chief of the armed forces. Twelve judges would constitute the supreme court. The upper house, the executive, and the judiciary would have lifetime terms. Under Hamilton's plan, all state laws contrary to the national interest could be declared invalid, and no state was permitted to have land or naval forces.

Revealing a passion for order and stability, the Hamilton Plan was too extreme, even for the advocates of a strong national government. It was rejected, and the issue again became whether to refine the Virginia Plan or to substitute the New Jersey Plan. By a vote of seven states to three, the New Jersey Plan was rejected, but several small states would still oppose the relinquishment of state equality in the national legislature.

To remove this impasse over representation, the Connecticut delegation proposed the "Great Compromise" whereby the lower house would be apportioned on the basis of population and an upper house, or Senate, would be organized on the principle of equal state representation. After much debate and refinement the convention adopted this proposal and established a two-house legislature wherein the number of state representatives in the lower house would be determined by a state's white population plus three-fifths of its slaves. (It is interesting to note that the northern states wanted to exclude all slaves from the population count and the South wanted to include all of them.) The upper house would consist of two senators from each state.

The task of structuring the executive branch was one of the most difficult issues facing the convention. Some delegates saw a single executive as no different from a king, especially if his term were lengthy and he was eligible to be reelected. Others opposed the direct election of the executive by the people, fearing that the masses were not qualified to make such a decision. Some were afraid that the larger states would have an advantage if the election of an executive were based on the popular vote. In all, five different methods of choosing the president were proposed.

Despite these apprehensions and reservations, the delegates reached a compromise by which a single executive would be elected for a four-year term. He would be chosen by electors from each state, these electors to be appointed in a manner devised by their respective state legislatures and to be equal in number to the total of senators and representatives each state had in Congress. As a check on the other two branches of government, the president could veto acts of Congress, his veto subject to an override by two-thirds of the membership of both congressional houses.

There was general agreement among the convention delegates on the need for a judicial system headed by a supreme court. The final draft of the Constitution included such a tribunal, with its judges nominated by the president and approved by the Senate. The new basic law also empowered Congress to establish such "inferior" federal courts as it thought necessary.

The Constitution gave the national government much of the authority that it lacked under the Articles of Confederation, including the power to regulate interstate commerce, to enforce the collection of taxes, to raise an army and navy, and to compel compliance with treaties. The central government could now act directly on individuals and bypass the states. It was given the "coercion of law" over its citizens. In addition, the Constitution was more flexible: it could be amended if three-quarters of the states assented, whereas the Articles had required unanimity. On the negative side, the document in three clauses (those dealing with congressional apportionment, the foreign slave trade, and fugitive slaves) sanctioned the system of slavery without mentioning the odious word explicitly.

"Signing the Constitution," a twenty-by-thirty-foot oil painting by Howard Chandler Christy (1873–1952), was dedicated in 1940 to hang in the United States Capitol. Though the work ranks high in popular esteem, Christy's pedantic biographer contends that the accuracy Christy claimed in the likenesses of the signatories and in the carefully recorded details was "defeated by his prettified, glossy treatment and by the monotonous overemphasis of all the parts." From the podium George Washington dominates the scene, as he dominated American public life during the last quarter of the eighteenth century. Painting by Howard Chandler Christy. Courtesy of the American Studies Center, Washington, D.C.

Responsibility for the final draft of the Constitution was given to a special Committee of Style headed by William Samuel Johnson of Connecticut and consisting of Gouverneur Morris, Alexander Hamilton, Rufus King, and James Madison. Morris was the prime draftsman. The proposed Constitution was approved by eleven state delegations (New York lacked a quorum) on September 17, 1787. Of the forty-two members still present, three refused to sign the document—Elbridge Gerry of Massachusetts and Edmund Randolph and George Mason of Virginia. The nonsigners objected because a bill of rights was not included. They wanted the state ratifying conventions to submit amendments to a second general convention.

The Constitution and the Confederation Congress

The Constitution was read in the Confederation Congress on September 20, 1787. Some members of Congress criticized the convention delegates for violating their instructions, the resolution of Congress calling the Convention, and the Articles themselves in providing for the ratification of the new Constitution by nine state conventions instead of by the unanimous approval of the state legislatures. Nevertheless, Congress voted on September 28 to transmit the Constitution to the states, recommending that the legislatures call special conventions elected by the people to consider the Constitution in accordance with Article VII of the proposed document, which stated that "the ratification of the conventions of nine states shall be sufficient for the establishment of this Constitution between the states so ratifying the same."

The Ratification of the Constitution

The states were divided over the merits of the Constitution. Its supporters, led by such nationalists as George Washington, Alexander Hamilton, James Wilson, and James Madison, were known as Federalists. Generally, they drew their following from the commercial interests, including exporting farmers. Federalists believed that only a strong central government could preserve the United States from internal conflicts, win respect from other countries, and protect the rights of the people.

The opponents of ratification, known as Antifederalists, were led by such prominent Revolutionary figures as Patrick Henry, Richard Henry Lee, and George Mason of Virginia; George Clinton of New York; and Samuel Adams of Massachusetts. Antifederalists argued that the United States was too large to be governed by one central government; to function effectively, they contended, such a government would need to be so strong that it would be dictatorial. Antifederalists, whose main numerical support came from subsistence farmers in more remote rural areas, believed that the smaller states would be dominated by the larger ones. They also claimed that under the Constitution the powers of the president would be like those of a king, and the role of Congress like that of Parliament—and kingship and Parliament were both institutions rejected by the Revolution. The Antifederalists' most formidable objection, however, was that the Constitution neglected to protect individual liberties from the strong central government by a bill of rights. Had a popular national referendum been conducted on the Constitution in December 1787, most historians of ratification believe Antifederalists would likely have prevailed by a narrow margin.

Both the supporters and the opponents of the Constitution wrote extensively to explain and promote their positions. Broadsides and pamphlets flooded the country, and the nation's almost 100 newspapers were filled with articles and letters for and against the new basic law. Samuel Adams of Massachusetts wrote, "If the several states in the union are to become one entire nation under one legislature . . . and its laws be supreme . . . the idea

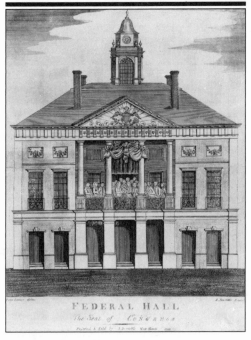

Federal Hall in New York City served as the U.S. Capitol in 1787 and as the meeting place of the Confederation Congress. Several delegates to that body also represented their states at the Philadelphia Convention and moved between the two cities. When the ordeal of constitution-making was over, Washington took his oath of office as the nation's first president on the balcony of Federal Hall on April 30, 1789, in the scene depicted by this contemporary print. Engraving (ca. 1790) by Amos Doolittle after a drawing by Peter Lacour, I. N. Phelps Stokes Collection, New York Public Library.

of freedom in these states must be lost." Adams predicted frequent insurrections by the states if the Constitution was adopted. Richard Henry Lee
of Virginia, who had introduced the resolution which led to the Declaration
of Independence, also opposed the Constitution. Lee wrote: "The plan of
government now proposed is evidently calculated totally to change, in time,
our condition as a people. When power is once transferred from the many
to the few, all changes become extremely difficult."

Two New York delegates, Robert Yates and John Lansing, who had
left the Philadelphia Convention in disgust long before the Constitution was
completed, rendering New York unable to participate, opposed ratification
because they believed the proposed national government would interfere with
the rights of the states. New York's governor George Clinton agreed with
this argument, as did Patrick Henry of Virginia.

The supporters of the Constitution were equally zealous in promoting ratification. The most notable work of these Federalists began with
a series of eighty-five essays by Hamilton, Madison and John Jay printed in
the New York City newspapers under the title *The Federalist*. The essays
(fifty-one by Hamilton, twenty-nine by Madison, and five by Jay) were published in two volumes in March and May 1788.

The Federalist was a skillful effort to convince the people of New
York and other states of the merits of the Constitution. Although clearly
propaganda in support of ratification, the arguments set forth by Hamilton,
Madison, and Jay won praise even from those who did not originally favor
the Constitution. Thomas Jefferson, for example, called *The Federalist* "the
best commentary on the principles of government ever written." Despite
their intrinsic excellence, however, these essays were geared to a learned
audience and had only a slight impact on public opinion in New York.

While the question of ratification was being argued, special conventions of the states were already taking formal action on the Constitution.
Tiny Delaware was the first state to make its decision. On December 7, 1787,
its convention unanimously endorsed the Constitution. Most of the smaller
states felt there were enough safeguards in the Constitution to protect them
from large-state domination, and they believed that their economic and military security would be enhanced by the new system of union.

After much local discussion, Pennsylvania became the first large state
to approve the Constitution. In general, residents from Philadelphia and other
towns with important commercial interests favored the document, while the
farming and frontier sections opposed it. Since the commercial interests were
able to dominate Pennsylvania's convention, the Keystone State approved
the new national charter on December 12, 1787, by a vote of 46 to 23.

Three smaller states were next to assent. Economically depressed
New Jersey and militarily vulnerable Georgia did so unanimously, the former

on December 18, 1787, and the latter on January 2, 1788. Connecticut approved by an overwhelming vote of 128 to 40 on January 9, 1788, with Sherman and future Supreme Court chief justice Oliver Ellsworth leading the way.

Many expected the Constitution to be defeated in Massachusetts, for the opposition, headed by Samuel Adams, appeared to outnumber the supporters. Federalists, led by Rufus King, however, turned the tide, striking a bargain with John Hancock by promising to support him for another term as governor of Massachusetts in return for his advocacy of ratification. On February 6, 1788, Massachusetts fell in line by a vote of 187 to 168, although it also proposed a number of amendments to the new basic law to appease Sam Adams and other Antifederalists.

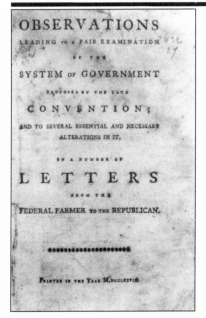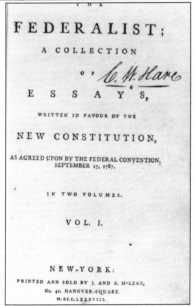

The question of adoption or rejection of the Constitution produced a newspaper and pamphlet war throughout the country. One of the most persuasive Antifederal tracts was the Letters from the Federal Farmer to the Republican *(1787). Alexander Hamilton, James Madison, and John Jay combined to write a series of anonymous newspaper essays advocating ratification, especially by New York; published in book form in 1788, these treatises—collectively called* The Federalist—*are among the most enduring statements of American constitutional theory. Title pages of* Letters from a Federal Farmer *(1787) and* The Federalist *(1788), from Robert G. Ferris, ed.,* Signers of the Constitution, *Washington: U.S. Dept. of the Interior, National Park Service, 1976.*

Rhode Island, fearing that a strong central government would prove oppressive, had not sent representatives to Philadelphia. When attempts to call a convention to ratify the Constitution failed, the question was submitted directly to the voters. Federalists believed this method of adoption was irregular and, knowing that they would be defeated in such a referendum, refused to participate. In late March 1788, with less than half of its six thousand qualified electors participating, Rhode Island defeated the Constitution by a margin of 2,711 to 243. Defiant Rhode Island thus became the only state to attempt a popular vote on the issue of adoption.

The Rhode Island result, coupled with adjournment of the New Hampshire convention on February 22, brought hope to the opponents of the Constitution, but it was short-lived. On April 28, 1788, Maryland ratified the proposed document by a vote of 63 to 11, despite determined resistance from the eloquent William Paca and Samuel Chase, both of whom had signed the Declaration of Independence. Maryland was followed on May 23 by South Carolina, whose talented Charleston-based Federalist leadership carried their convention by a comfortable margin of 149 to 73.

With the Constitution approved by eight states, New Hampshire now was anxious to cast the deciding vote for ratification. Its convention resumed, and on June 21, 1788, by a vote of 57 to 47, New Hampshire became the ninth state to ratify. Its convention also recommended twelve amendments to protect the rights of the citizens of the states.

Although the support of nine states met the constitutional requirement, most agreed the new basic law would not be effective if important and strategically located states such as Virginia and New York withheld their support. In Virginia, Patrick Henry, who had continued his Antifederalism, was winning supporters to his position. George Mason objected to the lack of a bill of rights and warned that its absence might lead to a monarchy or aristocracy. But with James Madison, George Washington, and Edmund Randolph in support of ratification, on June 25, 1788, the Virginia convention voted 89 to 79 to ratify. As a concession to Antifederalists, the convention also approved a proposal for a bill of rights, along with twenty other suggestions for changes in the Constitution.

In New York there was considerable opposition to the Constitution because of a deep-seated fear that a strong central government might abuse its authority. Led by the brilliant and energetic Alexander Hamilton and John Jay, Federalists managed to delay the vote on ratification long enough for the state's convention delegates to learn about the affirmative decisions by New Hampshire and Virginia. Hamilton stressed the difficult position New York would occupy if it remained aloof from the other states. This threat of isolation, coupled with an agreement to support a bill of rights to protect the interests of individuals and the states, helped overcome the Antifederalist arguments of Governor George Clinton and his faction. By a vote of 30 to 27, New York ratified the Constitution on July 26, 1788.

Although the participants at North Carolina's July convention were aware that nine states had already ratified, the opposition, led by Willie Jones, was in the majority. The fear that the states would lose their rights under the Constitution was a compelling argument against approval. Even though James Iredell and William R. Davie worked long and hard to convince the delegates that state sovereignty would not be surrendered, the Constitution was not ratified. Instead, by a vote of 184 to 84, the North Carolina convention recommended a bill of rights, along with twenty-six other amendments. Attitudes in North Carolina toward the Constitution began to change, however, after the new federal government was established. A congressionally proposed bill of rights and North Carolina's need for protection caused

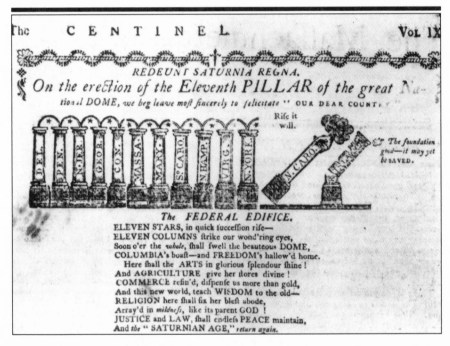

The metaphor of the federal structure supported by the state pillars was used elsewhere, but the Massachusetts Centinel *was the first newspaper to print an illustration bringing the metaphor to life. On January 16, 1788, a cartoon was printed under the heading "THE FEDERAL PILLARS," showing five pillars erected with a sixth pillar labelled "Mass." in the process of being raised. The cartoon was updated as each state ratified the Constitution. This version, showing New York raised, appeared on August 2, 1788.*

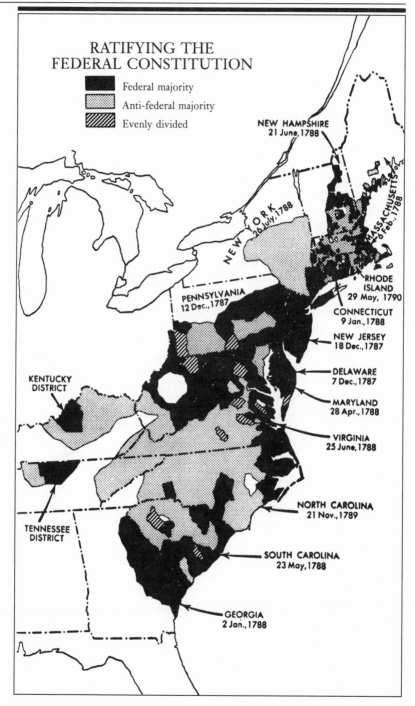

Ratification map. From Richard B. Morris, ed., Encyclopedia of American History, *6th ed. (New York, 1982).*

the state to relent. The result was a call for a second convention, which ratified the Constitution on November 21, 1789, by a vote of 194 to 77.

Rhode Island was now alone. With the other states threatening an economic boycott and some suggesting even stronger action, the recalcitrant state at last called a convention. The first session in March 1790 adjourned without voting, but in response to increased economic pressure by Congress, the convention reconvened in May. Finally, on May 29, 1790, by a vote of 34 to 32, the closest margin of any state, Rhode Island relented and made state support of the Constitution unanimous.

The Bill of Rights

Throughout the ratification debates it had become clear that additional guarantees of each citizen's liberties should be added to the Constitution. States such as Massachusetts, New Hampshire, Virginia, and New York, for example, specifically demanded a bill of rights, and other states ratified the Constitution based on a promise that it would be amended to protect individual liberties.

It was no surprise, therefore, that the new federal Congress in 1789 proposed, at Madison's urging, a series of nine constitutional amendments guaranteeing individual rights and liberties and three others dealing respectively with congressional apportionment, legislative pay, and the powers reserved to the states. Of the twelve amendments submitted to the states for approval, only those relating to apportionment and congressional pay failed to pass. The other ten, known as the Bill of Rights, were added to the Constitution on December 15, 1791, when Virginia became the eleventh state to ratify these guarantees.

The United States Constitution was the culmination of a long movement toward self-government, a movement that had been in progress since the early days of colonization. Yet the Constitution, for all its obvious importance, was only a giant step in the development of a new form of government. Much remained to be done. It was the responsibility of the first federal officials, and it continues to be the duty of their successors, to demonstrate that the Constitution-makers in Philadelphia established an enduring and practical foundation on which a strong republic could grow and flourish. In 1776, at the birth of the new nation, Thomas Paine proclaimed that "the cause of America is in great measure the cause of all mankind. 'Tis not the concern of a day, a year, or an age." The enduring union forged by the Constitution of 1787 has rendered Paine's words prophetic.

1
DELAWARE

Delaware Becomes the First State

HAROLD HANCOCK
Emeritus Professor of History
Otterbein College

ELAWARE, initially settled by Swedes at Fort Christina (Wilmington) in 1638, had a complex colonial existence. Swedish control was terminated by the Dutch in 1655, but these conquerors were soon displaced by the English. In 1682 Delaware's lands were included in a proprietary grant from James, Duke of York, to William Penn. This area—which became the Pennsylvania colony's three southeastern counties—agitated to regain its separate identity. In 1704 Penn, though retaining his position as proprietor, allowed his three lower counties their own legislature and their own identity as the colony of Delaware. In 1776 Delaware overthrew the proprietary government and took its position among the rebellious thirteen in the War for Independence.

Delaware after Independence

Delaware, in 1787, was quite a different state than it is today. The population of its three counties—New Castle, Kent, and Sussex—was less than sixty thousand, and the majority of the inhabitants were of English descent, with the Scots-Irish a significant minority. About 20 percent of the population was black, mainly held as slaves. As in the other original states, most of the inhabitants were subsistence farmers. A few people lived in comfortable surroundings, having inherited land or gained wealth from operating gristmills, shipping, or storekeeping. In contrast, life for many agricultural laborers, tenants, freedmen, and slaves was bleak, as their skimpy household possessions and food (in the form of cornmeal and large amounts of slab bacon) indicated. Wilmington, noted for its gristmills and thriving commerce, was the only large town, though its population was less than two thousand. No other place, including New Castle in the county of that name, Dover in Kent County, or Lewes in Sussex County, contained half as many inhabitants. Religiously, the Methodists were beginning to expand their numbers on their way to becoming the largest denomination in the state.

For Delaware the 1780s were a period of change and improvement: the state's first major newspaper commenced publication in Wilmington; John Fitch received a monopoly from the legislature to operate steamboats in the Delaware River; Oliver Evans began the mechanization of the Brandywine flour mills; and petitions to the General Assembly urged the abolition of slavery.

One thing that remained unchanged, however, was the form of Delaware's government, which had been established in 1776 at the time of the break with Great Britain. At the instigation of the legislature, a convention composed of thirty members—ten from each county—had convened in the town of New Castle late in August 1776 to frame a constitution, which established a two-house legislature consisting of a Legislative Council of nine members and a House of Assembly of twenty-one members. The majority of the members were usually farmers and landowners, but lawyers and physicians were also prominent in the deliberations. The president (governor) did not possess much power. An advisory council of four members aided the president, each house appointing two members who did not serve in the General Assembly. Levy courts, which administered the governments in the counties, were frequently a training ground for membership in the legislature. These courts made appointments to minor offices, heard petitions from citizens on almost any subject, and fixed tax rates.

Political rivalry in Delaware was between factions rather than between well-organized parties. Before the Revolution one group was called the Court or (Anglican) Church party and was friendly with the proprietary governor, while the other bore the name of Country or Presbyterian party and was less friendly. Appointments and election to office were often the issues of controversy.

During the Revolution, in Delaware as elsewhere in America, these opposing groups respectively took the names of Tory and Whig, using the same names for parties as in English politics. At first the Whigs were merely critical of the measures passed by Parliament concerning the colonies, but they eventually came to favor independence and were willing to fight to obtain that objective. They were strongest in New Castle County and had many Presbyterian supporters of Scots-Irish descent. The Tories were also critical of English laws governing the colonies but opposed independence and wished for continuation of British rule. They favored slower and more cautious change. They were strongest in Kent and Sussex counties, and some of their supporters were members of the Anglican Church.

In Delaware it is incorrect to use the word *Tory*, if that is intended to mean someone who was disloyal to the American cause. Certainly such political leaders as George Read, John Dickinson, and Dr. John McKinly cannot be regarded as disloyal in any sense, though they often disagreed with the opposing faction, which contained such "hotheads" as Caesar Rodney and Thomas McKean (Read, for one, was not yet prepared to vote for independence in July 1776, but later in the summer he did sign the Declaration of Independence). It is more accurate to refer to such persons as moderates rather than as Tories. Those Delawareans who joined the British forces, sold supplies to the British, and provided them with military information may be referred to as loyalists. In this study the name *Whig* has been retained, but the opposition is referred to as moderates. The people of Delaware

George Read (1733–1798), the son of a Welch mother and a Dublin-born father, signed both the Declaration of Independence (though he had voted against it on July 2, 1776) and the Constitution. A lawyer, Read held numerous governmental offices, and he was elected as one of Delaware's first two United States senators. After four years in the national legislature, he resigned to accept the position of chief justice of Delaware, an office he held for five years until his death. Portrait by C. W. Schreyler. Courtesy of the Delaware Bureau of Archives and Records Management.

understood the moderate stands of Read, Dickinson, and McKinly and rewarded them with high office.

In the midst of party battles Whigs might refer to Tories in the bitterest terms, but the key to understanding these accusations is the desire for office. Thus, in a 1787 pamphlet Dr. James Tilton, an ardent Whig, made a harsh attack upon "Dionysius, Tyrant of Delaware" (George Read), who, Tilton believed, controlled Delaware politics. In a similar fashion, when in 1804 Captain Peter Jaquett, another Whig, reviewed the political history of the state since the Revolution in a long letter to Caesar A. Rodney (Thomas Rodney's son, who later became U.S. attorney general under Jefferson), he found it displeasing that the opposition party was dominant, while veterans like himself were excluded from office.

Control of the General Assembly alternated between these factions. The moderates framed the constitution of the state in 1776 but lost control of the legislature after the British invasion of 1777. Following the British withdrawal from Philadelphia in 1778, the moderates gradually returned to power. John McKinly, a moderate and the first person elected to the office of president in February 1777, was captured by the British and taken prisoner to Philadelphia. Temporarily the office was then filled by Thomas McKean, the speaker of the House of Assembly and a Whig, until George Read, the speaker of the Legislative Council and a moderate, returned to Delaware from New Jersey, where he had fled when the British arrived in Philadelphia and forced the Continental Congress to adjourn.

Read did not wish to continue in this office because of the pressure of other business, and the General Assembly in 1778 elected Caesar Rodney, a Whig, president. This alteration of moderate and Whig continued in 1781, when John Dickinson, a moderate, was chosen as president, the only dissenting vote being cast by himself. The struggle for control of the legislature continued in the 1780s. In 1787 the Whigs carried New Castle County, and the moderates won in Kent County. Election irregularities led to a second election being held in Sussex County, and the legislature seated the moderate faction.

Two years before Dickinson became president, the legislature had approved the Articles of Confederation. Dickinson had been the chairman of the congressional committee which had prepared the plan of union and is regarded as its principal draftsman. The proposal had been submitted to the states in November 1777, but because of disturbances connected with the British invasion it was not presented to the General Assembly in Delaware until the fall of 1778. The legislature then voted its approval, but it wished to limit the boundaries of states extending to and beyond the Mississippi River, to secure a share of western lands, and to ensure that Delaware courts settled cases involving land rights within the state. On behalf of the state,

Thomas McKean signed the Articles on February 22, 1779, and other delegates, John Dickinson and Nicholas Van Dyke, did likewise on May 5, making Delaware the twelfth state to approve this document. Maryland held out until March 1781.

The Need for Additional Congressional Power

After the Articles of Confederation were adopted, Delaware consistently supported efforts to strengthen the powers of Congress. Nowhere was this more evident than in commercial matters—an area where Delaware was completely dominated by its giant neighbor, Pennsylvania.

Many of the imported goods that Delawareans consumed came indirectly from Philadelphia. Ocean-going vessels unloaded their wares in Philadelphia and merchants re-exported some of these products to Delaware.

John Dickinson (1732–1808) has been called the "Penman of the Revolution" for his authorship of several influential pamphlets and his chairmanship of the committee that drafted the Articles of Confederation. This brilliant, conservative political theorist held prominent governmental positions in both Delaware and Pennsylvania, including the presidency of both states. Dickinson declined to sign the Declaration of Independence. He was the only signer of the Constitution who did not personally affix his name to that document. Illness caused his early departure from Philadelphia, so Dickinson's name was placed on the Constitution by a fellow delegate. Portrait by C. W. Schreyler after a portrait by Rembrandt Peale. Courtesy of the Delaware Bureau of Archives and Records Management.

The importing merchants paid the Pennsylvania impost and added that tax to the price of the goods that consumers paid. Consequently, Delawareans, in an indirect way, paid a substantial revenue into the Pennsylvania treasury every year. In an effort to lure merchants to trade directly with Delaware and to forestall this outflow of money to Pennsylvania, Delaware on a number of occasions created free ports, none of which proved to be effective competitors with Philadelphia.

Unsuccessful in attracting direct foreign trade, Delaware pursued the next best policy—strengthening Congress' power over commerce. Delaware much preferred to pay a federal import duty to Congress for the mutual advantage of all the states as opposed to a Pennsylvania import duty for the exclusive advantage of that state. Thus, in November 1781, Delaware approved the Impost of 1781 which would have given Congress the power to levy a five percent duty on imported goods. This measure, however, failed to receive the required unanimous approval of all of the state legislatures and consequently died. In June 1783 Delaware gave its approval to a similar proposal from Congress, but that impost also failed to win the unanimous endorsement of the states. In February 1786 Delaware agreed to grant Congress special commercial powers for twenty-five years, but again the attempt to strengthen Congress failed.

The Turbulent 1780s

Legislators of the state felt that they faced difficult problems in the 1780s. The Black Camp Rebellion staged by moderates in the central part of Sussex County in 1780 spelled out the differences between the Whigs and their opponents on many points, such as oppressive taxation, a draft law that poor farmers considered unfair because it weighed more heavily on the poor than the rich, and harassment of the opposition party by Whig militia. In brief, these embittered farmers considered the Revolution to be a poor man's fight and a rich man's war. It is significant that their protests said nothing about King George or British oppression. The participants in the Black Camp Rebellion should be referred to as moderates rather than loyalists. In Massachusetts during 1786, a somewhat similar protest of poor farmers over economic grievances erupted as Shays' Rebellion.

In the case of the Black Camp insurrection, a group of poor farmers assembled in a swamp, preparing to attack and disarm Whigs, but militia soon appeared and arrested many participants. The ringleaders were sentenced to be drawn and quartered as traitors, but all seemed to have aged parents to support or to have many dependent children, and the General Assembly pardoned them.

Agricultural prices were depressed in the 1780s, and farmers could not keep up their mortgage payments and were losing their farms. A Kent County petition in 1785 claimed that the scarcity of money and prosecution for the non payment of debts had become universal. The unfeeling hearts of creditors were untouched by the cries of women and helpless children. The emotional petitioners asked for a three-year suspension of the payment of debts; otherwise, they asserted, they would be reduced to begging for bread or lying down to die, unless some guardian angel, like the legislature, appeared. A similar petition from Sussex County in 1786 claimed that creditors were purchasing property sold at auction to meet mortgage payments at one-third, one-fourth, one-fifth, and even one-tenth of its value. For relief, they asked for the issuance of paper money to be loaned to farmers.

These petitions, and others, stressed problems relating to paper money. Before the Revolution, Delaware paper currency was sound, being backed by land. Farmers applied to county loan offices for financial aid and pledged their farms as security. But during the war farmers began to pay off their mortgages with Continental currency, which had been declared legal tender by the legislature. The value of Continental currency rapidly declined, as it had no basis of support other than the backing of the Continental Congress. In 1780, by legislative action, Continental currency ceased to be legal tender, and in 1781 the General Assembly took the same steps concerning Delaware bills of credit. In February 1786 the legislature gave the state's inhabitants six months in which to surrender any Delaware notes in circulation at the rate of seventy-five pounds to one pound of lawful currency. After August 1, 1785, Delaware currency previously issued would no longer be redeemable. Thus currency problems complicated the payment of debts by farmers, who were paid for their produce in paper money.

The political situation, especially in Kent and Sussex counties, was difficult, and disturbances marred many elections. Whigs were determined that several classes of voters should not be permitted to exercise the franchise. Refugees who had fled to British lines were now trying to reestablish themselves within the state. "Act of Grace men," who were persons suspected of disloyalty and who had taken a special oath of loyalty, were barred from voting. In addition, many eligible voters had not taken the general oath of allegiance required by a legislative act of 1778. In Sussex County, Whigs wished to prevent Black Camp participants from taking part in elections.

In 1783 there were election disturbances at polling places in both Kent and Sussex counties. In Sussex County officers and soldiers appeared at the polling place with swords, bayonets, and clubs, intimidating many who wished to vote. By the use of such tactics the Whigs in Sussex County succeeded in carrying this particular election. If they had not won, one observer predicted, the Whigs would have fled to another state, probably west of the Allegheny Mountains.

The Annapolis Convention

By no means were these crises peculiar to Delaware. Many states faced problems about paper money, agricultural distress, and election disturbances. Delaware governors corresponded with officials in other states about these conditions, especially in the Middle Atlantic region. At the suggestion of Virginia, a conference was summoned to meet in Annapolis, Maryland, in September 1786 to discuss commercial relations. A committee of the House of Assembly recommended participation by the state. As delegates, the lower house proposed the names of George Read, Jacob Broom, Gunning Bedford, Jr., William Peery, and Eleazer McComb. When the members of the upper house were informed of these choices, they protested, pointing out that in the past such appointments had been made in a joint session. Subsequently, in a joint session the names of George Read, Jacob Broom, and Gunning Bedford, Jr., were retained, but the names of John Dickinson and Richard Bassett were substituted for those of Peery and McComb.

Dickinson, a lawyer and politician, was active in Delaware and Pennsylvania, and he was known both in America and England for his political writings. Read, a member of the legislature, had served in the Continental Congress and had been appointed by the latter body as a judge in the Court of Appeals. Bassett was a wealthy landowner who had served in the legislature. Broom was a Wilmington merchant and entrepreneur. Bedford was the state attorney general.

When the Annapolis convention met, it did little because only twelve delegates from five states attended. Delaware was represented by Read, Bassett, and Dickinson, who was chosen chairman. He signed the final report, which proposed that a convention be held in Philadelphia in May 1787 to "revise" the Articles of Confederation.

Delaware's Delegates to the Constitutional Convention

Delaware's General Assembly chose the same five delegates to represent the state in the Philadelphia Convention. Under the guidance of George Read, a member of the Legislative Council, instructions were approved by the legislature to have the Delaware delegates seek an equality with all other states in any legislative body that the convention might set up.

Of the Delaware delegation, Dickinson and Read had the most impact upon the deliberations of the Constitutional Convention. Delaware was the only state that gave instructions to its representatives, and these two men called attention to these directives when the convention moved towards advocating a national legislature in which votes would be allocated in proportion to each state's population. Read created alarm by mentioning the possibility of the withdrawal of the Delaware delegation should this large-state plan prevail. Bedford announced that if the Confederation dissolved, Delaware might seek a foreign ally, a statement which brought forth reprimands from other delegates, as well as an apology from Bedford.

During the debates Dickinson suggested a compromise on representation, recommending that there be equality among the states in the upper house of the legislative branch. Thinking apparently that Delaware might be swallowed up again by Pennsylvania, Dickinson also was interested in seeing that no portion of a state was taken over by another without its consent. Dickinson favored abolition of the overseas slave trade, but a convention compromise prohibited any congressional ban upon that nefarious commerce prior to the year 1808. Both Read and Dickinson wished for a strong national

Gunning Bedford, Jr. (1747–1812) was a native of Philadelphia and a Princeton roommate of James Madison. He served in the Continental army and, after moving to Delaware, held office as a state legislator, delegate to the Confederation Congress, and state attorney general (1784–1789). Bedford's prominent role in the Philadelphia Convention and his support of ratification earned him the appointment as Delaware's first federal district court judge. Portrait by Augustus E. Heaton. Courtesy of the Delaware Bureau of Archives and Records Management.

government, but Dickinson stressed that states should retain many powers. In discussions in the convention, Bedford seldom spoke. Neither Bassett nor Broom served on any committee, and Broom did not speak upon any question. All five voted on various issues.

Even though the compromise concerning representation in the Senate and House was not strictly according to their instructions, the Delaware delegates had no difficulty in accepting it, nor did the Delaware General Assembly. The work of the Philadelphia Convention was completed on September 17, and the document was signed by members of the Delaware delegation, except for the absent Dickinson, who gave his friend George Read permission to sign for him.

The Constitution in Delaware

It was obvious from the outset of the ratification contest that Delawareans favored the proposed Constitution. From Dover, Nicholas Ridgely, a lawyer who later became a member of the state's ratification convention, wrote in late August: "From the Convention at Phila. we must expect permanence and stability, or ruin and misery. Should a tolerable Government be formed, it will be wisdom to adopt it," as the present establishment is "tottering to a dissolution," and if it fails, "convulsions (and probably civil war)" will result. The *Pennsylvania Gazette* reported late in September that the document was received in Delaware "with universal satisfaction." A month later James Madison informed a friend that "Delaware will fall in of course." When Delaware's President Thomas Collins received broadsides and pamphlets in opposition from Pennsylvania, as soon as he discovered their nature he threw them into the fire.

The General Assembly was disappointed at not receiving a copy of the Constitution at its session in late August, as the next session would not be held until late October. Elections to the legislature took place on October 1, but riots in Sussex County prevented an election from being held there at that time. President Collins visited Sussex County and arranged an election for October 15. A Union ticket was formed of an equal number of persons from each party, and only fifty persons from each party would be permitted to vote. Petitions from Sussex County claimed that this unorthodox procedure was illegal and also mentioned minor irregularities on the day of the election. Without representation from Sussex County, the House of Assembly had difficulty in securing a quorum, and the legislature passed an act lowering the attendance figure required. In an attempt to settle the problem, the place of election in Sussex County, for the year 1787 only, was moved from Lewes to a spot near Vaughn's Furnace in Nanticoke Hundred not far from the center of the county. The returns from the balloting to be held there on November 26 would then be considered in the January session. Whigs claimed that the change of location was made so that the moderates could more easily control the election.

On October 24, the first day on which the House of Assembly had a quorum, President Collins sent to that body a congressional resolution of September 28 transmitting a copy of the Constitution, along with petitions favoring it from New Castle County. The House appointed a committee to consider the document, and it reported in its favor the following day, but further action was postponed because of the need to consider the results of the Sussex County election. On October 25 President Collins submitted similar material to the Legislative Council. George Read, one of the delegates, appeared and laid before that body a copy of the Constitution.

Having decided what to do about the irregularities in the Sussex County election, the legislature on November 9–10 directed that voting be held on November 26 for delegates to attend a convention in Dover to consider approving the federal Constitution. Resolutions summoning the members to the convention mentioned that petitions from the people of the state favored "speedy measures" for assembling such a body. Ten members were to be chosen from each county. Special attention was called to the fifth resolution, which proposed ceding to the national government land for a capital, as petitions had suggested.

In Sussex County the November contest was for delegates both to the convention and to the legislature. Two days after the election, on November 28, petitions were being circulated in Sussex County claiming that companies of armed men near the polling place in Nanticoke Hundred prevented Whigs from voting. A prejudiced Whig commentator, who called himself "Timoleon" (Dr. James Tilton), claimed that upon that occasion "sundry persons were insulted and violently assaulted professedly because they were Whigs, Presbyterians, or Irish-men; that one fellow in particular after assaulting a Whig with several blows, swore his teeth had grown an inch on that day that he might *eat* Presbyterians and Irish-men; that some huzzaed for the King, and others expressed a hope that they might again come under the old government."

According to the hyperbolic Timoleon, the Whigs of Sussex County did not wish to delay ratification in spite of these disturbances, and both factions united in supporting ratification. Members of the convention felt that that body lacked authority to send for witnesses and to conduct an investigation into election irregularities. Under these circumstances the convention allowed the members elected from Sussex County to be seated.

The State Convention

The state ratifying convention met in Dover on Monday, December 3. Most of the members were farmers and landowners, though some were physicians, lawyers, and gristmill owners. Many members had served in the state militia or in the Continental army. Two of the members, Gunning Bedford, Jr., and Richard Bassett, had been delegates to the Philadelphia Convention. President Collins on December 4 submitted to the Delaware convention a brief message and a copy of the federal Constitution. He also provided copies of the resolutions of the General Assembly concerning the document and called attention to the section recommending that land be offered in Delaware as a site for the national capital.

Unfortunately little is known about the work of this body, as the proceedings have not survived. French vice consul Antoine de la Forest, writing from New York City, suggested that the Delaware convention debated the Constitution for only a matter of hours before voting unanimously to ratify it, probably on December 6. All thirty delegates signed the document of ratification on December 7 (the signed original of the ratification document is one of the treasures of the Delaware State Archives). At the same time, the members passed a resolution to offer to the national government a site for the capital not exceeding ten miles square.

President Collins forwarded a certified copy of the ratification document to Secretary of State James Booth on December 22, asking him to give it to Nathaniel Mitchell, a Delaware member of the Confederation Congress, to present to that body. The document of ratification was read in Congress on January 22, 1788. President Collins delayed forwarding the resolution of the convention offering to cede land for the national capital until April 24, 1788, and it was read in Congress on May 13, 1788.

The action of Delaware in becoming the first state to ratify the Constitution, as well as the first to offer a site for the capital, was widely reported in the press. A Massachusetts newspaper headed an article "THE FIRST PILLAR of a great FEDERAL SUPERSTRUCTURE RAISED."

Two years later a Wilmington almanac reprinted "The Raising: A Song for Federal Mechanics," a poem about the Constitutional Convention and the ratification which compared the process to the raising of a house, with the states as rafters. The author was Francis Hopkinson of Pennsylvania, who in 1772 had been collector of the customs at New Castle. The last verse of the poem reads:

> The sons of Columbia shall view with delight
> Its pillars, and arches, and towering height;
> Our roof is now rais'd, and our song still shall be—

A federal head, o'er a people still free.
Huzza! my brave boys, our work is now complete,
The world shall admire Columbia's fair seat;
Its strength against tempests and time shall be proof,
And thousands shall come to dwell under our Roof.
Whilst we drain the deep bowl, our toast still shall be—
Our government firm, and our citizens free.

It was "Delaware's Greatest Glory," as one respected student of Delaware history has indicated in an essay, to have been the first state to ratify the Constitution, and Hopkinson's poetic predictions have come true.

Why was Delaware the first state to ratify the Constitution? No one reason explains this, but a number were involved. Sentiment in the state was so much in favor of the Constitution that the General Assembly expressed disappointment in late August when the work of the federal convention was not yet completed and the legislature therefore could not proceed to arrange for a state constitutional convention. Many Delawareans believed that a stronger government might solve many of the problems with which the Confederation Congress had not dealt. The Wilmington business community, which had close relations with Philadelphia, favored approval, and it is

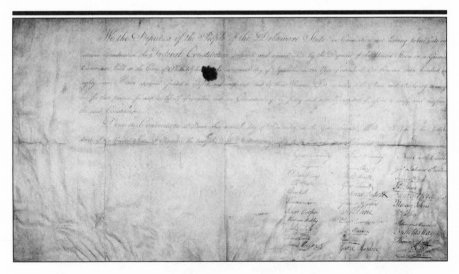

This faded manuscript is Delaware's most famous state paper—the ratification document of December 7, 1787, which made Delaware the first state to approve the handiwork of the Philadelphia Convention. Ten delegates from each of the state's three counties signed this ratification certificate, providing Delaware's margin of 30 to 0 in favor of the Constitution. Courtesy of the Delaware Bureau of Archives and Records Management.

significant that several petitions signed by businessmen and others in its favor came from New Castle County, where businessmen also hoped that the national capital might be located. Some Delawareans read Philadelphia newspapers, which printed essays for and against ratification, and they had plenty of time in which to make up their minds on the issue. George Washington had presided over the deliberations of the Federal Convention, and Revolutionary officers, some of whom were members of the state convention (among them were Allen McLane, Gunning Bedford, Jr., and James Latimer, its presiding officer), respected his integrity and had confidence in his leadership.

Both Whigs and moderates in Delaware supported ratification. An Antifederalist party did not appear in the state, even though Virginia's Richard Henry Lee, in passing through Wilmington on one occasion, did try to encourage the formation of such an opposition by speaking and handing out broadsides. Thomas Rodney was the only known Delaware politician who at first expressed doubts about whether the Constitution could provide better government. He thought that the proposed document did not promote national unity, gave the states too much power, and failed to provide an adequate balance among the different classes of society.

Both Whigs and moderates agreed in supporting ratification because they believed that chaos and confusion in state and local affairs should not

James Latimer (1719–1797), a New Castle County merchant and lawyer, was one of the wealthiest men in Delaware. He became a justice of the peace in 1769 and served on the Council of Safety in 1776. During the Revolution he was a lieutenant colonel in the Continental army. Latimer was elected president of the Delaware convention that ratified the Constitution. Portrait by Clawson Shakespeare Hammitt in Art in the United States Capitol *(Washington, D.C., 1976).*

continue. A stronger government than the existing Confederation Congress could more effectively face foreign nations, regulate commerce, provide a sound currency, and establish order. Timoleon, in the concluding paragraph of his partisan pamphlet, expressed the Whig view:

> Although every other means under Providence should fail us, we hope at least to derive some consolation from the NEW FEDERAL CONSTI-TUTION. From hence we may expect some standing institutions to walk by. Fraudulent retrospective laws will be no more. The injured and op-pressed army creditors of Delaware may hence expect a just reward to their patient virtue and hope to derive some emolument from their public se-curities. All good men will rejoice in the near prospect of an uniform act of naturalization, and that DELAWARE will not be destined as the sink of TORYISM. And although it should be long before virtue shall become triumphant over Vice, good men will nevertheless be more out of the reach and power of unjust and wicked oppressors than heretofore.

The moderates also could have subscribed to these sentiments with the change of a word or two. The Constitution offered hope of a better world to both factions, and this is what the thirty members of the Delaware convention voted for with unanimity and why they signed the document of ratification on December 7, giving Delaware the distinction of being the first state to ratify the federal Constitution.

Delaware: Essay on Sources

Contemporary sources relating to Delaware's ratification of the U.S. Consti-tution are meager, especially since the proceedings of the ratification convention are missing. Moreover, few letters and little contemporary material concerning the ratification process have survived. Fortunately, some 1787 issues of Delaware's only contemporary newspaper, the *Delaware Gazette*, have been preserved.

For the participation of Delawareans in the Philadelphia Convention, see James H. Hutson, "John Dickinson at the Federal Constitutional Convention," *William and Mary Quarterly*, 3rd series 60 (April 1983), 256–262; William T. Read, *Life and Corre-spondence of George Read* (Philadelphia, 1870); and Milton E. Flower, *John Dickinson: Conservative Revolutionary* (Charlottesville, Va., 1983). For legislative records about the ratification convention, see *Votes and Proceedings of the Legislative Council of the Delaware State . . .* [1787]; "Minutes of the Council of the Delaware State, from 1776 to 1792," *Papers* of the Historical Society of Delaware, 6 (Wilmington, 1887); *Votes and Proceedings of the House of Assembly of the Delaware State . . .* [1787] (Wilmington, 1787); and *Votes and Proceedings of the Delaware State . . .* [1788] (Wilmington, 1788).

Merrill Jensen, John P. Kaminski and Gaspare J. Saladino have conveniently compiled material about the state's ratification process in *The Documentary History of the Ratification of the Constitution*, vol. 3 (Madison, Wis., 1978), 36–117. An important partisan narrative, written in 1788, is John A. Munroe, ed., *Timoleon's Biographical History of*

Dionysius, Tyrant of Delaware (Newark, Del., 1958). This pamphlet, which attacked George Read, was written by Dr. James Tilton. The turbulent elections of 1787 in Sussex County are described in Harold Hancock, *The Loyalists of Revolutionary Delaware* (Newark, Del., 1977). These elections receive special attention in John Kern, "The Sussex County, Delaware, Election Riots of 1787," *Delaware History*, 22 (Fall–Winter 1987). For an interesting Whig account of politics at the time, see Peter Jaquett to Caesar A. Rodney, November 8, 1804, in Harold Hancock, ed., "Loaves and Fishes: Applications for Office to George Washington," *Delaware History*, 14 (1970–71), 150–158.

Accounts of Delaware's ratification are also presented in Henry C. Conrad, *History of the State of Delaware*, 3 vols. (Wilmington, 1908) and in J. Thomas Scharf, *History of Delaware*, 2 vols. (Philadelphia, 1888). Jeannette Eckman offers an interesting narrative in H. Clay Reed, *Delaware—A History of the First State*, 3 vols. (New York, 1947). A sound account of Delaware's reaction to the Constitution is found in John A. Munroe, *Colonial Delaware: A History* (Millwood, N.Y., 1978) and in his *Federalist Delaware, 1775–1815* (New Brunswick., N.J., 1954), as well as in Munroe's pamphlet *How Delaware Became a State* (Newark, Del., 1953).

Judge Richard S. Rodney displayed his wide knowledge and mastery of Delaware's eighteenth-century history in an essay entitled "Delaware's Greatest Glory," published in George Gibson, ed., *The Collected Essays of Richard S. Rodney on Early Delaware* (Wilmington, 1975). Two informative accounts by former directors of the Delaware State Archives are George H. Ryden, *Delaware—The First State in the Union* (Wilmington, 1938) and Leon de Valinger, Jr., *How Delaware Became the First State* (Dover, 1970). A pamphlet written to accompany an exhibit of constitutional documents from the Delaware State Archives provides general background information: William Williams, *Constitutional Documents of the First State* (Dover, 1987).

2
PENNSYLVANIA

From Revolution to Constitution

Pennsylvania's Path to Federalism

PAUL DOUTRICH
Associate Historian
Pennsylvania Historical Museum Commission

T HE AMERICAN REVOLUTION blossomed in Pennsylvania during the spring of 1776. In the fourteen
years that followed, the state experienced both revolution and counter-
revolution, with two political parties vying for control of the Pennsylvania
government. Central to this struggle were the debates that surrounded the
creation and ratification of the United States Constitution.

By early 1776 Pennsylvania's government was at the brink of revolution as three distinct political parties emerged. On one side were Tories
who supported the proprietary government established by William Penn in
1682 and maintained by his descendants. Tories opposed all talk of American
independence. Composed of wealthy Philadelphians, this party feared the
loss of property and position that would likely accompany a separation from
the mother country. At the other end of the political spectrum were Radicals
from the western counties, many of whom were Scots-Irish, and various
pockets of dissent in Philadelphia. Proponents of immediate independence,
Radicals argued that further conciliation with Parliament was impossible and

that independence should be accompanied by sweeping reform within the Pennsylvania government. Precariously positioned between Tories and Radicals were Moderates such as John Dickinson and James Wilson, who controlled the Provincial Assembly. Although they were opponents of the Penns' proprietary government, Moderates nevertheless resisted independence from England. Supported by relatively prosperous Philadelphia merchants and lawyers, they sought to rectify offensive British legislation through petitions. Though Moderates had gently pushed the province toward independence, the pace was not quick enough to satisfy Radicals.

In the months preceding American independence, several events added strength to the Radical cause. In January Thomas Paine, then a Philadelphia resident, published *Common Sense*, which advocated immediate independence. Many throughout the province cheered Paine's arguments. Meanwhile, Radicals laid plans for an April convention to establish a new Pennsylvania government. Since the previous October, Radicals had complained that western counties and portions of Philadelphia were being denied equitable representation in the Assembly. The proposed convention was called, in part, to provide additional seats for the underrepresented areas. In response to the growing demand for governmental reform, Moderate leaders in the Assembly resolved to admit seventeen new members and called for a special election in May 1776. While the resolution ended Radical plans for an April convention, it also intensified the political struggle in Pennsylvania.

All sides recognized what was at stake in the May 10 election. When the ballots were counted, candidates who opposed immediate independence had been elected to sixteen of the seventeen new seats. Considered a significant Moderate victory, the election did little to slow the growing wave of Radical protest. It was, however, the last election in which Tories participated. During the next few weeks political confusion reigned in Pennsylvania.

Upset by the election results, Pennsylvania Radical leaders found immediate support from like-minded representatives in the Continental Congress, which was meeting in Philadelphia. Proponents of independence and sympathetic to the call for a new provincial government, some congressional representatives recognized the importance of Pennsylvania to the independence movement, and less than a week after the May election they took steps to undermine the Moderate-controlled Assembly. On May 15 the Continental Congress resolved that all colonies should adopt new governments wherever the current governments failed to provide for the public well-being. Armed with this resolution, the way was clear for Pennsylvania Radicals to establish a new provincial government, bring the Revolution to Pennsylvania, and instruct the colony's delegates in Congress to vote for independence.

Radicals wasted little time in acting. The day after Congress passed the resolution, Radical leaders in Philadelphia called upon the provincial government to organize a convention. A few days later a rally of four thousand Philadelphians denounced the Provincial Assembly and demanded that a new frame of government be created for Pennsylvania. Though Moderates in the Assembly attempted to refute the claims made against them and tried to slow the revolutionary movement, there was no denying the Radicals. By June the Assembly, besieged by an unending barrage of charges, was unable to function. Radicals were now ready to write a state constitution that reflected their political concerns.

The call for a provincial constitutional convention was answered in mid-June. At a conference of Radicals on June 18, rules and regulations were drawn up which governed the election of delegates to such a gathering. Fearing Moderates might ultimately gain control of the proposed convention, Radicals devised rules to insure themselves an upper hand in the making of Pennsylvania's new government. Suffrage qualifications were extended to a broader portion of the population, thus enfranchising many Radical supporters who had previously been excluded from provincial elections. At the same time, various tests and oaths were adopted to limit opposition. Though the June conference was not sanctioned by law, it nevertheless initiated the creation of a new provincial government.

Prior to the election of delegates to the provincial constitutional convention, attention focused on the Continental Congress, then meeting in Philadelphia. On July 2 the delegates voted for independence. Benjamin Franklin, James Wilson and John Morton supported the separation from Great Britain; Thomas Willing and Charles Humphreys opposed it; John Dickinson and Robert Morris did not vote.

The election of delegates to the provincial constitutional convention went as planned, and on July 15 the convention opened with Benjamin Franklin as president. Usurping the responsibilities of the Assembly, the convention appointed a Council of Safety to act as the government of Pennsylvania until a new government came into being. As the delegates slowly proceeded to write the state's first constitution, the Council of Safety took steps to consolidate Radical authority throughout the state. Men sympathetic to Radical concerns were appointed justices of the peace. Penalties were meted out to those who opposed independence and military service. The council also directed military affairs, borrowed money, fixed commodity prices, prescribed oaths, called and supervised elections, and administered justice. Meanwhile the old Assembly, trying to preserve itself, met periodically until August 26; then, lacking a quorum, it adjourned, never to meet again. The adjournment further enhanced the Radical position in the state.

The Pennsylvania Constitution of 1776

Completed in late September, the Pennsylvania constitution of 1776 was the most democratic of its day. The document drew its inspiration from many sources. It exhibited philosophical influences of Locke and the liberal English political doctrine stemming from the Glorious Revolution of 1688. It called upon the traditions of liberty and tolerance embodied in Penn's Charter of Liberty in 1682 and the Charter of Privileges in 1701. The preamble and declaration of rights contained statements of the revolutionary rights proclaimed by the Stamp Act Congress, the First Continental Congress, and the Declaration of Independence. As with other state constitutions written during the Revolutionary period, the document announced that its goal was the "security and protection of the community." To fulfill these responsibilities, the new constitution guaranteed religious liberty, freedom of speech, protection from illegal seizure of person or property, and the right of trial by jury.

By taking formal steps to limit opposition to Radical leadership, the state's new frame of government reflected the fervor with which Pennsylvania embraced independence. Demonstrating a distrust of a privileged class, the constitution established a unicameral, or one-house, legislature with equal representation from all eleven counties. Fear that executive authority might be abused when vested in a single official resulted in the creation of an executive council rather than a governor. An independent judiciary appointed by the executive council was provided. Property qualifications for voting and for officeholding were abolished and replaced by oaths of allegiance to the state government. Oaths promising support of American independence were also required. These provisions established Pennsylvania's constitution of 1776 as the boldest of the period and guaranteed for Radicals control of the government for at least the early war years.

Radicals Consolidate Their Power

The implementation of Pennsylvania's first constitution completed one cycle of the Revolution and began another one. By November 1776, Radicals had replaced Moderates as the state's dominant political force. Radical policies were being carried out throughout the state, and most of the important governmental and military positions were held by Radicals. Nevertheless, the democratic character of the state's new constitution allowed Moderates to contend for power with Radicals on a relatively equal basis.

Though Radicals had been able to supplant the Provincial Assembly, the struggle for ultimate control of Pennsylvania was far from over. The difficulties facing Radicals stemmed from their own failure to understand the complexities of creating a new government. Radicals had few experienced people to fill government positions, and Moderates, who did have experience, refused to take government jobs because of the mandatory oath. The institution of a more rigid oath system in June 1777 only added to the Radicals' problems. In some counties new Radical officials were stymied by Moderates who refused to turn over county records. Meanwhile, the demands of the war with Britain gave Radicals little time to organize themselves once in power. Finally, Radicals were not above misusing their new authority in an effort to coerce all state voters to submit to the new government.

While Radicals had problems initiating a new government, the real threat to their authority came as a result of the state's economic woes. To keep the militia supplied, the state had to rely upon ever-depreciating Continental dollars and unsecured state notes. As inflation soared, Radicals took extraordinary steps to finance their regime. For example, they created local boards to regulate commerce and determine fair prices. Often these boards resorted to mob rule when enforcing price restrictions. Some merchants were accused of hoarding goods in an effort to push prices higher. Taxes were placed on anyone who did not actively support the Radical government, and in some cases property was confiscated from nonsupporters. Eventually Radicals came to manage the economy by edict. These methods alienated commercial and financial leaders as well as a growing number of farmers throughout the state. By 1781 Pennsylvania was on the verge of financial collapse. Even the militia, which had been a source of Radical strength since 1776, was on the brink of mutiny.

As conditions worsened, Moderates patiently awaited an opportunity to establish their leadership. In October 1780 their waiting paid off as Moderates won a small majority in the Assembly. For the next four years, Moderates tried to change the policies that their opponents had instituted during the previous four years. Despite their continued efforts, however, Moderates were unable to significantly alter the basic Radical program.

Economic Depression

By 1784 Moderates in control of the Assembly had launched a full-scale attack on the test oaths and the state's constitution. The campaign was turned aside only after Radicals boycotted the Assembly, thus preventing a quorum. After four years in power with a deepening postwar depression, Moderates lost control of the Assembly in the fall of 1784. Radicals immediately enacted an anti-depression program. They issued £150,000 of paper money on loan for real estate collateral, and they assumed payment of the federal debt owed to

Pennsylvanians. Finally, Radicals revoked the charter of the Bank of North America, the one stable financial institution within the state. These programs brought no immediate relief, and Moderates regained control of the Assembly in 1786.

Pennsylvania's economic problems were heightened by the deficiencies of the Articles of Confederation. Written to forge a union of states, the Articles created a general government that had little authority. Among other shortcomings, the Confederation government had no power to enforce the collection of taxes. As a result, interest and principal payments on public debts had to be suspended and foreign creditors went unpaid.

In addition to the economic problems and the shortcomings of the Articles, events in other states further alarmed Pennsylvanians. By the fall of 1786 farmers in western Massachusetts were ready to take up arms against their state government. There were also incidents of violence in New Hampshire, Connecticut, Vermont, Maryland, Virginia and South Carolina. In Rhode Island the radical elements gained control of the state government and started to implement their economic policy. The Articles of Confederation seemed incapable of handling these problems, and demands arose for separate confederacies or even a return to monarchy.

The Movement to Strengthen the Articles

Proposals to strengthen the Articles of Confederation failed to receive the required unanimous approval of the states. However, in January 1786 Virginia elected eight commissioners to meet with delegates from other states to consider the country's commercial problems. Following the Virginia election, resolutions were sent to the states inviting them to send delegates to a meeting at Annapolis in September. Pennsylvania Republicans (as the Moderates were now called) welcomed the idea, and in April the Supreme Executive Council appointed Robert Morris, George Clymer, John Armstrong, Jr., Thomas FitzSimons and Tench Coxe delegates to the Annapolis Convention. Coxe, a wealthy Philadelphia merchant, attended the convention alone while the other Pennsylvania delegates waited in Philadelphia for the New England delegates.

Tench Coxe went to Annapolis firmly believing that the central government needed the authority to regulate trade. He left the Maryland convention an ardent supporter of a completely remodeled and stronger national government. To Coxe, who served as the Annapolis Convention's secretary, the central problem of the times was finding a system which would assure that each state fulfilled its obligation to the Union. No longer could states be allowed to disregard the needs and directives of the general government.

Coxe also joined his colleagues at Annapolis in recommending that another convention of state delegates be held in May 1787 "to render the federal government adequate to the exigencies of the Union." Though he doubted that the Annapolis Convention had any real power to direct the Confederation Congress, Coxe had no doubts that if the Union was to survive, the Articles of Confederation had to be extensively revised or replaced altogether.

Pennsylvania and the Constitutional Convention

Pennsylvania wasted little time in preparing for the proposed convention of states. By the end of 1786 the Assembly, now controlled by Republicans, had appointed seven Philadelphians to represent the state at the May meeting. All had served in numerous posts in both the state and national government; and all, except for Jared Ingersoll, were Republicans who endorsed a strong central government. Three of those selected—Robert Morris, George Clymer, and Thomas FitzSimons—were prosperous Philadelphia merchants. Three other delegates—James Wilson, Gouverneur Morris, and Thomas Mifflin—were among the foremost lawyers of Philadelphia.

In March 1787 the Pennsylvania Assembly appointed an eighth member, Benjamin Franklin, to the state's delegation. Franklin, president of the Supreme Executive Council, had been left off the initial slate of delegates because it was thought he would not accept the appointment. Pennsylvania's elder statesman and one of the most distinguished men in America, Franklin brought considerable respect and esteem to the Philadelphia gathering and to the Pennsylvania delegation. With the addition of Franklin, the state had more convention representatives than any other state, and the distinguished delegation included four of the six convention members who had signed the Declaration of Independence.

In late May fifty-five delegates from twelve states—Rhode Island had refused to attend—began meeting in Philadelphia. Some delegates came prepared merely to revise the Articles of Confederation, while others, particularly the Virginia delegates, were ready to create a new frame of government altogether. Pennsylvania's delegates fell somewhere between these two extremes, though the Pennsylvanians clearly supported the idea of a strong national government. Representing one of the three large states in the country, they also agreed with the broad principles expounded by the Virginia delegation. These principles included the creation of a government with three branches, a system of checks and balances, and proportional representation based on population or wealth.

Among the important guideposts for the delegates were the state constitutions that had been written since 1776. Though more democratic than its counterparts, the Pennsylvania constitution of 1776 had much to offer the convention. As with other state constitutions, it was divided into three parts: a preamble, a declaration of rights, and a plan of government. The Pennsylvania document also stressed the representative character of the state's new government and announced that the primary objective of the state government was the protection of the commonwealth. In other ways, however, the Pennsylvania constitution differed significantly from its contemporaries and, therefore, provided a test case of sorts for convention delegates. For instance, Pennsylvania was one of the two states to have a unicameral legislature. Executive powers in Pennsylvania were held not by a governor, as in other states, but by a committee; and in Pennsylvania a Council of Censors met every seven years to review the state constitution and propose amendments where needed. These unique features made Pennsylvania's constitution particularly instructive to convention delegates—but primarily as a negative example not to follow.

Pennsylvania also provided some of the more active and vocal delegates to the Philadelphia Convention. One of the convention's most able

Benjamin Franklin (1706– 1790) was the elder statesman of the Philadelphia Convention and, with Washington, its most prominent delegate. Perhaps the most versatile American of the eighteenth century, Franklin distinguished himself as an author, publisher, diplomat, scientist, inventor, politician, philosopher, and philanthropist. Though he was hampered at the Constitutional Convention by age (81) and ill health, he worked to soothe passions and settle disputes, and he also lent the gathering added prestige and respectability. Etching, courtesy of the Pennsylvania State Archives.

participants was James Wilson, a well-respected Philadelphia lawyer. Wilson had come to America from Scotland in 1765 amid the Stamp Act crisis, and he soon became active in the growing debates between England and the colonies. As a student in John Dickinson's law office, Wilson was noticeably influenced by the philosophical bent of his mentor and became increasingly involved in the American cause. A member of the Second Continental Congress, he generally stood beside his former teacher and fellow delegate Dickinson in cautiously approaching independence. Though he was one of the three Pennsylvania delegates to vote in favor of independence, popular sentiment in the state soon moved beyond Wilson's position. Wilson bitterly opposed Radical rule and the Pennsylvania constitution of 1776. As Radical leadership within the state became oppressive and the shortcomings of the Articles of Confederation obvious, Wilson joined other Pennsylvania Republicans in calling for sweeping reforms.

With the exception of James Madison, no convention member understood the complexities that faced the delegates or was as well versed

James Wilson (1742–1798), after a turbulent career in Pennsylvania politics, achieved true distinction at the Philadelphia Convention. With the possible exception of James Madison, no member of that gathering was better versed in the study of political economy and governmental theory. Wilson was also the dominant force in the Pennsylvania ratifying convention and the state constitutional convention in 1789–1790. His learning and his nationalism made him Washington's choice as associate justice on the first U.S. Supreme Court. His land speculations, like those of his friend Robert Morris, landed him in deep financial difficulties at the end of his life. Painting, courtesy of the Pennsylvania State Archives.

in the politics of the times as James Wilson. Like Madison, Wilson staunchly believed that sovereignty ultimately rested with the individual and that the national government should represent more than a mere collection of states; rather, a strong national government should serve as a further guarantee of individual liberties. He rejected the idea of equal representation in the Senate as undemocratic and, unlike Madison, advocated the popular election of both the legislative and executive branches of government. During the debates about the executive branch, Wilson repeatedly argued that a vote of the entire nation should undergird the office of president. While keeping the immediate needs of the nation clearly in mind, Wilson nevertheless possessed a keen vision of the potential greatness of the United States.

The convention's most vocal member was another Pennsylvanian, Gouverneur Morris. A New Yorker by birth, Morris came to the state as a member of the Continental Congress and stayed in Philadelphia in the employ of Robert Morris. A Republican, Gouverneur Morris, unlike Wilson, took a very cynical view of democracy. Instead, he sought a government controlled by the rich and well-born. He preferred a president elected for life, with power to appoint a senate which also served for life. Morris argued that suffrage in national elections should be limited to freeholders. Any other solution, he believed, invited corruption. He also strenuously opposed equal representation in the Senate. Because of his aristocratic attitude, Morris contributed much to the convention debates about the powers and responsibilities of the new government.

A third Pennsylvanian who made noteworthy contributions to the convention was Benjamin Franklin. A man of remarkable achievements and international esteem, Franklin, who at eighty-one was the oldest delegate, brought a measure of respect to the convention. Though he did not participate as actively as either Wilson or Morris, Franklin's role was in many ways just as important. Perhaps his greatest contribution came during the early days of the convention, when delegates were embroiled in a potentially divisive argument about the method of representation in Congress. Franklin skillfully guided a conference committee through the differences and ultimately helped to devise an acceptable compromise, thus saving the convention from possible dissolution. Time and time again Franklin's wit and wisdom helped to steer delegates through troubled waters.

Called to order on May 25, 1787, the Philadelphia Convention was almost immediately faced with the question of whether merely to reform the Articles of Confederation or to create an altogether new frame of government. On May 29 the Virginia delegation presented the convention with fifteen resolutions that proposed sweeping changes. These proposals, which became known as the Virginia Plan, in effect advocated establishing a strong national government and limiting the authority of the states.

The Pennsylvania delegates enthusiastically supported the Virginia Plan. As one of the convention's foremost nationalists, James Wilson defended the democratic character of the plan on numerous occasions. Wilson

English-born Robert Morris (1734–1806) became one of Philadelphia's most prominent merchants in the years prior to the American Revolution. From 1781 to 1784 Robert (right) served as Superintendent of Finance and thus is known as the "Financier of the Revolution." During the Philadelphia Convention he was amazingly restrained for a man of his experience and influence. After ratification he declined Washington's offer of an appointment as secretary of the treasury and instead took a seat in the U.S. Senate. Ironically, this financial wizard—one of only two men to sign all three of America's founding documents—died in poverty after spending time in debtors' prison. Gouverneur Morris (1752–1816), who lost his left leg in a carriage accident, began his public career as a lawyer and politician in New York. In 1779 he moved to Philadelphia, where he became the principal assistant to Robert Morris (no relation), after the latter's appointment as Superintendent of Finance. Known for his brilliance, eloquence, and wit, Gouverneur Morris spoke more frequently in the Philadelphia Convention than any other delegate. In addition, he was the principal draftsman of the Constitution as a member of the Committee on Style. In later life the conservative and aristocratic Morris served as minister to France and U.S. senator. Painting by Charles Willson Peale, courtesy of the Pennsylvania Academy of the Fine Arts.

eloquently argued that the new government must be given extensive powers and that the will of the people should be the foundation upon which to build a national system. Without popular support and the power to enforce its authority, the government could not function. Popular consent would also serve as the ultimate check on governmental power. Wilson believed that a two-house legislature would provide an important check on power, for if one house should "depart from principles of the Constitution, it will be drawn back by the other house." Finally, one executive, rather than a committee as in Pennsylvania, would bring energy and responsibility to that branch of government. In the Virginia Plan, Wilson and his fellow Pennsylvania delegates saw a national government that balanced powers, incorporated obstacles to excessive power, and functioned with dispatch.

Through the convention the state's representatives consistently demonstrated a sophisticated philosophical understanding of government as well as an awareness of the potential benefits and pitfalls of their new creation. They realized that a national government could not be a creature of the states, as it had been under the Articles of Confederation, but rather had to be a separate and independent layer of government. Pennsylvania's delegates also recognized that the source of all potential power was the individual citizen and that for government to succeed, it must be responsive to the individual by protecting his rights and liberties.

Just as they had contributed to the debates, Wilson and Gouverneur Morris also made significant contributions to the actual writing of the Constitution. In late July, as a member of the Committee of Detail, Wilson was asked to help draw up a draft Constitution. A month later Morris was elected by his fellow delegates to serve on the Committee of Style, which was to produce a final version of the Constitution. Morris is given credit for having written the preamble as well as much of the rest of the Constitution. A fellow committee member, James Madison, later noted that "the finish given to the style and arrangement of the Constitution fairly belongs to Gouverneur Morris."

The Struggle to Ratify in Pennsylvania

With the Constitution written and approved by the convention, the next step in creating a national government was ratification by each state. Pennsylvania was considered crucial to ratification because of its location, size, and demographic diversity.

The state's delegates to the Constitutional Convention wasted little time informing the Assembly about the proposed Constitution. On September 18, just one day after the Constitution was formally signed, Benjamin

Franklin officially delivered a copy of the document to the Assembly, where it was read before the assemblymen and a large, receptive audience who stood in the Assembly gallery. Within a few days, every Philadelphia newspaper had printed the new form of government.

Despite the enthusiasm of many in the state Assembly, not all Pennsylvanians agreed that the Constitution should replace the Articles of Confederation. Radicals were concerned that the new national government would dominate the state government which they had created in 1776. They also feared that ratification would allow Republican lawyers and merchants centered in Philadelphia to permanently control state government and ultimately silence backcountry dissent. On the whole, Radicals saw the battle over ratification as their last chance to reassert the authority that they had once held within the state. Philosophically opposed to the idea of a national government and fighting for their political lives, they took every opportunity to slow ratification.

Even before the Constitutional Convention adjourned, Pennsylvania's Radical leaders met and planned their campaign against the new Constitution. Once it was made public, the Constitution became fair game, and Radicals attacked it with ferocity. They charged that the delegates to the Constitutional Convention had violated their instructions, the congressional resolution calling the convention, and the Articles of Confederation. They denounced the proposed new consolidated government that threatened to annihilate the states. They decried the lack of separation of powers in the new central government, and they predicted that the Senate would become an aristocratic body and the president would evolve into an elected monarch. In an obvious attempt to sway the influential Quaker population, Radicals (now called Antifederalists) condemned the constitutional provisions that sanctioned slavery and the slave trade. Most objectionable was the lack of a bill of rights. If the new Constitution were accepted without significant amendments, they said, the Revolution would have been fought in vain.

Antifederalists filled the newspapers with essays attacking the new Constitution. The most prolific and acerbic of the polemicists was "Centinel," who in eighteen numbers vilified the delegates to the Constitutional Convention. He maintained that the new Constitution was "a most daring attempt to establish a despotic aristocracy among freemen that the world has ever witnessed." He dismissed Franklin as too old and weak to know what the Constitutional Convention was really up to, and he asserted that George Washington, who was not an experienced legislator, had also been duped.

Republicans, now generally called Federalists, warmly supported the Constitution. The Articles of Confederation, they said, were too defective to amend—a wholesale change was necessary. Led by James Wilson, who was the first delegate from the Constitutional Convention to publicly explain the rationale of the convention, Federalists argued that a bill of rights was unnecessary because the Constitution created a federal republic with only delegated powers. Those powers not given to the central government were retained by the states.

The struggle to ratify the Constitution began in earnest in the Assembly in late September. Federalist assemblymen wanted to call a state ratifying convention before the legislature's scheduled adjournment on September 28. Antifederalists, hoping to regain control of the Assembly, wanted to postpone the call of a convention until after the state elections on October 9. Antifederalist assemblymen argued that the legislature should wait for official word from Congress before acting on the Constitution. Pennsylvania, they asserted, should act federally—not unilaterally.

George Clymer (1739–1813) was a prominent Philadelphia merchant who became a leader in opposing colonial rule because of the impact of British economic restrictions on his commercial enterprises. He served in Congress (1776–1777 and 1780–1782), where he signed the Declaration of Independence. Clymer served in the Pennsylvania Assembly (1784–1788) and as a delegate to the federal convention, where he spoke seldom but effectively and rarely missed a session. After signing the Constitution and working for its ratification, Clymer was elected a U.S. representative to the First Congress. After one term, Washington appointed him collector of excise taxes on alcoholic beverages in Pennsylvania, and the dignified Clymer found himself in the midst of the Whiskey Rebellion. After service on a presidential commission that negotiated a treaty with the Creek and Cherokee Indians, he retired from public life in 1796 and devoted his later years to business and civic activities. Portrait by Charles Willson Peale, courtesy of the Pennsylvania Academy of the Fine Arts.

On Friday morning, September 28, George Clymer, former delegate to the Constitutional Convention, proposed resolutions calling a state convention. After considerable debate, the assembly passed the first resolution approving a convention and then adjourned for lunch. When the Assembly reconvened in the afternoon, the nineteen Antifederalist assemblymen boycotted the session, thus denying the house its required two-thirds majority quorum. The sergeant-at-arms was sent to return two of the assemblymen so that the final resolutions, providing for the election, place of meeting, and pay of the convention, could be approved. But the sergeant-at-arms returned empty-handed, and the Assembly adjourned for the day.

When the Assembly reconvened on Saturday, September 29, the seceding assemblymen had not returned. During the night, however, word had come from New York by express rider that Congress had officially sent the Constitution to the states with a recommendation that ratifying conventions be called by the legislatures. Again, the sergeant-at-arms was sent to corral two Antifederalist assemblymen so that a quorum could be attained, and again he returned alone. A mob, however, succeeded in forcibly returning the necessary two seceding assemblymen, and the legislature completed its business. Delegates to the convention were to be elected on November 6 and would meet in Philadelphia two weeks later.

As expected, the election brought advocates of immediate ratification a decisive victory. While no Federalist in the Assembly ran for election to the ratifying convention, there were enough prominent supporters of the Constitution, including James Wilson and Chief Justice Thomas McKean, to provide a distinguished Federalist contingent at the convention. Although substantially outnumbered, Antifederalist delegates also played a significant role at this conclave. Led by Robert Whitehill, William Findley and John Smilie, Pennsylvania's Antifederalists argued that the Constitution lacked any guarantee of individual liberties and demanded a bill of rights before they would support ratification. While Federalists successfully countered most of the Antifederalist charges, the call for a bill of rights remained a formidable point of contention. Finally, on December 12, 1787, just five days after ratification by Delaware, Pennsylvania's convention voted by a 2-to-1 margin (46 to 23) in favor of the new Constitution.

A New State Constitution

With the Constitution ratified and Federalists entrenched as Pennsylvania's representatives on both the state and national levels, the victorious faction saw their opportunity to replace the Pennsylvania constitution of 1776. Radicals, or Antifederalists, recognizing the inevitability of change, could do little to stop the reform movement. In March 1789, as the new national government began to organize in New York, the Pennsylvania Assembly called for a state constitutional convention to be held the following November. Throughout the summer both parties campaigned vigorously; however, the election was generally free of the rancor and partisan attacks that had characterized state politics since 1776. As a result, an air of conciliation and cooperation dominated the convention.

In many ways the new state constitution of 1790 was patterned after the United States Constitution. It provided for a powerful governor who could veto legislation, grant pardons, and control the state militia. Instead of the unicameral legislature, a state Senate and a House of Representatives were created. All adult males who paid taxes were allowed to vote without being required to take an oath of any kind. In addition, the new state constitution guaranteed religious and civil liberty.

The implementation of the state constitution in September 1790 brought to a close a fourteen-year epoch of revolution and counterrevolution

Thomas McKean (1734–1817), like John Dickinson, carved out a political and legal career in both Delaware and Pennsylvania. He represented Delaware in Congress (1774–1776 and 1778–1783), where he signed the Declaration of Independence and served as president in 1781. In Pennsylvania, McKean served as chief justice from 1777 to 1799. Although he was not a delegate to the Grand Convention, he was active in securing Pennsylvania's approval of the Constitution as a leading member of the state ratifying convention. Comparing the arguments of the Antifederalists to "the feeble noise occasioned by the working of small beer," he pronounced the Constitution "the best the world has ever seen." McKean served as Democratic-Republican governor of Pennsylvania from 1799 to 1808. Etching from a portrait by Gilbert Stuart, courtesy of the Pennsylvania State Archives.

in Pennsylvania. During the political struggle that characterized those years, the debate surrounding the creation and ratification of the United States Constitution became pivotal. In essence, the constitutional contest in Pennsylvania became the final battleground for the state's two revolutionary parties and ultimately inspired a new frame of state government, one more attuned to the need of the times.

Pennsylvania: Essay on Sources

For anyone interested in exploring the role Pennsylvania played in the making of the U.S. Constitution, a number of sources are essential. James B. McMaster and Frederick Stone, *Pennsylvania and the Federal Constitution* (Lancaster, 1888) was one of the earliest studies and remains valuable. Two other early sources that should not be overlooked are James Madison's *Journals of the Constitutional Convention* and Paul Ford, comp., *Pamphlets on the Constitution of the United States* (Brooklyn, 1888). Robert Brunhouse, *The Counter-Revolution in Pennsylvania, 1776–1790* (Harrisburg, 1942) provides a detailed account of state politics during the period, with an emphasis on internal class conflicts, and Paul Selsam, *The Pennsylvania Constitution of 1776* (Philadelphia, 1936) offers a fine description of the state's first constitution.

In *The Creation of the American Republic, 1776–1787* (Chapel Hill, 1969), Gordon Wood spends much time discussing the Keystone State. Likewise, *The First American Constitutions* (Chapel Hill, 1980), by Willi Paul Adams, provides worthwhile information on the Confederation era.

An essential source for understanding the ratification process in Pennsylvania is *The Documentary History of the Constitution*, vol. 2: *Pennsylvania* (Madison, Wis. 1976), edited by Merrill Jensen, John P. Kaminski and Gaspare J. Saladino. Owen S. Ireland, "The Ratification of the Federal Constitution in Pennsylvania" (doctoral dissertation, University of Pittsburgh, 1966) is also excellent.

For general background, consult Philip S. Klein and Ari Hoogenboom, *A History of Pennsylvania* (New York, 1973). Important biographies are *James Wilson, Founding Father, 1742–1798* (Chapel Hill, 1956), by Charles Page Smith; *John Dickinson: Conservative Revolutionary* (Charlottesville, Va., 1983), by Milton E. Flower; *Gouverneur Morris and the American Revolution* (Norman, Okla., 1970), by Max M. Muntz; *James Wilson* (Milford, N.Y., 1978), by Geoffrey Seed; *Benjamin Franklin* (New York, 1938), by Carl Van Doren; *Franklin* (New York, 1976), by David Freeman Hawke; and *Franklin of Philadelphia* (Cambridge, Mass., 1986), by Esmond Wright. The serious scholar will also find *The Works of James Wilson*, 2 vols. (Cambridge, Mass., 1967), edited by Robert G. McCloskey, of great interest.

3

New Jersey and the Two Constitutions

MARY R. MURRIN
Research Associate
New Jersey Historical Commission

HE ENGLISH SETTLED NEW JERSEY in the mid-1660s, shortly after wresting the area from its original colonizers and their main commercial rivals, the Dutch. After the restoration of Charles II in 1660, his brother James, Duke of York, mounted a successful expedition against New Netherland. In 1664 James conveyed what is now New Jersey to two supporters of the royal court, John Lord Berkeley and Sir George Carteret. They had full title to the soil; they assumed they had governmental powers as well. The duke's chosen governor, Richard Nicolls, unaware of the duke's grant to Berkeley and Carteret, parceled out considerable acreage to various settlers.

Despite the uncertainty as to their legal right to rule, Berkeley and Carteret immediately drew up a frame of government for the new colony. Their "Concessions and Agreements" of 1665 offered liberal political and religious rights to prospective settlers. Yet initial harmony quickly yielded to conflict, largely over the payment of quit rents and the competing land claims caused by the duke's grants of power to both a governor and the two proprietors. A brief Dutch reconquest in 1673–74 was largely uneventful; but the retrocession to England brought with it significant change.

In 1674 Berkeley sold his share to Edward Byllynge and John Fenwick, and in 1676 Carteret agreed to a partition of the province into East and West Jersey. For the next quarter century West Jersey developed under Quaker influence, while Carteret's East Jersey became more heterogeneous, attracting not only English Quakers but Dutch immigrants from New York, Puritans from New England, Anglicans from England, and both Presbyterians and Quakers from Scotland. The West Jersey proprietors issued a liberal frame of government, the West Jersey Concessions, in 1677. Like its East Jersey counterpart, the Concessions were designed to attract settlers. Both guaranteed the basic rights of Englishmen, freedom of conscience, access to land, and participation in government. Both established general assemblies with elected lower houses. However, the West Jersey Concessions spelled out the powers of the assembly in greater detail and specified individual liberties, such as trial by jury, protection from arbitrary arrest, the secret ballot and a liberal code of laws. The East Jersey assemblies adopted a stringent criminal code modeled on the Duke's Laws of 1665.

During the period of division both Jerseys were beset by complicated questions of land ownership and by repeated challenges from New York to their independent status. In 1702 the proprietors, unable to rule effectively, surrendered all governing rights to the Crown. East and West Jersey became a single royal colony. Edward Hyde, Lord Cornbury, a cousin of Queen Anne, was New Jersey's first royal governor. Until 1738 the governor of New York also served, under separate commission, as governor of New Jersey, but beginning with Lewis Morris, New Jersey was permitted its own royal governor.

The proprietors retained their property interests, and New Jersey continued to be plagued with land disputes well after the Revolution. A Board of Proprietors of East Jersey (established in 1684 and headquartered in Perth Amboy) and a similar organization for West Jersey (established in 1688 and headquartered in Burlington) have continued in existence to the present day.

Problems Under the Articles of Confederation

At the close of the Revolutionary War, New Jersey faced many of the same difficulties besetting other states. However, internal differences complicated the state's response to problems of debtor-creditor relations, currency, and the Continental debt. Distinctive patterns of ethnicity, land use, trade, and religion established during the proprietary period, when New Jersey was two colonies, were still evident. But although the two regions, East and West Jersey, were at loggerheads on possible solutions to these postwar problems, a decade of experience trying to resolve them made the state as a whole receptive to the Constitution. New Jerseyans believed the

Articles of Confederation to be seriously flawed and were united on two major issues troubling the new nation—the disposition of western lands and Congress' need for a secure income.

The New Jersey legislature made its position on the Confederation quite clear in 1778. On June 16 it sent a remonstrance to the Continental Congress listing a number of objections to the proposed Articles of Confederation and urging their revision. The memorial New Jersey submitted devoted much space to issues of revenue, trade regulation, and western lands—topics of great importance during the next decade.

The legislature called for fixed state boundaries within five years, argued that Congress should have sole authority to regulate trade and impose customs duties, and observed that Congress should have authority over western lands so that all states might benefit rather than a few. On this last point the legislature observed plaintively,

> Shall such States as are shut out by Situation from availing themselves of the least Advantage from this Quarter, be left to sink under an enormous Debt, whilst others are enabled, in a short Period, to replace all their Expenditures from the hard Earnings of the whole Confederacy?

Congress listened, but it rejected the proposed revisions. In July, New Jersey delegate Nathaniel Scudder wrote to John Hart, the speaker of the New Jersey Assembly, urging the legislature to direct its delegates to ratify the Articles despite any disadvantages to the state. He pointed out that small states could be at a severe disadvantage if Congress began amending the Articles. Warning of the "fatal Consequences" should the Articles not be ratified and America be discovered to be "a Rope of Sand," Scudder asserted that "every State must expect to be subjected to considerable local Disadvantages in a general Confederation." In November, still convinced the Articles needed substantial revision, the legislature relented. New Jersey was the eleventh state to ratify, followed by Delaware and Maryland, two other small states that objected to the absence of any provision for the western lands.

New Jersey's objections were understandable. The Articles, which largely continued the constitutional relationship established under the Continental Congress, gave the Confederation Congress no power to tax, impose customs duties, or regulate trade (except by treaty). Under the Articles, and indeed after 1779, Congress no longer paid its bills simply by printing paper money. All governmental expenses, such as those required by the prosecution of the war and the servicing of the Continental debt, depended upon a system of requisition. Congress met its expenses by assessing each state a quota of the total amount. New Jersey had no source of income to satisfy these requisitions except by imposing direct taxes on its citizens. A small state with fixed boundaries, New Jersey had no western lands, no real port, and negligible foreign trade. Her merchants shipped through the ports of Philadelphia and New York City, and both New York and Pennsylvania exacted heavy import duties. As one historian has observed, New Jersey was like "a barrel tapped at both ends."

The Social Structure

New Jersey was an agricultural state: somewhere between 70 and 80 percent of the population of 150,000 owed its living in some way to the land. No town boasted more than 1,500 inhabitants. But despite the state's overall rural character, East and West Jersey exhibited important differences.

Dutch, English, Scots-Irish, Irish, and Germans made up the bulk of East Jersey's white population. Most of the state's black population of 10,000 (the majority slaves) lived in the northern part of the state, especially Bergen and Somerset counties. Economically, East Jersey was in New York City's orbit. It was a region of small family farms which produced little for sale. A few small manufactories and iron works and a number of artisans and shopkeepers completed the economic picture. Four of the state's largest towns—Newark, Elizabeth Town, Perth Amboy, and New Brunswick—were in East Jersey. English Calvinist and Dutch Reformed were the predominant religions; the Episcopal Church attracted fewer members.

West Jersey's population was more homogeneous, primarily English, with a few Germans, Finns, and Swedes. Politically it was dominated by Quakers who had not been enthusiastic supporters of either the war or measures to pay for the war. Economically the region looked to Philadelphia. Farms were larger, more prosperous than East Jersey's and produced some crops for sale. West Jersey escaped much of the devastation of the war, and few Continental creditors lived there.

Postwar Problems

The state, especially the northern part, was a major theater of battle between 1776 and 1780. One historian has called it "the cockpit of the Revolution." The clashing armies and the guerrilla warfare between patriots and the large loyalist population damaged and destroyed farms, houses, and towns. Farmers received payment for only a portion of the goods taken or destroyed. In 1779–80, when currency problems were at their height, federal officers left certificates or promises to pay. At war's end New Jersey was not only

58

devastated; her citizens, particularly those in East Jersey, held a sizable portion of the notes and certificates which constituted the Continental debt.

The economic depression of the mid-1780s had a profound effect on relations between New Jersey's creditors and debtors. People who had speculated in land and goods on the easy credit of the inflationary wartime economy found themselves in debt as the economy contracted. The depression affected the entire American economy. British closure of the West Indies to American shipping cut off a major trade outlet. American merchants, who had restocked their wares on credit as the war ended, found few customers for their goods. A series of crop failures brought severe hardship to New Jersey's farmers, already in difficulty from wartime devastation, debt, and high taxes. The number of lawsuits for recovery of debt mushroomed.

East Jersey legislators tended to support any measures, such as paper-money bills, that helped the many debtors among their constituents and to vote against measures which required the spending of money. West Jersey legislators, often wealthier than their East Jersey counterparts and representing fewer debtors, opposed measures favoring debtors, including paper-money bills.

A postwar dispute over the location of the dividing line between East and West Jersey significantly weakened the creditor influence within the legislature. The two boards of proprietors had surrendered political power when the Jerseys became a single royal colony in 1702, but they retained title to considerable amounts of land. The dispute over an improperly located dividing line occupied the attention of both groups of proprietors for several years as they argued the case before the legislature. Loath to offend potentially friendly legislators, the East Jersey proprietors mounted no opposition to prodebtor legislation. They won their case, but the two groups of proprietors, which might otherwise have combined to form a united procreditor front, exerted little or no influence on politics.

Paper Money

The Assembly passed a number of prodebtor measures in the early 1780s, including bills forcing creditors to accept paper money rather than specie, delaying court proceedings, releasing jailed debtors from confinement, and preventing the forced sale of debtor estates at reduced value. Creditors found the latter measure particularly reprehensible and believed that debtor-relief bills violated the sanctity of contracts and damaged public and private credit.

The 1785 session was marked by a fierce debate over a paper-money or loan office bill. The proposed loan office would issue paper money and lend it, at interest, to borrowers with sufficient landed security. Borrowers would repay the money in regular installments. As the loans were repaid, the principal would be withdrawn from circulation and destroyed. The interest payments would go to the state treasury for government expenses. The loan office had proved a convenient fiscal expedient in the past, especially in the middle colonies, and New Jersey's colonial experience with the device had been reasonably successful. The loan office debate provoked sharp exchanges from three of New Jersey's most influential political figures—Abraham Clark, William Livingston, and William Paterson.

Abraham Clark (1726–1794) was a figure of signal importance in New Jersey during the 1770s and 1780s. A signer of the Declaration of Independence, he either sat in the New Jersey Assembly or represented New Jersey in Congress for most of the period from 1776 to 1794. A man of fervent republican sympathies, he was the acknowledged champion of New Jersey's many indebted farmers, a position he eloquently presented in a series of anonymous newspaper essays and in a pamphlet entitled *The True Policy of New-Jersey, Defined.* Clark loathed privilege, distrusted lawyers, and had few kind words for merchants. At home he was a major advocate of paper money and other debtor-relief measures. In the wider arena he feared the economic power of New York and Pennsylvania over New Jersey and favored some expansion of congressional power, including a grant to the national legislature of authority over western lands. He represented New Jersey in the Annapolis Convention in September 1786, but he refused to accept appointment to the federal convention.

William Livingston (1723–1790) was governor of New Jersey from 1776 to his death in 1790. He served as one of New Jersey's delegates to both the First and Second Continental congresses before his selection as governor. Livingston was an accomplished polemicist, and his "Primitive Whig" essays made a forceful case for the hard-money, procreditor position. He served as one of New Jersey's delegates to the Constitutional Convention, but age and ill-health limited his contribution.

William Paterson (1745–1806) was a strong nationalist and, like Livingston, a vigorous Whig and staunch defender of property rights. A lawyer, Paterson was involved in two of the most divisive issues in New Jersey politics during the 1780s—the dividing-line controversy and debtor-creditor disputes. Paterson served in New Jersey's first and second provincial congresses, as New Jersey's attorney general, as one of New Jersey's delegates to the Constitutional Convention, and later as governor and then associate justice of the United States Supreme Court.

Advocates of the loan office bill argued that it would provide a necessary circulating medium for specie-poor New Jersey. Money did not circulate widely in the state's weak economy. In consequence, citizens found it difficult to pay either their debts or their taxes. Clark scornfully described the loan office opponents as "artful, designing men" and pictured creditors as "money-men ... wishing for greater power to grind the faces of the needy."

Opponents of the loan office bill argued that paper money was a direct attack on the sanctity of contracts because it inevitably depreciated. If debtors were allowed to pay creditors in depreciated currency, creditors would be cheated of the amounts rightfully owed them. According to their arguments, money was not scarce; debtors were simply lazy individuals attempting to evade the payment of lawful debts. Livingston described debtors as "idle spendthrifts" and looked forward to the day "when laws [would] be made in favor of creditors instead of debtors; and when no cozening, trickish fraudulent scoundrel [should] be able to plead legal protection for his cozenage, tricks, frauds and rascality." Paterson argued for a decrease in the amount of money available because such a measure would "introduce a Spirit of Industry & Frugality ... [and] compel people to work for the Bread they eat, and not go about seeking whom they may devour."

Abraham Clark (1726– 1794), a surveyor, farmer, lawyer, legislator, and signer of the Declaration of Independence, served in Congress from 1776–1778, 1780–1783, and 1786–1788. He represented the state in the Annapolis Convention and was selected to the Philadelphia Convention, but he refused to serve. Hesitant about the new Constitution because of the lack of a bill of rights, this spokesman for the agrarian interest was elected to the Second and Third Congresses and died in office in September 1794. Engraving from a painting by James Reid Lambdin of a original portrait by John Trumbull, courtesy of Independence National Historical Park and New York Public Library.

The legislature finally passed the paper-money bill in May 1786. The measure may have done little to relieve the situation of those in the most dire straits, but the legislature's attention to the agrarian discontent may have spared New Jersey from the kind of trouble Massachusetts experienced with Shays' Rebellion.

The weight of private debt made the problem of public debt more urgent. With no revenue from ports or western lands, New Jersey could meet congressional requisitions only by taxing its hard-pressed citizens, many of whom were the same Continental creditors Congress was raising money to pay. Not surprisingly, New Jersey was a strong advocate of alternative means to finance the central government.

During the war Congress and the states created several varieties of financial paper—certificates issued to pay for military supplies, notes given soldiers and militiamen in payment for services, and legal-tender paper money. Wartime inflation reduced its value nearly as fast as it was printed. Most of

William Livingston (1723–1790) rose to prominence as a lawyer and legislator in New York. His wife Susanna, who bore him thirteen children, was the daughter of a prosperous New Jersey landowner, a fact which prompted Livingston's move to the Elizabeth Town area in 1772. He became a leader in the movement for independence, serving in Congress from 1774 to 1776. He was elected the first governor of the state of New Jersey late in 1776. Amazingly, he held that position for fourteen consecutive years until his death. His gubernatorial duties lessened his role in the Philadelphia Convention, but he performed important committee work, especially as chairman of the body that formulated the three-fifths compromise. Livingston was a major force in New Jersey's rapid ratification of the Constitution. Portrait by Henry Harrison, courtesy of the New Jersey State Museum, Trenton.

this financial paper was issued by Congress and constituted the Continental debt. New Jersey's citizens held about one-eleventh of this debt, a large amount for such a small state. This high percentage was attributable to the state's situation as a major theater of war.

Congress made several attempts to deal with its currency and debt problems. In 1780 it called in the old currency at a proportion of 1 to 40 and asked the states to issue new paper money. New Jersey arranged to redeem the old currency, but the new issue depreciated rapidly despite the state's vigorous efforts to maintain its value.

Many New Jerseyans had little faith in the new currency and declined to accept it. The controversy over its value developed largely along sectional lines. West Jersey legislators, whose region had little to lose because it had little of the old currency, favored redemption of the new issue at current rather than face value. East Jerseyans favored redemption at the higher face value. This would benefit the region's creditors and satisfy its fiscal con-

William Paterson (1745– 1806), born in County Antrim, Ireland, was one of seven foreign-born signers of the Constitution. He studied law under Richard Stockton and became a leader in the Revolutionary movement. Paterson served as New Jersey attorney general from 1776 to 1783. At Philadelphia he introduced the New Jersey, or Paterson, Plan to protect the interests of the small states. In 1789 the New Jersey legislature chose him to be one of his state's first U.S. senators, and in that office he played a key role in the drafting of the Judiciary Act of 1789. Paterson was elected governor of New Jersey in 1790 and held that position until Washington appointed him an associate justice of the U.S. Supreme Court in 1793, a position he held until his death. Portrait by Edward Ludlow Mooney, Special Collections, Alexander Library, Rutgers University.

servatives, who viewed redemption at current depreciated value as a faithless repudiation of honestly incurred debt. Sectional divisions within the legislature prevented any resolution of the issue until after the October 1784 elections, when the political makeup of the Council (the upper house) changed. The Council and Assembly finally agreed on redemption at the depreciated value.

Western Lands

New Jersey's problems with the Confederation extended well beyond the currency issue. Many states were disturbed by the absence of any provision in the Articles for the disposition of trans-Appalachian lands claimed by some of the states under their colonial charters. New Jersey and other landless states, wanting to limit the western claims of states like Virginia, argued that the former Crown lands belonged in common to the Union. New Jersey's position was prompted both by its precarious economic situation and by the presence in the legislature of men who had invested in speculative land companies.

The land companies' claims to western lands were based on Indian deeds they had purchased. However, Virginia and other states, citing their original charters, claimed the same territory. In 1780 the New Jersey Assembly appointed a committee to investigate its citizens' western land claims. The Indiana Company, which counted many prominent citizens of New Jersey among its investors, was represented on the committee. Not surprisingly, the committee's report concluded that the lands belonged to the states in common. In December 1780 the Assembly sent Congress a memorial based on this report.

In January 1781 Virginia offered to cede the northern part of its western claim if all prior Indian claims were voided and Virginia's rights to the remaining territory were confirmed. New Jersey, among other states, objected strenuously. In October 1781 the New Jersey Assembly instructed its delegates to the Confederation Congress to oppose the cession and demand a resolution of the Indiana Company claim. Congress rejected Virginia's proposal in November, and the issue remained unresolved until March 1784, when Congress finally accepted the partial cession in a compromise which incorporated an understanding that the Indian grants would not be upheld.

Dissatisfied with the proposed compromise, New Jersey attempted to bring the land dispute before the Confederation as a suit between the states of Virginia and New Jersey. When this failed, New Jersey voted against the Virginia land cession. As late as March 1786, long after the land question had been resolved, New Jersey's legislature continued to instruct the state's delegates to oppose any western lands bill if the legislation might benefit one state exclusively.

New Jersey considered the western lands to be important, both as a source of revenue for the central government and as a prime area where the state's many impoverished farmers might seek a new start. However, the opening of the West to settlement depended upon the free navigation of the Mississippi River, and New Jersey's position on this issue differed from that of other northern states.

Britain had conceded the right to free navigation of the Mississippi River in the Treaty of Paris of 1783, but Spain actually controlled the region. To protect their territory, the Spanish closed the river to American shipping in 1784. Further, they demanded the renunciation of any American claim to free navigation of the Mississippi as the price of a commercial treaty.

Most of the northern states were quite willing to give up free navigation for a commercial treaty with Spain. A treaty would provide commercial opportunities for eastern cities hard-pressed by the postwar economic depression and give the new nation some commercial standing. Continued closure of the Mississippi River would prevent expansion into the West, an area all regions expected the South to dominate, and thus keep southern power in check.

The South promoted the opening of the West not only because expansion would increase its own influence but because the South feared the West might opt for independence if it were not brought into the Confederation quickly.

John Jay of New York, the American Secretary for Foreign Affairs, concluded that to insist on free navigation was futile, and he requested a change in his instructions. In August 1786 Congress agreed to Jay's proposed revision. Initially, two of New Jersey's three delegates supported revision. Virginia, convinced New Jersey might be persuaded that the opening of the West coincided with her best interests, directed James Madison to buttonhole Abraham Clark at the Annapolis Convention. Madison convinced Clark, who in turn helped persuade the New Jersey legislature to instruct the state's congressional delegates to restore the original demand for free navigation of the Mississippi.

A Spanish commercial treaty attractive to northern states blessed with ports and shipping industries was of little interest to a state with neither. The value of the western lands depended on opening the area for settlement. Once Congress controlled the western lands, New Jersey favored any course increasing their value.

New Jersey's Fiscal Problems with Congress

Congress' efforts to put its financial house in order did not end with the currency plan of 1780. In February 1781, before ratification of the Articles was complete, Congress asked the states to amend the document and give it the authority to levy a 5 percent tariff on certain imports—a move New Jersey favored heartily. Twelve states approved the 1781 impost, but passage required the assent of all thirteen. Rhode Island's negative vote killed the plan.

In September 1782 Congress made an emergency requisition on the states to pay the interest on the national debt. New Jersey's legislature took no action, an oversight which irritated the state's many Continental creditors. Stung by the public response, the legislature passed the required legislation in June 1783. In December the legislature moved to protect these creditors and bypass the requisition system it considered inequitable. It directed the state treasurer to pay the money directly to the federal public creditors resident in New Jersey rather than forward it to the Confederation treasury.

Meanwhile, Congress was again at work on a scheme to secure a regular source of income. In April 1783 it asked the states for the authority to levy a 5 percent tariff on certain goods for a period of twenty-five years. The proceeds would be used for public debt payments. In addition, it requested a supplemental revenue, also for twenty-five years, and the cession of all Crown lands still held by the states.

The New Jersey legislature had little reason to believe all thirteen states would agree to this impost when they had not approved the previous one. Nevertheless the legislature approved the duty and the land cession, but it delayed action on the supplemental revenue. In December 1783 the legislature authorized the necessary tax. It made it payable in paper money and ordered the printing of an amount equal to New Jersey's quota of the supplemental revenue. But as it did with the emergency requisition, it ordered the state treasurer to pay New Jersey creditors of the United States directly rather than forwarding any monies to the Confederation treasury. In December 1784 the legislature reaffirmed its decision and ordered the state treasurer to make no further payments on congressional requisitions until the states approved the impost.

As expected, all thirteen states did not ratify the financial plan. The significance of New Jersey's refusal to meet the requisition escaped notice because Congress made no new call for funds until September 1785 when it issued a requisition couched in language that enraged New Jersey's legislators. Congress announced it would not be responsible for interest payments made by any state to its own Continental creditors after January 1786. Further, it refused to issue interest certificates to public creditors of any state which failed to comply with the requisition.

The legislature fumed. New Jersey had expected to be reimbursed at some future point for the payments made to Continental creditors. In a December 9 letter to the state's congressional delegation, New Jersey assemblyman Abraham Clark noted that New Jersey had incurred considerable expense by shouldering the financial burdens of Congress and was now about to be penalized for doing so. He also observed that New Jersey's citizens had lent money to Congress as private citizens. No action of the legislature of the state where they resided should interfere with repayment. Supplying New Jersey's share of the requisition required oppressive taxes, said Clark; moreover, the state's hard-pressed citizens also paid tariffs to both New York and Pennsylvania, contributing handsomely to *their* state treasuries. Clark described the requisition as a scheme to subvert the impost, the only practicable means of raising a revenue. The requisition system of Congress was "a burden too unequal and grievous for this State to submit to." In February the legislature resolved to take no action on the requisition until the impost was passed. And until the impost was passed, the state's congressional delegation was to vote against any expense to New Jersey unless the measure benefited the state or the Union in general.

Congress was shocked by New Jersey's defiant posture and quickly dispatched Charles Pinckney of South Carolina, Nathaniel Gorham of Massachusetts, and William Grayson of Virginia to placate the legislators and plead with them to reconsider. Pinckney painted a gloomy picture of the dissolution of the Confederation should the New Jersey legislature remain recalcitrant, and he touched on the grim consequences of such a breakup for small states like New Jersey. He suggested that a proper remedy to the perceived difficulties with the Confederation might be a state call for a general convention to amend the Articles. The legislators discussed the matter for three days and agreed to rescind the vote, but they continued to insist that the requisition system was unreasonable.

New Jersey's change of heart was more cosmetic than real. The state took no steps to comply with the requisition. Indeed, few states made any attempt to supply the requisitioned funds. By June 1786 Congress was nearly out of money.

New Jersey's fiscal rebellion lent considerable weight to calls for some reform of the Articles. Congress had coped as best it could with the unwieldy requisition system. New Jersey's refusal to comply with that system, which it perceived as grossly unfair, made the fragility of the Union apparent.

New Jersey Delegates in the Constitutional Convention

Virginia's invitation to a September 1786 convention at Annapolis to discuss congressional power over trade followed closely upon New Jersey's refusal to honor the requisition. New Jersey sent three delegates—Abraham Clark, William Churchill Houston, and James Schureman—and equipped them with liberal instructions. The trio was authorized to examine the trade of the United States and the several states, to consider a uniform system of trade regulations, and to deal with other matters as well.

It was an interesting delegation. Clark advocated some expansion in the authority of Congress and was particularly concerned about the economic domination of New Jersey by New York and Pennsylvania. Houston (1746–1788) was a prominent lawyer whose specialties were tax and financial questions. Schureman (1756–1824) was a prominent New Brunswick merchant who had served in both the New Jersey Assembly and the Confederation Congress. He was a staunch nationalist and a determined opponent of all paper-money measures.

Delegations from New Jersey, Virginia, New York, Delaware, and Pennsylvania attended the convention. No delegation arrived with the same instructions. Delegates from New Hampshire, Rhode Island, Massachusetts, and North Carolina did not arrive in time; the other states ignored the call. Under these circumstances the convention could reach no conclusions. However, the delegates returned to their states with a report proposing that another convention be held in Philadelphia in May 1787 and noting that "the Idea of extending the powers of their Deputies, to other objects than those of Commerce which has been adopted by the State of New Jersey . . . will deserve to be incorporated into that of a future Convention." Congress approved the recommendation in February 1787.

New Jersey, Pennsylvania, Virginia, Delaware, and North Carolina named delegates to the Constitutional Convention before Congress even endorsed the idea. With the exception of Rhode Island, which ignored the convention entirely, the remaining states chose delegates between February and June, in part spurred by the specter of armed resistance raised by Shays' Rebellion in Massachusetts.

New Jersey finally settled on William Livingston, Jonathan Dayton, William Paterson, David Brearly, and William Churchill Houston as delegates. Houston did not attend, possibly because of illness.

David Brearly (1745–1790) was a prominent lawyer who had helped draft the New Jersey constitution in 1776. He was the chief justice of the New Jersey Supreme Court from 1779 to 1789 and a judge of the U.S. District

Court from 1789 to his death. He was a strong opponent of paper money and became a Federalist.

Jonathan Dayton (1760–1826) was the youngest man at the convention. He was a captain during the Revolutionary War but early established a reputation for imprudence. A member of a wealthy family, he owned large amounts of public securities and was an enthusiastic land speculator. At the convention he was a vigorous exponent of the rights of small states. Though considered Clark's protégé, Dayton became a Federalist.

Paterson proved to be the most important member of the delegation, though all five men went on to hold important state or federal office under the new Constitution.

The delegates to the Philadelphia Convention faced no easy task. First, they had to reach agreement on how radically to reform the Articles. Further, they had to achieve consensus on the amount of authority to be given the central government and how the states might be protected both from each other and from the central government.

Jonathan Dayton (1760–1824) was the youngest signer (age 26) of the Constitution. A Princeton graduate, he compiled a distinguished war record during the Revolution. Dayton arrived in Philadelphia on June 21 as a replacement for his patron, Abraham Clark. He later served in the U.S. House of Representatives (1791–1799), becoming speaker in the Fourth and Fifth Congresses. Then he served one term in the U.S. Senate (1799–1805). His national reputation suffered because of his involvement with Aaron Burr's intrigues in the southwest. A land speculator, Dayton owned 250,000 acres of Ohio land in the vicinity of the city that now bears his name. Portrait in Art in the United States Capitol *(Washington, D.C., 1976).*

Governor Edmund Randolph, head of the Virginia delegation, presented a series of resolutions on May 29. This Virginia Plan, drafted by Madison, called for a bicameral Congress with proportional representation. The lower house would be elected by the people, the upper house by the lower from a slate of nominees proposed by the state legislatures. Congress would choose the executive and could veto all state laws contravening the federal constitution. At least one supreme court and a system of inferior courts would make up the judicial branch. A council of revision consisting of the executive and several members of the judiciary would have a veto over the legislature.

The small states, including New Jersey, objected because the Virginia Plan would place them at a disadvantage. The larger states would control both houses and the executive. On June 15 Paterson presented a plan based on a reform of the Articles rather than an entirely new frame of government. This proposal would retain the Confederation's principle of equal representation for each state. In addition, Congress would receive limited power to tax and to regulate interstate and foreign commerce. The states would be freed from the requisition method of finance. Congress would control the disposition of western lands and could negotiate freely with foreign powers. The Paterson scheme also contained a provision making federal law and treaties "the supreme law of the respective states." This suggestion became the basis for the "supreme law of the land" clause in Article VI of the final document.

New Jersey's delegation was actually responsible for two proposals in support of equal representation. Brearly suggested that all existing state boundaries be redrawn, providing for thirteen precisely equal states. The convention made approving noises about the desirability of equitable boundaries, but it took no action.

The convention debated Paterson's scheme (also called the New Jersey or Small State Plan) for three days before rejecting it and deciding to use the Virginia Plan as the basis for debate. The small states continued to oppose proportional representation because it embodied some of their worst fears about the domination of small by large states. In July the convention broke the stalemate when it accepted a compromise calling for a two-house legislature, one house with representation based on population and the other with each state receiving equal representation.

Once New Jersey was assured of some form of equal representation, its delegation found the new Constitution quite a suitable frame of government, since it provided useful solutions for many of the problems New Jersey had first cited in 1778 when responding initially to the Articles.

The provisions allotting the federal government the power to regulate commerce (foreign and interstate), issue currency, and govern western lands, and the language upholding the sanctity of contracts, addressed the concerns of both East and West Jerseyans.

Stripping the states of the power to exact their own tariffs removed an economic burden from New Jersey and dissipated considerable hostility towards New York and Pennsylvania. The opening of the West would not only provide the new government a source of income but secure new opportunities for New Jersey's many impoverished farmers.

Throughout the Confederation period the state had suffered from depreciated currency and debt problems. New Jersey held a substantial portion of the Continental debt and had shouldered the heavy burden of interest payments to the state's Continental creditors, a burden the legislature believed should be the concern of the central government. There was little reason for any area of New Jersey to object to a new government which proposed to assume this debt. And New Jerseyans, appalled at the multiple and depreciating currencies and periodic repudiations of the Confederation years, were pleased with the prospect of a more stable financial system.

The form of government the convention produced owed more to Virginia's contribution than New Jersey's. Paterson's scheme rearranged the elements of the Confederation; Randolph's restructured the government. Still, New Jersey's contribution to the constitutional process was significant. The legislature's exasperation with the Confederation's mode of finance finally led to the flat refusal to comply with the requisition. This stand certainly encouraged the pursuit of more sweeping change among those states which sent delegations to Annapolis. New Jersey's broad instructions to its delegates were cited as a model, and the New Jersey Plan provided a useful corrective to the Virginia Plan.

The Constitution Ratified

The Philadelphia Convention's handiwork became public knowledge quickly. The full text of the Constitution appeared in the *Trenton Mercury* and in a New Brunswick broadside on September 25. In the first three weeks of October the legislature received several petitions from citizens of Salem, Gloucester, Middlesex, and Burlington counties calling for a ratifying convention. All expressed approval of the new frame of government; the most fervent was one from Salem, which read in part, "Nothing but the most immediate adoption of it can save the United States in general, and this state in particular, from absolute ruin."

Congress authorized the states to call ratifying conventions in late September. A month later, on October 29, the New Jersey legislature unanimously passed resolutions calling for a state convention. The elections were without incident, and on December 11 the delegates convened in Trenton at the Blazing Star tavern.

Information about the convention's deliberations is scanty. According to the account published in the *Trenton Mercury*, the delegates spent December 11–13 selecting officers, discussing rules, reading the legislature's authorizing resolution, and examining the Constitution. On December 14, 15, and 16 the Constitution was analyzed section by section. On December 18 the Constitution was again read, debated, and unanimously approved. A ceremonial procession to the courthouse for a public reading followed ratification. The celebration was punctuated by fifteen rounds of musket fire, thirteen for the new nation and one each for Delaware and Pennsylvania, which had ratified before New Jersey. The delegates then repaired to a nearby tavern, seeking a more convivial atmosphere for the expression of their satisfaction with the completed task. The newspaper account makes it plain

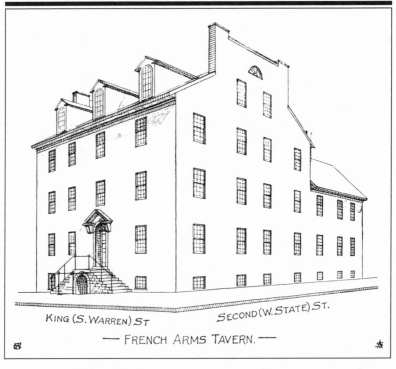

KING (S. WARREN) ST   SECOND (W. STATE) ST.

— FRENCH ARMS TAVERN. —

The New Jersey ratifying convention of December 1787 was held at the Blazing Star Tavern (later called the French Arms Tavern) in Trenton at the corner of King and Second streets (now South Warren and West State). India ink sketch by Carl W. Stead (ca. 1919) in Carlos E. Godfrey, The Mechanics Bank, 1834–1919 (1919) in Carlos E. Godfrey, The Mechanics Bank, 1834–1919 (1919).

that the joy of the occasion was fixed in every heart and expressed with liquid abandon. The convention adjourned on December 19, but not before passing a final resolution promoting a location in New Jersey for the nation's capital. Months later the New Jersey legislature offered a large site not far from Trenton, but to no avail.

New Jersey's hopes of luring the new federal capital (authorized by Article I, Section 8, of the Constitution) to a site on the Delaware may have added to the state's enthusiasm for the new Constitution. Congress had actually met in Princeton in 1783 after the delegates departed Philadelphia in some haste, fleeing an angry contingent of Continental soldiers demanding back pay.

New Jersey's attempt to capture the federal capital ran afoul of both sectional rivalries and the struggle between those favoring a strong national government and those who did not. Congress, in turn, voted first for a site on the falls of the Delaware, then for two sites (one on the Delaware, one on the Potomac), then again for the site on the Delaware. Victory seemed within New Jersey's grasp, but lack of money made state construction of the buildings impossible. Though the South eventually prevailed, a New Jersey site was still a possibility while the state was engaged in the ratification process.

New Jersey had every reason to view the Constitution favorably, and there is no evidence of any substantial opposition to it within the state. None of the commentaries from beyond the state's borders indicated any doubt that New Jersey would ratify and do so quickly. Indeed, most of the debate in the new nation over the Constitution took place after New Jersey ratified.

Abraham Clark, who could have registered significant opposition when the document was laid before Congress, remained quiet during ratification. Virginia's Richard Henry Lee proposed that Congress append a series of amendments detailing basic rights before forwarding the document to the states for ratification. His proposal, which included the provision for a second convention, might well have consigned the Constitution to defeat. Clark did not support Lee, and ten months later he explained his position in a letter to Thomas Sinnickson, a prominent Salem, N.J., merchant. Clark conceded he had not liked the Constitution because he believed it erected a consolidated rather than a federal government, and one which was unnecessarily oppressive. However, he had believed the document should be forwarded to the states as written, without approval or disapproval by the Confederation Congress, and he had hoped that the states would amend it as necessary.

The brief period of unanimity in New Jersey was not to last. Sectional divisions within the state had long been an important feature of political life. The two regions were different economically, socially, religiously, and ethnically. New Jerseyans were deeply divided over problems facing the state in the 1780s—debtor-creditor issues and the controversy over the loan office. The two regions agreed on little else but the deficiencies of the Confederation. The Constitution appealed to both sides. But the hostilities which had been expressed so forcefully in the loan office controversy and during the legislature's efforts to deal with the intense debtor-creditor situation reappeared during the first federal election. New Jersey's moment of concord then gave way to the accustomed pattern of sectional antagonisms, but these abated once more as the state achieved the distinction on November 20, 1789, of becoming the first to ratify the congressionally proposed Bill of Rights.

New Jersey: Essay on Sources

The major study of New Jersey during the Confederation period and the state's position on the Constitution is Richard P. McCormick, *Experiment in Independence: New Jersey in the Critical Period, 1781–1789* (New Brunswick, 1950). The New Jersey chapter in the present volume as well as a longer study, Mary R. Murrin, *To Save this State From Ruin: New Jersey and the Creation of the United States Constitution, 1776–1789* (Trenton, 1987), is based on McCormick's work.

For information on population, ethnic, religious, and land-use patterns, see Peter O. Wacker, *Land and People: a Cultural Geography of Preindustrial New Jersey; Origins and Settlement Patterns* (New Brunswick, 1975), especially chaps. 3–5. On politics and social structure, see Jackson Turner Main, *Political Parties before the Constitution* (Chapel Hill, 1973), chaps. 1, 6, 12, 13, and, by the same author, *Social Structure of Revolutionary America* (Princeton, 1965), chaps. 1, 3, 6. Information on wartime devastation can be found in Howard Peckham, ed., *Toll of Independence: Engagements and Battle Casualties of the American Revolution, 1763–1783: A Documentary History* (Trenton, 1975), which is a fertile source for quotations on wartime damage. On matters economic, see E. James Ferguson, *The Power of the Purse: A History of American Public Finance, 1776–1790* (Chapel Hill, 1961), chaps. 1–4, and John J. McCusker and Russell R. Menard, *The Economy of British America, 1607–1789* (Chapel Hill, 1985), especially chap. 9. On state and sectional rivalries, see Joseph L. Davis, *Sectionalism in American Politics, 1774–1787* (Madison, Wis., 1977) and Peter Onuf, *Origins of the Federal Republic: Jurisdictional Controversies in the United States, 1775–1789* (Philadelphia, 1983), chaps. 1, 2, 4, 7.

For biographical information on the major figures, see Paul A. Stellhorn and Michael Birkner, eds., *The Governors of New Jersey, 1664–1974: Biographical Essays* (Trenton, 1982), pp. 77–81, for Livingston; John E. O'Connor, *William Paterson, Lawyer and Statesman, 1745–1806* (New Brunswick, 1979) and James McLachlan, *Princetonians, 1748–1768: A Biographical Dictionary* (Princeton, 1975), pp. 437–440, for Paterson; Ruth Bogin, *Abraham Clark and the Quest for Equality in the Revolutionary Era, 1774–1794* (Rutherford, 1982); Richard A. Harrison, *Princetonians, 1776–1783: A Biographical Dictionary* (Princeton, 1981), pp. 31–42, for material on Dayton; and the McLachlan volume of *Princetonians*, pp. 643–47, for Houston.

74

Important sources of documentary material include Edmund C. Burnett, ed., *Letters of Members of the Continental Congress* (Washington, D.C., 1934; reprinted 1963), vols. 7, 8; Merrill Jensen, John P. Kaminski and Gaspare J. Saladino, eds., *The Documentary History of the Ratification of the Constitution* (Madison, Wis., 1976–), vols. 1, 3, 13; the "Primitive Whig" essays from the *New Jersey Gazette*, courtesy of the William Livingston Papers project at New York University; and the pamphlet now identified as the work of Abraham Clark, *The True Policy of New Jersey, Defined* (Elizabeth-Town, 1786), in the Special Collections Department at Alexander Library, Rutgers University.

Georgia: Security through Union

ALBERT B. SAYE

Emeritus Richard B. Russell Professor of Political Science
University of Georgia

ARLY IN THE CONSTITUTIONAL CONVENTION, Gunning Bedford of Delaware exclaimed: "Look at Georgia. Though a small state at present, she is actuated by the prospect of soon becoming a great one."

Georgia had cause to favor a strong union. Its geographic position was the most exposed of any of the states. Established in 1732 by James Oglethorpe—a statesman, philanthropist, and military strategist—as "a frontier to His Majesty's southern dominions," Georgia still held this frontier position. Florida had been ceded to England in 1763, but at the end of the American Revolution it was returned to Spain. In addition to having Spaniards in the south, Georgia had within its own borders, occupying five-sixth of its territory, the powerful Creek and Cherokee Indians with whom the Spaniards were ever conniving; and these Indians were determined to keep the territory they then possessed.

The Revolution

Vulnerable, poor, remote, and the youngest of the original thirteen, the royal colony of Georgia was a hesitant revolutionary and failed to attend the First Continental Congress. Three days after the start of the September 1775 session of the Second Continental Congress, however, the united colonies became the thirteen colonies when the first Georgia delegation appeared. The Georgia emissaries were Archibald Bulloch; John Houstoun, later governor; and the Reverend Mr. Johannes Joachim Zubly, who much impressed John Adams as "a clergyman of independent persuasion" from Switzerland, fluent in at least four languages. With Georgia thus mobilized, the colony proceeded towards the fateful break with England that Button Gwinnett, George Walton, and Lyman Hall ratified by affixing their signatures to the Declaration of Independence. Ironically, Zubly by that time had embraced loyalism.

When the extreme South was in the hands of the British during the War for Independence, a rumor spread that peace was about to be made on

In this composite portrait of Georgia's three signers of the Declaration of Independence, prepared by a modern artist, English-born Button Gwinnett (for whom no surviving likeness exists) is at the left, George Walton occupies the center, and Lyman Hall is on the right. None played a major role in the framing or adoption of the Constitution. Gwinnett died in 1777 from wounds sustained in a duel; Hall, who served as Georgia governor in 1783–84, had retired from active public service; and Walton, though appointed a delegate to the Philadelphia Convention, did not attend. Trust Company Georgia Collection, Atlanta Historical Society.

the basis of Britain's retention of South Carolina and Georgia as colonies. A lively anxiety developed in Georgia for the preservation of the Union. On January 8, 1781, George Walton, William Few, and Richard Howley, her delegates to the Continental Congress, published at Philadelphia their *Observation upon the Effect of Certain Late Political Suggestions*, containing weighty arguments against the scheme. They enumerated the various commodities produced by Georgia, emphasizing the value of its timber for shipbuilding, and pointed out the strategic value of Georgia to the union of the American states. "From all these considerations," concludes the pamphlet, "it inevitably follows that the State of Georgia is a material part of the Union, and cannot be given up without affecting its essential interests, if not endangering its existence."

Anticipation of greater security through a perpetual union with its sister colonies had been the prominent cause for Georgia's entrance into the American Revolution. Georgia was anxious to strengthen the union of the states and readily ratified the Articles of Confederation on July 24, 1778.

Georgia and the Confederation

The Articles were defective, to be sure, but the real cause for their failure is found more in the temper of the times and abuse by the several states than in any inherent weakness. Local jealousies prevented the amendment of the Articles that would have created a stronger national government for the decade of the eighties; the same jealousies rendered the established government impotent.

Had the people throughout America been as nationalistic as were the Georgians of the period, the history of the Confederation would have been a different story. Georgia was willing to amend the two notable defects of the Articles relative to commerce and taxation; Georgia enabled the United States "to commence and prosecute actions or suits in any of the courts in this State, for the recovery of their common rights and interests"; it sought to carry into execution the recommendations of the national Congress; and it was conspicuously honest in wanting to meet the requisitions levied upon it. In 1783 Georgia set up a sinking fund in the amount of £108,859, to be derived from the disposal of property confiscated from loyalists, from which to pay the state's quota of the national debt. At the same time, the state made special provisions toward paying its quota of the debts owed to France and Holland. It is true that the end of the Confederation found Georgia in arrears with its payments to the central government (in fact Georgia was the only state that had not paid anything on its quota of the federal requisition allocated by Congress), but this is an indication of its inability to pay rather than an unwillingness. "Desirous of adopting every measure which can tend to promote the interest of the United States" was a common phrase in the laws adopted in Georgia during this period. In essence, Georgia wanted a stronger central government to assist the states first against the British and then against the Indians, but it was not so willing to support that stronger government with anything but words.

Georgia's Delegates to the Constitutional Convention

Georgia was not represented at the Annapolis Convention of 1786, but the state legislature responded readily to the invitation to send delegates to Philadelphia, being the fifth state thus to act. On February 10, 1787, Georgia's unicameral legislature named Abraham Baldwin, William Few, William Houstoun, Nathaniel Pendleton, William Pierce, and George Walton as "commissioners" to the Philadelphia Convention. Any two or more of them were authorized to join with delegates from other states "in devising and discussing all such alterations and provisions as may be necessary to render the Federal Constitution adequate to the exigencies of the Union."

Of the six delegates appointed to represent Georgia at the convention, four were members of Congress, two of whom (Few and Pierce) were actually attending its sessions in New York. The legislature probably made these appointments to ensure that some of the delegates would attend. It is interesting to note that the two not then members of Congress (Walton and Pendleton) never served in the convention. William Pierce furnishes the following pithy sketches of the four Georgia delegates who did participate:

> Mr. Few possesses a strong natural Genius, and from application has acquired some knowledge of legal matters;—he practices at the bar of Georgia, and speaks tolerably well in the Legislature. He has been twice a Member of Congress, and served in that capacity with fidelity to his State, and honor to himself. Mr. Few is about 35 years of age.
>
> Mr. Baldwin is a Gentleman of superior abilities, and joins in a public debate with great art and eloquence. Having laid the foundation of a compleat classical education at Harvard College, he pursues every other study with ease. He is well acquainted with Books and Characters, and has an accommodating turn of mind, which enables him to gain the confidence of Men, and to understand them. He is a practicing Attorney in Georgia, and has been twice a Member of Congress. Mr. Baldwin is about 38 years of age.
>
> Mr. Houstoun is an Attorney at Law, and has been a Member of Congress for the State of Georgia. He is a Gentleman of Family, and was educated in England. As to his legal or political knowledge he has very little to boast

of. Nature seems to have done more for his corporeal than mental powers. His Person is striking, but his mind very little improved with useful or elegant knowledge. He has none of the talents requisite for the Orator, but in public debate is confused and irregular. Mr. Houstoun is about 30 years of age of an amiable and sweet temper, and of good and honorable principles.

My own character I shall not attempt to draw, but leave those who may choose to speculate on it, to consider it in any light that their fancy or imagination may depict. I am conscious of having discharged my duty as a Soldier through the course of the late revolution with honor and propriety; and my services in Congress and the Convention were bestowed with the best intention towards the interests of Georgia, and towards the general welfare of the Confederacy. I possess ambition, and it was that, and the flattering opinion which some of my Friends had of me, that gave me a seat in the wisest Council in the World, and furnished me with an opportunity of giving these short Sketches of the Characters who composed it.

William Few arrived in Philadelphia as early as May 19 and attended the opening meeting of the convention on May 25. Since the resolution of

William Few (1748–1828), a self-educated lawyer, was a leader in the drive for independence. He represented Georgia in Congress from 1780 to 1782 and 1786 to 1788, and his duties in that body kept him from actively discharging his duties as a delegate at the Philadelphia Convention. Nevertheless, he became one of Georgia's two signers, worked to secure congressional approval of the Constitution, and became the only Georgia delegate to the Philadelphia Convention to attend the state ratifying convention. After serving Georgia as a U.S. senator (1789–1793) and federal district judge (1796–1799), at age 52 he unexpectedly moved to New York City, where he prospered both as a politician and a banker. Courtesy of the Special Collections Division, University of Georgia Libraries.

the Assembly of Georgia naming its delegates had authorized any two or more of them to act, and since the convention rules required at least two delegates for a state to be officially represented, it was not until the arrival of Pierce on May 31 that Georgia was given a voice in the proceedings. From that time on, Georgia's representation on the floor of the convention was maintained. Houstoun arrived on June 1 and Baldwin on July 11.

When judged by either the number, length, or content of their speeches, Georgia's delegates played little part in the debates of the convention. The largest number of speeches recorded by James Madison for any delegate from Georgia is eight by Baldwin, and all of these were so short that their total length would be less than that of any one of the several long speeches by more influential members. Houstoun spoke seven times; Pierce, four times; and William Few seems never to have spoken before the convention.

The Georgia delegation supported the plan of the large states to establish a strong central government. William Pierce, one of the most perceptive members of the convention, delivered a brilliant speech on June 29 in which he declared:

Abraham Baldwin (1754–1807), a Connecticut-born minister, lawyer, and legislator, moved to Georgia in 1784. He represented Georgia in Congress in 1785 and 1787–1788. Although he played only a minor role in the Philadelphia Convention, he performed important service to his adopted state as a founder of the University of Georgia, a member of the U.S. House of Representatives (1789–1799), and a United States senator (1799–1807). Politically, he sided with the Democratic-Republican party of Jefferson and Madison. Courtesy of the Special Collections Division, University of Georgia Libraries.

The great difficulty in Congress arose from the mode of voting. Members spoke on the floor as state advocates, and were biassed by local advantages.—What is federal? No more than a compact between states; and the one heretofore formed is insufficient. We are now met to remedy its defect, and our difficulties are great, but not, I hope, insurmountable. State distinctions must be sacrificed so far as the general government shall render it necessary—without, however, destroying them altogether.

In an address before the House of Delegates of Maryland after the adjournment of the convention, Luther Martin explained:

It may be thought surprising, sir, that Georgia, a State now small and comparatively trifling in the Union, should advocate this system of unequal representation, giving up her present equality in the Federal Government and sinking herself almost to total insignificance in the scale, but, sir, it must be considered that Georgia has the most extensive territory in the Union. This system being designed to preserve to the States their whole territory unbroken and to prevent the erection of new States within the territory of any of them, Georgia looks forward to when, her population being increased in some measure proportional to her territory, she would rise in the scale and give law to the other States, and hence we found the delegation of Georgia warmly advocating the proposition of giving the States unequal representation.

William Houstoun (1757–1812), one of four Georgia delegates present in Philadelphia, was an English-educated lawyer who represented Georgia in the Congress (1784–1786). He engaged briefly in debate but left before the convention finished its work. After 1787 he held no major political office. He moved to New York in 1788. Courtesy of the Special Collections Division, University of Georgia Libraries.

Clearly, Georgia was an advocate of a strong union, but the emphasis placed upon this point here and in the foregoing pages is not to be taken as suggesting that Georgia would have favored discarding state distinctions altogether. Its delegates were decidedly opposed to any federal control over slavery, an institution initially banned in Georgia. The delegates from Virginia, a state with a large and rapidly multiplying slave population, spoke of the evils of the institution and advocated an extension of power to the central government to tax or prohibit further importations. Oliver Ellsworth of Connecticut pointed out the weakness of this argument by stating that if the question were to be considered in a moral light, the convention should go further and free the slaves already in the country. Simply to prohibit or to place a duty upon further importations, argued Ellsworth, would not be just to South Carolina and Georgia, where slaves were needed and could, under the proposed plan, be procured only by purchase at augmented prices from the states advocating the restrictions.

At this point in the slave-trade debate Baldwin came to the defense of his adopted state. "Mr. Baldwin had conceived national objects alone to be before the Convention," wrote Madison in his notes for the day, "not such as like the present [that] were of a local nature. Georgia was decided on this point. . . . If left to herself, she may probably put a stop to the evil."

On one notable occasion, perhaps the decisive moment in the convention, Georgia's delegation was divided, Baldwin voting with the small states and Houstoun with the large states. It is necessary to give some of the circumstances leading to this unusual vote in order to explain it.

The second proposal included in the resolutions introduced by Edmund Randolph on May 29 was "that the right of suffrage in the National Legislature ought to be proportioned to the Quotas of Contribution, or to the number of free inhabitants, as the one or the other rule may seem best in different cases." The following day this provision was considered, and a motion was made to the effect that the states should not be represented equally in the new government as they had been under the Articles. George Read of Delaware announced that his state would accept no change in representation, and that the restrictions in the commissions of the delegates from Delaware made it their duty to retire from the convention in case such change was fixed upon. Gouverneur Morris of Pennsylvania replied that while the valuable assistance of these delegates could not be lost without real concern, the question of representation was so fundamental that it could not be dispensed with. Here at the very opening was seen the fundamental difference between the large and small states. The matter was passed over for the time being, but all realized that the basis of representation had to be settled before much could be accomplished.

On June 29, immediately after Ellsworth's timely proposal of the Connecticut Compromise, Baldwin stated that "he would vote against the motion of Mr. Ellsworth, 'tho he did not like the Resolution as it stood in the Report of the Committee of the Whole." (The committee of the whole had provided that representation in the second branch should be the same as in the first, i.e., proportional to population.) Baldwin thought it would be wise to follow the example of the constitution of Massachusetts, where the first branch of the legislature represented the people and the second represented property.

On Monday, July 2, the decisive vote regarding representation in the Senate was taken. Five states—Connecticut, New York, New Jersey, Delaware, and Maryland—stood in favor of a motion for equal representation; five states opposed it—Massachusetts, Pennsylvania, Virginia, North Carolina, and South Carolina. Georgia's vote was divided, Houstoun voting nay, Baldwin aye. John Fiske, in his *Critical Period of American History*, describes the situation as follows:

> It was Abraham Baldwin, a native of Connecticut and lately a tutor in Yale College, a recent emigrant to Georgia, who thus divided the vote of that state, and prevented a decision which would in all probability have broken up the convention. His state was the last to vote, and the house was hushed in anxious expectation, when this brave and wise young man yielded his private conviction to what he saw to be the paramount necessity of keeping the convention together. All honour to his memory!

It is generally accepted that Baldwin voted against his convictions in order to save the convention from dissolving. He abandoned his previously held position of June 29, as recorded by Madison, that "he should vote against the motion of Mr. Ellsworth." According to Luther Martin, Baldwin did not change his vote because of any change of opinion, but "from a conviction that we [the delegates from the small states] would go home and thereby dissolve the Convention, before we would give up the question." A consideration of the circumstances and the conciliatory nature of Baldwin supports this assessment. It should be remembered that Baldwin was a native of Connecticut, and his association with the delegates from that state afforded him ample opportunity for understanding the fears of the small states and the seriousness of their threats to withdraw.

Although only Abraham Baldwin and William Few signed the Constitution on behalf of Georgia, William Houstoun and William Pierce would also have signed had they been present on September 17. A letter from Pierce to St. George Tucker, dated New York, September 28, 1787, indicates his approval of the document:

> You will probably be surprised at not finding my name affixed to it; and will, no doubt, be desirous of having a reason for it. Know then, Sir,

that I was absent in New York on a piece of business so necessary that it became unavoidable. I approve of its principles, and would have signed it with all my heart had I been present. To say, however, that I consider it as perfect, would be to make an acknowledgement immediately opposite to my judgment. Perhaps it is the only one that will suit our present situation. The wisdom of the Convention was equal to something greater; but a variety of local circumstances, the inequality of the states, and the dissonant interests of different parts of the Union, made it impossible to give it any other shape or form.

Georgia Ratifies the Constitution

Antifederalists subjected the Constitution to scathing criticism in most of the states, but as in Delaware and New Jersey, there was little opposition to the Constitution in Georgia.

William Pierce sailed from New York on the sloop *Friendship* on October 3, bringing with him a dispatch from Congress relative to the Constitution. He arrived in Savannah on October 10. The next day the Savannah *Gazette of the State of Georgia* printed, with slight alterations, the text of the Constitution sent to Governor George Mathews on September 17 by Abraham Baldwin and William Few.

Governor Mathews had earlier called the Georgia Assembly into special session to consider the danger of an Indian war. A quorum of this session was not obtained until October 18, when, according to Mathews, the first order of business would be defense. For a week Indian matters occupied the Assembly. Then, the Assembly passed resolutions calling a state convention to consider the Constitution.

The resolutions directed the state's eleven counties to elect three delegates each on December 4, the date set for the annual election of assemblymen. The convention was to meet in Augusta, the state capital, on December 25, one week before the scheduled meeting of the new Assembly. A majority of delegates was declared a quorum, and the state's prohibition against dual officeholding was waived so that state officeholders could be elected to the convention. The resolutions, unlike any other state resolutions calling ratification conventions, empowered Georgia's conclave "to adopt or reject any part or the whole" Constitution, thus opening the door for a partial ratification. An astonished George Washington commented on this provision: "Georgia has accompanied her act of appointment, with powers to alter, amend, & what not;—But if a weak State, with powerful tribes of Indians in its rear, & the Spaniards on its flank, do not incline to embrace a strong *general* Government there must, I should think, be either wickedness, or insanity in their conduct."

The manuscript minutes of Georgia's ratifying convention are preserved in the State Archives in Atlanta. But unfortunately, relatively few documents remain detailing the public and private debate over the Constitution in Georgia. On October 18 James Jackson, writing as a militia commander, mentioned in passing that he hoped the legislature would give the new Constitution its "immediate attention." Three other letters from Georgians expressed some concern about the Constitution, but the writers all hoped for ratification. James Habersham, a Savannah merchant and planter, writing to his brother John from Augusta on October 17 while waiting for a quorum of the legislature to assemble, observed that the new "system of government, like all other human productions, may have, and no doubt has, its faults, but I imagine its defects will be generally thought to be fewer than could reasonably be supposed in framing a Constitution in which so many different interests are involved—it has its enemies and its friends here . . . it is very well calculated to promote the general Welfare—certain it is that any government is better than the one we have and under which I am certain we could not much longer exist as a people." Joseph Clay, a Savannah merchant and assemblyman, believed that the new Constitution would "be adopted with us readily; the Powers are great, but of two evils we must choose the least." Almost a month later, Clay wrote Judge John Williams of North Carolina that most of "the considerate part of our Community hope the new fœderal System" will, if adopted, remove "the want of sufficient energy in our Government."

On December 17, 1787, General Lachlan McIntosh, a Camden County planter, wrote an insightful letter to state auditor John Wereat, soon to be elected president of the state convention. McIntosh said that "the popularity of the Framers is so great, that the public view seems to be for adopting the Constitution in the Lump on its appearance as a perfect System without enquiry or Limitation of time or Matter. Such hasty Resolutions have Occasioned all the Misfortunes that ever happened in Governments." McIntosh was surprised to see so many people willing to yield everything to Congress when many had been reluctant to grant Congress the temporary power to lay a tariff on imports just a few years earlier.

McIntosh himself felt torn. The country needed a strengthened central government, but McIntosh believed that the objections raised by Antifederalists such as Elbridge Gerry of Massachusetts, "Centinel" of Pennsylvania, and others were "very weighty" and that "the Remedy" might "prove Worse than the Disease." McIntosh hoped that Georgia and "some other States, especially the Southern States," would devise a compromise. The prudent policy would be "to adopt the Constitution only for a certain period of time during which they will have a fair tryal of its Effects." The states could then adopt the Constitution again for a period of time with or without amendments that might be thought necessary. McIntosh suggested that Georgia might ratify the Constitution for twenty years. At that time, in 1808, Congress could constitutionally prohibit the importation of slaves, "which however Just may not be convenient for us so soon as for them, especially in a New Country & hot Climate such as Georgia."

Georgia's two newspapers printed relatively little about the Constitution. Between mid-October and the end of 1787, about fifty articles from other states appeared in these papers. Only five expressed concern about the Constitution, including an excerpt from "Centinel" I and Elbridge Gerry's objections as written in a letter to the Massachusetts legislature. The most important Federalist item reprinted in Georgia was James Wilson's speech given in the Pennsylvania State House yard on October 6, which appeared in the Augusta *Georgia State Gazette* in two installments on December 22 and 29.

The Savannah *Gazette of the State of Georgia* also had its own domestic-produced debate over the Constitution. "A Georgian," printed on November 15, expressed serious concerns about the Constitution, asserting that the South should have been given greater representation in the House of Representatives. As the system now stood, the North would exploit the underrepresented Southern States. "A Georgian" also believed that the President's powers should be further limited, the federal judiciary should be curtailed, and the rights of habeas corpus, trial by jury in civil and criminal cases, and liberty of the press should "be forever sacred and inviolable." Characterizing the Constitution as a counter-revolution, he asked his audience to read the Declaration of Independence "and compare it with the Federal Constitution; what a degree of apostacy will you not then discover."

"Demosthenes Minor" severely attacked "A Georgian" as a demagogue, an adventurer, a knave, a blockhead, and probably a former Hessian. The ensuing essays by "A Citizen," "A Briton," and the two original correspondents tended to avoid reasoned discussion of the Constitution while concentrating solely on personalities.

Only twenty-nine delegates actually participated in the convention. William Few alone of the four delegates to the Philadelphia convention was present, and it is probable that he took an active part. Among the other prominent delegates were Governor George Mathews; past governors John Wereat, Edward Telfair, and Nathan Brownson; future governors George Handley and Jared Irwin; and John Milton, Henry Osborne, Joseph Habersham, William Stephens, James McNeil, and Christopher Hillary.

The ratifying convention, called to meet on December 25, did not attain a quorum until Friday, December 28. John Wereat, from Richmond County (in which Augusta is located), was elected president and Isaac Briggs secretary. The convention lasted for a week. The minutes of the convention indicate no division of opinion, but according to Chatham County delegate Joseph Habersham, the convention considered the Constitution "paragraph by paragraph with a great deal of temper." On Monday (December 31) it was "resolved, Unanimously, that the proposed Federal Constitution be now adopted." On Wednesday (January 2, 1788) twenty-six delegates representing ten counties signed the act of ratification. "As the last name was signed to the Ratification, a party of Colonel [James] Armstrong's regiment quartered

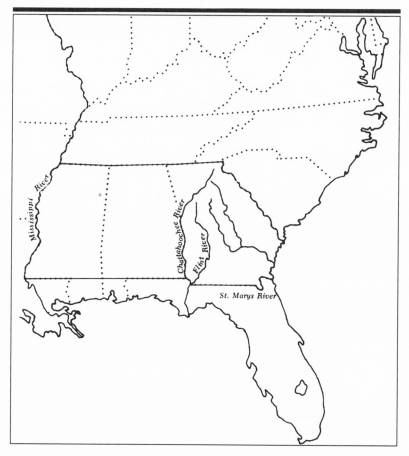

In 1787 Georgia was a frontier state. Within and outside its borders were unfriendly Spaniards and Indians. Georgia extended westward from the Atlantic to the Mississippi, and it did not cede its lands beyond the Chattahoochie River to the federal government until 1802. Georgia's exposed and vulnerable location helps to explain its support for a strong national Union. Georgia map, from Albert B. Saye, Georgia History and Government *(Austin, 1982).*

in this town [Augusta] proclaimed the joyful tidings outside the State-house by thirteen discharges from two pieces of artillery." On Saturday (January 5), before final adjournment, the Georgia convention directed that along with the formal ratification the following letter should be sent to the president of Congress:

> Sir, We have the honor to transmit, to the United States in Congress assembled, the Ratification of the Federal Constitution by the State of Georgia.
>
> We hope that the ready compliance of this State, with the recommendations of Congress and of the late national Convention, will tend not only to consolidate the Union but promote the happiness of our common Country.

Georgia was the first state in the South and the fourth in the nation to ratify the Constitution. It was a small state, but its action was significant and maintained the Federalist momentum.

Georgia and the Bill of Rights

Since the requisite number of states (eleven) voted to approve the Bill of Rights, thus appending it to the Constitution as Amendments 1 through 10, prior to Georgia's action on these congressionally proposed changes, Georgia (along with Connecticut and Massachusetts) saw no need to conduct a ratification process. Not until 1939, as a token gesture in celebration of the 150th anniversary of the Bill of Rights, did these three states formally ratify the first ten amendments to the Constitution of the United States.

A New State Constitution

Much has been written about the influence of the early state constitutions on the federal Constitution; more should be written about the influence of the federal Constitution on the state constitutions. Consider, for example, the experience of Georgia.

On January 31, 1788, less than a month after Georgia ratified the federal Constitution, the House of Assembly proceeded to appoint "three fit and discreet persons for each County," as the House *Journal* records, "to be convened . . . by the Executive as soon as may be after official information is received that nine States have adopted the Federal Constitution, to take under their consideration the alterations and amendments that are necessary to be made in the Constitution of this State." In May of the following year Georgia adopted a new state constitution.

The new basic law, announced the *Augusta Chronicle*, was "an assimilation to the Federal Constitution." It firmly established the basic principle of the separation of powers by vesting the legislative, executive, and judicial powers in three distinct branches of government. The state's unicameral legislature gave way to a General Assembly, composed of a Senate and a House of Representatives. The unit of representation was the county; so following the federal model, each county was given equal representation in the state Senate. Representation in the House was by population. The plural executive of the first state constitution of 1777 gave way to a single chief executive, vested with a veto over legislation that could only be overridden by a two-thirds vote of both houses of the legislature. Judges of the state courts would have a competent salary established by law, not to be diminished during their continuance in office. The beneficial influence of the Constitution of the United States in Georgia was unmistakable.

Georgia: Essay on Sources

Modern histories of Georgia in one volume include Kenneth Coleman, ed., *A History of Georgia* (Athens, Ga., 1977); E. Merton Coulter, *Georgia: A Short History* (Chapel Hill, 1960); and Albert B. Saye, *A Constitutional History of Georgia* (Athens, Ga., 1970). The most extensive bibliography for both primary and secondary sources is the *Catalogue of the Wymberly Jones DeRenne Georgia Library at Wormsloe, Isle of Hope, near Savannah*, 3 vols. (privately printed, 1931).

The classic authors on eighteenth-century Georgia are William B. Stevens, *A History of Georgia*, 2 vols. (New York, 1847); and Charles C. Jones, *The History of Georgia*, 2 vols. (Boston, 1883). Jones's study is detailed, scholarly, and superior in literary style but lacks the synthesis of Stevens' work. Albert B. Saye's *New Viewpoints in Georgia History* (Athens, Ga., 1943) depicts Georgia as primarily a military colony in its origins and traces political developments from 1732 to 1789.

The chief documentary sources for Georgia's eighteenth-century history are *The Colonial Records of Georgia* (26 vols.) and *The Revolutionary Records of Georgia* (3 vols.), both edited by former governor Allen D. Chandler and published by the state between 1904 and 1913. A few additional volumes edited by Kenneth Coleman have been published subsequently. *The Diary of John Percival, First Earl of Egmont*, 3 vols., edited by the British Historical Manuscripts Commission (London, 1920–23), is the key source on the origins of the colony of Georgia, while Merrill Jensen, John P. Kaminski and Gaspare J. Saladino, eds., *The Documentary History of the Ratification of the Constitution*, vol. 3: *Georgia* (Madison, Wis., 1978) is definitive on its topic.

Walter McElreath's *Treatise on the Constitution of Georgia* (Atlanta, 1912) conveniently reprints copies of Georgia's early constitutions. The charter of 1732 has been lost. A photostatic reproduction of the copy in the British Patent Roll is given in *Georgia's Charter of 1732* (Athens, Ga., 1942). The original copy of the constitution of 1777 has also been lost, and there is little information about the convention that framed it other than fragmentary minutes accompanying copies of the constitution printed in Savannah by William Lancaster in 1777 (copy in the Library of Congress, Hazard Pamphlet No. 33). Manuscript journals of the three conventions held to frame Georgia's constitution of 1789 are available in the Georgia State Department of Archives in Atlanta.

Convenient compilations of the laws of Georgia for the formative period are George and Robert Watkins, *A Compilation of the Laws of Georgia* (Philadelphia, 1800 and 1801) and Horatio Marbury and William H. Crawford, *Digest of the Laws of Georgia from 1755 to 1800* (Savannah, 1802). Georgia's two newspapers published during 1787–88 were the Augusta *Georgia State Gazette* and the Savannah *Gazette of the State of Georgia*.

Short biographies of early patriots of Georgia can be found in the *Dictionary of American Biography* and in the *Dictionary of Georgia Biography*. See also Charles C. Jones, *Biographical Sketches of the Delegates from Georgia to the Continental Congress* (Boston, 1891).

Georgia's Signers of the Declaration of Independence (Atlanta, 1981) is a collaborative work of merit by Edmund C. Bridges, Harvey H. Jackson, Kenneth H. Thomas, and James A. Young. A biography containing a wealth of information on the Constitutional Convention of 1787 and the early years of the United States government is E. Merton Coulter's *Abraham Baldwin: Patriot, Educator, and Founding Father* (Arlington, Va., 1987).

Sovereignty Finessed

Roger Sherman, Oliver Ellsworth, and the Ratification of the Constitution in Connecticut

CHRISTOPHER COLLIER
Professor of History, University of Connecticut
Connecticut State Historian

ROGER SHERMAN, at Philadelphia as a delegate to the First Continental Congress in 1774, was asked one day by Patrick Henry, "Why are the People of Connecticut more zealous in the cause of liberty than the people of other states?" Sherman is reported to have answered, "Because we have more to lose than any of them." Sherman was referring specifically to Connecticut's royal charter of 1662, which gave the colony virtually full local self-government. Thirteen years later, in 1787, despite the intervention of a successful war for independence from the Crown, Connecticut was still ruled by its charter of 1662; and Sherman continued to believe the colony, now a state, had more to lose than any of the others.

Why, then, at a state convention to ratify a constitution that would fundamentally undermine the charter and severely limit the state's autonomy, did three-quarters of 168 delegates vote aye? Did the majority disagree with the sentiments expressed by Sherman? Was it bamboozled by a little oligarchy of self-interested leaders? Was it persuaded that the safety of Connecticut's liberties could be guaranteed only by the risky expedient of surrendering its sovereignty and joining a union of other—though very different—states? Or is there another set of reasons entirely that explain the radical transformation of opinion in Connecticut?

The Election of Delegates to the Constitutional Convention

The call to the Philadelphia Convention came to Connecticut, said one politician, at "a time of jealousy when all men are on tiptoe." Noah Webster, a self-styled disillusioned former republican, described the fac-

Roger Sherman (1721–1793), despite his humble origins, became one of two Americans (wealthy Robert Morris was the other) to sign all three founding documents of the Republic: the Declaration of Independence, the Articles of Confederation, and the Constitution. He served in Congress from 1774 to 1781 and 1783 to 1784. Within Connecticut he was a member of the Council (1766–1785), Superior Court judge (1766–1789) and mayor of New Haven (1784–1793). Sherman served as one of his state's three delegates at Philadelphia and was a major architect of the Connecticut (or Great) Compromise, which broke the deadlock between large and small states over congressional representation. He was one of the Federalist leaders in the state ratifying convention, and he wrote at least two newspaper series in support of the Constitution. He finished his career by serving terms in the U.S. House (1789–1791) and Senate (1791–1793). Sherman was also active on the home front—twice married, he fathered fifteen children. Portrait by Ralph Earl, courtesy of Yale University Art Gallery, gift of Roger Sherman White.

tionalism that had rent the deferential harmony of the pre-Stamp Act years as "two parties . . . jealous of each other; federal men and antifederal. The federal men supposed the antifederal to be knaves, designing artful demagogues. The antifederal suppose the federal to be ambitious tyrannical men, who are aiming at power and office at the expense of the people at large." At the time of the call from the Annapolis meeting of September 1786 (which Connecticut failed to attend), there was a standoff in the Connecticut General Assembly, and nothing was done about the convention until Congress issued a formal invitation in February 1787.

Federalists, who supported a strong, more effective national government, persuaded Governor Samuel Huntington to delay responding until the regular session of the Assembly met in May. They were afraid that the Antifederalists would carry the day. "Connecticut," David Humphreys wrote to George Washington in March, "is under the influence of a few such miserable, narrow-minded, and I may say wicked politicians, that I question very much whether the legislature will choose members to appear in the Convention." When the Assembly met, however, it set right to work debating the question of sending delegates. The debate was only about two hours long, and we know little about it. Those opposed to Connecticut's participation raised the spectre of "arbitrary power" and "regal government." One Antifederalist thought the convention would be "dangerous to the liberties of the people," another claimed that alterations to the Articles of Confederation "would have a tendency to produce a royal government in this country," and a third warned "that the state would send men that had been delicately bred and who lived in affluent circumstances, that could not feel for the people in this day of distress." Humphreys told Washington that the farmers in the Assembly "effect to persuade the people . . . that they are only in danger of having their liberties stolen away by an artful designing Aristocracy." The proponents pointed to the necessity of paying the national debt, regulating interstate and foreign trade, and preserving peace among the states. In the end, a majority voted to take part, and the Assembly elected three delegates.

One of those elected was Erastus Wolcott of East Windsor. Wolcott, sixty-six years old in 1787, was one of the leading agrarian localists, despite the fact that his brother, the lieutenant governor, was among the strongest nationalists. Wolcott was elected a delegate to the old Congress in 1787 but resigned, and at the last elections for that body in 1788 he was elected again. He never went. And now he followed his pattern and refused to go to Philadelphia. He was too old, he said, and anyway was afraid of catching smallpox in that distant city. But Wolcott undoubtedly wanted to disassociate himself from the convention. He thought that reform in Connecticut was the best way to continue "democratical government which had lasted through

150 years . . . unruffled through the most trying scenes." Wolcott's resignation deprived the agrarian provincials of their one really committed partisan. They had counted on him to balance the representation and had required that the states not be bound but by the vote of at least *two* delegates.

The original slate of delegates was elected "after a long discussion" in the lower house on Saturday, May 12. Wolcott resigned on the 14th, and to replace him Roger Sherman was chosen on the next day. Final authorization was passed on May 16, but funds were not provided till several days later.

Connecticut Wants to Strengthen the Federal Government

The official appointments furnished to the three delegates—Sherman, William Samuel Johnson, and Oliver Ellsworth—authorized any *one* or more of them to "Act in said Convention and to discuss upon such Alterations and Provisions agreeable to the General Principles of Republican Government as they shall think proper to render the federal Constitution adequate to the exigencies of Government and the preservation of the Union." The charge included the phrase, taken from the February act of Congress, "for the sole and express purpose of revising the Articles of Confederation," and it certainly was the understanding of the Connecticut delegates that a revision was all that was called for. It was mere alterations they had in mind, certainly not a whole new document premised on a whole new concept of the federal relationship. As Ellsworth remarked in convention debate, they ought to avoid "razing the foundations of the building, when we need only repair the roof." Sherman, it was rumored, wanted only to "patch up the old scheme." His maiden speech in Philadelphia warned of making "too great inroads on the existing system."

Certainly the precious charter government, with its prevailing system of internal republicanism and external sovereignty, was not to be tampered with. Connecticut had consistently refused to countenance parliamentary restrictions on local government throughout the colonial period. By 1775 Connecticut and Rhode Island (which had a similar corporate or self-governing charter) were much the freest and—in format, at least—the most "democratical" of all the colonies in America. Their citizens' sense of independence was greatly enhanced by events of the decade following 1776. State sovereignty implied equality in the national councils, and this determined Connecticut's delegation against giving up the one state–one vote system of the Articles.

Nevertheless, many Connecticut citizens and most of the economic and political leadership did see considerable advantage in altering the national system in some respects. The changes they wanted, however, were economic rather than political. First and most important, both farmers and merchants wanted freedom from paying import duties to support other state governments. Such duties should be levied only by the central government, so that they would be uniform; and the income should be used to benefit all the states, particularly by paying off the Revolutionary War debt. But in no case could Connecticut citizens permit export taxes—taxes that would ruin their economy, based as it was on trade with the West Indies. They would want also an equitable system of taxation. The rule under the Articles was that quotas of money would be levied proportional to the value of real estate in each state. But the difficulty of appraising the real estate had made this scheme unworkable, and as a matter of practice quotas were based on relative populations, counting all the whites and three-fifths of the blacks. Connecticut would want this de facto system continued and—despite its own recent refusal to pay—would want some teeth put into the mechanism for making the collections.

The mercantile sector of Connecticut society also wanted authority to make treaties with foreign nations to be granted exclusively to the central government, along with authority over interstate commerce; and they wanted some coercive power put in the hands of Congress so that these authorities could be made effective. In addition, merchants wanted to take away from the states—and from the United States, too—any right to print paper money. Many in Connecticut did not want this kind of restriction, but they were not represented in the trio that the state dispatched to Philadelphia. Everyone, but especially the farmers, so many of whom had emigrating sons, wanted protection for Connecticut's control over its western land claims (the Western Reserve) built into any alterations in the Articles.

Connecticut Delegates in the Constitutional Convention

The Philadelphia Convention opened on May 25, but Ellsworth didn't arrive until the 28th; Sherman came on the 30th; Johnson got there on June 2. Ellsworth stayed continuously to August 23, but he left then and was not present to sign the document. Sherman and Johnson departed for a Connecticut visit on July 20 and returned to Philadelphia on August 6, when the Convention reconvened after a ten-day recess. They both stayed to the end and signed the Constitution on September 17. Thus Sherman served for ninety-six days, Johnson for ninety-three, and Ellsworth for ninety. Sherman, a signer of both the Declaration of Independence and the Articles of Confederation, was by far the most experienced of the three and did most of the talking. Historians have suggested that the others decided to put him forth as their spokesman and that his statements represent positions taken by a united delegation.

Of course, the best-known role played by the Connecticut delegates in the convention was as architects of the compromise that resolved the dispute between the most populous states and the least populous states. The large states wanted representation in both legislative houses to be in proportion to population; the small states wanted, at best, to continue the single house with equal representation or, at least, to have an equal vote in both houses if a two-house legislature was unavoidable. The system familiar to Americans today, a Senate with each state represented equally and a House with representation based on population, is the result of the famous Connecticut Compromise. What local factors lay behind the Connecticut promotion of this idea? Why didn't the ardently state-rights Connecticut delegation stand firmly behind the concept of equality of representation? Why did it desert Maryland, Delaware, and New Jersey on this issue?

The answer to these questions lies on two bases. One was the state's middle position in population—sixth out of thirteen. The other lies in the pragmatic politics that was the necessary practice of any politician who sought success in Connecticut's republican society. Compromise was the name of the game there, and consensus lay behind every major legislative move.

Roger Sherman was the principal engineer of the compromise. As far back as 1776, in the early days of the Second Continental Congress, it was clear to him that any national measure must have the support not only of a majority of the state governments but also of a majority of the people. Just on the basis of efficiency, the pragmatic Sherman pointed out, "there must always be a majority of States as well as a majority of the people on the side of public measures"; otherwise the central government will lack "decision and efficacy." Even in the single-house Congress under the Articles, he had proposed a dual form of voting: "The vote should be taken two ways; call the Colonies, and call the individuals, and have a majority of both." Now, eleven years later, demonstrating the perseverance for which he was famous, he brought the idea forward again. Voting in the House "should be according to the respective numbers of free inhabitants; and ... in the ... Senate, each State should have one vote and no more." And this— with the important modification of allowing each state two senators—became the system that went into the Constitution and remains the system we have today. Except for the Connecticut delegation, it probably satisfied no one;

but by the middle of July, when it was accepted, everyone knew that it was the best solution that could be hoped for.

The major negative objective of the Connecticut delegation to Philadelphia was to guard against unnecessary encroachments on the state's sovereignty. The positive one was to bring about a national system of commerce that would allow Connecticut's intimately integrated domestic and foreign economy to flourish. As we have seen, the state's major economic concerns were threefold: to enable the U.S. government to make and enforce commercial treaties with foreign nations; to regulate foreign and interstate trade; and to draw an income from import—but not export—duties levied equally on all the states and used for the benefit of all the states, primarily to pay off the national debt.

On all these matters but one, the Connecticut trio was in tune with the orchestra it found in Philadelphia, where only two or three members played off-key. The convention was overwhelmingly nationalist on economic matters. The one point essential to Connecticut, where the delegates had to face down the nationalists, was the matter of taxing exports. And here they had the support of the representatives from South Carolina, whose wealth, based on the export of indigo and rice, was so important to the Union that it gave their voices extra strength and their votes undue weight. The Connecticut–South Carolina axis depended for its success on the support of Georgia and North Carolina in the South, Massachusetts in New England, and whatever other states would join from time to time. The arrangement was strictly pragmatic politics. The northerners would not contest the continuance of slavery and the slave trade, and the southerners would not stand in the way of congressional control over commerce. The hinge of this coalition was the Connecticut–South Carolina axis, which was held together by each state's intransigent stand against export taxes. And in the end they had their way.

The Constitution authorized Congress to lay and collect taxes, duties, imposts, and excises which would be uniform throughout the United States, providing that no tax or duty should be laid on articles exported from any state. The proceeds from such duties were to be used to pay the national debt and provide for the national defense and welfare. No longer would thousands of dollars be paid by Connecticut consumers of foreign goods into the New York treasury, a situation that existed under the Confederation because of New York's tariff on imports.

The paper-money men in Connecticut had never been numerous and had almost no influence in the Assembly at all. Even Erastus Wolcott, the agrarian tax reformer, would not have opposed the unambiguous antipaper provisions of the Constitution. Sherman had been campaigning against paper money for thirty-five years. Now in the convention Sherman "thought this a favorable crisis for crushing paper money," and in his major break with state sovereignty he urged a provision that would prohibit state emissions of such fiat money.

William Samuel Johnson had revivified his political life on the basis of his successful negotiations that led to Connecticut's acquiescence in the loss of its Pennsylvania land claims in exchange for the Western Reserve, a large tract in present-day Ohio bordering on Lake Erie. He, no doubt, was sent to Philadelphia to watch out for that valuable piece of real estate. Sherman, too, had long been a friend to Connecticut pioneers, and the pair made certain to strike down any threat to the state's claims. In fact, the Reserve was never seriously threatened in Philadelphia (though it was ceded to the national government in 1800 and became part of the state of Ohio three years later).

William Samuel Johnson (1727–1819), son of the first president of King's College (now Columbia University), was one of the most highly educated delegates to the Philadelphia Convention. During the Revolution, Johnson worked for peace between England and the colonies rather than separation, and this stand caused an interruption in his political career. He returned to favor and served in Congress from 1784 to 1787. At Philadelphia the learned Johnson played a major role in the debates and chaired the Committee on Style, which crafted the final document. After helping to secure Connecticut's ratification, he served for two years in the U.S. Senate before resigning to devote full time to his other post—the presidency of Columbia College. Portrait by James Weiland after an original by Gilbert Stuart, courtesy of the Connecticut State Library.

Thus it was that the Connecticut delegates came away from Philadelphia with a document they thought they could recommend in good conscience to the jealous Connecticut provincials and enthusiastically to the nationalist merchants as well. But perceptions differ, and in Connecticut, as well as in other areas of the United States, men felt different parts of the elephant. Ratification in Connecticut would be quick and easy, but not without objection.

The Debate in Connecticut

In the fall of 1786 Connecticut's politics was dominated by provincial farmers who distrusted Congress and protested efforts to expand its powers by amending the Articles of Confederation. As late as March 1787, high nationalist David Humphreys warned that if Connecticut sent delegates to Philadelphia, "my apprehension is still greater that they will be sent on purpose to impede any salutary measures that might be proposed." Both Connecticut delegates to Congress, Stephen Mix Mitchell and William Samuel Johnson, voted against the call to the Philadelphia Convention—the only state delegation to do so. Johnson considered the gathering "a very doubtful measure at best."

A little over a year later, however, a state convention ratified, by the lopsided vote of 128 to 40, a new constitution that altered in the most fundamental ways the state's control over its most important economic concerns, and indeed severely undermined that precious sovereignty for which so many had risked and lost life and limb in the recent Revolution. How can we explain this rapid and radical transformation from a determined states' rightism to total surrender to nationalism?

The answer lies in a widespread acknowledgement among Connecticut farmers and merchants of the real economic gains under the proposed Constitution; the failure of the Connecticut delegates to the Philadelphia Convention—Sherman and Ellsworth, at least—to face up to and explain the true nature of the revolutionary impact that the new government would have on the states and the people; a barrage of Federalist propaganda; and suppression of Antifederalist polemic throughout the state.

The economic arguments were made by newspaper writers and speakers at the state ratifying convention. The most prominent of these was Oliver Ellsworth, who wrote thirteen "Letters of Landholder." "Landholder" tied together the economic interests of the farmer and the merchant. "Your property and riches," he told the farmers, "depend on a ready demand and a generous price for the produce you can annually spare. Every foreign prohibition on American trade is aimed in the most deadly manner against the holders and tillers of the land, and they are the men made poor. Your only remedy is such a national government as will make the country respectable; such a supreme government as can boldly meet the supremacy of proud and self-interested nations. The regulation of trade ever was and ever will be a national matter."

"Landholder" also pointed out that the Constitution, in prohibiting states from levying import duties, would stop the flow of Connecticut money—estimated at $40,000 to $50,000 a year—into the New York State treasury, since an estimated seven-eighths of all goods imported into Connecticut came through New York. Under the proposed Constitution such sums would be collected by the U.S. government for the benefit of all the states. Though

Oliver Ellsworth (1745–1807) abandoned studies for the ministry in favor of a legal career, then went on to play a prominent role in Connecticut's Revolutionary effort. He served in Congress (1778 to 1783), on the state Council (1780–1785) and on the Connecticut Superior Court (1785–1788). He was also influential at Philadelphia, taking an active part in debates and committee work, although he departed early and did not sign the document. During the battle for ratification, Ellsworth labored for approval and wrote the widely circulated "Landholder" essays. Once the new Union was formed, his political career blossomed. Ellsworth served successively as U.S. senator (1789–1796), chief justice of the U.S. Supreme Court (1796–1800), and peace commissioner to France to end the limited naval war with our former ally (1799–1800). Following his diplomatic service, he returned to state politics, serving on the Council from 1802 until his death. Portrait by James Weiland after an original by William P. Chappel, courtesy of the Connecticut State Library.

no one pointed it out, it was also true that since Connecticut citizens were owed proportionately much more of the national debt than citizens of any other state, a good share of the national income would tend to flow Connecticut's way.

Also persuasive were the benefits to be achieved by stopping interstate trade restrictions and levies and by granting the central government a monopoly of the income from import duties, enabling it to put such revenues to use for all states and making it able to pay the domestic national debt. These arguments alone, however, were not decisive, because Connecticut citizens were fiercely determined to maintain their freedom to act as they chose and to govern themselves as they always had. The fear of an overweening national government was widespread and deep, and it was the strongest objection to which the advocates of the Constitution were forced to respond.

Perhaps the defenders of the Constitution overreacted and overstated their position, but it is clear that they either deliberately or mistakenly misrepresented the force that the new government would have. Take Roger Sherman, for example. Sherman was the least nationalistic of Connecticut's three delegates and the most effective states' rightist at the federal convention. He went to Philadelphia convinced that the central government had to be strengthened in only three respects: it must have an independent income; it must have the exclusive authority over interstate and foreign commerce; and it must have an effective mechanism, civil and military, against internal and foreign attacks on government. Sherman would let the Articles—with its single house, equal state representation, and legislative dominance—stand; change would come through amendment.

After participating as a most influential debater throughout the convention, after negotiating some of the crucial compromises, and after accepting a wholly new document, Sherman seemed to believe that the only changes that had actually been made were those which he had been willing to accept in the first place. Thus, as Connecticut Antifederalists proclaimed their fear of a new dominating government that would circumscribe their individual freedoms and undermine the sovereignty of the state, he insisted that almost nothing would be altered under the new government.

Sherman apparently did not understand or was unwilling to accept the theoretical underpinning on which James Madison had built the structure. Central to Madison's theory was the concept that government was the enemy of liberty and was necessary only to protect individuals as individuals from themselves acting in groups. A republican form of representative government was the best way to channel the desires of the people in such a way that individual liberty was protected; but republican government was also a hazard because it was prone to majoritarianism, which often led to tyrannization of individuals and minorities.

The scheme developed by Madison, as finally incorporated in the Constitution, granted the central government ample authority and sufficient power, but it curbed the exercise of power through three mechanisms: dividing it between the states and the United States; separating governmental functions into three different branches; and spreading the system over the entire United States—in what Madison called an "extended republic"—so as to include such a diversity of economic, ideological, and sectional views as to make it virtually impossible for any but transitory majorities to develop.

Sherman and Ellsworth rejected the modern republicanism of Madison, built as it was on the "science of politics" that proclaimed mankind as vice-ridden and representative government a congeries of competing self-interested factions. Their perception of republican society reflected the Connecticut in which they practiced politics. They viewed republican government as organically connected to society, an elite chosen for their virtue—i.e., selflessness and wisdom—to rule a hardy, hardworking, patient yeomanry and their families, whose principal virtue was their ability to elect their betters to office and to defer to them thereafter. In such a society, government was neither the servant nor the enemy of the people, but rather the kindly father who always knew best. Representative assemblies consisted of the best of the yeomen and the most honest of the merchants, who had been nurtured in the same soil as their constituents and from time to time returned to it to maintain their common perspective. There was no need for a bill of rights or separation of powers. Liberty was best protected by practicing the virtues of labor, thrift, patience, regularity, and moderation, and electing one's most virtuous neighbors to run the government.

No amount of Madisonian tinkering with governmental mechanisms like checks and balances and extended republics could protect ordered liberty, for "were it ever so perfect a scheme of freedom," wrote Ellsworth, "when we become ignorant, vicious, idle, and regardless of the education of our children, our liberties will be lost—we shall be fitted for slavery, and it will be an easy business to reduce us to obey one or more tyrants."

Sherman and Ellsworth failed either to understand or to subscribe to the "new science of politics" which underlay Madison's plan for the Union. Thus their efforts to persuade Connecticut citizens to accept the Constitution were directed toward placing the document in the older concept of republicanism. This required them to minimize the reach of the proposed new national government and insist—against any fair reading of the document—that only minor changes were involved.

Take, for instance, the absence of a bill of rights. This was the single strongest objection to the Constitution, not only in Connecticut but in every other state as well. When a bill of rights had been proposed at the Philadelphia Convention, Sherman alone spoke against it. "State Declarations of Rights are not repealed ... and being in force are sufficient," he said, perhaps forgetting that the supremacy clause of the Constitution made all state constitutions and laws subject to revision by Congress—a fact that was pointed out to him at the state convention. His fundamental position was that state governments since 1776 had been sovereign, possessing all authority. The real safety of the people lay in their choosing virtuous rather than self-interested men to represent them. Not all citizens were virtuous; indeed, even the minority who were voters could not always be trusted to elect virtuous men to represent the whole society. National legislators, he said in the federal convention, should not be elected by the people directly; the people, said Sherman, "should have as little to do as may be about the Government. They want information and are constantly liable to be misled." Thus the government was not the servant of the people, but rather it constituted—when it worked right—the wisest and most virtuous part of the society and therefore should not be fettered by restrictions written out on paper. "No bill of rights," he wrote, "ever yet bound the supreme power longer than the *honeymoon* of a new married couple unless the rulers were interested in preserving the rights; and in that case [in Connecticut] they have always been ready enough to declare the rights and to preserve them when they were declared." And as long as the representatives are drawn from the very society that would suffer from legislative abuse, Sherman reasoned, there need be no fear that rights would be violated.

Writing as "Landholder," Ellsworth too made this point, perhaps more succinctly than his mentor. "Bills of Rights," he wrote, "were introduced in England when its kings claimed all power and jurisdiction, and were considered by them as grants to the people. They are insignificant since government is considered as originating from the people, and all the power the [new national] government now has is a grant from the people. The constitution they establish, with powers limited and defined, becomes now to the legislator and magistrate, what originally a bill of rights was to the people. To have inserted in this constitution a bill of rights for the states, would suppose them to derive and hold their rights from the federal government, when the reverse is the case."

Despite his articulation at the federal convention of the important principle that the new system was "partly national and partly federal," Ellsworth here lost sight of the fact that the Constitution was not only an agreement of union among the states but also a body of national law operating directly on individuals without reference to the states. Since Connecticut had no constitution in the modern or late eighteenth-century sense of the term, it was easy for him to fall into this error, and of course he found an accepting audience in Connecticut. After all, Ellsworth asserted (apparently blind to Article I, Section 10, to the supremacy clause, and to several other parts of the document he helped to write), "No alteration in the state governments is even now proposed, but they are to remain identically the same as they are now." A year later Ellsworth, as author of the Judiciary Act of 1789, wrote the single most nationalizing piece of legislation in all American history.

Division of powers was another modern complexity that Roger Sherman saw only through the simple plan that he had carried in his head to Philadelphia. "The General and particular [i.e., state] jurisdiction ought in no case be concurrent," he insisted. "The immediate security of the civil and domestic rights of the people," he wrote on the eve of the ratifying convention, "will be in the governments of the particular states. And as the different states have different local interests and customs which can be best regulated by their own laws, it would not be expedient to admit the federal government to interfere with them any further than may be necessary for the good of the whole." What "further powers" that "may be necessary" seemed clear enough to Sherman in 1788, even if it took a generation longer for Congress and the Supreme Court to come to understand the terms so well. "The objects of the federal government will be so obvious that there will be no great danger of any interference," he concluded. So much for the "necessary and proper" clause and the interpretation that would be given it by such practicing nationalists as Alexander Hamilton and John Marshall.

If Sherman misunderstood the operation of the division-of-powers system established in the Constitution, he categorically rejected the practice of separation of powers. Historian Gordon Wood, among the most authoritative voices on the matter, writes: "Perhaps no principle of American Constitutionalism has attracted more attention than that of separation of powers. It has in fact come to define the very character of the American political system." If this is true, then surely Roger Sherman propounded a constitution that he didn't understand at all.

In Connecticut, still operating under a 1662 royal charter, separation of powers did not exist. Reflecting this political system, Sherman saw the mixing of legislative and executive functions in the presidential veto and appointive power shared with the Senate as positive attributes of the new Constitution. He always thought that the legislature, as the "supreme will of the Society," should appoint the national executive, which was "nothing more than an institution for carrying the will of the Legislature into effect." The chief executive should be "absolutely dependent" on the legislature, which "should have the power to remove [him] at pleasure." The idea that the executive and legislative powers "ought to be entirely distinct and unconnected," Sherman wrote, was a "gross *error* in politics."

Sherman and Ellsworth also dismissed a long list of major and minor objections raised by Antifederalists not only in Connecticut but in other states as well. The new government would be no more expensive than the old, Sherman assured worried farmers; Congress would not have to sit for more than "two or three months in a year"; the executive departments would be no larger than they were under the Articles (which was a total of about twelve men); the security against standing armies would be strengthened by prohibiting Congress from appropriating money to support the military for more than two years; direct taxes were unlikely because of the new national impost, but in any event they would be small and proportionate to population. Even the U.S. Supreme Court, created by Article III, was no threat, because it would deal only with great national issues; and it was probable that state courts would try federal cases, so that no new lower federal courts would be established. And, he told his infamously litigious constituents in a state swarming with lawyers, "it is not probable that more than one citizen to a thousand will ever have a cause that can come before a federal court."

Thus the Connecticut delegates articulated what was to most members of the Philadelphia Convention an unspoken fiction—the integrity of state sovereignty under the new Constitution. But what Madison and other practitioners of "the new science of politics" knew to be a fiction, Roger Sherman and perhaps Oliver Ellsworth believed to be a republican truth. It was this misperceived version of the new government that was sold to the Connecticut convention that ratified a document which would have been drummed out of the state if Hamilton's or Madison's or even Elbridge Gerry's or Luther Martin's version had come to light in Hartford.

The version of the Constitution presented to Connecticut voters by Sherman and Ellsworth might not have been so persuasive had an opposition voice been heard. But the Federalists had firm and determined allies in all the state's printers. Though pages and pages of polemic in support of ratification were published, only a single article written by a Connecticut Antifederalist saw print, and it was not reprinted anywhere. The newspapers even suppressed the fact that several town meetings had rejected the document. Vast amounts of pro-Constitution material reproduced from out-of-state newspapers appeared in Connecticut, but only five out-of-state articles against the Constitution found their way into local newspapers.

Virulent attacks on the integrity, wisdom, learning, and character of Antifederalist leaders in Connecticut filled the papers. James Wadsworth of Durham, a longtime spokesman for the agrarian majority, took the brunt of the attack. Wadsworth was a seasoned politician who had served a term in Congress, and in 1788 he was a member of Connecticut's upper house and state comptroller. Ultimately he was able to hold the agrarian towns of New Haven County to their Antifederalist stance, and it is from there that the largest bloc of votes against ratification came. For this, Wadsworth was removed from office by a Federalist-dominated General Assembly, ostensibly for refusing to swear an oath to uphold the U.S. Constitution under a law repealed the day after he was replaced as judge and comptroller.

The State Convention

On October 17, 1787, the General Assembly passed a resolution calling for meetings in each town to elect delegates to a January convention to consider the Constitution. Benjamin Gale, who labeled the Constitution a "dark, intricate, artful, crafty, and unintelligible composition," charged that the Connecticut establishment had "managed the matter that they have not left . . . a fortnight to weigh and consider the most important affair that ever came before you." And indeed the General Assembly had mandated town meetings for November 12—only five weeks after the Constitution had been published in Connecticut papers—for the election of delegates to the state convention. Officially the meetings were merely to elect delegates, but a few

James Wadsworth (1730–1817) was town clerk of Durham from 1756 to 1786 and represented the town in the state Assembly from 1759 to 1785 and 1788 to 1789. A lawyer by profession, Wadsworth served in Congress in 1784, in the state Council from 1785 to 1788, and as state comptroller from 1786 to 1788. He emerged as Connecticut's leading Antifederalist and voted against the Constitution in the state convention. His vigorous opposition to the Constitution precluded him from holding important political offices in the aftermath of its ratification. Portrait courtesy of Yale University.

did debate the Constitution, and seven of them instructed their delegates to reject the document.

The ratifying convention met at Hartford on January 3 at the State House, but it adjourned to the First Church, North Meeting House, where spectators could sit in the balcony. Of the 174 men who had been elected, 172 were present and 168 voted.

It cannot be said with certainty that in January 1788, when the ratifying convention met, a majority of Connecticut voters were Antifederalist, but that is a good possibility. The old Revolutionary war-horse Hugh Ledlie thought the Constitution "a gilded pill" and asserted there were many in Connecticut who agreed. The Antis had articulate leadership in Benjamin Gale of Killingworth and James Wadsworth of nearby Durham. Wadsworth, wrote Ledlie, "is one of the many steeds that has behaved in character against the new constitution and stood firm not withstanding all the scoffs, flirts, browbeatings, flings, coughs, shuffles, threats, and menaces of the opposite faction." Ledlie himself thought the Constitution "will work the ruin of the freedom and liberty of these thirteen dis-united states."

Just as the newspaper debate was wholly dominated by the nationalists, so was the debate at the ratifying convention. Ledlie was told that while opponents of the Constitution were speaking, galleries stacked by the nationalists, along with some convention members, were "shuffling and stamping [their] feet, coughing, talking, spitting, and whispering.... All these menaces and stratagems were used by a junto who tries to carry all before them in this state." Federalists had the old establishment of Congregational ministers and perpetual officeholders firmly behind them—indeed, establishment members made up the hard core of the movement to ratify.

Thus, though perhaps lacking quantity, the nationalists commanded quality in Connecticut. Or as Hugh Ledlie put it, the convention was stacked with "the very men that framed the new Constitution at Philadelphia, together with our present governor, lieutenant governor, judges of our superior and inferior courts, present delegates to Congress, judges of probates, lawyers, ragtag and bobtail, with some reverend divines, and placemen, salarymen, sinecures, and expectants of every denomination whatsoever." These were, of course, the same men who as state officeholders might be supposed to have the most to lose under an overweening national government, a logical problem not addressed by Antifederalists.

One old establishment figure described the membership of the convention somewhat differently, pointing out that the pro-Constitution forces included two governors, one lieutenant governor, six members of the upper house, a judge of the Superior Court, two ministers, eight generals, eighteen colonels, seven majors, thirteen captains, and sixty-seven others, including many county judges and justices of the peace. On the other side were only one member of the upper house (the soon-to-be-deposed James Wadsworth), two generals, four colonels, one major, three captains, a lieutenant, and a sprinkling of county judges and justices of the peace.

All three delegates to the Philadelphia Convention, who had been over every point and every argument many times, were present to put forward the case for ratification and answer all the charges against the new system. Ellsworth did most of the talking, but Sherman and Johnson both contributed speeches. The balconies were packed with supporters of the establishment, and the lone newspaper reporter was an ardent Federalist. He reported that the Constitution "was canvassed critically and fully. Every objection was raised against it which the ingenuity and invention of its opposers could devise. . . . Suffice it to say that all the objections to the Constitution vanished before the learning and eloquence of a Johnson, the genuine good sense and discernment of a Sherman, and the Demosthenian energy of an Ellsworth."

The last words in debate were given to Governor Huntington, Lieutenant Governor Wolcott, and Superior Court Chief Judge Richard Law, a

Samuel Huntington (1731– 1796) rose from the trade of cooper to the governorship of Connecticut. Desirous of political involvement, he abandoned his trade for the study of law and began practice in Norwich in 1760. He became a judge of the Superior Court (1773– 1785) and a member of the state Council (1775–1784), and he represented Connecticut in Congress (1776– 1781, and 1783), where he signed the Declaration of Independence and the Articles of Confederation. He served as president of Congress from September 1779 to July 1781. He was lieutenant governor from 1784 to 1786 and was then elected governor, a position he held until his death. Huntington strongly supported Connecticut's ratification of the Constitution as a delegate to the state convention. Sketch from Connecticut Magazine, 6 (May–June, 1900), No. 4, p. 247.

triumvirate of power that finally won over anyone still wavering. As one disgruntled Anti put it, "The sophistry, coloring, and smooth speeches of those great men which spoke last gave a turning cast to the whole and thereby gave the weaker brethren a different turn of mind from what they had when they came from home and or the instructions they received from the towns to which they belonged." Hugh Ledlie wrote a friend that the business "was carried on . . . with a highhand against those that disapproved thereof," who "were browbeaten by many of those Ciceroes, as they think themselves, and others of superior rank, as they call themselves."

Finally, on January 9, the vote was taken and counted: 128 for to 40 against. Thus the great revolution was wrought; and the Connecticut freemen, without violence though with less than total equanimity, surrendered—perhaps unknowingly—the sovereignty that had been "the darling" of the people for a century and a half. And though the new order was constitutional and may have been representative, they put their government and themselves under a dominion that was ultimately far more restrictive and dominating than any they had ever known under Parliament, Crown, and Empire before the bloody years of revolt and revolution.

Connecticut: Essay on Sources

Writing about the ratification of the U.S. Constitution in Connecticut has been greatly simplified by the publication of vol. 3 of *The Documentary History of the Ratification of the Constitution* (Madison, Wis., 1978), edited by Merrill Jensen, John P. Kaminski and Gaspare J. Saladino. The volume has an excellent introductory essay on Connecticut's ratification. Three invaluable dissertations on Connecticut's economy and politics during the Revolutionary era are Gaspare John Saladino's "The Economic Revolution in Late Eighteenth Century Connecticut" (University of Wisconsin, 1964); Philip H. Jordan, "Connecticut Politics during the Revolution and Confederation" (Yale, 1962); and Harvey Milton Wachtell's "The Conflict between Localism and Nationalism in Connecticut, 1783–1788" (University of Missouri, 1971). One older essay still worth consulting is Bernard C. Steiner, "Connecticut's Ratification of the Federal Constitution," *Proceedings* of the American Antiquarian Society, new series, 25 (October 1915), pt. 2.

The Jensen *Documentary History* includes, either in print or in an accompanying microfiche supplement, every scrap of relevant matter that anyone knows about today. Newspaper polemic, private letters, public records, and minutes of town meetings are all collected and presented with appropriate scholarly apparatus. For the Connecticut story, there is hardly a need for research beyond this volume.

Other helpful sources are largely biographical. William Samuel Johnson was biographed fifty years ago by George C. Groce (New York, 1937) and recently in a thorough, scholarly work, Elizabeth P. McCaughey, *From Loyalist to Founding Father: The Political Odyssey of William Samuel Johnson* (New York, 1980). There is no recent biography of Oliver Ellsworth William Garrott Brown, *The Life of Oliver Ellsworth* (New

York, 1905) must be supplemented with an excellent short monograph, Ronald J. Littieri, *Connecticut's Young Man of the Revolution: Oliver Ellsworth* (Harvard, 1978). Roger Sherman is the subject of one twentieth-century scholarly work, Christopher Collier, *Roger Sherman's Connecticut: Yankee Politics and the American Revolution* (Middletown, Conn., 1971), which can be augmented with Henry Lewis Boutell's *The Life of Roger Sherman* (Chicago, 1896), a volume that deals more thoroughly with Sherman's legal career.

Important articles are Ronald J. Littieri, "Connecticut's 'Publius': Oliver Ellsworth, *The Landholder Series*, and the Fabric of Connecticut Republicanism," *Connecticut History*, 23 (April 1982), 24–25, and Larry R. Gerlach, "Towards 'a more perfect Union': Connecticut, the Continental Congress, and the Constitutional Convention," *Bulletin* of the Connecticut Historical Society, 33 (July 1969), 64–78.

Massachusetts and the Creation of the Federal Union, 1775–1791

JOHN J. FOX
Professor of History
Salem State College

S THE WINTER OF 1775–1776 melted into spring, the Second Continental Congress moved cautiously along the road to independence. Elbridge Gerry, recently appointed to Congress by the Massachusetts provincial assembly, was sure that among the delegates "some timid minds" were "terrified at the word independence." But he was more certain than ever that the day of independence was at hand. John Adams was also hopeful. Since May 1775 he had been in attendance and had become convinced that "independence was the general sense ... of a considerable majority." The delegates tingled with excitement when Richard Henry Lee introduced his motion "that these United Colonies are, and of right ought to be free and independent states" and that a form of confederation government ought to be created. After sixteen months of debate it accepted a final version of the Articles of Confederation and sent it to the states for consideration.

In a democratic spirit, the Massachusetts General Court (the state's legislature) sent the Articles to the towns. Although approving the Articles in principle, many towns proposed amendments. In keeping with local wishes, the General Court, while not submitting any amendments, instructed its congressional delegates to support those which would not endanger "the union proposed." In the early summer of 1778, Massachusetts joined seven other states in ratifying the Articles. By January 1779 Maryland was the lone holdout.

With the formation of the new republic, the people hoped that the country would get on with its business. But this would not be an easy task. The Articles had been written by men who feared the power of government, and as a result Congress found it difficult to conduct business.

The Need to Strengthen the Articles

Several times prior to 1787 Congress attempted to amend the Articles, but to no avail. While seemingly sympathetic to the plight of Congress, the political leaders in Massachusetts did not view the situation as critical. Rufus King spoke for many when he wrote John Adams that there was "no cause of despair." But by July 1785 the General Court began to worry about the drift. Feeling that something needed to be done, but not sure what, it instructed its congressional delegates to petition Congress to call a convention of the states. The delegates dragged their feet. Elbridge Gerry, Samuel Holten, and Francis Dana were one in believing that a convention would be "ill judged and very dangerous." They were apprehensive that a convention would be dominated by nationalists and aristocrats. Being warned by its congressional delegates that such a combination would work to undermine the cherished republican nature of the Union, the legislature rescinded its instruction. But as Massachusetts soon discovered, the idea of a convention had been on the minds of others.

Virginia, a state that wanted a strengthened central government, issued a call for a meeting in Annapolis, Maryland, in September 1786. Ignoring the warning of its congressmen, the General Court appointed delegates, but to its surprise, they declined to serve, as did a second set of appointees. By the time willing delegates were found, it was too late; the convention had adjourned.

Massachusetts was not alone in its tardiness. Only five states were represented at Annapolis. Recognizing that little could be done, the attending delegates called for a new convention to meet in Philadelphia on the second Monday in May 1787, a summons the Massachusetts legislature debated in the early fall. Appearing before the House of Representatives, Rufus King, completing his third year in Congress, warned that the call was improper. The Articles of Confederation, he pointed out, gave Congress the exclusive power to issue a call. For only it, with the approval of the state legislatures, could amend the Articles. The General Court took heed and did not act.

Shays' Rebellion

While the General Court dawdled, the response of the state's rural areas to the crushing financial burden and unbearable taxation played into the hands of those who wanted a stronger national government. By the late summer of 1786, when tax relief was not forthcoming from the General Court,

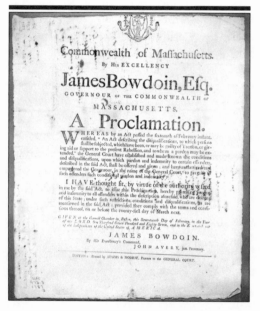

In August 1786 an uprising consisting mainly of debtor farmers began in central and western Massachusetts. Eventually Daniel Shays became its leader. The insurgents demanded various debtor-relief legislation. When the protesters prevented county courts from sitting to hear debt cases, Governor James Bowdoin called out the state militia. After numerous incidents and several deaths, the rebellion was suppressed in February 1787 by General Benjamin Lincoln. This proclamation pardoned all except the leaders of the uprising, but even Shays was forgiven in June 1788 after the administration of Governor John Hancock, Bowdoin's successor, sponsored several measures to meet the debtors' demands. The rebellion set off a wave of backcountry resistance to debt recovery and tax collection that extended as far as South Carolina. These protesters gave a sense of urgency to the nationalists, who now recognized that in addition to setting up a more efficient government with powers over taxation and commerce, there was a need for a strong central government that could maintain order and stability in the states and protect the interests of creditors. Bowdoin proclamation (1787), courtesy of the Essex Institute, Salem, Massachusetts.

embittered farmers, having learned well the art of resistance, began to meet in county conventions. The more militant farmers, known as Regulators and led by Daniel Shays, took up arms. These angry men led mobs in closing the courts. Their action, bordering on rebellion, brought a degree of relief. When not sitting, the judges could not approve foreclosures, nor could they send debt-burdened farmers to debtors' prison. Faced with what many believed to be an insurrection, Governor James Bowdoin called the General Court into a special fall session. Frightened that the government might be toppled, the legislators passed several measures which they prayed would bring relief to debtors and end the prowling, angry mobs.

When the representatives returned in early January 1787, their prayers were unanswered. Sam Adams, "the father of the American Revolution" and now president of the upper chamber, wanted the uprising crushed before it destroyed all that he and the patriots of '76 had bled for. He was able to convince the General Court to declare that a rebellion existed and to urge Bowdoin to crush it. To make the stern measures acceptable to the people, rumors were circulated that the rebels were being supported by Tories and directed by British agents. The state's harsh attitude was motivated more by political expediency than by a concern that the Regulators (who were thought to have a leveling spirit) desired to destroy the republican system.

Crushing Shays' Rebellion did not end the enmity which existed between the urban creditors and the rural debtors. The harshness of the political establishment toward the beleaguered debtors reverberated throughout the commonwealth and was a major factor in the annual spring election. John Hancock defeated Governor Bowdoin and many legislators were not returned. The politicians who survived read the message loud and clear; the electorate was unhappy with the treatment of the Regulators. As the rebellious incident subsided, its waves were felt throughout the nation.

It would be misleading to claim that Shays' Rebellion was the major impetus in bringing about the Philadelphia Convention. The constitutional movement was well along by the time the mobs began to gather. What the rebellion did do, however, was to strengthen the hands of those who were fearful of mobocracy and wanted a stronger national government. To them, the rebellion was the final nail in the Confederation's coffin.

Massachusetts' Delegates to the Constitutional Convention

The rush to convention gained momentum in late 1786. Before Congress issued its own call, several states had appointed delegates. King reluctantly recognized that the movement was unstoppable and that his state might choose delegates without waiting for Congress to act. In January he counseled Gerry that if the General Court should appoint delegates, "for Godsake be careful who are the men; the times are becoming critical." Five weeks later he indicated that "although my sentiments are the same as to the legality of this measure," he would no longer flow against the flood tide. "I think," he wrote, "we ought not to oppose, but to coincide with this project." In the waning days of winter, he came to accept the idea that "events are hurrying us to a crisis." It was important, therefore, that "prudent and sagacious men should be ready to seize the most favorable circumstances to establish a more perfect and vigorous government."

King was not the only one to recognize the momentum of the movement. Without any reference to the Annapolis meeting, Congress on February 21, 1787, called for a convention to meet in Philadelphia for the purpose of amending the Articles of Confederation. In responding, the General Court paid careful attention to its selection of delegates, choosing Francis Dana, Elbridge Gerry, Nathaniel Gorham, Rufus King, and Caleb Strong. With the exception of Strong, all had served or were serving in Congress. Strong, a lawyer from Northampton, had served in the state Senate. No attempt was made to include anyone who represented the interests of the Regulators, debtors, or farmers. This was not surprising, for these interests lacked strong and articulate spokesmen in the General Court.

While neither the legislature nor its agents were supportive of the movement to abandon the Articles, their connections to the merchants caused them to favor a strengthened central government. A successful meeting in Philadelphia would ensure, they hoped, the political existence of the new nation. They were desirous that it would provide the commercial interests with the type of support that could come only from a government that had the power to regulate commerce and to raise and collect revenue.

On the day the convention opened, Massachusetts was represented only by Rufus King; but soon he was joined by three others. Francis Dana, who was very sick, never arrived in Philadelphia. From the outset, King, Gerry, and Gorham took an active part in the deliberations. Strong, a quiet man, tended to follow the lead of Gerry.

In the early days it became evident that there was a split in the Massachusetts delegation. While all shared a commitment to strengthening the government, they disagreed on how this best could be done. By the time they arrived in Philadelphia, King and Gorham had moved closer to the nationalist position. They were troubled that without a strong government the states would not be able to protect the interests of the commercial class. They were still haunted by the specter of Shays' Rebellion. Gerry, perhaps more affected by Shays' Rebellion than the other delegates were, opposed the direct involvement of the people in government, but he was also apprehensive about framing a government that would have the potential of becoming tyrannical. To protect the people from such a threat, he could support only a government based on the federal principle.

When debate began on the Virginia Plan, Gerry complained that the scheme went beyond the instructions of Congress and certainly beyond the General Court's commission. He warned his fellow delegates that "if we have a right to pass this resolution, we have a right to annihilate the confederation." His colleagues from Massachusetts sat quietly by, not showing any signs of support for Gerry's apprehensions.

Rufus King (1755–1827), like several framers, had a career spanning two states, as befitted a person of his nationalistic outlook. Born in the Massachusetts province of Maine, King graduated from Harvard College in 1777 and, after brief military service, began the practice of law. He then served successively in the Massachusetts legislature (1783–1786), Congress (1784–1787), and the Philadelphia Convention. An ardent foe of slavery, the eloquent King helped fashion its ban in the Northwest Ordinance of 1787 and spoke against it in Philadelphia. King's marriage to a wealthy New York heiress prompted his move to that state in 1789. Amazingly, he was immediately chosen as one of New York's U.S. senators in the First Congress, where he later became a leading member of the Federalist Party. After able service as minister to Great Britain (1796–1803), he became the Federalist candidate for vice president (1804 and 1808) and president (1816). In his presidential bid he was the standard-bearer of a party tainted by sectionalism, pitted against former Antifederalist James Monroe, who ran on a platform espousing economic nationalism. King's later career included a return to the U.S. Senate (1813–1825) and to his English diplomatic post (1825–1826). Painting by John Trumbull, courtesy of Yale University Art Gallery.

The split in the delegation became well defined when the convention turned its attention to the issue of representation in the national legislature. King and Gorham sided with those who favored representation based on population and election by popular vote. Gerry and Strong, on the other hand, wanted elections for federal offices to be by the state legislatures. Fearing democracy with its "leveling spirit" as much as tyranny, Gerry believed that if the people had the power to elect, they could be manipulated by selfish politicians or by the "respectable, united and influential" Society of the Cincinnati, a national hereditary organization composed of retired Revolutionary War officers. When the convention could not agree, the issues of election and representation were referred to a special committee chaired by Gerry.

The committee's report recommended Connecticut's solution—proportional representation in the lower house and equal representation of the

Elbridge Gerry (1744–1814), a Harvard-educated merchant, became a protégé of Sam Adams and a leading Massachusetts radical prior to the Revolution. Gerry represented Massachusetts in Congress from 1776 to 1780 and from 1783 to 1785, signing both the Declaration and the Articles of Confederation. Gerry represented Massachusetts at the Philadelphia Convention, where he was active, if inconsistent, in debate. He passed up the opportunity to sign his third founding document because he found the Constitution "full of vices." In 1789, after declaring his intention to support the newly ratified Constitution, he was elected to the U.S. House of Representatives, where he served until 1793. In the ensuing twenty years he held such varied positions as commissioner to France during the XYZ affair; Democratic-Republican governor of Massachusetts (1810–1812), where his redistricting scheme brought the word "gerrymander" into the language; and James Madison's vice president (1813–1814). Engraving by Albert Rosenthal, in Clinton Rossiter, 1787: The Grand Convention (New York, 1966).

states in the upper chamber. Money bills were to originate only in the former house with no amendments to them in the latter. The large states were angered by the recommendations. Gorham, who chaired the committee of the whole and who supported proportional representation in both houses, demanded that Gerry explain how his committee had arrived at its recommendations. Reeling under the attack, Gerry declared that while he had some reservations concerning the proposal, it was a compromise, intended to move the proceedings along. He warned that if the convention was unable to arrive at a solution to this key question, a new order might be imposed by a foreign power.

After more than a week of discussion and maneuvering, the convention accepted the report on a vote of five states to four. The division in the Massachusetts delegation played an important role in the success of the compromise. When the question was put to the delegation, it divided evenly, with Gerry and Strong supporting the report and King and Gorham opposed. Because of this deadlock Massachusetts' vote did not count in the final tally. If Dana were in attendance, he would have joined King and Gorham and the compromise would have gone down to defeat. This would have insured that at another point in its deliberations the convention would have been forced to debate the large states' contention that the compromise was unfair.

Other issues on which the delegation divided included the length of terms for representatives, the size of electoral districts, and the right of national officeholders to sit in Congress. Influenced by their Massachusetts experience, Gerry and Strong supported the idea of annual elections. King and Gorham sided with those favoring longer terms and larger electoral districts.

Gerry's fear of a strong government misusing its powers heightened as the convention moved towards completion of its work. On September 12 he proposed that a committee be established to prepare a bill of rights. The convention unanimously defeated his motion by a vote of 10 to 0, with Massachusetts abstaining. When a second attempt to include a bill of rights was unsuccessful, Gerry, along with Edmund Randolph and George Mason of Virginia, reluctantly withheld his name from the Constitution. He took this action not from spite, he told his colleagues, but because the proposed ordinance of government did not secure the rights of citizens.

On adjournment day Benjamin Franklin encouraged all the delegates to sign. Although he remained obstinate, Gerry withheld his signature with some reluctance. He was not, he maintained, an enemy of the national government. Though he always had felt the convention violated its charge from Congress, he supported the strengthening of the government. He had not come with preconceived ideas of the structure that should result. Diligently he had worked to create a document which he could support. He wished that he could honor the great doctor's call for unity, but he could not. The new Constitution was in most parts acceptable, but it did not insure the "liberties of America."

After adjournment Gerry's mood appeared to mellow. In a letter to the state legislature, he indicated that he understood that "the welfare of the Union requires a better Constitution than the Confederation." He saw it as his duty "as a citizen of Massachusetts, to support that which shall be finally adopted, sincerely hoping that it will secure the liberty and happiness of America." Gerry said that he had "no objection" to the people "trying on the fœderal chains, for such I am persuaded they will find the bonds of this constitution eventually to be."

The Massachusetts Convention

The convention had proposed that the Constitution be submitted to the states and, upon ratification by nine state conventions, replace the Articles of Confederation as the new basic law among the ratifying states. Abiding by the instructions of Congress, the General Court issued the call for a ratification convention to convene in early January 1788. Of the 401 communities in the commonwealth, 46 did not send representatives.

The men who came to Boston in the second week of January were already knowledgeable concerning the Constitution, for it had been published in newspapers throughout the state. Since October there had been public meetings, numerous gatherings, and a running debate between Federalists—those who supported the Constitution—and Antifederalists, who opposed it.

Many convention delegates were concerned by Elbridge Gerry's refusal to stand for election to the Massachusetts convention. As a delegate to Philadelphia, he should have been sent to the ratification convention, they felt. Federalists, having little choice, acquiesced when Antifederalist leader Samuel Adams requested that Gerry be invited to attend the convention and to respond to questions directed to him by the delegates. Federalists, however, made certain that the invitation did not provide the nonsigner with an opportunity to participate in the give-and-take of debate. Wanting to lend support to those who favored his position, and possibly feeling a need to justify his actions in Philadelphia, Gerry accepted the invitation.

Having carefully observed the election of delegates, Federalists knew that they did not control the convention. As King wrote to James Madison, "Our prospects are gloomy, but hope is not entirely extinguished." Politically cunning, Federalists were determined to use every ploy that would help achieve their goal. Aware of the popularity of Governor Hancock, they backed him for president of the convention, even though it was suspected that he was not a warm supporter of the Constitution. It was known that he shared with Gerry a concern that it did not contain a bill of rights.

Hancock had apparently not yet made up his mind by the time the convention met. He conveniently became ill with the gout and remained away until January 30. As some of his contemporaries whispered, he may have used this excuse to determine which side was going to win. Federalists were not unhappy with his absence; they could use the time to plead their case.

For several days Gerry observed the restrictions placed upon him. When the discussion turned to the congressional compromise, however, he attempted to speak. Before he had a chance, Francis Dana and other delegates were on their feet insisting that he was out of order. To restore sanity to the brawling chamber, the convention was adjourned. This unplanned disruption surprised Federalist leaders. They were fearful that the incident would widen the split between the sides and make their selling job more difficult. If there was a bright lining to a dark cloud, it was that the confrontation had taken place on Saturday. Sunday, hopefully, would provide enough time for cooling off.

When the uneasy delegates were seated on Monday, Gerry was not to be seen. Feeling humiliated, he was determined not to give his enemies a second chance. He would return only if he was allowed an opportunity to defend himself. Federalists, happy that he had removed himself from the convention, would see that Gerry's desire would never be granted.

In the early weeks of the convention, Federalists were certain that there were enough opposing votes to defeat ratification. To be victorious, they needed to delay a final tally until the numbers were right. Thus they quivered when Antifederalists attempted to speed up the debate. To their surprise, Federalists were saved by Samuel Adams, who unexpectedly chided those who would rush the proceedings. The delegates, he scolded, should not "be stingy of our time." Given this concession, Federalists needed to develop a strategy that would move moderates to their side.

On January 12 the *Massachusetts Centinel* had published an essay from a "Republican Federalist" suggesting ratification, with the addition of proposed amendments. Two weeks later, after failing to win over enough support to ratify the Constitution, Federalists were willing to give the plan a try. But if it was to work, they knew that it had to be presented to the convention by someone whom moderates could trust. It was now time to court John Hancock. Federalists believed they understood the game the governor was playing; as Rufus King predicted, the governor's illness would end "as soon as the majority is exhibited on either side."

Hancock had the respect and admiration of rural debtors. He had shown concern in the aftermath of Shays' Rebellion. A political opportunist who enjoyed the public spotlight and admiration, Hancock would do anything which would enhance his public reputation and his political career. He wanted to be re-elected governor and harbored dreams of national leadership. Give him guarantees and he would strike a political bargain.

The deal was struck. Federalists would provide Hancock with amendments which he could introduce as his own. In turn, they pledged their support in the upcoming gubernatorial election. To sweeten the pot, they led him to believe that they would back him for vice president and, if Virginia failed to ratify, for president. Hancock did not spend a great deal of time agonizing over the propriety of what he was about to do. Both he and Federalist leaders knew that his standing among the moderates would influence their vote.

Even after working out the terms of the agreement, Federalists were unsure that Hancock would sustain them. "If Mr. Hancock does not disappoint our present expectations, our wishes will be gratified," King wrote

John Hancock (1737-1793), a Harvard-educated merchant of great wealth, joined the Revolutionary protest when British regulations and their arbitrary enforcement impinged upon his huge commercial operation. To give their cause respectability, rebels like Sam Adams pushed the prestigious and vain Hancock into the vanguard of the protest movement. He represented Massachusetts in Congress (1775-1778) and presided over that body when the Declaration of Independence was approved and signed (his signature being the most prominent). Elected the commonwealth's first governor under its famed constitution of 1780, Hancock served as chief executive from 1780 to 1785 and again from 1787 until his death in 1793. Though not at Philadelphia, Governor Hancock chaired the Massachusetts ratifying convention, and his support of the Constitution (though rendered firm by a political deal) was a critical factor in his state's approval. Engraving by L. B. Forrest from a painting by John Singleton Copley, courtesy of the Essex Institute.

to James Madison, "but his character is not entirely free from a portion of caprice."

Ratification was still not assured. There was some anxiety about Samuel Adams. If he spoke against the plan, he could cause much trouble. It was necessary, therefore, to bring him into the Federalist camp or, at the least, to neutralize him. Adams could not be politically tempted. The one thing that might move him would be the desire of the people that he claimed to represent—the workingmen of Boston.

In the past few years Boston had suffered economically. Federalists had spread the word that ratification would bring prosperity. On the eve of the convention, Boston's tradesmen met at the Green Dragon Tavern on Union Street in the North End and threw their weight behind the Constitution. Paul Revere, who was one of them, communicated this information to his old friend. When Adams was told the crowd overflowed into the street, he wanted to know how great was the overflow. There were "more . . . than there are stars in the sky," Revere told him. With his political ally John Hancock now supporting the Constitution, Adams felt reluctant to keep up the battle. The death of his son as the convention sat also sapped Adams's ability to fight.

While there is no historical evidence to verify the exact reason for Adams's willingness to ratify the Constitution, his constituents' strong expression of support for the Constitution may have been the key to his willingness to ratify the document if it were amended. For Federalists, such amendments were not too high a price to pay, especially if they were only proposals and would be considered only after the new government had been formed. Federalists were now on the way to victory.

On January 30 Hancock attended the convention for the first time. The next day, after the stage had been set, he proposed a series of amendments, eventually fixed at nine. The most significant was the reservation to the states of all powers not "expressly delegated" by the Constitution to the general government. His motive, Hancock said, was to pave the way for the adoption of "a form of government as may extend its good influence to every part of the United States, and advance the prosperity of the whole world."

Samuel Adams played his role by moving that the amendments, which he referred to as "conciliatory propositions," be taken under consideration. He assured delegates who were still sitting on the fence, or who wanted to return the Constitution to a second national convention for amending, that the Massachusetts plan was the best way of dealing with their misgivings. The failure of Massachusetts to ratify, Adams warned, could have repercussions throughout the nation and lead to the breakup of the Union, and he feared "the consequence of such disunion."

Fully aware that Federalists were willing to compromise, Adams saw a chance to push a little further. On adjournment day he introduced some additional amendments which were intended to protect more fully the liberties of the people. They dealt with freedom of the press, freedom of conscience, the right to bear arms, the right to petition, and protection against unreasonable search and seizure. Federalists were angered by this last-minute maneuver, but after long debate, when no support came forth, Adams withdrew his amendments from consideration. Before the vote on ratification was called, he reassured the delegates that all was in order.

The debate and political manipulation came to an end on February 6; the time was then at hand to decide on ratification. Federalists had been

Samuel Adams (1722–1803), called "the Firebrand of the Revolution," was a restless and turbulent leader more adept at denouncing injustice than in creating a system to prevent it. As a writer, a propagandist, and an organizer of protest, he was unsurpassed in the decade preceding the Revolution. The Sons of Liberty and the committees of correspondence were two of the vehicles he helped fashion to protest the policies of the mother country. Adams signed the Declaration of Independence and served in Congress from 1774 to 1781. As a leader of the state senate (1780–1788), he refused to attend the Philadelphia Convention because he feared a stronger central government would result from that gathering. At the outset of the ratification struggle, he observed: "As I enter the building, I stumble on the threshold. I meet with a National Government instead of a Federal Union of Sovereign States." In the end, however, Adams cautiously gave his support. His long career was capped by service as lieutenant governor (1789–1793) and governor (1794–1797) of Massachusetts. Painting by John Singleton Copley, courtesy of the Museum of Fine Arts, Boston.

bolstered following the introduction of the "conciliatory propositions" when three outspoken opponents indicated that they would support ratification. Of the trio, William Symmes, an articulate young lawyer from Andover, was the most important. Symmes refused to apologize for switching sides, for "in so doing," he stated, "I stand acquitted to my own conscience; I hope and trust I shall to my constituents, and I know I shall before God."

Staunch Antifederalists, fearing that their numbers were eroding, moved for adjournment. It was their hope that they could return home and rouse their constituents against ratification. If nothing more, the delay might derail the Federalist bandwagon. The motion was soundly defeated. Federalists were now certain that they had moved the moderates away from the Antifederalist camp. To apply a little more pressure to those who might still be uncertain, Governor Hancock rose and reinforced his call for ratification.

When the vote was tallied, Federalists heaved a sigh of relief, for they had squeaked through with a narrow victory of 187 to 168. Some were concerned that the struggle for ratification had developed hostility between the factions that would be difficult to overcome; so when a few Antifederalist delegates promised to accept the results and called upon their constituents "to live in peace under and cheerfully submit to" the Constitution, Federalists were pleasantly surprised.

At the end of the day, a happy Rufus King dashed off a quick note to Madison to tell him that "the majority, although small, is extremely respectable, and the minority are in good temper." Federalists made every effort to overcome any hard feeling that might have been harbored by the opposition. After the vote everyone was invited to adjourn to the Senate chamber, "where," it was reported, "the toasts given were truly conciliatory." Two days later Boston hosted a grand procession, and again the victors did everything to ensure that their "country friends were accommodated to their wishes."

Hancock's efforts on the part of ratification did not go unnoticed. They were memorialized in a ballad:

> Then 'Squire Hancock, like a man
>   Who dearly loves the nation,
> By a concil'atory plan,
>   Prevented much vexation.
>   Yankee doodle, keep it up!
>   Yankee doodle, dandy!
>   Mind the music and the step,
>   And with the girls be handy.

He made a *woundy* Fed'ral speech,
    With sense and elocution;
And then the 'Vention did beseech
    T' adopt the Constitution
        Yankee doodle, &c.
The question being outright put,
    (Each voter independent)
The Fed'ralists agreed t' adopt,
    And then propose amendment.
        Yankee doodle, &c.
The other party, seeing then,
    The people were against 'em,
Agreed, like honest, faithful men,
    To mix in peace amongst 'em.
        Yankee doodle, &c.

The narrow victory speaks volumes about the split that existed within the state. The rural counties—Middlesex, Bristol, Worcester, Hampshire, and Berkshire—voted against the Constitution better than 2 to 1: 60 votes for and 128 against. The Federalists' strength was found in the urban coastal counties of Suffolk, Essex, Plymouth, and Barnstable. Out of 119 delegates, only 19 voted against ratification—a margin greater than 5 to 1. In the counties where the creditor and commercial interests were dominant, Federalists won handily. The delegates from these areas were committed to limitations on state governments and to a stronger national government which would honor its debts and be vigorous enough to pursue policies which would allow the commercial interests to compete in world markets.

If the people of the commonwealth had been allowed to vote directly, they would have determined against ratification; so would a majority of delegates if they had been asked to cast their vote in the early days of the convention. The issue that decided the vote for the moderates was not whether the Constitution would make for a stronger, more viable government but whether or not it would establish a government that had the potential to oppress the people. Aided by Hancock and Adams, they decided that it would not.

The ideologues within the ranks of the Antifederalists were not moved by any pleas or promises intended to remove this fear of governmental tyranny. They were unalterably opposed to the proposed Constitution, and Federalists, being political realists, made no attempts to convert them. The supporters of the Constitution achieved victory, rather by convincing the moderates that all, including liberty, would be secure under the new government.

The Bill of Rights

A few moderates left the convention, sensing that Federalists might fail to honor their pledge to amend the Constitution. When the first session of Congress got under way on April 1, 1789, most members were in no hurry to proceed with the revisions. They felt that there was more pressing business at hand. Madison was one who believed that the promise had to be kept.

On June 8 the Virginian proposed several amendments and called upon Congress to take immediate action on the question. His call went unheeded. Even Congressman Gerry was reluctant to move ahead quickly. He felt that it was more important to get "our political ship . . . under way"; then, in "a period of tranquility and leisure," Congress could turn its attention to "a momentous subject . . . Very near [his] heart."

Fisher Ames, a Federalist stalwart from Massachusetts, saw no need to amend, yet he recognized that "it may do some good towards quieting men who attend to sound only." He was willing to keep the pledge, but the amendments, he wrote a friend, "should not be trash, such as would dishonor the Constitution."

Congress referred Madison's proposal to a special committee consisting of one member from each state. The committee's report was debated for three weeks. In the end the House approved seventeen amendments and sent them to the Senate for action. When the two chambers could not agree, a conference committee was established. Following its report, the House agreed to twelve amendments, all of which the congressional delegation from Massachusetts unanimously supported.

The ratification process moved quickly. Within six months eight states had consented to ten of the twelve proposals that would become the Bill of Rights. By January 1790 both houses of the Massachusetts General Court had given preliminary approval to nine of the amendments, rejecting articles 1, 2, and 12, which dealt with, respectively, apportionment, congressional pay, and the reservation to the states or the people of all powers not delegated to the national government. At this stage the legislature bogged down. Some Antifederalist lawmakers did not feel that the amendments addressed the issues raised at the time of ratification. To placate them, a joint committee was established "to consider what further amendments are necessary to be added to the Federal Constitution."

Toward the end of February the committee reported back with a recommendation for twelve additional amendments. These were intended to define the powers of Congress and to secure the sovereign powers of the states. Neither chamber took any action; the Federalist majority in the General Court had no intention of tampering with the Constitution. The legislators also failed to take final action on the amendments proposed by Congress. The journals of the General Court provide no indication that the joint committee which had been appointed to bring in a bill or resolution for ratification ever submitted a report.

The action of the legislators seems contradictory in light of the promises made at the ratifying convention. But the failure to complete the ratification process or to send to Congress the amendments proposed by the joint committee may not have been a breech of political faith. Federalists did not feel a strong commitment to amending the Constitution, being satisfied with the document as it stood. The political leaders perceived that since the convention the acceptance of the Constitution by the majority had lessened the need to fulfill the promises.

Massachusetts, the state which started it all on April 19, 1775, did not ratify the Bill of Rights until March 2, 1939. The General Court took this action to commemorate the bill's 150th anniversary and to finish the business which began in Philadelphia on May 25, 1787.

Massachusetts: Essay on Sources

The starting point for a study of Massachusetts history in the Confederation era is Van Beck Hall, *Politics Without Parties: Massachusetts, 1780–1791* (Pittsburgh, 1972), which uses quantitative research to support the thesis that socioeconomic influences were the driving force behind the politics of the times. The split between the coastal commercial centers and the inland rural/agricultural regions which Hall highlights is brought into sharp focus by Robert J. Taylor, *Western Massachusetts in the Revolution* (Providence, 1954); Lee N. Newcomer, *The Embattled Farmer: A Massachusetts Countryside in the American Revolution* (New York, 1953); and Robert Zemsky, *Merchants, Farmers and River Gods: An Essay on Eighteenth-Century American Politics* (Boston, 1971).

Agrarian discontent is discussed in David Szatmary, *Shays' Rebellion: The Making of an Agrarian Insurrection* (Amherst, Mass., 1980). Edward Bellamy provided a fictionalized account of the rebellion in *The Duke of Stockbridge* (Boston, 1900). Robert A. Feer, "Shays's Rebellion and the Constitution: A Study in Causation," *New England Quarterly* 42 (1969), 388–410, convincingly argues that the rebellion had little or no influence on the calling of the Constitution Convention; see also his "Shays's Rebellion" (doctoral dissertation, Harvard University, 1958). Ronald P. Formisano, *The Transformation of Political Culture: Massachusetts Parties, 1790s–1840s* (New York, 1983) puts the era's political maneuvering into a larger historical perspective. Robert A. Gross, *The Minutemen and Their World* (New York, 1976) and Samuel Eliot Morison's classic *The Maritime History of Massachusetts, 1783–1860* (Boston, 1921; reprinted 1979) provide a further understanding of this period.

Although there are no monographs on the subject, the role that the Massachusetts delegates played in framing the Constitution can be culled from several works. The major primary sources are Max Farrand, ed., *The Records of the Federal Convention*, 4 vols. (New Haven, reprint ed. 1967) and James Madison, *Notes of Debates in the Federal Convention of 1787* (New York, 1966).

The major primary sources on Massachusetts ratification are *Debates and Proceedings in the Convention of the Commonwealth of Massachusetts, Held in the Year 1788, and Which Finally Ratified the Constitution of the United States* (Boston, 1856) and Jonathan Elliot, ed., *The Debates in the Several State Conventions on the Adoption of the Federal Constitution*, vol. 1 (New York, 1888). The latest monographic work on Massachusetts ratification is Thomas H. O'Connor and Alan Rogers, *This Momentous Affair: Massachusetts and the Ratification of the Constitution of the United States* (Boston, 1987). Although published nearly a century ago, Samuel B. Harding, *The Contest Over the Ratification of the Federal Constitution in the State of Massachusetts* (New York, 1896) is still a valuable work. Also of major importance is Charles R. King, ed., *The Life and Correspondence of Rufus King*, 6 vols. (New York, 1894).

Most of the major Massachusetts figures in the framing and the ratification of the Constitution has been the subject of one or more biographies since the nineteenth century. These include John C. Miller, *Sam Adams: Pioneer in Propaganda* (Stanford, Calif., 1936); Robert Ernst, *Rufus King: American Federalist* (Chapel Hill, 1968); George A. Billias, *Elbridge Gerry: Founding Father and Republican Statesman* (New York, 1976); and William M. Fowler, Jr., *The Baron of Beacon Hill: A Biography of John Hancock* (Boston, 1980). Nathaniel Gorham and Caleb Strong still await biographers.

There are a few contemporary works which will give the reader a feel for the period. *The Diary of William Bentley* (Salem, 1905–14), written by a learned Unitarian clergyman, perceptively surveys local events from 1784 to 1819; George Richards Minot, *The History of the Insurrections in Massachusetts in the Year of 1786 and the Rebellion Consequent Thereon* (Boston, 1788) is an account of Shays' Rebellion written by a political figure who was horrified by it; Mercy Otis Warren, *History of the Rise, Progress, and Termination of the American Revolution* (Boston, 1805) was written by a politically connected woman who opposed the Constitution.

Insightful essays and articles of a specialized nature include Robert A. East, "The Massachusetts Conservatives in the Critical Period," in *The Era of the American Revolution*, edited by Richard B. Morris (New York, 1939); Joseph P. Warren, "The Confederation and Shays' Rebellion," *American Historical Review*, 11 (1905), 42–67; Richard B. Morris, "Insurrection in Massachusetts," in *America in Crisis*, edited by Daniel Aaron (New York, 1952); Oscar and Mary F. Handlin, "Radicals and Conservatives in Massachusetts after Independence," *New England Quarterly*, 17 (September 1944), 343–355; George Henry Haynes, "The Conciliatory Proposition in the Massachusetts Convention of 1788," *Proceedings* of the American Antiquarian Society, new series, 29 (1919), 294–311; Charles Warren, "Elbridge Gerry, James Warren, Mercy Warren, and the Ratification of the Constitution in Massachusetts," *Proceedings* of the Massachusetts Historical Society, 64 (1930–32), 143–164; and "Elbridge Gerry, Gentleman-Democrat," in Samuel Eliot Morison, *By Land and By Sea* (New York, 1953).

Necessity, the Mother of Union

Maryland and the Constitution, 1785–1789

GREGORY STIVERSON
Assistant State Archivist
Maryland State Archives

WHEN MARYLAND'S RATIFICATION CONVENTION convened in Annapolis in late April 1788, friends of the Constitution everywhere anxiously awaited the final vote. Maryland's support was uncertain. A small number of men, noted for their contrariness and conservatism, dominated Maryland politics. This was the state that had nearly refused to join in the vote for independence from Britain in 1776 and that had delayed for years the implementation of the Articles of Confederation.

Maryland's supporters of the Constitution had overwhelmed their opponents in the county elections for delegates to the ratification convention, but with Maryland one could never be sure. What appeared certain on the surface could crumble under a barrage of argument and secret deals when the delegates actually met. And Maryland's ratification was essential. In the two months before, Massachusetts had adopted nine amendments to accompany its ratification, New Hampshire had refused to ratify, Rhode Island had balked at even calling a convention and then rejected the Constitution in a statewide referendum. Maryland's approval as the seventh state was essential to restore momentum to the ratification drive. If Maryland failed to ratify unconditionally, support for the new Constitution could be irretrievably lost.

The Uniqueness of Maryland

There was, in fact, much in the proposed Constitution that did not fit well with Maryland's political experience. Maryland had always been a bit different from the other states—not really northern or southern, but a mixture of both. A tobacco-staple colony in its early years of settlement, Maryland had developed a diversified agricultural and commercial base by the War for Independence. Merchants and tradesmen in the port city of Baltimore had propelled Maryland to a leadership position in trade with the expanding hinterland and in shipbuilding and shipping. A tiny village in the 1750s, Baltimore ranked as the country's fifth largest and fastest-growing city after the Revolution. The aggressive entrepreneurs and tradesmen of Baltimore enthusiastically endorsed the Constitution, because they believed a strong national government would resolve the economic uncertainties that had prevailed since the war.

But Baltimore had little voice in Maryland's politics in the 1780s. That remained the province of an entrenched and powerful elite. Reluctant rebels in 1776, Maryland's political leaders had crafted the most conservative constitution of any of the new states. Property qualifications limited the size of the electorate and severely restricted the number of individuals eligible to hold office. The indirectly elected state Senate, which served as the model for the federal Constitution's electoral college, provided a severe and frequently used check on the actions of the directly elected lower house, or House of Delegates.

Maryland's political elite was close-knit and self-assured, confident that it knew best how to govern the citizens of Maryland. This confidence had been gained in the decades-long struggle for power with the proprietor, who until the Revolution owned Maryland and enjoyed by charter right virtual kinglike authority over his colony. The first proprietor, George Calvert, first Lord Baltimore, envisioned Maryland becoming a feudal fiefdom, with him and his male descendants at the pinnacle, surrounded and supported by manor lords beholden to and supportive of his prerogatives. But the charter King Charles I granted to George Calvert also provided for an assembly of freemen. From the first sitting of this assembly in 1635, the issue of who would really govern the province of Maryland was joined.

For the next 140 years, political debate in Maryland pitted the lower house of the General Assembly against its constant adversaries, the proprietor and his placemen in the colony. The culmination of this struggle came in June 1774, when the first of nine extralegal conventions assembled in Annapolis and effectively took control of the legislative branch of government. By June 1775 an executive body, called the Council of Safety, had been added. Local control was ensured by county committees of observation and committees of correspondence. Similar extralegal bodies appeared in other colonies in the early 1770s as part of the movement toward rebellion. In Maryland, however, the revolution was directed at the proprietor, not the king and Parliament. By 1775 Marylanders had won their revolution. The extralegal government had replaced the proprietary regime in what amounted to a bloodless coup. With victory achieved, Maryland political leaders had no stomach for more revolution. They had risked so much to wrest power from the proprietor, and their victory had been so complete, that they were content to remain loyal subjects of Britain. Only at the last minute, when it was clear that the vote for independence would be taken with or without them, did Maryland cast its lot with the other rebellious colonies. Maryland would fight for independence from Britain because it had no choice. Its political leaders were determined, however, to keep the revolutionary movement at bay when it came to the internal affairs of the state.

Once Maryland joined the struggle for independence, it did so with a commitment equaled by few other states. It became the "breadbasket of the Revolution," and its troops acquitted themselves so admirably on the battlefield that General Washington himself is said to have bestowed on Maryland the appellation "Old Line State." From the heroic stand of Major Mordecai Gist's troops at the Battle of Long Island in 1776 to the men and materiel the state supplied for the final victory at Yorktown, Maryland gave its all for the cause of American independence.

But Marylanders did not sacrifice so much during the War for Independence merely because of the nation. Instead, they fought and died and gave generously of their resources to preserve their own form of government, their own sovereignty as an independent state. The war against Britain was simply an extension of their struggle against the proprietor. The Declaration of Independence had proclaimed that each state was free and independent, and the Articles of Confederation had affirmed that each state retained its own sovereignty and that the central government was merely a "firm league of friendship"—an arrangement much to the liking of Maryland's political leaders. When the Confederation Congress, then sitting in Annapolis in the new Maryland State House, ratified the final draft of the Treaty of Paris in January 1784, Marylanders looked forward to being able to govern themselves once again without outside interference.

Post-Revolution Maryland

As a matter of political faith, state sovereignty was a potent force in motivating Maryland to work with the other states during the War for Independence. But once the war was won, the state quickly returned to a parochial concentration on what was in the best interests of itself and its citizens. This turning inward was both natural and predictable. It attempted to reestablish the colonial focus of government, which rarely extended beyond the colony's boundaries, and it conformed to the accepted political thinking of the day, which argued for a republican form of government that was geographically compact and close to the people it governed. The idea of a strong national government would have been considered dangerous and absurd by most Marylanders in 1783.

But Marylanders soon learned that revolution leaves little unchanged. Nothing was quite the same anymore. State government and its functions had grown enormously during the war, and its expanded role could not be immediately curtailed with the cessation of hostilities. Keeping track of the more than a quarter million acres of loyalist land that had been confiscated and sold to support the war effort, for example, would require years of work before the state had been paid and the new owners had clear title. This bigger state government meant more officeholders and more expenses, all of which had to be supported by more taxes on an already overburdened public.

Marylanders did not immediately appreciate what a vacuum had been left when they finally and permanently severed connection with Britain. British law had regulated colonial trade, British money had provided a monetary standard for the colonies, British merchants had provided credit and banking services, British manufacturers had provided the colonists with everything from clothing to medicine, furniture to fine coaches. The American colonies had exported vast quantities of agricultural products, lumber, fish, flour and bread, iron, and other products of the land and sea to pay for British goods and services. When the war with Britain was won, the Americans had their independence, but they had lost forever their place in the secure, if exploitative, British commercial system.

The permanent disruption of traditional trade patterns was a serious problem for a state as deeply involved in the export trade as Maryland, but paying accumulated war debts was another important concern. Maryland had financed a large part of its contributions to the war by printing paper money. Liquidating the debt represented by this paper would require taxing the state's citizens at a high rate for years to come.

Maryland was not the only state faced with economic dislocations and the necessity of maintaining high taxes after the war. In Maryland, as elsewhere, people who could not pay their taxes risked losing their farms at tax sales or being consigned to debtors' prison. But war debts were not the only financial obligations that loomed over Maryland's residents. According to the terms of the peace treaty with Britain, all prewar debts were to be honored, and Marylanders owed in excess of £130,000 sterling to British merchants. Nearly every state experienced local disturbances as disgruntled and often desperate citizens turned their anger on their government.

The most serious threat to Maryland's internal stability occurred in July 1786, when "a considerable number of disorderly persons" in Charles County converged on the courthouse at Port Tobacco and forced an attorney to remove from the docket prewar debt cases he had filed on behalf of a British creditor. While no violence was done to any of the court officials, Governor William Smallwood took the disturbance seriously. He issued a proclamation condemning those who had engaged in the "riotous and tumultuous behaviour" and demanded an end to all such "violences and outrages" upon threat of punishment to the full extent of the law. Smallwood also launched a detailed investigation to determine why the Charles County justices had been unable to maintain peace and good order in their jurisdiction.

Some states printed new paper money as a quick fix for the economic problems their citizens faced after the war, and considerable support for such a plan existed in Maryland. A shortage of circulating currency had, in fact, exacerbated Maryland's economic problems. Expenditures to pay for imported goods that flooded into Maryland after the war accounted for part of the shortage of cash, but the state's method of retiring the war debt also contributed. The state government destroyed tax-revenue money earmarked for the war debt, either by burning it or by defacing it so that it could not be used again. This practice gave positive proof of progress in retiring the debt, but it severely constricted the amount of circulating currency necessary to sustain the state's already beleaguered economy.

Support for a new emission of paper money was centered in the popularly elected lower house of the General Assembly. The lower house unanimously passed a paper-money bill in December 1785 and another bill for the same purpose a year later. Both bills were unanimously rejected by the conservative Senate, which opposed any artificial increase in the money supply. Instead, the Senate passed its own bill to "prevent frivolous appeals" in debt cases.

The confrontation between the two houses of the General Assembly over paper money and debtor relief set the stage for a protracted and bitter public debate. Both the merits of paper money and, more generally, the responsibility of a government to respond to the financial plight of its citizens were discussed. Following the Senate's veto of the second paper-money bill, Samuel Chase and William Paca, both signers of the Declaration of Independence, led infuriated House members to adjourn the General Assembly to take their case directly to the people. The House expected the counties to adopt resolutions urging passage of a paper-money bill and denying that the indirectly elected Senate was exempt from the electorate's instructions. The senators and their defenders, however, launched a vigorous and effective counterattack. As a result, most of the resolutions returned to Annapolis in the late winter and spring of 1787 opposed paper money and supported the independence of the Senate.

When the General Assembly reconvened in April 1787, a chastened House and a more conciliatory Senate agreed to work together on a bill to provide relief by allowing installment payment of debts. This effort too foundered when the Senate bill could not be reconciled with the more liberal

Samuel Chase (1741–1811) is one of the most enigmatic figures of the founding period. An outspoken, ardent revolutionary in the 1770s and a signer of the Declaration of Independence, he was severe in dealing with political protesters of the 1790s when he sat on the Supreme Court as an associate justice. A highly successful political figure, he was the subject of a war-profiteering scandal in 1778, an attempt by the Maryland legislature in 1792 to remove him from the office of chief judge of the General Court, and an impeachment and trial by the Democratic-Republican Congress in 1804–5. He survived every ordeal. Writing over the signature of "Caution," Chase opposed the adoption of the Constitution and was one of eleven members of the Maryland ratifying convention to cast a negative vote. Nevertheless, he became a staunch member of the Federalist Party in the 1790s and gained from Washington an appointment to the U.S. Supreme Court, where he served from 1796 until his death. Portrait by John Beale Bordley, courtesy of the Maryland Commission on Artistic Property, Maryland State Archives.

House draft, so more than two years of wrangling ended in stalemate. If it accomplished nothing else, however, the paper-money issue of 1785–87 heightened awareness in Maryland about the precarious nature of the state's economy, and it convinced many political leaders that sustained prosperity would require an adequate supply of a stable circulating currency.

The Weaknesses of the Articles of Confederation

Maryland's problems in the postwar years were not unique, and each state found that it had to grapple with its difficulties alone. The structure of government that united them—Congress under the Articles of Confederation—was powerless to do anything about the growing turmoil and instability that became ever more apparent in the mid-1780s.

Maryland itself had provided the incipient Confederation with its first stiff test by refusing to ratify the Articles until those states with expansive western land claims ceded their holdings to the central government to create a national domain. Because the Articles required the unanimous ratification of all of the state legislatures, Maryland's obstinacy prevented the Articles, approved by the Second Continental Congress in November 1777, from becoming operational until March 1, 1781. This ability of one state to impede the functioning or improvement of the Confederation government continued during the 1780s as that system's major defect.

Burdened with war debts and nearly bankrupt, Congress lacked the power to compel the states to contribute to its support. With its army and navy effectively disbanded, Congress even lacked the means to provide for the common defense, even though the Spanish in the south and west and the British in Canada posed a clear threat to the territory the United States had won in the war.

To make matters worse, the states began to turn on each other. Instead of cooperating to help restore the prosperous prewar trade in which they all had shared, they competed against each other, hoping to gain at the expense of their neighbors. Free to set their own trade regulations under the Articles of Confederation, some states went so far as to impose high tariffs on goods imported from adjacent states while offering beneficial terms to foreign shippers.

England contributed to the growing economic distress. The English government declared that all trade with the former colonies had to be carried in English ships, and it prohibited American vessels from trading with the British West Indies.

The Attempt to Strengthen the Articles

The country was at a low ebb by 1786. Something had to be done, but with the Confederation Congress consisting of thirteen jealous states, each with an equal voice, the initiative would have to come from the states themselves. The first encouraging step in this direction occurred in March 1785, when delegates from Maryland and Virginia met at George Washington's Mount Vernon home to discuss mutual problems of trade and commerce on the Potomac River and Chesapeake Bay. Virginia owned the land that formed the capes at the mouth of Chesapeake Bay, and it threatened to restrict Maryland shipping. Maryland retaliated by citing its charter, which designated the state's southern border as the Virginia shore of the Potomac River. The task of the delegates to the Mount Vernon conference was to draft an agreement that would ensure the free navigation on the Chesapeake and Potomac that was vital to each state.

Real progress was made at Mount Vernon. The delegates adopted an agreement known as the Mount Vernon Compact, which offered solutions for many of the problems that had plagued the two states since independence. Approved by the Maryland legislature in November 1785, the Mount Vernon Compact provided for future meetings to continue the discussion of trade and commerce. In forwarding its ratification document to Virginia, Maryland suggested that the other two states involved in trade on the Chesapeake, Delaware and Pennsylvania, be invited to the next meeting held between the states.

Virginia accepted this suggestion, but it expanded the call to include all thirteen states. Virginia's governor, Patrick Henry, wrote to his counterparts in the other states asking them to appoint delegates to a commercial convention that would be held in September 1786 in Annapolis, Maryland. The purpose of this Annapolis Convention would be to "take into consideration the trade and commerce of the United States, [and] to consider how far a uniform system in their commercial intercourse and regulations might be necessary to their common interest and permanent harmony."

The fact that all the states were invited to convene in Annapolis to discuss something as vital as trade and commerce reflected the impotence of Congress. Increasingly, thoughtful people in all parts of the country were coming to the realization that if anything were to get done, if any positive steps were to be taken to solve the dangerous problems facing the United States, it would have to be done outside of Congress. The call to Annapolis, in fact, encouraged discussion among political leaders about the eventual need to strengthen, or entirely replace, the weak Confederation government.

But the time was not yet ripe for such drastic action in early September 1786, when the first delegates began to assemble in Maryland's capital city. The idea of a strong national government posed a direct challenge to the sovereignty for which each state had fought during the War for Independence, a sovereignty which was guaranteed to them by the Articles of Confederation. What was needed was a catalyst that would transform mere dissatisfaction with the Articles, and the growing belief that the country was in real peril, into a constructive movement for change.

Through the dog days of August 1786, anticipation that the Annapolis Convention could come to grips with the frightening economic situation that threatened the states and the fragile Union itself continued to build. Newspapers expressed the hope that the delegates to the convention would be able to solve "this particular crisis of our affairs."

Despite the urgency of the situation, Congress did nothing. That body had become so ineffective, in fact, that often a quorum of state delegations failed to attend its meetings, and thus Congress could conduct no business of substance. Because of the ineffectiveness of Congress, the Annapolis Convention assumed a special importance. Perhaps this meeting of delegates from all thirteen states, free of the restraints imposed on Congress by the inflexible Articles of Confederation, could solve the country's economic problems. If the thirteen states could reach such an agreement, it would be, in the words of James Monroe, "the source of infinite blessing to this country."

But the thirteen-state gathering never happened. Some states failed to respond to the call to Annapolis. Others, including Maryland, refused to participate in a meeting that so directly challenged the authority of Congress under the Articles of Confederation. The lower house of Maryland's General Assembly nominated delegates to the Annapolis Convention, but the Senate balked. In explaining their reasons for refusing to concur in the appointment of delegates to the convention that would be held in their own capital city, the senators expressed the belief that the meeting might "produce other meetings, which may have consequences which cannot be foreseen. Innovations in government, when not absolutely necessary, are dangerous, particularly to republics, generally too fond of novelties, and subject to change."

The Annapolis Convention was supposed to begin on Monday, September 4. When James Madison of Virginia arrived in town on that day, he found only two other delegates present. As the days passed, a few others trickled into town, but on Friday, September 8, Madison had to conclude that "the prospect to make the meeting respectable is not flattering." The delegates who traveled to Annapolis waited a whole week before deciding that the meeting could be delayed no longer.

When the Annapolis Convention finally convened on Monday, September 11, there were just twelve men from five states present. The states represented were New York, New Jersey, Pennsylvania, Delaware, and Virginia. Though their number was small, the men at Annapolis included some of the best-informed individuals in the country, including Alexander Hamilton of New York, Abraham Clark of New Jersey, Tench Coxe of Pennsylvania, James Madison of Virginia, and John Dickinson of Delaware, "the Penman of the Revolution," who was elected chairman of the convention. These men and their fellow delegates settled at Mann's Tavern, the town's most commodious inn, which offered both accommodations and meeting rooms for the convention sessions.

As the delegates to the Annapolis Convention drifted into town during the week before the convention sat, they found that despite the poor turnout there was remarkable agreement among them that the condition of the country was precarious. Trade and commerce had brought them together, but the roots of the problem lay deeper and affected many other areas as well. The real difficulty, the attendees agreed, was the Articles of Confederation itself. Devising a solution to the problem of trade and commerce would require a fundamental change in the existing form of government, but under the Articles such a change would require unanimous consent of the thirteen contrary states.

Hampered by representation from a minority of the states, but convinced of the urgency of addressing the critical condition of the nation, the delegates to the Annapolis Convention seized the initiative. They could not reach a consensus on trade and commerce, because too few states were represented. But the delegates refused to leave Annapolis empty-handed. Instead, they appointed a committee on September 11 and charged it with drafting a report. The committee reported back to the convention two days later, and on September 14 the full convention unanimously approved the report and agreed to send copies of it to Congress and to the governors of all the states.

In this report the delegates to the Annapolis Convention called for another convention of all the states, to be held in Philadelphia in May 1787. This Philadelphia convention should not be limited to discussing a single issue, but instead it should be empowered to discuss everything necessary to "render the Constitution of the federal government adequate to the exigencies of the Union."

The Annapolis Convention did not originate the idea of an interstate convention to revise the Articles of Confederation. Political leaders in several states had been arguing privately that a new convention was necessary, although most doubted that the time was right for such an assembly. The importance of the Annapolis Convention is that it provided a focus for the growing disillusionment and discontent with the government under the Articles, and it proposed a specific course of action.

The Annapolis Convention's call to Philadelphia could have fallen on deaf ears and resulted in nothing. But thoughtful men throughout the country saw the necessity of a new convention. They mobilized the local press and argued their case with other political leaders.

Even these efforts might have been in vain, but the need for a new convention achieved a heightened sense of urgency with developments in New England. Just as the Annapolis Convention's call to Philadelphia began appearing in newspapers around the country, reports began to circulate of penal legislation imposed upon creditors by the debtor-controlled government of Rhode Island and of a frightening uprising of economically beleaguered citizens in Massachusetts. The new nation, and Congress under the Articles of Confederation, faced the test that many had predicted and all feared.

In Massachusetts, farmers exasperated by the economic collapse that threatened their farms and livelihood had taken up arms against the government of their own state. This rag-tag rebellion, named after its reluctant leader, Daniel Shays, began in August 1786. Congress was powerless to do anything about the uprising, so the Massachusetts militia responded to the alarm. In January 1787 Shays and his men mounted an assault on the arsenal at Springfield, hoping to get the arms and ammunition they needed to press their fight on to Boston. They were met by heavily armed troops. A single artillery volley from the militia was all that was needed to cause the insurgent debtors to break and run.

Shays' Rebellion made a powerful impression on everyone. George Washington expressed an opinion undoubtedly shared by many Marylanders when he wrote of the disturbance: "What stronger evidence can be given of the want of energy in our governments than these disorders? If there exists not a power to check them, what security has a man of life, liberty, or property?"

Happening as it did just as the Annapolis Convention was adopting its report calling for a new convention in Philadelphia, Shays' Rebellion gave the call an urgency that it otherwise would have lacked. As a result, the Annapolis Convention's summons for another convention met with little resistance. First Virginia, then other states, took the call to Philadelphia under consideration and appointed delegates. In Maryland none were more concerned about the government's need to protect the "life, liberty, and property" alluded to by George Washington than the members of the conservative Senate. The scruples that in the spring of 1786 had prevented it from allowing Maryland to participate in the Annapolis Convention were conveniently forgotten in its post-Shays deliberations. When the proposition came before it, the Senate "cheerfully" joined with the lower house in agreeing to appoint delegates to Philadelphia.

However, the Maryland General Assembly was so preoccupied with the paper-money controversy in the fall and winter of 1786–87 that it did not turn its attention to the appointment of delegates until April. Before the state's five-member delegation was filled, fully a dozen men had declined nomination, including political leaders like William Paca, Samuel Chase, and Charles Carroll of Carrollton, all signers of the Declaration of Independence.

Why so many Marylanders refused to represent the state in Philadelphia is uncertain, although at least three declined because of ill health. Others may have feared that their political opponents, especially in the paper-money cause, would take advantage of their absence. The heavy demands of the season, particularly for those involved in planting, and Philadelphia's reputation for unhealthiness in summer may also have been factors. Perhaps most important, however, is that no one at the time knew that the Philadelphia Convention would write the Constitution or that the framers would become known as Founding Fathers and be preeminent in the American pantheon of heroes.

Maryland's Delegates to the Constitutional Convention

Despite the difficulty of assembling a delegation, the five men Maryland sent to the Constitutional Convention were able, experienced, and well connected. James McHenry, a native of Ireland who came to Baltimore in 1772, was a physician (although no longer practicing) and merchant who had served during the Revolution as an aide to both General Washington and the Marquis de Lafayette. Daniel of St. Thomas Jenifer, a Charles County planter, had served in both the proprietary government before the war and in the Revolutionary government. Daniel Carroll, a Roman Catholic, was a large landowner from Montgomery County and a distant cousin of signer Charles Carroll of Carrollton, who had also held high office during and after the Revolution. John Francis Mercer, a Virginian by birth and a former member of the Virginia legislature, had moved to Anne Arundel County in 1785 upon his marriage to the wealthy heiress Sophia Sprigg. Luther Martin, a Baltimore resident who had been born in New Jersey, was a brilliant lawyer with a flourishing practice who since 1778 had also served as attorney general of Maryland.

The Philadelphia Convention convened on May 25 and conducted its business in secret through the next four months. Maryland's delegation did not play a major role in the convention, although Luther Martin, from the day he arrived on June 9, was a frequent and outspoken critic of the proceedings. In particular, Martin opposed the Virginia Plan, arguing that allocating representation in Congress according to population would greatly expand the influence of the large states of Massachusetts, Pennsylvania, and Virginia. Martin advocated instead the federalism implicit in the New Jersey Plan, which he helped draft. Martin also objected to the lack of a bill of rights in the proposed Constitution. He was prepared to offer a resolution establishing a committee to draft one for the consideration of the convention, but he was unable to secure a second for his motion.

Martin was not the only Maryland delegate displeased with the way the Constitution was taking shape, and before the convention ended, both he and John Francis Mercer had left Philadelphia in disgust. Nearly everyone agreed that the central government needed more authority and power. Martin himself had called the government under the Articles of Confederation "weak, contemptibly weak." But the proposed Constitution created a strong national government by giving it many of the powers formerly held by the states. In

Daniel of St. Thomas Jenifer (1733–1790) was a wealthy Charles County landowner of English and Swedish descent. The origin of his distinctive middle name is unknown. He held a variety of political, financial, and judicial offices prior to the Revolution and served the patriot cause in Congress from 1778 to 1782. An ardent nationalist, Jenifer was one of the Maryland commissioners at the Mount Vernon Conference. At the Philadelphia Convention he had an excellent record of attendance but was not active in debate. He signed the Constitution with enthusiasm, and when Luther Martin declared that he would be "hanged" if the people of Maryland approved the document, Jenifer humorously advised Martin to remain in Philadelphia lest he hang in his home state. Etching from an original portrait by Albert Rosenthal (1888), courtesy of the Maryland State Archives.

addition to curtailing state sovereignty, the document did not expressly protect some of the rights of individuals that were specifically guaranteed in many of the state constitutions.

The Philadelphia Convention finished its work on September 17. Thirty-nine of the forty-two delegates then attending signed the Constitution, including McHenry, Carroll, and Jenifer for Maryland. The Constitution was forwarded to Congress with the request that it be sent to the states for ratification.

The Constitution in Maryland

To become the new basic law of the United States, the proposed Constitution had to be ratified by nine of the thirteen states. The first five states ratified quickly with little or no opposition. Then, on February 21,

Daniel Carroll (1730–1796), one of the two Roman Catholic signers of the Constitution, was a brother of John Carroll, America's first Catholic bishop, and a cousin of Charles Carroll of Carrollton, who would become the last surviving signer of the Declaration of Independence. As a member of one of Maryland's first families, Daniel was a man of education and great wealth. As a delegate to Congress (1781–1783), he signed the Articles of Confederation. During the struggle for ratification he wrote a judicious and persuasive letter to the Maryland Journal *in refutation of an Antifederalist letter by Samuel Chase. Carroll was chosen a Maryland representative to the First Congress and then became commissioner of the newly created District of Columbia (1791–1795). Etching by Albert Rosenthal from an original portrait (1888), courtesy of the Maryland State Archives.*

1788, the New Hampshire convention adjourned without voting on the Constitution. Two weeks earlier Massachusetts had narrowly ratified as the sixth state, but only after Federalists, who were a minority in the convention, agreed to support a list of nine proposed amendments. In March, Rhode Islanders by popular referendum overwhelmingly rejected the handiwork of the Philadelphia Convention.

All eyes then turned to Maryland, which would be the critical seventh state. If Maryland refused to ratify, or conditioned its ratification with amendments, many believed the momentum needed to approve the Constitution

Luther Martin (ca. 1748–1826) was born in obscure surroundings to a New Jersey farm family (even his year of birth is uncertain) but rose to eminence as a lawyer. He became the first attorney general of the state of Maryland, a post he held for nearly thirty years (1778–1805, 1818–1820), as well as a member of Congress (1784–1785), a delegate to the Philadelphia Convention, and, with his longtime colleague Samuel Chase, a leader of Antifederalism in Maryland. Before the convention was over, the turbulent Martin walked out with John Francis Mercer and returned home to fight ratification. His "Genuine Information" about the Constitutional Convention was published in twelve installments in the Baltimore Maryland Gazette *and as a pamphlet. In the 1790s Martin became an archfoe of Jefferson and served as counsel for Samuel Chase at his removal trial and for Aaron Burr in his trial for treason. Both of his controversial clients prevailed. In later life alcoholism, extravagance, and illness left Martin destitute, prompting the Maryland legislature to pass a resolution requiring every lawyer in Maryland to pay an annual license fee of five dollars, to be placed in trust for Martin's support. Etching by Albert Rosenthal from an original portrait, courtesy of the Maryland State Archives.*

would be lost forever and the country would continue in a perilous state of uncertainty and confusion.

The outcome in Maryland should never have been in doubt. The genius of the Constitution is that the long months of debate and compromise in the Philadelphia Convention had resulted in a document that pleased no one entirely, but that did offer something important to virtually every individual and constituency. Large states got proportional representation in the House of Representatives; small states got an equal voice in the Senate. Merchants were promised tariff protection and a national currency; slave owners got an assurance that Congress would not immediately interfere with the slave trade and that runaway slaves would be returned. The new government promised to be strong enough to quell internal disturbances and defend against foes from abroad, while encouraging the trade, commerce, and industry that would ensure prosperity for every section of the country.

Most Marylanders who read the proposed Constitution liked what they saw. When elections for delegates to the state's ratification convention were held in early April 1788, the results showed that Federalists outnumbered Antifederalists by a margin of 64 to 12. Still, Federalists worried about the outcome. As late as the night before the convention assembled, James McHenry wrote George Washington that he feared Antifederalists would be able to force a postponement of Maryland's vote or encumber the state's ratification with binding amendments.

One reason Federalists were concerned about Maryland's convention was that the proposed Constitution had failed to generate much popular support in the state. Apathy, not strong feelings on one side or the other, characterized much of the state's electorate. Voter turnout in Maryland was usually low because of a long tradition of deferring to the local gentry for virtually all elective offices. But in the elections for delegates to the convention, less than a quarter of the electorate appears to have voted. In fully three-quarters of the state's twenty political subdivisions, there was no recorded opposition to the delegates who were chosen.

Furthermore, a fact of special concern to proponents of the proposed Constitution was that Maryland politics had long been characterized by shifting coalitions and temporary alliances rather than by identifiable parties or dependable factions. In the absence of explicit instructions from their constituents, even members of the popularly elected lower house had always felt free in legislative assemblies to be convinced by argument and to vote their conscience on any issue. Although avowed opponents of the Constitution numbered only a handful among the delegates elected to the convention, that small group included two masterful political strategists and experienced debaters whose opposition to anything could not be taken lightly. They were former governor William Paca and the eloquent Samuel Chase, labeled "the Demosthenes of Maryland," and they opposed the Constitution on principle.

The energetic duo of Paca and Chase must surely rank as one of the oddest, but most politically effective, twosomes in Maryland history. Paca was refined, wealthy, socially secure, and cerebral; Chase was more than a little rough around the edges, always in or near bankruptcy, the fiery patriot equally skilled at arousing passions in legislative assemblies or in the streets. Paca and Chase had worked together on every major political cause from the Stamp Act repeal in the mid-1760s to the Declaration of Independence to the fight for debtor relief in the mid-1780s. Now they would be together again, fighting against odds as tough as any they had faced before. Their goal was not simply to defeat the Constitution but rather to establish the principle that certain fundamental rights must have written guarantees in any form of government.

William Paca's principal objection to the proposed Constitution was its lack of a bill of rights that would protect individual liberties and assure a role for the states in the new national government. The Constitution offered much that Paca wanted badly. Having served as governor from 1782 to 1785, he was acutely conscious of the need for a strong central government that could restore order to the economy and provide for the common defense. But Paca also knew that American freedom had been won at a very high cost, and he had experienced government tyranny firsthand. Others were willing to overlook the absence of a bill of rights in the Constitution or to accept the Federalist assurances that a bill of rights was unnecessary. Paca insisted that the only way to guarantee rights to the citizens and the states was to write them down and incorporate them in the Constitution itself. Paca was determined to fight for amendments on the floor of Maryland's convention, and he knew he could count on support from his old friend and ally Samuel Chase.

With only twelve Antifederalists in the convention of seventy-six members (two elected members did not attend), Paca and Chase could not hope to mount a direct assault on the Constitution when the Maryland convention convened on April 21, 1788. The Federalist leadership was intent upon ratifying the Constitution quickly and without qualification, and they had the votes to control the discussion on the floor. The domineering Federalists agreed not even to discuss amendment of the Constitution in full convention or to respond to criticisms raised by its opponents. They also voted to consider the Constitution only in its entirety, precluding a section-by-section analysis and debate. By agreeing to remain silent on the floor of the convention, Federalists effectively blunted their opponents' most effective weapon: the ability of Paca and Chase to present a compelling case when permitted to engage in a free-wheeling debate.

Too greatly outnumbered to have any effect on the preliminaries of the convention, Paca and Chase delayed attending until Thursday, April 24, after the second reading of the Constitution. Chase arrived first, accompanied by Luther Martin, whose sore throat prevented him from adding his arguments to the one-sided debate. After speaking for more than two hours, Chase resumed his seat and the convention broke for dinner. When the gathering resumed, William Paca announced his arrival and stated that he

William Paca (1740–1799) was a lawyer by profession. He had been a leader in the movement toward independence and spent several thousand dollars of his own funds to outfit troops. In 1778 he was appointed chief judge of the Maryland General Court, and beginning in 1782 the legislature elected him governor of Maryland for three successive one-year terms. As a delegate to the ratifying convention, Paca offered twenty-two amendments to the Constitution (page one of his draft is shown here), but when the convention decided to accept or reject the proposed document without alteration, Paca voted for adoption. His acquiescence earned the eminently qualified Paca Washington's appointment as Maryland's first federal district court judge. Portrait by John Beale Bordley, courtesy of the Maryland Commission on Artistic Property, Maryland State Archives; Paca's manuscript amendments, courtesy of the Maryland State Archives.

intended to offer amendments to the proposed Constitution. He asked permission to submit his additions the next morning, and the convention obliged by adjourning for the day.

When Paca attempted to introduce the twenty-two amendments he had prepared, one member from each Federalist county rose to successfully challenge his right even to speak. With Paca's offensive blunted, Antifederalists spent the rest of the day vainly attempting to engage Federalists in debate by raising a variety of objections to the Constitution. By the sixth day of the convention, Saturday, April 26, the Constitution was just one step away from being ratified, and Paca had not been able to say a word about his amendments.

Pragmatic as well as principled, Paca struck a deal with the Federalist leadership. He would vote for the proposed Constitution if he would be allowed to present his amendments to a special committee after the vote for unconditional ratification was held. Federalists agreed, and the vote was taken. Maryland ratified the Constitution unconditionally by a margin of 63 to 11. Paca was the lone defector from the Antifederalist ranks, but his maneuver brought Antifederalists a chance to convince their opponents that the Constitution was seriously flawed.

The amendments Paca proposed to the special committee have a startlingly modern ring. They sought to guarantee the right to petition the legislature for redress of grievances; to ensure the right to a trial by a jury; to limit the use of search warrants; to prohibit establishment of a national religion; to guarantee freedom of speech and the press; and to secure to the states all powers not expressly delegated to the federal government by the Constitution. These rights are guaranteed to every American in the first ten amendments to the Constitution—the Bill of Rights—and they are today held as sacred as the Constitution itself. And yet the Constitution that was proposed to the states, and that Maryland ratified overwhelmingly, left each of these fundamental rights and privileges unprotected.

When Paca finally got a chance to present his proposed amendments to the special committee, he was faced with a membership composed of nine Federalists and just four Antifederalists. Nevertheless, over the course of two days Paca and Chase, using their well-honed combination of reason and rhetoric, secured committee approval of thirteen amendments. Fearing the results if these amendments were introduced to the convention, the Federalist majority on the special committee suddenly rescinded its support, and Paca was refused permission to debate the amendments on the convention floor

But Paca had made his point. He had demonstrated that there were serious, potentially fatal flaws in the proposed Constitution. He and Chase, when given the chance to debate the issues, had convinced a Federalist majority on the special committee that at least some of the Antifederalists' concerns were justified. But the overbearing Federalist majority in the Maryland convention was too large for Paca and his allies to extract any sort of victory, despite the validity of the principles involved.

Maryland took pride in its decisive vote as the seventh state to ratify the Constitution. Its unconditional ratification on April 28, 1788, restored momentum to the ratification drive. But Maryland's small band of Antifederalists made an important contribution too: despite overwhelming odds, they focused attention on the need for amendments and kept the movement for a bill of rights alive until it could reach other states where Antifederalists were more numerous. As a result, when the first Congress assembled in 1789, it proposed a list of amendments to the Constitution for the consideration of the states.

On December 19, 1789, Maryland became the second state to ratify these proposed amendments, the Bill of Rights. These additions perfected the U.S. Constitution in ways some Federalists never thought necessary. But to Maryland's Antifederalists, a written guarantee preserving fundamental liberties to individuals and to the states was not simply a matter of form; it was an essential, unchallengeable matter of principle.

From the perspective of two hundred years, it is clear that Marylanders played a vital role in the seminal events of the 1780s that shaped our constitutional form of government and cemented the thirteen states into a viable union. But to say that Maryland's political leaders recognized fully the impact of their actions, that they perceived themselves as active participants in the creation of a political system that would not only endure but enable the nation to grow and prosper as had no country before it, is tempting but far from the mark.

Given a choice, Maryland's political leaders undoubtedly would have preferred simply to be left alone to govern at home as they saw fit. But circumstances and change made isolationism both dangerous and impractical. Independence from Britain ensured that the new states could govern at home without outside interference, but removal from the orderly British commercial system meant that politics could no longer be confined to parochial matters. What one's neighboring states did now mattered as never before, and it mattered in ways that directly affected the security and pocketbooks of everyone.

Necessity, not lofty political ideals, convinced Maryland to join in the War for Independence against Britain. Necessity, not neighborly benevolence, led Maryland to join with Virginia in drafting the Mount Vernon Compact of 1785. Necessity, not informed conviction, prompted Maryland to dispatch delegates to the Philadelphia Convention of 1787. And necessity, not enlightened judgment, persuaded most Marylanders to support the Constitution, even though its implementation could jeopardize not only the state's cherished sovereignty but the fundamental rights of its citizens as well.

The Maryland experience suggests that the 1780s was a period characterized by increasingly desperate men in desperate times. Other people in other places have reacted to such situations in different ways, from civil war to sniveling fatalism. Rarely have a people turned to a representative assembly and charged it with the responsibility of working together for the good of the whole. Reasoned debate and compromise are not the usual products of crises. The Maryland experience also suggests that the too frequent portrayal of the Founding Fathers as being providentially assembled and divinely inspired misses the point. Instead, it was desperation and a shared conviction of impending calamity which produced the accommodation and compromise that enabled the United States Constitution to emerge as the remarkable document that it is.

Maryland: Essay on Sources

The best source for the background of Constitution-era Maryland is Aubrey C. Land, *Colonial Maryland: A History* (Millwood, N.Y., 1981), although Charles Albro Barker, *The Background of the Revolution in Maryland* (Hamden, Conn., 1940, 1967) remains a classic for the late colonial period. The best textbook treatment of Maryland history is Susanne Ellery Greene Chappelle, ed., *Maryland: A History of Its People* (Baltimore, 1986).

Maryland's role in the creation and adoption of the U.S. Constitution was first detailed in Philip A. Crowl's seminal work *Maryland during and after the Revolution: A Political and Economic Study* (Baltimore, 1943). Also significant is Crowl's "Anti-Federalism in Maryland," *The William and Mary Quarterly*, 3rd series, 4 (October 1947), 446–469. Norman K. Risjord's *Chesapeake Politics, 1781–1800* (New York, 1978) offers some useful insights, but the author's characterization of many Maryland events and individuals fails to ring true. Although it has been largely superseded by more recent works, Bernard C. Steiner's "Maryland's Adoption of the Federal Constitution," *American Historical Review*, 5 (October 1899, January 1900), 22–44, 207–224, is still worth reading. A provocative recent study that concentrates on that hotbed of Federalism, Baltimore Town, is Charles G. Steffen, *The Mechanics of Baltimore: Workers and Politics in the Age of Revolution, 1763–1812* (Urbana and Chicago, 1984). Especially helpful in terms of understanding the political climate in the state on the eve of Maryland's ratification convention is Melvin Yazawa, ed., *Representative Government and the Revolution: The Maryland Constitutional Crisis of 1787* (Baltimore, 1975).

Several publications issued by the state archives as part of Maryland's celebration of the U.S. Constitution's bicentennial provide new information on Maryland's role in the formation of the Union, particularly Edward C. Papenfuse, *Maryland and the U.S. Constitution: Five Delegates to Philadelphia* (Annapolis, 1987); the *Maryland Bicentennial Gazette* (Annapolis, 1986); the *Annapolis Convention Fact Pack* (Annapolis, 1986); and Shirley V. Baltz, *A Closer Look at the Annapolis Convention* (Annapolis, 1986).

Biographical data on virtually every Marylander involved in politics during the 1780s can be found in Edward C. Papenfuse et al., *A Biographical Dictionary of the Maryland Legislature, 1635–1789*, 2 vols. (Baltimore, 1979–85). Biographical information on persons elected to the Maryland ratification convention who are not included in the two-volume *Biographical Dictionary* has been compiled by the Legislative History Project team and is on file at the state archives in Annapolis. Other helpful biographical sources are James Haw et al., *Stormy Patriot: The Life of Samuel Chase* (Baltimore, 1980); Paul S. Clarkson and R. Samuel Jett, *Luther Martin of Maryland* (Baltimore, 1970); and Bernard C. Steiner, *The Life and Correspondence of James McHenry* (Cleveland, 1907). Less helpful, but still worth consulting because of the importance of their subjects in Maryland's constitution-making efforts, are Gregory A. Stiverson and Phebe R. Jacobsen, *William Paca: A Biography* (Baltimore, 1976) and Sr. Mary Virginia Geiger, *Daniel Carroll, A Framer of the Constitution* (Washington, D.C., 1943).

South Carolina

A Conservative Revolution

JEROME J. NADELHAFT
Professor of History
University of Maine-Orono

I AM NOW BY THE WILL OF GOD brought into a new world, and God only knows what sort of a world it will be," a committed South Carolina rebel, Henry Laurens, wrote to his son in 1776. "What may be your opinion of this change I know not." John Laurens, studying law in England on the wealth his father had amassed as slave trader, merchant, and plantation owner, was unequivocal: If his country submitted to British oppression, he would forget he was an American; if it was steadfast and triumphant, he would "glory in the name which will thenceforth raise the associate Ideas of brave and free." Father and son, however, foresaw serious problems. The older Laurens worried about the effects of warfare: "horrible butcheries" resulting from British-encouraged Indian attacks and slave insurrections, and "fraud, perjury & assasination" resulting from splits within the white community. But both Laurenses had political fears. In 1776 the elder Laurens denounced the idea that "no Man is now supposed to be unequal to a share in Government," while John Laurens raced home from England to fight despite concern that the conflict was overturning established rules of political behavior. He "most heartily lament[ed]" that some people who were "illy calculated to move in the most limited ministerial spheres [were] unfortunately suffered to have a voice in matters of the greatest Intricacy and Importance." But the political disruption that the Laurenses and other aristocrats feared, many Carolinians saw as opportunity. The tensions and struggles among various groups, reflected in three constitutions adopted between 1776 and 1790, complicated by years of war and postwar economic difficulties, revolved around the meaning of independence. Was it more than freedom from England? Was it, in fact, opportunity for political change, even for social revolution?

Colonial Background

South Carolina (or Carolina, as it was initially called) was first settled in 1670 at Charles Town under the auspices of a group of aristocratic adventurers, foremost of whom was Anthony Ashley Cooper. King Charles II had granted these speculators and court favorites all the lands south of Virginia and north of Spanish Florida by charter in 1663.

When its initial site proved unhealthful, Charles Town was moved a few miles up the peninsula in 1680 to its present location, where it immediately prospered by developing close commercial ties with the British West Indies. The colony's promoters (called the lords proprietors) sought to transplant the feudal system of landholding to America under the provisions of a document drafted in 1669 by Cooper or his secretary, John Locke. This formulation, called the Fundamental Constitutions of Carolina, also attempted to establish an hereditary aristocracy. The early legal history of Carolina was turbulent because of the proprietors' demand that their colonists adopt this basic law. Such insistence, coupled with the government's unpopular trade and land policies, caused political dissent, occasionally accompanied by violence. The explosion came in 1719, after many specific grievances had built up an intense hostility toward the proprietors and their successors, when the militia mobilized against the proprietary government itself.

Rather than suppress the revolt, the English government welcomed it, bought out the rights of the remaining proprietors, and made South Carolina a royal colony in 1720. The designation "South" resulted from the fact that the wild northern part of the Carolina grant, settled mostly by outcasts and dissenters from Virginia, had already broken away from proprietary rule in 1712 and gained the status of a separate colony.

The events of 1719–20 only replaced a group of hereditary aristocrats with wealthy, planter aristocrats of the home-grown variety. Until the Revolution, South Carolina's colonial government was run by a small, close-knit political oligarchy entrenched in the lower house of the legislature. In the 1760s the forty-eight man Commons (or lower) House represented only a small area of the colony, the lowcountry, which consisted of the sea islands, the neighboring coast, and the lower pine belt, making a strip of land roughly sixty miles wide. After 1769 the area was divided into three circuit court districts: Georgetown, extending from the North Carolina border to the Santee River; Charleston, the land between the Santee and Combahee rivers; and Beaufort, the land between the Combahee and Savannah rivers, which separated the colony from Georgia. In time the lowcountry came to be dominated by plantations, a slave labor force, and the staple crops of rice and indigo. Representatives of these areas, like many of their constituents, were rich.

Members of the Commons, who were barred from the Council, or upper house, by a British policy of appointing English placemen, acquired prestige while serving the colony and protecting their own interests. Convinced of their own abilities and cherishing the independence wealth allowed them, they had not divided into permanent factions as in some other American colonies. Rather, they were intimately acquainted, related, and intermarried. Between 1762 and 1768 seventy-five people sat in the Commons, at least forty-seven of whom were related to others by marriage or blood (first cousins or closer).

The closeness was partly based on the need for protection from a self-imposed danger. Lowcountry settlers were surrounded by black slaves whose behavior was thought to be unpredictable, whose nature, according to whites, was "barbarous, wild, [and] savage." Because of the danger, Henry Laurens thought factional divisions within the colony "more awful and more distressing than Fire, Pestilence or Foreign Wars." In times of stress or crisis, anxiety grew, and in the 1760s and 1770s fear of insurrection was great.

The Division between East and West

But despite the unanimity among Carolina leaders in their dealings with slaves, and their near unanimity on what Henry Laurens called "the grand essential points"—remaining free from English tyranny being paramount—there were serious divisions among Carolinians. In simple but inadequate terms, the most dangerous split was between east and west, lowcountry and backcountry; in reality, sometimes the lowcountry parishes or counties in the immediate vicinity of Charleston stood against the rest of the colony. Nor was the city of Charleston free of dissension.

Beginning in 1730, settlement of the interior was encouraged to provide the lowcountry with greater protection from slaves, Indians, and the agents of competing European governments. Townships stretching across the frontier were established by Germans, Swiss, Dutch, Irish, Scots, Scots-Irish, Welsh, and English. While most lowcountry settlers were Anglican, the inland settlers belonged to the Presbyterian, Lutheran, Baptist, French Huguenot, and Quaker churches. New settlement came in the 1760s, after the Cherokee War, swelling the population of the interior from about 20,000 in 1759 to over 50,000 in 1775. Almost all settled small farms where, without the aid of substantial numbers of blacks, they produced corn and wheat and, in some areas, tobacco and indigo.

In the late 1760s settlers in the backcountry and northeastern part of the lowcountry, responding to problems caused by rapid growth, ruinous Indian raids, disease, and an almost unbelievable influx of criminals, denounced their lowcountry rulers and took the law into their own hands to punish those terrorizing them. Calling themselves Regulators, the defiant settlers aired old complaints, some perhaps trivial to the unaffected but, taken together, testifying to the daily burdens that could wear people down. Their spokesman, the Reverend Charles Woodmason, summed up most of the grievances: "Is it not Slavery to be without wise Magistrates—Without Religion—Without Laws—Without Police—Without Churches—Without

Henry Laurens (1724–1792) was one of the old guard in South Carolina. He had been a leading Charleston merchant since 1763. Except for one year, he served in the colonial assembly from 1757 until the Revolution. He represented South Carolina in Congress (1777–1779), serving as president from November 1777 until December of the following year. He was appointed to negotiate a loan with Holland but was captured by the British in 1780 and imprisoned in the Tower of London for over a year. He was named a peace commissioner in Paris, but he arrived two days after the signing of the preliminary treaty. Laurens stayed in Europe until 1784. He was elected to the Philadelphia Convention but did not attend. Portrait attributed to John Singleton Copley, from Art in the United States Capitol *(Washington, D.C., 1976).*

Clergy . . . ? And is it not Slavery," he asked, "for to have no Roads, Ferries, or Bridges . . . ?" Fundamental was the lack of backcountry representation in the legislature, there being no one, Lieutenant Governor William Bull thought, to "state their Grievances and . . . point out and urge effectually the proper Remedies." Before 1765 the unresponsive legislature had laid out only one backcountry parish, St. Mark.

The attitude of the legislators shifted somewhat in the 1770s. Low-country visitors to the backcountry, impressed by its beauty and potential, began to buy large quantities of land. And for the lowcountry, the difficulties with England and the threat of slave rebellions made accommodation desirable.

If the need to win over the backcountry made change likely, so too did divisions within the lowcountry. One division was visible when the extralegal Provincial Congress met in Charleston in January 1775. A bitter debate took place over a plan adopted by the Continental Congress to allow the exportation of rice but no other agricultural product. The opposition focused on that partiality and disclosed an agricultural division within the lowcountry which is often overlooked.

Too often the lowcountry has been described as a monolithic region of plantations producing both rice and indigo. But the most important indigo lands were separate and distinct. Indigo was grown in the backcountry, in Orangeburg, Camden, and Cheraw districts. It was grown, too, in the sea islands off the southern coast, and in Georgetown District.

Like the backcountry, Georgetown had been settled late, without large numbers until the 1740s and 1750s, and many settlers were non-English. Again like the backcountry, both Georgetown and Beaufort districts were hopelessly underrepresented and politically deprived. In 1771, the predominantly rice-growing Charleston District, with its thirteen parishes, elected thirty-six of the forty-eight members of the lower house. With roughly the same area, and at least half the white population of Charleston District (the city included), Georgetown elected only four; the smaller Beaufort District, with perhaps half Georgetown's white population elected five. Few politically important people came from areas outside Charleston District. Some people in Georgetown District were as troubled by the lack of courts and sufficient local officials as the backcountry settlers. They too became Regulators.

The other lowcountry division involved the city of Charleston, where artisans and mechanics, without voice in the running of the unincorporated city, which was governed by the legislature, seized the opportunity to assume a public importance. The changing times were indicated by their success in pushing through a nonimportation plan, with planter support but in the face of merchant opposition, in 1769. They highlighted that success, and the very legitimacy of their participation, by joining with others to create a committee of enforcement that included equal numbers of planters, merchants, and mechanics. But by 1774 everyone, "the Gentleman & Mechanic, those of high and low life, the learned & illiterate," was discussing politics and "American affairs" and influencing policy. A new political system which included westerners and city workers had begun to take form.

In July 1774, not yet four months after England closed the port of Boston, 104 inhabitants, drawn to Charleston by letters sent to every parish and section of South Carolina, met until midnight on three consecutive days to consider American rights and the election of delegates to the First Continental Congress in Philadelphia. Then they set up a General Committee to run the colony. The meetings, said Peter Timothy, editor of the *South Carolina Gazette*, were "such an example of pure democracy as has rarely been seen since the days of the ancient city republics."

In November 1774, after the return of delegates from Philadelphia, the General Committee called for the election of a Provincial Congress to better represent the entire colony. Fifty-eight of the 184 seats were set aside for backcountry spokesmen; and when elections were held, thirteen men closely identified with Charleston's artisans and mechanics were chosen in addition to the new westerners. The new groups were active, brought to a state of political awareness either by England and the actions of Carolina's rulers or through instinctive response when presented with their first real opportunities.

A New State Constitution

In March 1776 South Carolina's Provincial Congress adopted a temporary plan for governing the colony until the "unhappy differences" between England and America should be settled. The constitution confirmed many familiar arrangements and introduced some change. Two years later the state adopted another constitution, which, while reaffirming some old practices, was revolutionary. Given the starting point, the total domination of colonial affairs by a few people and a small area around Charleston, the internal revolution confirmed by the constitution was dramatic.

Eight states wrote constitutions in 1776, two more in 1777. Almost everywhere there was intellectual excitement, lengthy debate, a clash of ideologies as people tried to make what they could out of the Revolution. For some the mood was exultant, for the Revolution was an opportunity to start over, "boldly to chalk out a new plan," to "exclude kings ... [and] tyranny," to enter "a new era in politics." But in South Carolina the dominant moods among the constitution writers were reluctance and satisfaction. The reluctance was evident in the attempts to delay the formation of a regular government—the Provincial Congress had to order many to attend—while the satisfaction was apparent in the terms of the government formed.

The constitution of March 26, 1776, based on a report of a committee totally dominated by representatives of Charleston District, gave South Carolina a government more democratic in form, yet more suited to the native aristocracy, than that enjoyed or endured through the British connection. The most noticeable and important change from the colonial period was the creation of a large Assembly of 202. Charleston District, retaining its 96 representatives from the Congress, continued to dominate, but it was no longer able to govern without due regard for other areas. The lowcountry parishes far from Charleston still had only 30 representatives, but the backcountry's representation was increased from 58 to 76, partly through the creation of new districts. While representation was still not adequately apportioned according to population, the colonial imbalance had been considerably corrected.

Fearing executive power, people of other states stripped their new governors "of most of those badges of domination, called prerogative," and turned them into figureheads, weak officers surrounded by suspicious people. Six of the nine states besides South Carolina writing constitutions in 1776 and 1777 provided for the annual election of governors; seven limited the number of successive years they could serve. All denied governors the power to veto legislation.

In South Carolina the governor, now called the president, remained a real part of the political process. Elected by the legislature for a two-year term, he, like the vice president and privy councilors, was perpetually re-eligible. A fixed salary, denied royal governors and other American revolutionary executives, gave him additional freedom of action. Most importantly, South Carolina's president could veto legislation.

The General Assembly was elected for a two-year term. Almost all states created upper houses to utilize the wisdom of "men of worth" whose lack of "popular qualities" might prevent them from winning elections. Chosen usually by the people, senators served longer terms than representatives. And since balance in government would be achieved through the clash of interests, the senates were either composed of men possessed of more property than those in the lower houses or elected by owners of larger amounts of property. Any other arrangement, it was felt, would be to form "only two Houses of Assemblymen" and thus to miss the benefits of mixed government. But South Carolina's Legislative Council was elected by the General Assembly "out of their own body" for the same two-year term. New elections filled the seats vacated in the Assembly by the election of thirteen councilors.

As in the colonial period, white adult males owning a "settled" plantation and ten slaves or property valued at £1,000 currency were eligible for election. Non-Protestants could qualify as freemen according to the provisions of the first state constitution.

Constitution writers in South Carolina had seen no need for drastic experimentation. For the hitherto powerless settlers outside the Charleston area, the constitution did little but grant fixed representation. No provision was made for reapportionment; nothing promised to redress complaints about the inadequacies of the legal system. And because the Anglican Church of the lowcountry leaders remained the established church, the thousands of dissenters who formed the vast majority of the state's white population were liable to be taxed for its support.

Another New State Constitution

Criticism of the constitution quickly surfaced. Although no final action was taken, proposed amendments attacked the president's power and the "capitol and adjacent Parishes," whose political advantage, one legislator feared, would "in time" cause the government to "degenerate into an oligarchy." The danger of the oligarchy came largely from the upper house, chosen in a manner that let the old habit of deference operate to its fullest and gave inordinate power to a small area, as the first election demonstrated. Because several men resigned to fill other positions or declined to serve, seventeen men had to be chosen by and from the members of the lower house before the thirteen-man Council could be completed. Eleven were from parishes in or close to Charleston, four from the backcountry, and only two from the coastal parishes near Georgia; none came from the parishes north of the Santee River in Georgetown District.

The dissatisfaction soon led to a new constitution, which was almost certainly the work of overlapping groups of dissenters, backcountry settlers, distant lowcountry planters, Charleston radicals, and opponents of the Rutledge family, which had emerged from independence as the dominant political clan. John Rutledge had been elected the state's first president; his brother Hugh was president of the Legislative Council and a member of the Privy Council, while his other brother Edward was a representative of Charleston.

The changes in the nature of government and the relations between church and state introduced by the new plan of 1778 were numerous and important. The Anglican Church was disestablished, although the "Christian Protestant Religion" became the established religion. Only Protestants now could be elected to office, and ministers were declared ineligible. Jews and other non-Protestants, however, could still vote; all free white men resident one year in the state and meeting the old property requirements—ownership of fifty acres or a town lot or payment of a tax equal to that on fifty acres—

could vote if they acknowledged "the Being of a God, and . . . a future State of Rewards and Punishments."

In its effort to effectively protect freedom and liberty, the new plan of government resembled the plans of other states. The governor was still elected by the legislature, but he was denied a veto and a fixed salary. And no man could be reelected for four years after the expiration of his two-year term. Furthermore, neither the "Father, Son, or Brother to the Governor" was eligible for the Privy Council.

Recognizing that government officials might be guilty of "mal and corrupt Conduct," Carolinians, like the people of six other states before them, gave their legislature the power of impeachment. And further to reduce corruption, remove temptation, and remove even the suspicion of wrong-doing, the constitution limited plural officeholding.

John Rutledge (1739–1800), brother of Edward Rutledge, who signed the Declaration of Independence, was probably the richest lawyer in South Carolina. He served regularly in the colonial assembly until the Revolution, when he was elected governor. Under the new state constitution of 1776 he was elected president, but he resigned after vetoing the constitution of 1778. He was again elected governor in January 1779 and served his maximum two-year term. He served in Congress in 1782 and 1783 and in the state Assembly from 1784 to 1790. In the Constitutional Convention he was chairman of the Committee of Detail. He was appointed to the first U.S. Supreme Court but resigned in 1791 after his election as chief justice of South Carolina. Appointed by President Washington as chief justice of the United States in 1795, Rutledge presided over the court for one term before the Senate rejected his nomination because of his vehement opposition to the Jay Treaty and his intermittent periods of insanity. Portrait by James Peale, courtesy of the J. B. Speed Art Museum, Lousiville, Kentucky.

The new constitution made the government more representative of people throughout the state and set forth a few inviolable rights. The Legislative Council was abolished, and in its place a Senate was established, chosen not by the lower house but by the people voting by parish or district. Higher property qualifications were set for senators than for representatives. Although apportionment in the lower house remained the same, the new composition of the upper house seriously lessened the power of Charleston and the neighboring parishes, which could now elect thirteen senators, while Beaufort and Georgetown were to elect five and the backcountry eleven. Seven years after the new constitution was written, and every fourteen years after that, representation in the lower house was to be reapportioned on the basis of the number of white inhabitants and the amount of taxable property. Correcting one of the oversights of the first constitution, the legislators provided for future amendments with the approval of a majority of the members of the Senate and House of Representatives.

On March 5, 1778 Governor John Rutledge vetoed the new constitution, reasoning that he had taken an oath to govern the state according to the constitution of 1776. One of his objections, perhaps the most important one, reemphasized the conflicts over the extent of change: the new plan was too democratic. "The people preferred," Rutledge said, "a compounded or mixed government to a simple democracy, or one verging toward it," because the effects of democratic power "have been found arbitrary, severe, and destructive." He specifically repudiated the new upper house, because it was less likely to have "persons of the greatest integrity, learning and abilities." And he objected to the loss of an executive veto.

After preventing passage of the constitution, Rutledge resigned (his term expired in a month), and Rawlins Lowndes inherited the position and the new plan of government.

Postwar South Carolina

Repeated battles among South Carolinians regarding the nature of their government occurred in the postwar years. Attacks on bad government, tyranny, the aristocracy, and the constitution continued. The new political atmosphere, along with an economic depression and the continuing hostility towards Great Britain, helped to produce a federal constitution and still another state constitution.

Arthur Bryan, a Charleston merchant, sensed the political change. "The great people had an entire sway" before 1784, he wrote, but then "a violent opposition" in the city almost "totally ruin[ed] the Aristocracy, for if they now carry any thing in the assembly it is by deception."

Edward Rutledge lamented that the "worthless" and "foolish" elements of society, who had become important "whilst the enemy were in the country," had not fallen "back in the ranks" where they belonged.

Conflicts erupted first in 1782 over Governor John Mathews' agreement, later confirmed and extended by the legislature, to allow British merchants to remain in Charleston after British troops left. Some native merchants, led by William Logan, Alexander Gillon, and the newly formed Marine Anti-Britannic Society, protested that the British competition would hinder their own ability to recover from the war. The protests became more vocal when the legislature modified the 1782 acts confiscating the property of loyalists (also called Tories).

After the legislature's adjournment in March 1783, the more vehement opponents of the British merchants and reinstated Tories began to use the newspapers and streets of Charleston to mobilize their allies. The intense propaganda was probably designed to bring about a political and economic alliance between backcountry residents—and some from the lowcountry—and the mercantile followers of Gillon and Logan. "The old inhabitants of the town are becoming very uneasy respecting the admission" of British merchants, wrote one Charlestonian. "Riots," he added, had already occurred.

The disorders were taken seriously. "A spirit has gone forth among the lower class of people to drive away certain persons whom they are pleased to call Tories," wrote David Ramsay, unhappily predicting at the same time that "the licentiousness of the people" would not disappear for half a century. In response, a small number of legislators, representing the area with most at stake, met in the summer of 1783 and acted quickly to quiet Charleston, not by considering complaints or redressing grievances, but by incorporating the city, thereby creating the machinery to suppress demonstrators. Opposition continued. When the legislature again modified the confiscation acts in 1784, it touched off new disturbances.

But Gillon and his supporters never were able to control the city or dominate elections to the legislature. Their goals and arguments certainly guaranteed them the opposition of the wealthy. Their rhetoric played down their own middle-class background and divided the opposing forces into rich and poor, undoubtedly antagonizing those who expected to rise into the upper class and those who feared the lower orders more than they worried about British merchants or aristocratic tendencies.

The Emergence of the Backcountry

By the mid-1780s politics in the interior regions of the state, quiet for a few years after the war, was awakening. Perhaps only twice, in 1783 and 1784, did the area exert much influence, the first time when the legislature passed a confiscation act affecting backcountry landownings, and the second time when it altered the system of taxation. Before the war backcountry settlers had been angered by the uniform property tax, proposing instead a graduated land tax placing heavier burdens on more valuable rice and indigo lands. The change came in 1784, when the usually quiet representatives from "the remoter and poorer districts" obstinately opposed an attempt to raise the land tax "equally over the entire state." The act of 1784 placed a tax of one percent on the value of all land. In the Charleston area, land was valued from six pounds an acre down to five shillings an acre. Backcountry land was valued as low as one shilling an acre. The law also doubled the tax on slaves. The tax may have had a political side as well. Since the constitution dictated reapportionment in 1785 according to the size of the white population and the amount of taxable property, increased taxes may have been the price planters agreed to pay to justify their political dominance.

Before 1785, however, the backcountry was unable to pull itself together to demand more. Many people there, as well as in Georgetown and Beaufort, seemed unable to rise above their immediate pressing circumstances. The vicious warfare had left interior regions physically desolated; many inhabitants were demoralized and incapable of considering broad or long-range issues. The burning of houses, the plundering, the often wanton destruction of the war, "so reduced" some people, wrote a backcountry legislator and tax collector, that they could not "procure even the necessarys of life." Observers also pointed to problems caused by criminals who "peeled, pillaged, and plundered" the people. Judge Aedanus Burke was horrified to discover in November 1784 that people were "worried & half ruined by . . . an outlying Banditti that constantly beset the roads, rob the inhabitants & plunder their dwellings."

But as conditions improved, residents became more demanding. In 1785 the people around the Little River in Ninety Six District demonstrated a new attitude when, in one petition, they suggested revising the constitution for the people's welfare, moving the seat of the government inland for the backcountry's convenience, reapportioning the legislature (since property was "larger represented than the free white inhabitants"), recording important votes in the legislature, establishing counties, reducing the fees and salaries of officers on the civil list, and granting rewards for the heads of outlaws ravaging the frontier. As settlers began to speak out, so also did their representatives. Perhaps the swelling population gave them confidence.

Simultaneous with suggestions and demands for increasing the government's dependence on the people by moving the capital, recording votes, and, as some Charlestonians were arguing, electing only those who would bind themselves to follow instructions, came another threat to established rulers. Time and again backcountry districts petitioned for a convention to write a new constitution. Part of the pressure stemmed from the idea that the constitution of 1778, "being only an act of the legislature," was not "found on proper authority." It was repeatedly "set aside" by the legislature.

In 1784, 1785, and 1787, backcountry legislators who desired an overhaul of the constitution were defeated by sectional votes in the upper house. In 1787, for example, eleven senators—eight from the backcountry, two from the Charleston area, and one from a distant lowcountry parish—favored a meeting of a constitutional convention. They were defeated by an alliance of nine senators from the lowcountry, two from parishes some distance from the Charleston area, and one from the backcountry. The vote in the lower house was not nearly as sectional, but the strongest support came from the backcountry and the most opposition from the Charleston area.

Outside the legislature, and not mentioned by the newspapers which were most accessible to Charlestonians, there may have been more radical demands. Judge Henry Pendleton, of backcountry Saxe-Gotha, in a speech urging reapportionment, had apparently expressed a fear that somehow the people might take it upon themselves to call a convention, which would be attended by "consequent horrors," and that "another revolution might be expected to follow." Another backcountry representative, Patrick Calhoun, was apprehensive because "the general mass of the people were so much bent for a democratical government, that . . . a convention . . . would do more harm than good." Perhaps more was implicit in backcountry calls for a new constitution written by a new body. Inland representatives were asking only for changes that would have altered the balance of power between east and west, leaving most of the same people in office. New settlers might have gone further. They had moved to a state where they were first without the right to vote for three years and then disenfranchised until the legislature saw fit to declare them full citizens. Some, coming from Pennsylvania or Virginia—states with more democratic provisions for voting and officeholding—could try to abolish or lower the property qualifications for voting and officeholding as well as the residency requirement for officeholding. Probably few were disenfranchised by the fifty-acre property requirement, but all were affected by the provision that no man could be a senator or representative unless he had been resident in the state for three years. And most people were removed from consideration by the provisions that representatives had to own "settled" plantations and ten slaves or property worth £1,000 currency, while senators had to own property worth £2,000.

Depression and Debtor Legislation

From 1784 onward, South Carolina, like the other states, experienced a severe postwar economic depression which threatened the status and power of lowcountry planters. The backcountry was growing populous, and tobacco cultivation and plantation slavery were spreading, while the lowcountry was growing poor. The situation contained elements of both hope and despair. Indeed, the lowcountry's desperate plight necessitated an emergency session of the legislature in 1785.

Obviously pleading for special legislation in September 1785, Governor William Moultrie placed before the legislature the "situation between Creditor and debtor." Unprotected, the fate of the debtor would "fall little short of ruin." The urgency of the financial problem stemmed from the seriousness of lowcountry distress. Planters had commanded and used vast amounts of credit, but rice and indigo crops had failed every year since the war. The distress was apparent in tax returns. Making payments between 1785 and 1787, Christ Church's planters paid about £394 on their 1785 tax. They should have paid more than £1,200. Together, all the lowcountry parishes, excluding those in Charleston, should have paid approximately £37,700, but instead they put into the state treasury only £7,100.

Presented with evidence of overt opposition to judicial and legal power, evidence of upper-class "anarchy and confusion," in September 1785 the governor called for relief. "Necessity ... obliges an interposition of the Legislature in private Contracts," he asserted. Others joined in. In 1787, when the legislature again rescued debtors, John Julius Pringle, a lawyer and speaker of the lower house, justified legislative interference with a sweeping statement: "There is no general principle or maxim that may not admit of relaxation and exception under extraordinary circumstances," he declared.

The legislature did act, and in a manner partial to the state's "wealthier" debtors. The defense of debtors' property took two forms. The legislature first passed a valuation bill providing that no property could be sold at sheriffs' auctions for less than three-fourths its appraised value. In practice, debtors with diversified holdings offered worthless property, which creditors refused. The other defense was to issue paper money, which, more clearly even than the valuation act, exposed the nature of the relief legislation. The state set up a loan office to put in circulation £100,000 of paper money. The money was to be loaned for five years at 7 percent annual interest to individuals who borrowed no more than £250 and no less than £30 and who gave a mortgage on their land equalling three times the amount borrowed, or gold or silver plate worth twice the amount. The money could be used to pay duties and taxes. One provision, stating that no one could make use of the valuation act if a creditor demanded payment in paper, was repealed in 1786.

Most backcountry residents could not meet the loan requirements, since their land, at least for tax purposes, had little value. In real terms also, backcountry land values were low because the state, between mid-1784 and the end of 1787, had sold over 3,000,000 acres of land at about 2½ pounds per 100 acres.

Clearly, a greater percentage of qualified property owners resided in the lowcountry, and they could and did take advantage of the land bank. Of the 124 people listed on a tax return for Christ Church in 1788, 78 would have qualified for loans. In fact, the loan office appealed to people with far more than the minimum amount of property. Only 9 of about 450 borrowers borrowed £50 or less. No one borrowed £30. But 254 people borrowed £250 each. For poor debtors, or for those with moderate amounts of property, the bank and its paper currency were obviously useless.

The legislature acted again in 1786, extending the valuation act, and in 1787, adopting an installment law allowing debtors to discharge their obligations in three annual, equal payments beginning in March 1788. The installment act met with at least the partial approval of some creditors, for it seemed to promise that debts would eventually be paid. And one clause gave particular pleasure. Because of economics and not humanitarianism, the legislature prohibited the importation of Negroes for three years. Charleston District representatives favored the ban by a vote of 33 to 11 (the city's vote was 14 to 1); other lowcountry representatives cast 7 votes for and 11 against the proposal, while members from the backcountry cast 18 votes for it and 31 against. Apparently some lowcountry planters not only wanted to correct the state's imbalanced trade but also hoped to sell a few slaves to tobacco farmers in the interior. While creditors might feel more reassured over the debtor legislation of 1787, there were qualifications: the legislature would reevaluate debtors' problems whenever necessary, and installments could be postponed.

The Need to Strengthen Congress

The debt, indeed, was bound to surface again, not only in the state's political arena but in the national one as well. Following passage of the new debtor legislation, and partly because of it, many merchants and lawyers looked with "anxious expectation" to the national Constitutional Convention that was to meet in Philadelphia, hoping that its work would prove "effectually useful" in creating a sound economy. It was a time to look forward and beyond South Carolina.

It would, however, be easy to misunderstand the connection between the new federal Constitution and South Carolina's debtors. When the Constitution was up for ratification, some Carolinians sought to characterize the opposition as the immoral, debtor class. With a strict and narrow economic interpretation, Charles Cotesworth Pinckney maintained that "if we were allowed to pass Installment & valuation Laws as heretofore, an antifederalist would be a rare *avis* in this state." But that was a crass, false statement, and Pinckney knew it. It neither accounted for past legislation, explained the fight over the Constitution, nor anticipated sentiments and actions only a few months away. Had South Carolina's ratifying convention been held in October 1788 rather than May, Pinckney would have had difficulty distinguishing between a Federalist and an Antifederalist by their stand on debtor laws. The fight over the Constitution reflected economic divisions within the state, although not those between creditors and debtors; it also mirrored political divisions apparent since the troubled years before the Revolution.

A great many Carolinians, as different as Alexander Gillon and William Logan, popular leaders in Charleston, and John and Edward Rutledge, Ralph Izard, and Thomas Bee, the spearheads of the "Nabob Phalanx" of wealthy planters, agreed that the central government was too weak. They felt that Congress needed power to regulate foreign trade to force open old markets for Carolina rice and to exclude British products for the benefit of Charleston's artisans and mechanics. Backcountry settlers, too, favored a strengthened Congress that could threaten England. The unanimity on the issue was to Thomas Bee "a pleasing alteration."

Charles Cotesworth Pinckney (1746–1825) received his legal training in England and France and returned to America in 1769. He was an aide to General George Washington and was captured by the British in the fall of Charleston in May 1780. When he was exchanged in November 1782, he was promoted to brigadier general. He served in both the Constitutional Convention and the state ratifying convention as a strong supporter of the Constitution. President Washington offered him appointments on the U.S. Supreme Court and as secretary of war and secretary of state, all of which he declined. Portrait courtesy of Independence National Historical Park.

But the unanimity did not extend to the document which emerged from the Philadelphia Convention. Though Edward Rutledge characterized the opposition as "tedious but trifling," it was important. Few people objected to the specific economic powers granted to the new central government, which indicated that in most such matters the Carolina delegates had represented fairly the interests of the state. But in political matters they had not. Their ideas on government reflected the interests of only a small part of the state; hence, the debates in South Carolina were political and sectional in nature.

South Carolina and the Constitutional Convention

South Carolina dispatched four able and articulate delegates to the Philadelphia Convention. All represented the lowcountry and its conservative

Charles Pinckney (1757–1824), second cousin of Charles Cotesworth Pinckney, was a Charleston lawyer. He served in Congress from 1784 to 1787. In the Constitutional Convention he was one of the most frequent speakers, often opposing the direct participation of the people in government. Pinckney also proposed to the convention a comprehensive plan of government that possibly exerted considerable influence on the drafting of the Constitution. In April 1788 he married a daughter of Henry Laurens, then turned his ardor towards South Carolina's ratification effort. After a year on the state privy council, Pinckney served two years as governor (1789–1792). In 1796 he was again elected governor and two years later won a seat in the U.S. Senate. From 1801 to 1805 he was U.S. minister to Spain. He was elected to his fourth gubernatorial term in 1806 and served one term in Congress from 1819 to 1821. Portrait courtesy of the American Scenic Historical Preservation Society.

political views. John Rutledge and Charles Cotesworth Pinckney were English-trained lawyers and political leaders of long experience. Charles Pinckney, like Rutledge and his older cousin, Charles Cotesworth, was a lawyer, but the Revolution had prevented him from studying abroad. Although he was only twenty-nine when the convention met, his political experience was already broad. He had been a privy councilor and was a member of the lower house. From 1784 to 1787 he represented South Carolina in the Confederation Congress. Irish-born Pierce Butler, the fourth South Carolina delegate, was as worldly as Rutledge and the older Pinckney, but he had traveled in a different direction, resigning a British army commission in 1773 and joining the Carolina government. He represented a lowcountry parish in the lower house almost throughout the Confederation period but sometimes championed backcountry demands.

Charles Pinckney, as a member of Congress, saw the weakness of the national government. In 1787, he drew a distressing picture of America: "Our government is despised—our laws are robbed of their respected terrors—their inaction is a subject of ridicule." Relations with other nations, their lack of respect for America, alarmed, embarrassed, and humiliated the delegates. But they were also frightened, perhaps more so, by the anarchy, "or rather worse than anarchy," they found within individual states. "Go through each state," Charles Cotesworth Pinckney said, "and be convinced that a disregard for law hath taken the place of order." While the general statements in favor of order and stability apparently met the approval of the lowcountry planters who were their constituents, some of the supporting evidence did not, for the Pinckneys, Rutledge, and Butler denounced debtor legislation as a sign of anarchy. Many lowcountry planters, however, worried not only about the future of the state and the nation but about their own economic problems. Considering government intervention in private contracts a genuine necessity, they disagreed with their delegates concerning the justice and propriety of the recently enacted debtor legislation.

All members of the South Carolina delegation were in attendance on May 25 for the opening session of the Philadelphia Convention, at which Rutledge seconded Robert Morris' nomination of Washington as convention president. Immediately following that decision, Major William Jackson, formerly of South Carolina, was chosen secretary of the gathering. Nominated by wartime colleague Alexander Hamilton, Jackson defeated Benjamin Franklin's grandson, William Temple Franklin, for the post.

On May 29, the day that Edmund Randolph introduced Madison's Virginia Plan, Charles Pinckney also advanced a formal proposal to strengthen the national government. The Pinckney Plan, based in part upon constitutional reforms he had urged in 1786 as a member of the Confederation Congress, has produced endless and inconclusive historical debate.

The details of the Pinckney draft (which did not emerge from the committee of the whole to which it was assigned) did not come to light until 1818, when Secretary of State John Quincy Adams requested a copy for an official edition of convention documents. The version Pinckney furnished to Adams contained over thirty provisions that were embodied in the completed Constitution. But soon James Madison and pioneer historian Jared Sparks successfully challenged the authenticity of the document that Pinckney sent to Adams, and the South Carolinian was discredited.

During this century, however, several historical detectives, using the convention notes of James Wilson, have rehabilitated the brilliant, egocentric Pinckney, though Irving Brant, Madison's chief biographer, still calls him "a sponger and a plagiarist." Today's prevailing view is that Pinckney's proposal, though not innovative or original, was comprehensive, well thought out, and influential in bringing many issues to the attention of the delegates. Since the original draft or a copy thereof has never been verified, Pinckney's impact on the Grand Convention will remain a subject of speculation and controversy. Perhaps the contemporary assessment of Georgia delegate Wil-

Pierce Butler (1744–1822) was born in Ireland and served as a major in the British army. His father was a member of Parliament and a baronet. In 1771 Butler married a South Carolinian and moved to America two years later after resigning his army commission. He was a state assemblyman from 1778 to 1789 and strongly supported the backcountry demands for increased representation and the removal of the capital from Charleston. He was elected to Congress and the Constitutional Convention in March 1787. As a Federalist, he was elected to the first and second U.S. Senates, resigning in protest of the Jay Treaty in 1796. In 1802 he was again elected to the Senate and four years later he again resigned. Portrait courtesy of the New York Public Library.

liam Pierce is not far from the mark: "Mr. Charles Pinckney is a young gentleman of the most promising talents . . . in possession of a great variety of knowledge. . . . [He is] intimately acquainted with every species of polite learning and has a spirit of application and industry beyond most men. He speaks with great neatness and perspicuity and treats every subject as fully, without running into prolixity, as it requires."

The South Carolina delegation, especially Charles Pinckney, made frequent contributions to specific areas of the constitutional dialogue. They stoutly defended slavery, opposed Luther Martin's proposal to levy a tax on imported slaves, and fought against an outright ban on the foreign slave trade. Pierce Butler shaped the fugitive slave clause, while Charles Pinckney was instrumental in fashioning the three-fifths compromise dealing with House representation. The ratio was based upon a 1783 formula devised by Congress to determine what money the individual states should contribute to the Confederation government.

The delegation was unanimous in supporting the concentration of executive power in one person. Though they argued for a strong executive, the conservative quartet opposed his direct election by the people. Pierce Butler, anticipating modern experience, wished to give the president the power to declare war. He reasoned, however, that the president would make war only when the nation would support it.

The political conservatism of South Carolina's lowcountry delegates also extended to the judiciary. Charles Pinckney felt that federal judges should be required to swear under oath that they were possessed of an estate of specific value to indicate that they were independent of political or financial pressure. John Rutledge concurred with Pinckney's view. Pinckney, a strong nationalist and champion of the propertied interest, also wanted to provide a method of appeal on specified issues from the highest state court to a federal court system.

When the long, hot summer of debate ended on September 17, Rutledge, Butler, and both Pinckneys affixed their signatures to the completed Constitution and headed back to Charleston to convince an anxious lowcountry and a suspicious backcountry of the merits of the new national frame of government which they had helped to shape.

South Carolina Debates the Constitution

South Carolina's debate over the adoption of the Constitution took place in two phases. Extensive formal discussion first occurred in January 1788, when Federalists introduced a measure calling for the election of a ratifying convention to be held in Charleston. During that controversy Rawlins Lowndes of Charleston surprisingly emerged as the principal Antifederalist opponent of such a convention while raising numerous criticisms of the Constitution. Because of its concecssions on commerce and the slave trade, he regarded the document as a capitulation to the Northern States, and he predicted that with its adoption "the sun of the Southern states would set, never to rise again." Except for slight assists from General Thomas Sumter, James Lincoln, and a handful of other western legislators, Lowndes waged his verbal battle almost single-handedly. When the crucial tally was taken on January 19, the legislature easily endorsed the idea of a state convention to be held the following May. The House, however, divided on the location of the convention—the backcountry lost their fight against Charleston by a one-vote margin, 76 to 75. Ironically, Lowndes, hoping to alter the proposed Constitution, voted in favor of the ratifying convention, along with the other twenty-four assemblymen from Charleston.

Lowndes' anti-Constitution tirade in the legislature caused his townsmen to bypass him as a delegate to the May convention. Although the citizens of St. Bartholomew's Parish elected him to their delegation, the slighted Lowndes declined to serve, and thus the Antifederalists lost their most effective spokesman.

After the election results were counted, it was clear that Federalists had swept the coastal regions while the western counties went Antifederalist. Since the lowcountry benefited from legislative malapportionment, the Federalist side entered the conclave with a majority of approximately 2 to 1. The site of the gathering further favored the Constitution's supporters, for Charleston Federalists wooed, flattered, cajoled, and entertained the delegates from the time of their arrival until their departure. On May 13, the first day a quorum was present, the delegates chose Governor Thomas Pinckney (the like-minded brother of Charles Cotesworth) as convention president, and on the following day debate began.

Antifederalist objections to the Constitution, whether raised by state legislators in January when the convention call was argued or in May during the ratifying session itself, ranged from the sectional suspicions of the North uttered by aristocrat Lowndes to agrarian denunciations of aristocracy voiced by frontier opponents of the close-knit lowcountry "nabobs." Federalists defended not only with oratory but by controlling both the mechanisms of government and the press.

At the Constitutional Convention the state's delegates had sought to decrease the role of the people in the proposed government, speaking against the popular election of senators and representatives because it was "impracticable" or because "the people were less fit Judges" than state legislatures. Although members of the state ratifying convention did not know the arguments advanced by their delegates to the Philadelphia Convention, the opponents of the Constitution understood their aims.

Both supporters and opponents spoke of the people's voice, the American Revolution, and liberty. Francis Kinloch welcomed the shift back toward a system like the one they had "destroyed some years" before, because Americans did not have "virtue enough for that free form of government." Charles Pinckney thought the Constitution showed that "all power of right belongs to the people, and is delegated to their officers for the public good." Patrick Dollard, from a remote lowcountry parish, found the voice of the people to be the voice of God. But unlike Pinckney, Dollard thought they would not accept the Constitution unless a standing army rammed "it down their throats with the points of bayonets." For James Lincoln, from Ninety Six District, the people would be rushing "from a well-digested, well-formed democratic" government into an aristocratic one. Why should they throw away "all that human wisdom and valor could procure?"

To Antifederalists, the government did not seem sufficiently responsive to the people, nor did it adequately protect people from tyranny. Only one branch of the legislature was popularly elected, a shortcoming, said Rawlins Lowndes, that Carolinians had eliminated from their 1778 constitution. Another error was the absence of a doctrine of rotation in office, an idea fundamental not only to the Articles of Confederation but to many early state constitutions, South Carolina's included. James Lincoln remarked that there was nothing to prevent a president from repeating his four-year term fourteen times. "You do not put the same check on him," Lincoln said, "that you do on your own state governor, a man born and bred among you, a man over whom you have a continual and watchful eye." The absence of rotation was more serious because the government was located far from Carolina. Liberty was entrusted to men "who live one thousand miles distant."

Antifederalist issues such as rotation in office, the remoteness of the capital, and the election of senators had divided Carolinians throughout the revolutionary period. Federalists did what they could to answer the charges, labelling rotation a political mania that was ruining the state and arguing that as long as the Senate was independent of the lower house, as it was when elected by state legislatures, there was clearly no danger. (It would have embarrassed Federalists if the delegates' true reasons for opposing popular elections had been known.)

During the rambling ratification debate, Lowndes expressed his skepticism about the Federalist argument that opponents were not to "be uneasy, since every thing would be managed in [the] future by great men," who were "infallible." At another time it was noted that if Charles Pinckney favored—as citizens knew he did—a government with an absolute veto over all state legislation, and if he feared "pure democracy," Antifederalists could rightly

174

conclude that he was interested not only in increasing the powers of the central government but also in depriving westerners of their newly-won political power. Their power decreased when state governments were weakened. Pinckney's satisfaction was cause for alarm.

Regardless of the debate, ratification was effortless. The only potential allies for the backcountry spokesmen who led the attack were the Charlestonians who had in the past criticized the political ideas of the aristocracy. But the Charlestonians were willing to forgo their ideological objections to get a government with power to strike at Britain.

On May 23, 1788, the state convention ratified the Constitution by a lopsided margin of 149 to 73. A united lowcountry voted 121 to 16 in its favor, the backcountry 28 to 57 against. Seventeen of the 28 backcountry votes for ratification, and only one of the 57 votes against, came from four election units bordering lowcountry parishes. The delegates opposed to the Constitution, however, probably represented a majority of the state population, and Antifederalism was stronger in the state at large than the ratification vote indicated.

The economic division over the Constitution was determined by one's geographical location rather than from one's stand on debtor legislation. Federalists came from different areas and were wealthier than Antifederalists, owning larger amounts of public securities and more slaves. Wealthy Federalists were richer than wealthy Antifederalists. The gulf between Federalists and Antifederalists outside the convention was still wider, since backcountry settlers sent to the convention the same propertied people they sent to the legislature.

Like Charles Cotesworth Pinckney, Federalist author and physician David Ramsay sought to link Antifederalists and debtors. Ramsay alleged that Antifederalists feared that the Constitution, by prohibiting states from emitting bills of credit or passing laws interfering with contracts, would force people to pay debts. This assertion ignores the fact that in 1785 the lowcountry planters had passed the debtor legislation. By October 1788 Pinckney acknowledged that backcountry legislators had agreed to debtor laws only "in compliance with the wishes of the lower country gentlemen."

Another State Constitution

Ratification of the Constitution was the final impetus for calling a state constitutional convention. No longer would the legislature annually elect delegates to Congress, and no longer could the governor, with the legislature's consent, declare war, make peace, or enter into any binding treaty. And some lowcountry leaders thought the structure of the new government worth copying.

Delegates to the state constitutional convention met in Columbia from May 10 to June 3, 1790, with Charles Pinckney presiding over this reform-oriented body. The constitution of 1790 introduced few changes, but these few, along with those in the previous constitution, gave South Carolina a government quite different from what had existed before 1778. Even though William Loughton Smith, another English-trained lawyer and a Federalist member of Congress, thanked conservative Charlestonian Edward Rutledge for inserting "such advantages for the Low Country" into a constitution which was "much better than the former one," the new plan was not an improvement over the government of 1778 for the old rulers. If lowcountry leaders were satisfied, it was because they had not been forced to make greater concessions than they did. More than some contemporaries openly admitted, and more than historians have subsequently realized, the constitution of 1790 was a major advance for the newer areas of the state.

South Carolina's third state constitution extended political rights by accepting full religious toleration. No religious qualifications for officeholders or voters were established. The free exercise of religion was allowed as long as the peace of the state was not disturbed. Continued limitations on the governor protected the people from arbitrary rule, and yet, despite the example of the federal Constitution, he was again denied a veto and automatically rotated out of office. Officials under the national or state government were prohibited from sitting in the state legislature. Property qualifications for voting and holding office remained similar to those set in 1778, but legislators were allowed compensation. Perhaps lowcountry delegates won a victory in making further amendments more difficult: the constitution could not be changed unless a bill to that effect was passed by a two-thirds vote of the whole membership, published three months before an election, and then passed again by two-thirds of the new legislature.

But success for individuals or groups did not depend on rotation, legislators' pay, amendments, a governor's veto, or even property qualifications. Rarely in the 1780s had property qualifications been an issue. Apportionment and the location of the capital had been and remained the significant issues of the day.

Thus, in a real victory for the lowcountry, the convention defeated proposals to base representation on numbers of white inhabitants or on a specific combination of wealth and numbers. Apparently lowcountry delegates feared that soon the backcountry would be prosperous as well as populous. Instead, without mentioning property but obviously considering it, the constitution established the number of legislators for each parish and county, with no provision for future changes. The lower house was reduced to 124 members; the Senate, with 29 in 1778, was enlarged to 37. With change in size came reapportionment. In 1778 the backcountry had elected 37.9 percent of the senators and 37.6 percent of the representatives. In 1790 it elected 45.9 percent of the senators and 43.5 percent of the representatives, while Georgetown and Beaufort combined increased their share of the Senate from 17.2 percent to 18.9 percent, and their presence in the lower house from 14.8 percent to 17.7 percent. The backcountry emerged from the convention as the most powerful section in each branch of the legislature.

Reapportionment took on greater meaning with the decision to establish the government in Columbia. Attendance at the convention even reminded people of the issue's importance. Because of "ill health," "unexpected circumstances," or other reasons, at least nineteen lowcountry delegates informed the governor that they would not attend the convention. Elections filled the vacancies, but the resignations highlighted both what was at stake and the lowcountry problem. The lowcountry lost the first vote on keeping the government inland, 105 to 104. Eighty-six of the 87 backcountry delegates voted in favor, while 103 of 122 lowcountry delegates opposed the interior location. But 22 lowcountry delegates were absent, compared to only 8 from the interior.

The Bill of Rights

South Carolinians were generally happy with their new federal and state constitutions. Those who had fears that the federal government might impinge on individual rights were placated when Congress proposed amendments to the Constitution in September 1789. Less than four months later, on January 18, 1790, the state House of Representatives resolved to adopt the new Bill of Rights, and the next day the Senate concurred. The legislature also resolved that it would be "inexpedient" to hold a second constitutional convention as requested by New York when it had ratified the Constitution in July 1788.

Overview

What, then, was the Revolution in South Carolina? Independence led to a bloody civil war, economic chaos, and, throughout the period, political change. It was controlled change, steady and unrelenting, but not overwhelming at any one time. Lowcountry leaders who participated in and led the opposition to England up to and after independence never completely lost control; nor did they have to be ousted from power in order for responsive government to emerge. But Charlestonians and backcountry settlers, and some from the lowcountry, were nonetheless presented with opportunities which they did not waste. They demanded change year after year, and change came. In analyzing the range of reforms implemented from 1776 to 1790 and their impact upon South Carolina, one might employ this laconic assessment: some people would have preferred to give up less, others to gain more.

South Carolina: Essay on Sources

The best general sources on South Carolina during the Revolutionary era are Jerome J. Nadelhaft, *The Disorders of War: The Revolution in South Carolina* (Orono, Maine, 1981); Charles Gregg Singer, *South Carolina in the Confederation* (Philadelphia, 1941); David Duncan Wallace, *South Carolina: A Short History, 1520–1948* (Chapel Hill, 1951); Jeffrey J. Crow and Larry E. Tise, eds., *The Southern Experience in the American Revolution* (Chapel Hill, 1978); and Raymond G. Starr, "The Conservative Revolution: South Carolina Public Affairs, 1775–1790" (Ph.D. dissertation, University of Texas, 1964). For a contemporary's point of view, see David Ramsay's *The History of the Revolution of South-Carolina from a British Province to an Independent State*, 2 vols. (Trenton, N.J., 1785) and his *The History of South Carolina from Its First Settlement in 1670 to the Year 1808*, 2 vols. (Charleston, 1809).

For colonial background, see M. Eugene Sirmans, *Colonial South Carolina: A Political History, 1663–1763* (Chapel Hill, 1966); Robert M. Weir, " 'The Harmony We Were Famous For': An Interpretation of Pre-Revolutionary South Carolina Politics," *William and Mary Quarterly*, 3rd ser., 26 (October 1969), 473–501; "Charleston in 1774 as Described by an English Traveler," *South Carolina Historical and Genealogical Magazine*, 47 (July 1946), 179–180; Frederick P. Bowes, *The Culture of Early Charleston* (Chapel Hill, 1942); David Morton Knepper, "The Political Structure of Colonial South Carolina, 1743–1776" (Ph.D. dissertation, University of Virginia, 1971); and Richard Maxwell Brown, *The South Carolina Regulators* (Cambridge, Mass., 1963). For special studies in the Revolutionary years, see George C. Rogers, Jr., *Charleston in the Age of the Pinckneys* (Norman, Okla., 1969); Richard Walsh, *Charleston's Sons of Liberty: A Study of the Artisans, 1763–1789* (Columbia, S.C., 1959); Benjamin R. Baldwin, "The Debts Owed by Americans to British Creditors, 1763–1802" (Ph.D. dissertation, University of Indiana, 1932); and W. Robert Higgins, "A Financial History of the American Revolution in South Carolina" (Ph.D. dissertation, Duke University, 1970). Studies of South Carolina's constitutional development include William A. Schaper, "Sectionalism and Representation in South Carolina," American Historical Association *Annual Report* (1900), I, 243–463; D. Huger Bacot, "Constitutional Progress and the Struggle for Democracy in South Carolina following the Revolution," *South Atlantic Quarterly*, 24 (1925), 61–72; Fletcher M. Green, *Constitutional Development in the South Atlantic States, 1776–1860: A Study in the Evolution of Democracy* (Chapel Hill, 1930); and George C. Rogers, Jr., "South Carolina Ratifies the Federal Constitution," South Carolina Historical Association *Proceedings* (1961), pp. 41–62.

For biographical studies, see George C. Rogers, Jr. *Evolution of a Federalist: William Loughton Smith of Charleston* (Columbia, S.C., 1962); Frances Leigh Williams, *A Founding Family: The Pinckneys of South Carolina* (New York, 1978); Marvin R. Zahniser, *Charles Cotesworth Pinckney: Founding Father* (Chapel Hill, 1967); Harriet Horry Ravenel, *Life and Times of William Lowndes of South Carolina, 1782–1822* (Boston, 1901); Richard Barry, *Mr. Rutledge of South Carolina* (New York, 1942); Malcolm Bell, *Major Butler's Legacy: Five Generations of a Slaveholding Family* (Athens, Ga., 1987); and Lewright B. Sikes, *The Public Life of Pierce Butler, South Carolina Statesman* (Washington, D.C., 1979). Little of any length has been written on Charles Pinckney, but George C. Rogers, Jr., is currently preparing what should be the definitive study of him. Until then, one may consult Andrew J. Bethea, *The Contribution of Charles Pinckney to the Formation of the American Union* (Richmond, Va., 1937); J. Franklin Jameson, "Portions of Charles Pinckney's Plan for a Constitution, 1787," *American Historical Review*, 8 (April 1903), 509–11; Charles C. Nott, *The Mystery of the Pinckney Draft* (New York, 1908); Andrew C. McLaughlin, "Sketch of Charles Pinckney's Plan for a Constitution, 1787," *American Historical Review*, 9 (July 1904), 735–747; and S. Sidney Ulmer, "Charles Pinckney: Father of the Constitution?" *South Carolina Law Quarterly*, 10 (Winter 1958), 225–247. In varying degrees, all these studies support Pinckney's role as a major influence on the drafting of the Federal Constitution.

For group portraits, consult Ernest M. Lander, Jr., "The South Carolinians at the Philadelphia Convention, 1787," *South Carolina Historical Magazine*, 57 (July 1956), 135–155; and Alexander S. Salley, *Delegates to the Continental Congress from South Carolina, 1774–1789* (Columbia, S.C., 1927).

For primary sources dealing with various South Carolinans, see Joseph Barnwell, ed., "Diary of Timothy Ford, 1785–1786," *South Carolina Historical Magazine*, 13 (1912), 132–147, 181–204; Robert L. Brunhouse, "David Ramsay on the Ratification of the Constitution in South Carolina, 1787–1788," *Journal of Southern History*, 9 (1943), 549–555; Anne Izard Deas, *Correspondence of Mr. Ralph Izard, of South Carolina, from the Year 1774 to 1804 with a Short Memoir* (New York, 1844); Felix Gilbert, ed., "Letters of Francis Kinloch to Thomas Boone, 1782–1788," *Journal of Southern History*, 8 (1942), 87–105; and Philip M. Hamer, George C. Rogers, Jr., and David R. Chesnutt, eds., *The Papers of Henry Laurens*, 10 vols. to date (Columbia, S.C., 1968–). Also valuable is the *Journal of the Convention of South Carolina which Ratified the Constitution of the United States, May 23, 1788*, indexed by A. S. Salley (Atlanta, 1928).

9
NEW HAMPSHIRE

Ideology and Hardball

Ratification of the Federal Constitution in New Hampshire

JERE DANIELL
Professor of History
Dartmouth College

A T 1:00 P.M., June 21, 1788, a convention of town delegates meeting at Concord, New Hampshire, ratified the proposed federal Constitution by a margin of 57 to 47. The vote capped a lengthy and often acrimonious constitutional conflict which had divided state inhabitants for more than nine months. The opponents of ratification—initially a majority of the convention delegates—deeply distrusted the idea of voluntarily granting to any distant and unknown political authority powers recently won at such personal and collective sacrifice. Supporters of the new plan of union felt just as deeply that a strengthened national government was necessary to fulfill the promise of successful revolution and that New Hampshire citizens would gain far more from union than they would lose. These ideological lines were drawn early in the conflict; relatively few individuals subsequently changed their minds.

Hard-nosed politics decided the issue. Federalists, those supporting ratification, simply outmaneuvered Antifederalists. They used influence in the state government to delay consideration of the plan until neighboring

Massachusetts acted and to maximize their representation when ratification proceedings did begin. When the convention first met in February, Federalists arrived early, elected a committee to determine convention procedures, skillfully used those procedures to prevent a final vote—which they feared would be negative—and obtained adjournment until June. In the interim they prepared long and hard for the June session. The final vote provided convincing evidence of their political skills.

Sectional Strife in Colonial New Hampshire

The ratification struggle took place in a state with a recent history of extended constitutional debate. Disputes over the proper structure of government had erupted in the mid-1770s and continued throughout the war years. The disputes reflected both ideological disagreements and competition for power among inhabitants of New Hampshire's three major subregions, the watersheds of the Piscataqua, Merrimack, and Connecticut rivers. Piscataqua residents, from Portsmouth and Exeter especially, had dominated the pre-Revolutionary government and accumulated a great deal of wealth, largely through external trade. Not surprisingly, their constitutional arguments indicated a desire to preserve as much of the status quo as possible. Citizens in the rapidly growing central part of the state drained by the Merrimack River had been poorly represented in the colonial government and used the Revolution to assert themselves at the expense of the seacoast. Their fundamental constitutional stance emphasized local rather than state authority and control of state government by town delegates elected to a broadly representative legislature. Leaders in the Connecticut River Valley communities tended to articulate beliefs which would free them from subordination to the more populated eastern parts of the state.

The first serious trouble occurred before passage of the Declaration of Independence. The only province in New England without a formal charter of incorporation, New Hampshire was left without legal government when the last royal governor, John Wentworth, fled in the summer of 1775. Town delegates from throughout New Hampshire created an extralegal Provincial Congress which gradually took over responsibilities previously exercised by Wentworth and the General Court. The Congress, which contained far broader town representation than its colonial predecessor, adopted a written constitution in January 1776. The constitution legitimized the Congress by making it New Hampshire's official House of Representatives and by authorizing the new house to create an upper legislative body called the Council.

Adoption triggered a brief but dramatic protest movement. Western spokesmen criticized the new arrangement because it perpetuated eastern political domination. A few seacoast writers also complained about the specific form of government, but more argued simply that adoption of any constitution was premature. Portsmouth's delegates at the Congress returned home and helped call a town meeting which voted unanimously to petition for reconsideration. Portsmouth also voted to send letters urging other towns to "remonstrate likewise." By the end of January eleven different Piscataqua communities and twelve individual Provincial Congress delegates had submitted formal protests. The Congress as a whole compromised by asking the Continental Congress if taking up government had been a mistake. That body, however, never replied, and the formal Declaration of Independence ended conflict over adoption of the state's first constitution.

New Hampshire and the Articles of Confederation

The next testing of constitutional attitudes had to do with national, not state, government. In late 1777 New Hampshire was asked to ratify the Articles of Confederation. Partly because of the earlier controversy, the legislature decided to submit the document to individual towns before acting. The towns, although most reported general approval, made clear their commitment to state sovereignty. The citizens of Hawke (now Danville) complained that binding all states by a vote of only nine was "too prerogative"; Wilton argued that giving Congress the right to declare war bestowed "a power greater than the King of Great Britain in Council ever had"; numerous towns worried about New Hampshire's interests being compromised by insensitive federal officeholders. Not a single town suggested that the Articles provided the Confederation Congress with insufficient power. Complaints about the Articles granting too much power were concentrated in areas where Antifederalism subsequently became strong.

Internal Strife in Revolutionary New Hampshire

Meanwhile, two major and closely interrelated constitutional problems had begun to buffet the state. Both were triggered by dissatisfaction with the document so hastily adopted by the Provincial Congress early in 1776. A group of town leaders from the Connecticut River Valley renewed complaints that the new form of state government left their communities underrepresented and demanded that a convention be called to rewrite the constitution. Portsmouth-area critics of the state government joined in the demand for a constitutional convention. The legislature, after testing public sentiment, voted to hold such a gathering in the summer of 1778. By that time the western rebels had decided their towns would be better off joining the self-created state of Vermont across the river. Thus New Hampshire wrestled simultaneously with its own secession crisis and with a constitutional reform movement where existing authority supposedly was accepted. It took nearly five years to put down the western rebellion. Obtaining approval for a new plan of government took even longer.

The western rebellion was more than a constitutional conflict. It involved a complex mix of legal, demographic, geographic, and political factors all related to New Hampshire's colonial history. Constitutional questions, however, dominated the reasoning of the malcontents. They argued that the Revolution had severed all governmental bonds of allegiance except those of the individual to his town. Towns therefore had the right to join whatever state their voters chose. According to this argument, New Hampshire's constitution, which classed small towns together for purposes of representation, had violated the fundamental right of each town to elect a member to the General Court, a right which towns in Connecticut and Rhode Island enjoyed. Furthermore, the constitution created a government with serious structural weaknesses which virtually guaranteed that seaboard inhabitants would dominate. Vermont's constitution, on the other hand, recognized the fundamental equality of all towns, accorded them representation, and in general seemed based on sound constitutional principles. In 1778 sixteen valley towns east of the river formally voted to join Vermont.

Constitutional issues were subordinated in the latter stages of rebellion. Vermont first accepted, then rejected the seceding towns. When community leaders on both sides of the river launched a campaign to have all towns east of the Green Mountains become part of New Hampshire, Vermont's legislature reannexed the original sixteen plus twenty-two more. This "second union" lasted until leaders in both state governments withdrew support from the idea of any change in state boundaries. Meanwhile, several spokesmen for the Continental Congress, including George Washington, expressed disapproval of the entire secession movement. The rebellion ended by 1783.

The New State Constitution of 1784

Acceptance of existing state authority by western leaders stemmed in part from constitutional reform within New Hampshire. The convention which met in 1778 had not accomplished much; its proposals were overwhelmingly rejected by the voters when submitted to town meetings for approval. But the existing constitution had been enacted only for the duration of hostilities. As it became apparent the war would soon end, the legislature called a second convention and ordered it to remain in session, amending its proposals, until ratification by the citizenry.

That proved easier said than done. The convention first met in the summer of 1781. Dominated by Portsmouth-area delegates—including John Langdon and John Pickering, who would play key roles in ratifying the federal Constitution—it first recommended a constitution which eliminated town representation entirely and provided such high property qualifications for state officeholding that few supporting votes could be obtained. A second, more moderate proposal was similarly rejected. Finally, in the fall of 1783, the convention submitted a document which a majority of those voting accepted. The constitution provided for a popularly elected president (i.e., governor), a Senate made up of county delegates, and a House of Representatives which gave each town with 150 voters the right to choose a member. Smaller communities would be "classed," or combined, for purposes of representation. The rapidly growing western towns then could see their influence increasing as the years passed. The following June a state government chosen under the new system met for the first time.

Thus, by the middle of the 1780s, the politically active portion of New Hampshire's population had extensive experience in constitutional matters. Citizens shared certain assumptions. They believed in representative government. They believed that such government should have separate executive, legislative, and judicial branches and that the powers of each should be defined by a written constitution. Constitutions, in turn, should be drafted by individuals representing subunits of government—towns for state constitutions and states for any national constitution—and all proposed constitutions should be subject to close examination by voters in those subunits. New Hampshire's citizens accepted the basic logic of a three-tiered system of local, state, and national authority. The whole arrangement they labeled "federated republicanism."

Within that pattern of shared assumptions, however, there was much disagreement. Individuals differed on how authority should be distributed among the three levels of power; until now controversies had concentrated on local and state relationships, but that would soon change. Two regions of the state—the eastern seacoast area and the western Connecticut River Valley—had long histories of dissatisfaction with constitutional arrangements shaped largely by community leaders from central New Hampshire. Compromise was achieved, but sectional differences remained. Finally, there existed both attraction to and deep distrust of the whole idea of constitutional reform. The past made clear that proposals for constitutional change should be carefully scrutinized to prevent loss of popular liberties.

Round One: Preparation for a Decision

New Hampshire, like other states, experienced serious economic and political troubles in the postwar era. A short-lived commercial revival collapsed soon after mid-decade. The newly formed state government found itself torn by factional disputes, in part because it proved unable to combat the recession effectively. Accusations of corruption, favoritism, and insensitivity were leveled at public officials. In 1786 groups of irate citizens began meeting to pressure state government. In September 1786 a mob of angry farmers, demanding an issuance of state paper money, surrounded the legislative hall in Exeter and had to be dispersed by the local militia. Disillu-

John Langdon (1741–1819) represented New Hampshire at the Philadelphia Convention and coastal Portsmouth at the state ratifying convention, where he played a key role in organizing the Federalist victory. A prosperous merchant, Langdon was a leading figure in the political and military events of the Revolution, during which he outfitted privateers, served as speaker of the New Hampshire Assembly (1777–1783, 1786–1787, 1788), represented his state in Congress (1775–1776, 1787), and commanded militia units at the battles of Saratoga and Rhode Island. After his return from Philadelphia he was chosen chief executive, or president, of New Hampshire (1785–1786, 1788–1789), and in that position he wielded much influence on behalf of ratification. From 1789 to 1801 he served in the U.S. Senate, becoming the first president pro tem of that body. In politics he was a staunch Democratic-Republican. During the latter stages of his career, Langdon served in the New Hampshire legislature, twice holding the post of speaker, and also presided again as governor for several terms. Portrait by Edward Savage, courtesy of the New Hampshire Historical Society.

sionment became so great that the following spring nearly 40 percent of the towns in the state refused to send legislative representatives.

Given the context, it is not surprising that many citizens looked to the Confederation Congress for help, and when efforts to beef up its powers failed, they began discussing other forms of interstate cooperation. In 1786 the legislature appointed delegates to a commercial convention to be held in Annapolis, Maryland. None of the appointees attended, but when that convention called for a general meeting of state delegates in Philadelphia, the legislature authorized any two of its four Confederation Congress members to attend the meeting. John Langdon and Nicholas Gilman, both prestigious seacoast merchant-politicians, eventually made the trip south. Although they arrived two months late (on July 23) and contributed little to the constitutional discussion, they supported the final proposals, then joined Congress to make certain its members did nothing to hinder ratification. Langdon and Gilman also promised to campaign for approval in New Hampshire.

Between September 29 and October 6, 1787, the three Portsmouth newspapers printed the new federal Constitution. Debate on its merits had begun even before then, and it continued unabated until ratification. New Hampshire's five newspapers printed article after article emphasizing the potential benefits of adoption. Ministers throughout the state devoted sermons to the subject; in general, they too supported the Federalist position. Both Federalists and Antifederalists circulated pamphlets defending their stances and engaged in lengthy discussions in parlors, taverns, ship cabins, and any other place an interested audience gathered.

Proponents articulated a variety of arguments. Ratification would be of immense economic benefit to merchants, landholders, mechanics, farmers, and taxpayers. It would help solve the current political crisis by reducing interstate rivalries and circumscribing both the authority and responsibilities of state legislatures. It would give the United States a better international reputation. Ratification, in short, promised to solve all the problems of New Hampshire and its fellow states. "Many people look upon the adoption of the new constitution," wrote one newspaper correspondent, "as the millenium of virtue and wealth."

Critics saw no such millenium on the horizon. Deeply committed to decentralization, they worried about too powerful a central authority. Merchants might benefit from increased commerce, some argued, but New Hampshire's many farmers would not. If state officials responsible to their electors could not be trusted, what could be expected of national rulers? The proposed federal judiciary would put decisions in the hands of distant authorities insensitive to local circumstances. Lack of religious qualifications for national officeholding—only Protestants were eligible in New Hampshire—seemed fraught with dangerous implications. The proposed Constitution, many concluded, provided much too radical a change. The state should vote against ratification.

There were no professional polltakers in the 1780s, so it would be fruitless to attempt any quantitative assessment of public opinion. Several things, however, quickly became clear. Federalist attitudes dominated only in areas with a long history of constitutional disaffection—the seacoast and Grafton County, the center of the western rebellion. Secondly, most critics of the Constitution were not cowed by the fact that a very high percentage of the state's economic, political, and intellectual elite favored ratification. And finally, no one could be certain which side would win.

The proposed Constitution itself dictated where the initial round of formal fighting would take place. Article VII stated simply that "Ratification of the Conventions of nine States shall be sufficient for the Establishment of this Constitution." It was up to the state legislature to decide when, where, and with what membership the New Hampshire convention would meet. Actions taken by the legislature, leaders on both sides knew, would help determine the eventual outcome.

Individuals of known Federalist commitment controlled state planning for the upcoming convention. The next scheduled legislative session was set for late January. John Sullivan—seacoast resident, president of New Hampshire, a former Revolutionary War general, and an outspoken unionist—decided that pro-Constitution individuals would have a better chance of controlling a special legislative session than the regular one, and he hastily convened such a meeting in December and urged his fellow Federalists to attend. The tactic worked. Of the ten senators who gathered, eight were from towns eventually voting for ratification. When the House had a quorum, attending members were evenly divided in sentiment, even though the total membership contained a decided Antifederalist majority. The speaker, Thomas Bartlett, strongly favored ratification.

Decisions made in December reflected the superiority of Federalist forces. Both houses agreed to form a joint committee to make recommendations for the convention. Bartlett selected an equal number of Federalist and Antifederalist members; the Senate, however, selected all Federalists. Not surprisingly, the committee recommendations had a Federalist flavor. The convention should be held at Exeter, in the heartland of Federalism. It would not convene until mid-February; by that time, it was hoped, six states, including neighboring Massachusetts, would have ratified. The state would pay expenses, and each town or class of towns could send as many delegates as it had in the House. An apparently innocuous qualification stated that towns presently unrepresented could elect delegates if they chose. Finally, the state's exclusion bill, which prohibited most appointed state officials from simultaneously representing their towns in the legislature, would not apply to the convention. This made possible the participation of such influential Federalists as Superior Court chief justice Samuel Livermore of Grafton County and state treasurer John Taylor Gilman.

Antifederalists in the House, led by Nathaniel Peabody of Atkinson, knew they had been bested and made one effort to change the joint-committee's recommendations. They tried to have the number of convention delegates doubled, hoping thus to dilute the influence of powerful Federalists like Sullivan and Langdon. Since that would also have doubled the cost of the convention, the motion failed badly. The vote provided the last flurry of round one. Judge's decision: a clear Federalist victory.

Round Two: Decision Postponed

The election of convention delegates by the various towns and classes of towns came next. Copies of the Constitution were printed and distributed,

John Sullivan (1740-1795), president (i.e., chief executive) of New Hampshire when the state government called the ratifying convention, became president of that gathering as well. An ardent Federalist, Sullivan had played a leading role in the military events of the Revolution, serving in the lofty post of major general. He commanded American troops in the Battle of Rhode Island (1778) and conducted a highly successful campaign against the loyalists and Iroquois in western New York (1779). The son of Irish immigrants, Sullivan was a lawyer by profession, having studied under Samuel Livermore. He held numerous civil positions in addition to the governorship. These included delegate to Congress (1774-1775 and 1780-1781), state attorney general (1782-1786), speaker of the state assembly (1785 and 1788), and New Hampshire's first federal district court judge (1789-1795). Portrait by Adna Tenny, located in the New Hampshire State House, Concord.

selectmen began to post warrants for special town meetings, public curiosity about results intensified, and local leaders of both persuasions discussed strategy. Antifederalists, coached by men of like sentiment in Massachusetts and warned by returning legislators that Federalists already seemed effectively organized, belatedly developed their own communication network that operated most effectively in the Merrimack River Valley.

Antifederalist tactics dictated the internal dynamics of many town meetings. The plan was simple: elect Antifederalist delegates and bind them by written instructions so they would not be talked out of voting nay at Exeter. It was inevitable that in some communities the delegates chosen would object to binding instructions—after all, they could and did argue that the purpose of the convention was to discuss the Constitution and make a reasonable judgment about its merits based on that discussion. In such cases instructions were especially important, for unwillingness to accept them indicated potential softness of commitment. The matter of instructions seemed more and more important as New Hampshire's Antifederalists watched an initial majority in the Bay State convention gradually slip away. Only a handful of delegates there had formally been instructed.

These Antifederalist tactics produced some elaborate and exciting local political contests. In Walpole, for example, Major General Benjamin Bellows was elected but refused to accept binding negative instructions. A few days before the Exeter convention, and shortly after news arrived of ratification in Massachusetts, a quickly convened town meeting replaced Bellows with an Antifederalist. Keene also held a second meeting, but a Federalist majority voted both to keep the same delegate and to pass over the article warrant on instructions. Town after town either voted against the Constitution itself or appointed a committee which advised against adoption.

Surviving records, however, are neither plentiful nor clear enough to calculate the overall results with precision. Contemporary estimates of instructed delegates reached as high as forty. A more likely figure is about twenty-five, all but two or three of whom were advised negatively. Whatever the exact total, Antifederalists had a large base from which to operate. The total number of elected delegates would not be much over one hundred. With negatively instructed delegates and a similar number of uninstructed but opposed delegates, the Constitution might be defeated.

Federalists, meanwhile, prepared just as aggressively. They continued to flood newspapers with articles, including many critical of binding instructions. They also made every effort to maximize the number of pro-Constitution delegates. The inhabitants of Newcastle, which had not elected a legislative representative for some time, chose a convention delegate when merchants in neighboring Portsmouth explained the need for more votes. Previously, Canterbury and Northfield had shared a legislator; soon after the former chose an Antifederalist, the latter voted to send its own pro-Constitution delegate. Up in Grafton County, Samuel Livermore lined up support and convinced elected delegates they should make the long trek to Exeter. Bellows, Aaron Hall of Keene, Benjamin West of Charlestown, and other town leaders in Cheshire County fought successfully to limit the number of binding instructions.

The most important form of Federalist preparation involved the convention itself, not the local elections. The regular legislative session, which convened in Portsmouth on January 23, provided the first good opportunity to gather accurate information about developments at the local level. What Sullivan, Langdon, and their allies learned must have been distressing. Inhabitants in the interior apparently did not share seacoast enthusiasm for the new Constitution. The problem of binding instructions was more serious than anticipated. Antifederalists had found an effective leader in the influential legislator Nathaniel Peabody, who seemed confident of victory at Exeter. Given the uncertainty, Federalist leaders decided they should have a contingency plan for Exeter. They should be prepared to engineer an adjournment if ratification could not be guaranteed.

The contingency plan, hatched in early February, involved tactics similar to those used in the December legislative session. It is unclear who coordinated things, but Sullivan, Langdon, Gilman, Livermore, and West—all convention delegates and former members of Congress—undoubtedly knew beforehand what would happen. Federalists were told to arrive as early on February 13 as possible. As soon as anything close to a quorum appeared, the convention would be called to order and a rules committee formed. This committee, chosen by Federalists in attendance, would check the delegates' credentials. It also would prepare procedural ground rules which would maximize the possibility of adjournment, should that become necessary. By the time everyone arrived, the procedures would be in place.

This bold plan worked to perfection. The convention journal for February 13 tells the story. The first paragraph reads, "About fifty members being assembled, they proceeded to the choice of a chairman, and the Honorable Josiah Bartlett Esq. was chosen." Of the "about fifty" recorded in attendance, thirty-three voted in June for ratification. Five of these thirty-three had quietly left the nearby legislative session, which Sullivan did not adjourn until late that afternoon. Among the legislators remaining in Portsmouth were about two dozen delegates, a majority of them Antifederalist. The choice of Bartlett as temporary chairman may also have been pre-arranged. Bartlett was a highly respected judge and a close friend of Peabody, and he was uncommitted publicly on the issue of ratification. His election to the chair would give what followed the appearance of legitimacy among all convention delegates.

The second paragraph of the journal reports the choice of Livermore, Gilman, and West as "a Committee to receive the returns of members elected"; they were also appointed "a Committee to prepare and lay before the Convention such rules as they shall judge necessary for regulating the proceedings in said Convention." The committee, in short, was to determine, not to recommend, the rules. Then the meeting broke up.

Attendance, swollen by legislative adjournment, doubled the next day. John Calfe, a Federalist and longtime clerk for the House of Representatives, was chosen secretary, and President Sullivan was elected convention president by secret ballot. No doubt he received all the votes of those informed beforehand of the Federalist strategy.

Early in the afternoon the rules committee reported. Three key procedural rules helped prepare for possible adjournment. No individual's

Josiah Bartlett (1729–1795), a physician by profession, was chosen temporary chairman of the first (February) session of the ratifying convention. In early 1788 Bartlett was associate justice of the New Hampshire Superior Court, and he became chief justice later in that year. He had been a leader in the Revolutionary movement, represented New Hampshire in Congress (1775–1776, 1778–1779), and signed both the Declaration of Independence and the Articles of Confederation. In the ratifying convention he became an earnest advocate of ratification. According to his biographer, Bartlett's "personal efforts to allay the opposition of the smaller towns during the three months' interval between the two sessions of the convention" contributed significantly to New Hampshire's affirmative vote. Bartlett was chosen by the assembly to be one of New Hampshire's first U.S. senators, but he declined. Elected president (governor) by a wide margin in 1790, he served in that office until 1792. Engraving by Henry B. Hall from Cirker, Dictionary of American Portraits *(1967).*

vote would be recorded except on the question of adoption, which would enable those bound by negative instructions to vote for adjournment without their fellow townsmen ever finding out. Second, a motion to adjourn would take precedence over any other motion; this routine legislative provision could be used to prevent a final vote on adoption. And finally, no vote could be reconsidered without as many members present as made the initial vote. If Federalists got in deep trouble, they could sneak in a delaying vote, then walk out. Calfe wrote simply that the report was "considered, received, and accepted." Antifederalists later regretted the acceptance.

Debate on the Constitution began soon thereafter and continued until the following Thursday. The Constitution was read and discussed section by section. The form of the debates quickly became routinized and predictable. Antifederalists explained why they found the section unacceptable, and Federalist spokesmen defended its logic. Joshua Atherton, a lawyer from the inland town of Amherst, spoke most frequently and effectively for the opponents, most of whom were content, as one observer wrote, "to remain silent . . . until the vote comes." Several Federalists shared responsibility for answering objections. Sullivan (who accepted the presidency only on condition he be allowed to participate in discussions), Langdon, Livermore, Pickering, and two seacoast ministers, Benjamin Thurston and Samuel Langdon, played the most important roles as defenders of the proposed plan of government.

Only four parts of the Constitution stimulated lengthy debate. Antifederalists objected strongly to the two-year term for congressmen and the six-year term for senators—in New Hampshire, annual elections occurred for both. Section 8 of Article I, on congressional powers, compromised state authority far too much, according to several spokesmen. Atherton spoke at length against a federal judiciary. The debate on the last paragraph of Article VI, which stated that "no religious Test shall ever be required as a Qualification to any Office or public Trust under the United States," lasted nearly a full day. Its critics wanted officeholding limited to Protestants.

While the discussions dragged on, leaders of both sides tried to count noses. Everyone agreed that Antifederalists had an initial advantage. Sullivan later estimated the difference at 70 to 30, but the best evidence suggests a much narrower margin, perhaps 50 to 40, with the rest—including some restricted by negative instructions—uncertain as to how they would vote. During dinner parties, convention recesses, and any other occasions when the opportunity arose, Federalists tried to add to their ranks. They also tested the willingness of delegates to vote for adjournment. By February 21, when debate ended on the last article, no one could predict the outcome with confidence. "It is very doubtful," wrote Portsmouth postmaster Jeremiah

Libbey, "how the numbers are. Each party think they have a majority, and yet appear afraid of each other."

A proposal by eleven of the instructed delegates determined the next move. The group approached Langdon and said they would consider supporting adjournment, but they could not vote for the Constitution. Almost immediately Langdon made the motion for which he and others had so carefully prepared. By general agreement the vote was postponed until the following day. That evening a bargain was struck. If the adjournment motion passed, the convention would reconvene in June at Concord, a more convenient site where the June legislative session was scheduled to meet, although in the Antifederalist heartland. Whether Sullivan, Langdon, and other Federalist leaders promised anything in the way of state appointments or other rewards cannot be determined. In any case, the motion passed. According to Pickering, who seems to have been in charge of tabulating delegate sentiment, the margin was only 56 to 51. Convention minutes note simply that after "some general observations were made," the "question was put and it was voted to adjourn to some future day."

Judge's decision on round two: a draw. Crowd reaction was mixed. Federalists breathed a huge and collective sigh of relief. They knew a vote on the Constitution itself would have lost.

Round Three: Ratification

The vote on adjournment gave both sides hard information on which to plan strategy for the next four months. Antifederalists had about 50 solid votes; Federalists about 45. Since the maximum number of delegates who might attend in June was around 110, every vote counted. Momentum lay with Federalists—they already had exhibited more skill in converting the undecided than their opponents—but the outcome was still in doubt. In late March one perceptive seacoast resident reported that there was a "probability" New Hampshire would ratify, "although considerable danger" that it would not.

Antifederalists tried as best they could to prevent further erosion in their ranks. Led by Nathaniel Peabody, who had refused to serve as a delegate but remained active outside the convention, they convinced one town which had not yet chosen a delegate to elect an opponent of the Constitution for the June session. Attempts were made in at least three towns to impose negative instructions on delegates who had voted for adjournment. Antifederalists in Boscawen convened a town meeting which voted to replace the elected delegate, who refused to promise a nay vote, with one who would. All in all, however, Antifederalists were relatively quiet in the interim between sessions. They knew that had a vote been taken at Exeter, the Constitution would have been defeated. Their majority, they hoped, would hold at Concord.

Federalist leaders could not afford merely to bide their time. To no one's surprise, they continued to flood the press with pro-ratification articles. The constitutional arguments differed little from those used before, but press coverage overall involved two fresh ingredients. One was widespread circulation in Cheshire and Grafton counties of the Hartford *Connecticut Courant*, which contained numerous articles explaining why Connecticut had ratified so readily and emphasizing the benefits of union to all Connecticut River Valley inhabitants. Since many of the potential swing votes were from southwestern New Hampshire, circulation of the *Courant* had a large potential payoff.

Personal attacks on leading Antifederalists were the second new ingredient. Atherton provided a particularly inviting subject. At the beginning of the Revolution he had been a loyalist. Now Federalists accused him of "wishing to prevent the adoption of a system only because it will put it out of the power of Britain to subjugate us." Citizens were told that Peabody, still a major force in the legislature, opposed ratification primarily because it might undermine his influence over appointments to political office. Several writers linked Antifederalism to participation in the paper-money riot of September 1786 and to the well-publicized personal financial problems of Peabody and others.

Federalists supplemented their publicity campaign with hard-nosed politicking at the local level. Benjamin Bellows somehow managed to regain the convention seat from Walpole: either a third town election was held or, as town clerk he doctored the records to validate the results of the initial election. Whatever the reasons, Bellows' credentials were accepted at the Concord session. Both Charlestown and Derryfield (now Manchester) repulsed efforts to force unwanted instructions on Federalist delegates. The Derryfield member, who had not gone to Exeter, showed up in Concord. Hopkinton held a special town meeting and released its delegate from binding negative instructions. Federalists in Boscawen drew up a petition which asserted that the recent town vote to change delegates had been illegal. Livermore produced two new supporters from Grafton County, one who had been elected but had not gone to Exeter, the other representing Lincoln and Franconia, which together had fewer than a hundred residents. The latter delegate, Isaac Patterson, lived in Piermont, part of a class of towns which had chosen the county's one Antifederalist. All in all, interim town meetings provided Federalists with six badly needed new votes and prevented at least one potential defection.

Meanwhile, Federalist leaders worked on individual convention members trapped between the Antifederalist sentiment in their towns and their personal willingness to support ratification. Not attending the Concord session was one possible solution to their dilemma. Four of the five delegates who did not attend the Concord session had been at Exeter and probably were among those voting for adjournment. One of them had been given negative instructions, and two others had been counted in the opposition camp by Federalist tabulators. The fifth nonattendee, Nathaniel Ladd from strongly Antifederalist Epping, missed both sessions.

These developments made Sullivan, Langdon, Livermore, and their associates optimistic as decision time approached. External factors added to the optimism. Since the February adjournment, Maryland and South Carolina had ratified, thus bringing the total to eight ratifying states, just one short of the required nine. Virginia's convention would meet on June 2 and the New Hampshire and New York conventions both would meet in mid-June. If New Hampshire moved rapidly, it could, as one writer put it, provide the "Keystone of the Federal Arch." It was an opportunity not to be missed. Federalists gained further encouragement from the legislative session held in Concord early in the month. Langdon, who replaced Sullivan as state president, gave ratification a ringing endorsement in his inaugural, and the legislative response suggested that resistance to the Constitution had weakened. Even more important, the session gave Federalist organizers an opportunity to gather additional information about how delegates were apt to vote. Victory by a thin margin looked probable, but much depended on who showed up, and when.

The convention's first day, Wednesday, June 18, went well for Federalists. Ninety of 113 delegates attended, and of the missing 23, 16 were from Antifederalist towns. Sensing a golden opportunity, Federalist delegates pushed through votes settling the Walpole and Boscawen disputed elections in their favor. Meanwhile, the credentials of all members chosen during the interim—including those of the Piermont resident supposedly representing Lincoln and Franconia—were examined by the rules committee and accepted. Then the meeting adjourned.

Encouraged by these successes, Federalist leaders decided to push rapidly for ratification. Their plan was to forgo the extensive debate and behind-the-scenes politicking which had been so necessary at Exeter. They would—like their counterparts in several other states—support a series of constitutional amendments to correct "deficiencies" pointed out by Antifederalists. The critical vote would come when someone, probably Atherton, moved for conditional ratification, i.e., that New Hampshire ratify only on condition that all the proposed amendments become part of the Constitution.

Federalists would seek postponement of that motion, substitute a motion for unconditional ratification, and then vote to ratify.

Everything seemed in place by Friday, June 20. All but one of the known Federalists had arrived, and four probable Antifederalists were still absent. Early in the day an amendment committee, chaired by Langdon, was appointed. It reported after the noon meal, at which point Atherton made his expected motion. The ensuing debate proved perfunctory, so Livermore, seconded by several delegates, tested sentiment by proposing postponement. He also announced that if postponement passed, he would move unconditional ratification. Postponement of Atherton's motion was voted, and by common agreement the meeting dispersed until the following morning.

Saturday's events confirmed what by now everyone suspected. Atherton tried unsuccessfully to obtain an adjournment. As the vote on the main motion neared, at least one delegate torn between negative instructions and personal commitment left the building. He and three others—all in similar

The North Meeting house in Concord was the site of the decisive June session of the New Hampshire ratifying convention. Here the framers' mandate of ratification by nine states (Article VII) was achieved when the Granite State approved the Constitution on June 21, 1788, by a margin of 57 to 47. Engraving (ca. 1860) courtesy of the New Hampshire Historical Society.

circumstances—were recorded as in attendance but not voting. The final tabulation was 57 yeas and 47 nays. The ten-vote majority surprised even the most optimistic Federalist leaders. Secretary Calfe recorded the precise time as 1:00 p.m. in case Virginia ratified the same day and made claim to having been the ninth.

Round three required no judge's decision.

The Statewide Division over the Constitution

In the last century historians have exerted a good deal of energy analyzing votes in the various ratification conventions. Several generalizations can be made about New Hampshire. To begin with, the mutually reinforcing factors of geography and past constitutional experience correlate neatly with divisions on the proposed plan of government. Federalism was concentrated in the seacoast area and the upper Connecticut River Valley, where inhabitants had a long history of attempted constitutional reform. Similarly, Antifederalism centered in regions whose inhabitants had resisted such reform. Secondly, Federalism was strongest among the upper classes. Of those listed in convention records as judges, esquires (justices of the peace), generals, doctors, or reverends, thirty-three voted yea and only fourteen nay; misters, captains, and lieutenants, on the other hand, voted sixteen for and twenty-seven against ratification. Third, there was a clear Federalist bias among state citizens with "Continental" experience: six former delegates to Congress served as convention delegates, and all worked hard for ratification. Finally, the eventual vote masked the closeness of the struggle. Only the calculated and imaginative political maneuvering of men like Sullivan, Langdon, and Livermore made possible New Hampshire's claim to the label "Keystone of the Federal Arch."

Whatever historians make of the ratification conflict, adoption gained quick acceptance in New Hampshire. Portsmouth celebrated with a parade, fireworks, and free liquor. Ratification by Virginia four days after New Hampshire, and by New York in late July, increased jubilation among citizens already optimistic about the newly established national government. Antifederalists swallowed their disappointment and advised acquiescence. Even Atherton gave up after New York's approval. "The language" among New Hampshire opponents, he lamented to a friend, has become "It is adopted, let us try it." Few, in subsequent years, regretted the attempt.

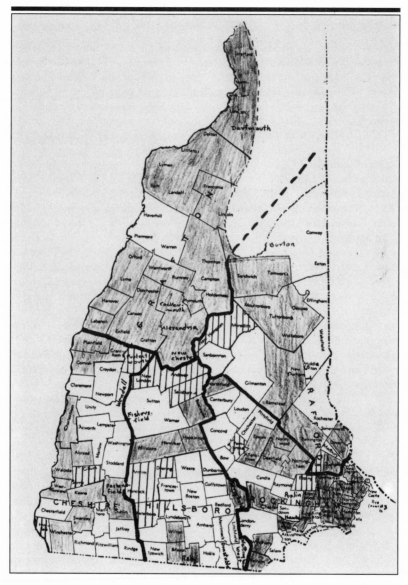

This map depicts the geography of delegate voting in the New Hampshire ratifying convention. Delegates from shaded areas voted Federalist, those from unshaded areas Antifederalist. The lined areas cover towns where no delegates were elected. Town and county lines are roughly equivalent to those existing in 1788, except that boundaries among "classed" towns have been eliminated. Town names are those in common use in 1788. Courtesy of Jere Daniell.

New Hampshire: Essay on Sources

The most comprehensive treatment of the Revolutionary era is Jere Daniell, *Experiment in Republicanism: New Hampshire Politics and the American Revolution, 1741–1794* (Cambridge, Mass., 1970). Useful older studies include Richard F. Upton, *Revolutionary New Hampshire* (Hanover, 1936); the relevant parts of Jeremy Belknap's *History of New Hampshire*, vols. 2 and 3 (Boston, 1791, 1792; republished New York, 1970); and Walter F. Dodd, "The Constitutional History of New Hampshire, 1775–1792," *Proceedings of the Bar Association of the State of New Hampshire*, new series, 2 (1904–8), 379–400.

Numerous historians have written previously about New Hampshire's ratification of the federal Constitution. The most detailed discussions appear in two unpublished studies, Nathaniel J. Eiseman, "The Ratification of the Federal Constitution by the State of New Hampshire" (master's thesis, Columbia University, 1937) and Nancy B. Oliver, "Keystone of the Federal Arch: New Hampshire's Ratification of the United States Constitution" (doctoral dissertation, University of California at Santa Barbara, 1972). Shorter narratives are provided in Daniell, *Experiment*; Forrest McDonald, *We the People: Economic Origins of the Constitution* (Chicago, 1958); Lynn Turner, *The Ninth State: New Hampshire's Formative Years* (Chapel Hill, 1983); and Joseph B. Walker, *Birth of the Federal Constitution: A History of the New Hampshire Convention . . .* (Boston, 1888). Walker's centennial piece was republished after the sesquicentennial along with other material in Francis H. Buffum, ed., *New Hampshire and the Federal Constitution* (Concord, 1940). Laurence G. Straus, "Reaction of Supporters of the Constitution to the Adjournment of the New Hampshire Ratification Convention—1788," *Historical New Hampshire*, 23 (Autumn 1968), 37–50, discusses that subject systematically. See also Richard G. Kalkhoff, "Toasting the Constitution: New Hampshire's Celebrations of 1788," *Historical New Hampshire*, 43 (Summer 1988).

Full biographies exist for only two convention members: Laurence S. Mayo, *John Langdon of New Hampshire* (Concord, 1937) and Charles P. Whittemore, *A General of the Revolution: John Sullivan of New Hampshire* (New York, 1961). Shorter biographical sketches of the delegates include Charles R. Corning, *Samuel Livermore* (Concord, 1888); Frank C. Mevers, *Guide to the Microfilm Edition of the Papers of Josiah Bartlett, 1729–1795* (Concord, 1976); a series of seventeen notes in Nathaniel Bouton, ed., *Provincial and State Papers: Miscellaneous Documents and Records Relating to New Hampshire*, vol. 10 (Concord, 1877), 8–11; and articles on delegates from towns in Grafton County which appeared in *The Granite Monthly*, 11 (1888), 310–312, 367–368, and 12 (1889), 36–38, 59–61, 310, 340–341. The *Dictionary of American Biography* has entries on seven delegates (Josiah Bartlett, John Taylor Gilman, John and Samuel Langdon, Samuel Livermore, John Pickering, and John Sullivan) and one on Nicholas Gilman, who represented the state in the Philadelphia Convention. Both Eiseman ("Ratification") and Oliver ("Keystone") have combed the numerous histories of New Hampshire towns for biographical material on convention delegates.

Published primary material on the ratification process itself is scarce. The convention attendance records and minutes appear in Bouton, ed., *Provincial and State Papers*, vol. 10, pp. 2–7, 12–22. Records for the relevant legislative sessions are in vol. 11 (Concord, 1892) of the same series. My present interpretation of the ratification process in New Hampshire is based as much on miscellaneous manuscript materials encountered in a quarter century of research on early state history as on published primary material.

Virginia

The Cement of the Union

ALAN V. BRICELAND
Associate Professor of History
Virginia Commonwealth University

IRGINIA, founded in 1607 at Jamestown, was the oldest of the thirteen original colonies. From the outset it was also the most heavily settled, with a population that doubled every twenty-five years. By 1790 Virginia's inhabitants (including the District of Kentucky) numbered 821,287, about 21 percent of the national total and almost 350,000 more than second-ranked Massachusetts. Although Virginia became a royal colony in 1624, since 1619 it boasted a lower legislative chamber—the House of Burgesses—elected by the colonists themselves, or, more precisely, by those who met the stringent suffrage requirements.

Along with influential Massachusetts and contrary Rhode Island, the Old Dominion (as Virginia was nicknamed for its loyalty to the Stuarts in the English Civil Wars of the seventeenth century) played a leadership role in the events preceding the War for Independence. In 1769 Virginia initiated a boycott of British goods to protest the controversial Townshend Acts. In 1773 it became the first colony to establish an intercolonial committee of correspondence in response to the British investigation under way in Rhode Island following the burning there of the royal revenue sloop *Gaspee*. When the First Continental Congress assembled in September 1774, it chose Virginia's Peyton Randolph as its president.

The Old Dominion boldly instructed its delegates to move for independence at the Second Continental Congress in 1776, and the congressional resolution "that these united colonies are, and of right ought to be, free and independent states" was introduced by one Virginian, Richard Henry Lee, and justified by another, Thomas Jefferson, in the Declaration of Independence. During the war to vindicate that declaration, Virginia's George Washington served as commander in chief of the Continental army; and on Virginia soil, at Yorktown on October 19, 1781, British general Charles Cornwallis surrendered to Washington, effectively ending the military conflict.

The Road to Philadelphia

Peace brought its problems too, especially in the area of interstate relations, as thirteen "squabbling sovereignties" set about the difficult task of achieving political and economic stability. The common waterways of Virginia and neighboring Maryland became one of the more serious of many points of confrontation that threatened the internal harmony of the new nation.

In order to reach world markets, Maryland tobacco and grain had to pass through a section of the Chesapeake Bay controlled by Virginia. Commerce destined for the citizens of northern Virginia and the Shenandoah Valley had to navigate the Maryland-controlled Potomac River. During the depression years following the Revolutionary War, Maryland raised taxes on Virginia commerce that used the Potomac, while Virginia threatened to tax Maryland-bound ships that entered the capes of the Chesapeake. Between 1784 and 1786 the geography of the Chesapeake, coupled with the boundary provisions of the two states' colonial charters, would produce a train of events destined to alter the course of American history.

In 1784 James Madison of Montpelier in Orange County was chairman of the Virginia Assembly's Committee on Commerce. Madison convinced the Assembly to invite Maryland to confer on joint use of the Chesapeake and the Potomac. Although Maryland authorities agreed to meet at Alexandria, Virginia, in March 1785, Governor Patrick Henry of Virginia forgot to notify his own commissioners of Maryland's acceptance. Thus, when Samuel Chase and the Maryland delegation arrived in Alexandria, no Virginia commissioners were present to greet them.

Learning of the Marylanders' plight, George Washington attempted to rectify Virginia's apparent lack of courtesy by inviting the Maryland delegates to enjoy the hospitality of his Mount Vernon home. Once the hastily assembled Virginia delegation gathered, what would later become known as the Mount Vernon Conference proceeded expeditiously. Since Maryland and Virginia each controlled interests vital to the other, accord was easily reached on Potomac and Chesapeake issues. Virginia commis-

sioners were so pleased with the conference that they concluded by recommending that the two states hold annual conferences on common commercial problems. Responding to this recommendation, in December 1785
the Maryland legislature proposed that both Pennsylvania and Delaware be
invited to the next meeting.

James Madison, who had long favored uniform commercial regulation encompassing all thirteen states, saw Maryland's proposal to enlarge the
conference as an opportunity to hold a national convention. In January 1786
he drafted a resolution inviting attendance by all the states. However, because
many in the Virginia Assembly were suspicious of Madison's national outlook, John Tyler agreed to introduce the resolution. The Tyler Resolution,
presented on January 21, the last day of the 1785–86 session, called for a
meeting of state representatives empowered "to examine the relative situ-

*George Washington (1732–
1799) served as president of
the Philadelphia Conven-
tion and, more than any
other delegate, lent that
body legitimacy and re-
spectability. Washington
was a great leader whose
ability to command support
derived more from his im-
posing presence, forceful
personality, and austere de-
meanor than from the
power of his intellect or his
skill at oratory. In his major occupations, this
wealthy member of Virginia's landed gentry was a surveyor, a planter, and a soldier. His courageous military service in the French and Indian War, together
with his social position, prompted the Continental Congress to appoint him commander in chief of American forces during the Revolution. His tenacity and in-
spirational leadership gained him victory and the enduring affection of his coun-
trymen. After ratification, Washington became the unanimous choice of the
Electoral College to be the nation's first president. After serving a second term,
also won by unanimous vote, the general retired to Mount Vernon, where he died
less than three years following his departure from office. Portrait by Charles Willson Peale, courtesy of the Pennsylvania Academy of the Fine Arts.*

ations and trade of the United States" and "to consider how far a uniform system in their commercial regulations may be necessary to their common interest and their permanent harmony." Since the proposed meeting was an outgrowth of the Mount Vernon agreements, Virginia suggested that the commercial convention should meet in Annapolis, Maryland. Not only was Annapolis centrally located, but the city was a neutral site in a world of intense commercial rivalries.

With less than eight months between the call and the meeting, only nine states designated delegates, and half of those failed to reach Annapolis

James Madison (1751–1836) was the most influential figure at the Philadelphia Convention. He contrasted markedly with Washington in height (five feet four inches to six feet three inches), temperament (contemplative vs. practical), and leadership style (persuasion rather than prestige), but not in nationalist sentiment. Madison, a Princeton-educated scholar, was constructive, patient, companionable, and learned. His self-restraint and his ability to carry motions without making enemies were external marks of a mildness not appreciated by those who preferred fiery politicians and thunderous oratory. Madison was a delegate to the Annapolis Convention and a leader in the move to call the Philadelphia Convention. He drafted the Virginia Plan, the blueprint for the Constitution; kept detailed notes of the convention debates; acted as a leader in those debates; spearheaded Virginia's move for ratification; coauthored The Federalist, *explaining the principles of the Constitution; and emerged in the First Congress as the leading sponsor of the Bill of Rights. After the ordeal of ratifying the Constitution, Madison served in Congress from 1789 to 1797 and became a principal founder of the Democratic-Republican party, secretary of state (1801–1809), and the nation's fourth president (1809–1817), compiling a record that has prompted historians to call him America's ablest champion of constitutional republicanism. Portrait by Charles Willson Peale, courtesy of the Thomas Gilcrease Institute, Tulsa, Oklahoma.*

within a week of the appointed time. The twelve delegates who arrived in the Maryland capital by early September 1786 represented New York, New Jersey, Delaware, Pennsylvania, and Virginia. After a week of waiting for late arrivals, the delegates issued a report on September 14 concluding that "it will be inexpedient for this Convention, in which so few states are represented, to proceed to the business committed to them." Madison, however, was not about to accept failure. He and Alexander Hamilton of New York convinced the delegates to call for another convention to meet in Philadelphia in May of 1787. Furthermore, it was proposed that at this convention state-appointed delegates should be empowered to consider and act not only upon commercial issues but upon any and all problems facing the nation as it struggled under its first constitution, the Articles of Confederation.

Hamilton prepared a draft of an address to the states. An ardent nationalist, he stressed the current dire condition of the Confederation and proposed a strengthening of the powers of the national government. Edmund Randolph, Virginia's popular attorney general, objected that Hamilton's strident nationalism would frighten many states into boycotting the Philadelphia Convention, and among them would be Virginia. Madison, who saw the wisdom in not unduly alarming the defenders of state sovereignty, prevailed on Hamilton to moderate his indictment of the Articles and to leave to the individual imagination what the convention might propose as remedies.

The call of the Annapolis Convention, unanimously adopted on September 14, 1786, simply declared "that there are important defects in the system of the Federal Government," defects sufficient "to merit a deliberate and candid discussion." The thirteen states were therefore requested to appoint delegates empowered "to devise such further provisions as shall appear to them necessary to render the constitution of the Federal Government adequate to the exigencies of the Union."

When the Confederation Congress delayed the Annapolis call in committee, Madison rushed to Richmond to prod the Virginia Assembly into setting an example for the other states. Under Madison's direction the Assembly proclaimed on October 16 "that the Crisis is arrived at which the good People of America are to decide the solemn Question whether they will by wise and magnanimous Efforts reap the just fruits of ... Independence." Seven Virginians were appointed to join with the delegations from other states "in devising and discussing all such Alterations ... as may be necessary to render the Federal Constitution adequate to the Exigencies of the Union." The Virginia delegation was composed of George Washington, James Madison, Edmund Randolph, George Mason, George Wythe, John Blair, and—because Patrick Henry, Thomas Nelson, and Richard Henry Lee refused to serve—James McClurg. Initially, Washington, like Henry, declined the appointment, but Madison and others pleaded and cajoled until the general yielded.

Several of the Virginia delegation played critical roles during the Philadelphia Convention. Edmund Randolph, now governor of the state, introduced a proposal for an overthrow of the Confederation and the establishment of a radically different Madison had authored the plan, but the proposal would become known to many as the Randolph or Virginia Plan. George Washington brought prestige to the proceedings and insured that

Edmund Randolph (1753–1813) came from a distinguished Virginia family that produced three king's attorneys (attorneys general for the Crown). His father, who held that high legal post, was a loyalist who departed for England at the outbreak of the Revolution. Edmund espoused the patriot cause and became the first attorney general of the new state of Virginia (1776–1786) at the age of twenty-three. He served in Congress in 1779 and from 1781 to 1782, and he was a delegate to the Annapolis Convention in 1786. From 1786 to 1788 Randolph was governor, and in that position he led the Virginia delegation at Philadelphia, where he introduced Madison's plan on behalf of Virginia and served on the important Committee of Detail. In company with George Mason, he stayed until the convention's adjournment but refused to sign the finished Constitution, since he thought the document was "insufficiently republican" and regarded "a unity in the Executive magistry" (a single president) as a "fœtus of monarchy." In the state convention, however, he voted for ratification, asserting that "the accession of eight states reduced our deliberations to the single question of Union or no Union." Washington appointed Randolph the nation's first attorney general (1789–1794). Randolph's last major office was that of secretary of state, a position he filled for over twenty months during the bitter controversy over the Jay Treaty (1794–1795). Portrait by F. J. Fisher, courtesy of the Virginia State Library.

the convention's work would receive a respectful hearing from the American people. Madison's leadership earned him the deserved reputation as "Father of the Constitution."

Fifty-five of the most prominent men in America had participated in the convention. These men, representatives of twelve of the thirteen newly independent American states, had created through reason, argument, and compromise a proposed plan of government, a document styled the "Constitution of Government for the United States of America." Signed by thirty-nine of them (though not by Randolph or Mason), this plan was then sub-

Patrick Henry (1736–1799), a noted Revolutionary leader and outspoken foe of British colonial policy, was born on the Virginia frontier to a family of moderate wealth and influence. After an unsuccessful start as a storekeeper, Henry turned to law as a profession. Here his intensity, forcefulness, and great oratorical skills won him immediate success. In 1765 he entered the House of Burgesses, where, as a leader of backcountry Virginia, he contended against both the Crown's policies and the traditional leadership of the eastern, or Tidewater, politicians. After serving in Congress in 1774 and 1775, Henry became the state's first governor in 1776 and was twice reelected, serving until succeeded by Jefferson in 1779. Henry again became governor in 1784 and held that position until 1786. He was chosen as a delegate to the Federal Convention but firmly declined to participate. In the ratifying convention of 1788, Henry led the opposition to the Constitution because it created a "consolidated government" under which "our rights and privileges are endangered and the sovereignty of the States will be relinquished." In a complex turn of events, Henry (an avowed foe of Jefferson and Madison) became a member of the Federalist party in the 1790s. In 1795 Washington offered him the position of secretary of state and in 1796 that of chief justice, but the ailing revolutionary declined. Portrait by Thomas Sully, courtesy of Colonial Williamsburg.

mitted to the states. The framers asked each state to authorize a convention of its citizens in order to approve or reject their proposed concept of nationhood.

Virginians Divide over the Constitution

It was clear from the beginning that the ratification contest in Virginia was going to be close and hard fought. Powerful men stood arrayed on both sides. George Washington and James Madison—who had no qualms

George Mason (1725–1792), one of the convention's elder statesmen and one of its foremost advocates of individual liberty, was a highly respected lawyer and the wealthy proprietor of Gunston Hall, a large plantation on the Potomac close to Mount Vernon. Though he disliked public office and seldom sought it, Mason played a major role in Virginia politics as adviser and legal counsel to Washington, Jefferson, Madison, and other prominent leaders. In 1776, as a member of the Virginia constitutional convention, Mason became the principal draftsman of Virginia's new basic law and the framer of the state's Declaration of Rights, the latter of which was drawn upon by Jefferson for the Declaration of Independence and widely copied in the other colonies; eventually it became the basis for the federal Bill of Rights. Like most members of the Virginia gentry, Mason was a prominent Anglican, but he supported disestablishment. Though he was a slaveholder, he strongly opposed the slave trade and advocated compensated emancipation. Despite his prominent role in the Philadelphia Convention, Mason refused to sign or support the Constitution, primarily because it protected the foreign slave trade and lacked a bill of rights. Portrait courtesy of the Virginia State Library.

about the Constitution—knew that success for the Federalist, or Constitution, cause depended on the votes of men such as Edmund Pendleton, who entertained doubts. A strategy was needed to unify all who were basically sympathetic to the Constitution. Washington and Madison determined whenever possible to shift the emphasis of the contest from the merits of the Constitution to the issue of union or disunion. Washington firmly believed that the only real choice lay between "The Constitution or disunion."

Patrick Henry, who declined to attend the Philadelphia Convention because he "smelled a rat," led the largest group of Virginia Antifederalists, the "Virginia First" faction. The Henryites could countenance no subordination of Virginia's interests to national interest. George Mason, who attended the convention but refused to sign its handiwork, was the best known of the unregenerate radical faction of Antifederalists. Henry's primary loyalty was to Virginia, while Mason's was to the philosophical principles of revolutionary, egalitarian radicalism. Mason considered the proposed government not so much a threat to Virginia as to individual liberty. The national government would be not only too distant for the people to control but also too powerful to be restrained. Even before the Philadelphia Convention had adjourned, he had penned and begun to circulate his "Objections." "There is no declaration of rights," trumpeted the opening words. The author of the Virginia Declaration of Rights expected readers to comprehend immediately the profound and terrible significance of this omission.

Mason went on to identify other heresies in the Constitution. "In the House of Representatives there is not the substance, but the shadow only of representation." Senators, elected directly by state legislatures, would not be "the representatives of the people, or amenable to them." They would, however, be in a position "to accomplish what usurpations they please, upon the rights and liberties of the people." The federal judiciary would "absorb and destroy the judiciaries of the several states . . . enabling the rich to oppress and ruin the poor." The president would "be directed by minions and favorites." He and his executive officers would fall into "dangerous or oppressive measures." If challenged, they would "shelter themselves, and prevent an inquiry into their own misconduct in office." If the wrongdoers were brought to trial, the president would use his pardoning power to "screen from punishment those whom he had secretly instigated to commit the crime."

Between the Antifederalists and Federalists, Governor Edmund Randolph occupied the middle ground. He insisted that he was a friend to the Constitution (which he also refused to sign), but he argued that the way to prevent the document's outright rejection was to advocate prior amendments, particularly a bill of rights.

The Debate in Virginia

The period from the fall of 1787 to March 1788, when the elections for convention delegates were held, was essentially a drawn-out election campaign. Leading partisans wooed the support of locally prominent men, for it was from their ranks that the delegates would be chosen. Because of Virginia's great distances and poor roads, the ratification contest can best be understood by considering it not as a statewide contest but as many local contests. There were no political parties, no party organizations, and no mass media.

Each of Virginia's eighty-four counties would elect two delegates. The boroughs of Norfolk and Williamsburg each would elect one delegate. The result would be a constitutional convention of 170 members.

Several prominent Virginians did not seek election. Washington declined nomination in a belief that his moral influence, not his involvement as an active partisan, would do the Federalist cause the most good. Richard Henry Lee communicated his ideas through George Mason. Thomas Jefferson was abroad as minister to France.

Patrick Henry's election was a foregone conclusion. So popular was he in Prince Edward County that he could hardly have prevented it had he tried. Mason's residency in Fairfax, a Federalist stronghold, posed a temporary problem. A candidate was not, however, required to live in a county in order to be chosen to represent it. Citizens of nearby Stafford County invited Mason to run there. He did so and was elected easily.

Madison and Randolph faced stiff tests. Madison did not intend to stand for election, but friends informed him that the election of a Federalist from Orange County depended on his candidacy. Madison reached Orange "to find the County filled with the most absurd and groundless prejudices against the federal Constitution." He felt compelled for the first time in his political career to mount the rostrum and harangue the election-day crowd. This election then produced a majority of nearly 4 to 1 in the Federalists' favor.

By mid-April the voting patterns were broadly evident. Tidewater, Northern Neck, the Shenandoah Valley, and the Alleghenies were overwhelmingly Federalist. Southside, the Southwest, and Kentucky were just as strongly Antifederalist. The Piedmont north of the James was something of a checkerboard.

In the wake of the election results, many observers became convinced that Virginia held the key to the whole ratification question. After six consecutive Federalist victories—Delaware, Pennsylvania, New Jersey, Georgia, Connecticut, and Massachusetts—the string had been broken when the New Hampshire convention had met in February and adjourned without decision until mid-June. Even if Maryland and South Carolina ratified in the interim, as it appeared they would do, there could be only eight of the needed nine ratifications by the time the Virginia convention met in June. Moreover, all of the remaining states—Virginia, New Hampshire, Rhode Island, New York, and North Carolina—were Antifederalism's strongest bastions.

A small bombshell of sorts exploded in mid-May at the Maryland convention. Although Thomas Jefferson was abroad, his support for tactics to force the inclusion of a bill of rights in the Constitution was made known through the unauthorized publication of a private letter. The event proved to be an embarrassment to Virginia Federalists, since Jefferson had implied that Virginia should withhold ratification in support of a bill of rights.

Thus by late May the talk in Virginia centered on the subject of amendments to the Constitution, although various groups in the ratification struggle viewed the prospect of amendments in different ways. The Henry faction planned to use prior amendments to gut the Constitution. The Mason-Lee faction sought them to protect individual rights, along the lines suggested by Jefferson. The Randolph faction sought them to garner enough votes to establish the Union. Believing a bill of rights unnecessary, the Madison-Washington faction thought that prior amendments would lead to disunion rather than union.

The Virginia Convention: The Opening

On an early June day in 1788, 170 specially elected delegates crowded into the Academy building on Shockoe Hill in the city of Richmond. They had journeyed from as far as the Ohio and Mississippi River valleys. In 1788 Virginia, the largest of the states, encompassed what is now West Virginia and Kentucky.

Patrick Henry was in his element here. In the arts of emotional appeal, he had no equal. He had the singular ability to bring about "a perfect stillness throughout the House and in the galleries." During the convention he would speak long and often. His speeches alone constitute a fourth of all the deliberations. At one point a frustrated Governor Randolph chided the delegates for tolerating Henry's prolonged, rambling orations. "If we go on in this irregular manner," he protested, ". . . Instead of three or six weeks, it will take us six months to decide this question."

The responsibility for rebutting Henry generally fell to Madison and Governor Randolph. Madison's style contrasted strikingly with that of the flamboyant Henry. His manner was quiet. Sometimes he was barely audible. He relied on a coldly logical presentation. After Henry's dramatic orations on the threat which this or that section of the Constitution posed to the liberties of the American people, Madison would rise and quietly expose the flaws in Henry's reasoning, the inappropriate nature of his historical examples, and the distortions inherent in his interpretation of the language of the document.

Only a few individuals actively took the Federalist side in the proceedings. As president of the convention, the revered old war-horse Edmund Pendleton was able to keep the parliamentary reins in Federalist hands. In the sessions when the convention was assembled as a committee of the whole, he spoke on several critical occasions. George Wythe, the famous Williamsburg law professor and tutor of Jefferson and Marshall, chaired the body when it convened to debate as a committee of the whole. He controlled the order of speaking and ensured that the proper Federalist was recognized to rebut each Antifederalist assault. But "*Madison* took *the principal share in the debate* for it," James Monroe observed. "He was," Monroe added, "somewhat assisted by [James] Innes, H. Lee, [John] Marshall, [Francis] Corbin, and G. Nicholas." Although the convention numbered 170 members, in practice the debate was carried on between half a dozen men on each side. One hundred forty-nine delegates said nothing before the body during the entire four weeks.

Madison had been anticipating Henry's strategy well in advance of the convention. "The preliminary question will be whether previous alterations shall be insisted on or not," he had predicted. "Should this be carried in the affirmative, either a conditional ratification, or a proposal for a new convention will ensue. In either event, I think the Constitution, and the Union will be both endangered," because the states that had already ratified would not graciously submit to "alterations prescribed by Virginia." The working out of differences would necessitate a second convention. The polarization preceding such a convention would extinguish every hope for a spirit of accommodation. Madison and the Federalist floor leaders therefore had to head off any movement for a conditional ratification.

One overriding fact colored the development of convention strategies on both sides—the knowledge that Federalists, with eighty-six votes, had a slim majority in delegate count. If the majority held, it meant victory. Antifederalists counted eighty firm adherents. Half a dozen votes won and the day would be theirs, but they had to win those crucial votes.

Henry's tactic was to excite and alarm, to expose the chains of tyranny lurking in every clause of the Constitution, and to fasten these imagined chains around every possible interest group. In speech after speech he played upon the fears and private interests of the delegates. "The trial by jury is gone," he thundered at the small debtor farmers. "British debtors will be ruined by being dragged to the federal courts," he told the larger planters. "The majority of congress is to the north, and the slaves are to the south," he warned the slaveholders. He threatened the men of the Shenandoah Valley with the loss of their lands and the men of the west with the loss of their navigation. He threatened everyone with the loss of individual liberty. Time and again he returned to the theme of northern dominance of the new government, with the consequent loss of southern rights.

Antifederal strategists believed the weakest link in the Federalist chain to be "the four Counties which lie on the Ohio between the Pennsylvania line and Big Sandy Creek." These were the counties of Greenbrier, Ohio, Harrison, and Montgomery, the first three of which were located in present-day West Virginia. How could they be turned against the Constitution? Over and over in the course of the convention, Henry reminded the delegates of the willingness of the northern commercial states to relinquish to Spain navigation rights on the Mississippi in return for commercial advantage for themselves.

Federalist leaders had their own problems. They had to avoid any action that could be construed as unfair. The slightest hint of manipulation could drive men with a strong sense of fair play into opposition and would strengthen the resolve of the Antifederalists to fight to the last ditch. "I have thought it prudent," Madison would explain, "to withhold, by a studied fairness in every step on the side of the Constitution, every pretext for rash experiments."

Knowing that they did not have the votes, Mason and Henry needed time—time for Mason's logic and Henry's passion to work upon those delegates who were only weakly committed to the Constitution. The Antifederalist convention strategy was one of delay and attrition. On June 3, immediately after convention preliminaries had been concluded, Mason sought recognition. He declared that "the fullest and clearest investigation" into the Constitution was "indispensibly necessary." He therefore moved that the convention should systematically examine and separately debate each and every section of the Constitution. To his great surprise, Madison rose immediately to support the proposal. The procedure was ideal for Madison's purpose of focusing the convention on the Constitution rather than on amendments. The Federalists' margin was too thin for them to risk an immediate vote. Discussion clause by clause would take time; but it was, from the Federalists' standpoint, less dangerous than an open-ended discussion dominated by Henry. Federalist facts, knowledge, and logic could be focused more effectively on specific points in the Constitution than on its broad tendencies.

To make absolutely certain that the debate would last several weeks, Mason moved that no vote for ratification should be taken "until the said Constitution shall have been discussed clause by clause, through all its parts." Again Federalists acquiesced, and the rule passed unanimously. The stage was set. Antifederalists would have the time they needed, but the fight was to be on grounds advantageous to Federalists.

Nonetheless, a clause-by-clause discussion of the Constitution did present a risk to the document's supporters. Madison feared that Antifederalists planned deliberately to "procrastinate the debates" until a weariness of debating, the heat of Richmond, and the convening of the state legislature at the end of June would provide an excuse for the members to "yield to a postponement of the final decision to a future day." Over sixty of the convention delegates were also members of the General Assembly, which was scheduled to meet on June 23. Two weeks into the convention Madison informed New York Federalist Alexander Hamilton that "we have conjectured for some days that the policy is to spin out the Session in order to receive overtures from your Convention; or if that cannot be, to weary the members into an adjournment without taking any decision."

The Virginia Convention: The Debate

Wednesday, June 3, was the first day for debating the Constitution and for discussing the proposed plan of government clause by clause in the committee of the whole. Before the clerk could read the first section, however, Henry sought and gained recognition. In disregard of the vote of the previous day, Henry intended single-handedly to shift the debate onto grounds favorable to his own position. He called for the reading of the "act of [the Virginia] Assembly appointing deputies to meet at Philadelphia to revise the Articles of Confederation—and other public papers relative thereto." Everyone now realized that Henry was laying the groundwork from which to challenge the legality of the proposal before the convention. He obviously was going to argue that the Philadelphia Convention had exceeded its authority by proposing a new government when it should have proposed only amendments to the Articles of Confederation. If he were successful, serious doubts might be raised, and a vote to reject might bring the proceedings to a quick end.

There was a stirring, and Pendleton was helped to stand with the aid of crutches to speak on whether the documents should be read. Whether the federal convention exceeded its powers "ought not to influence our deliberations," he declared. "Although those gentlemen were only directed to consider the defects of the old system, and not devise a new one," he continued, "if they found it so thoroughly defective as not to admit a revising, and submitted a new system to our consideration which the people have deputed us to investigate, [then] I cannot find any degree of propriety in reading those papers." The people were the key. The people were sovereign.

Whether the Philadelphia Convention exceeded its instructions was of no consequence. One fact overrode all questions of legality: "The people have sent us hither to determine whether this government be a proper one or not." That, Pendleton declared, was the authority on which the convention and the Constitution, if ratified, would rest.

It is ironic that Henry, who had been thrust into prominence as the voice of the sovereign people, could not accept the fact that the people might choose to speak through some voice other than his own. Henry must have sensed that the power of Pendleton's logic had crushed any doubts he had raised, for he thereupon withdrew the request and took his seat. The clerk read the preamble of the Constitution and a part of Article I. George Nicholas of Albemarle County had agreed to speak in support of this section. His prepared speech lasted two hours. Such lengthy speeches would be the norm during the next twenty-one days.

After Nicholas concluded, Henry again sought recognition, but his objections were not addressed to the single section before the body. He had prepared himself to challenge the authority of the federal convention, and he was going to do so. "Who authorized them to speak the language of, *We, the people* instead of *We, the states?*" Henry demanded. This was no confederation with which the people were comfortable. "If the states be not the agents of this compact, it must be one great, consolidated, national government, of the people of all the states," he reasoned. *Consolidated*—that was the scare word. It conveyed the impression that Virginia's affairs were being decided by outsiders. Time and again over the next three weeks, Federalists would have to parry this form of attack by explaining that they supported a federal system of divided or dual sovereignty, and not a consolidated or unitary system of national sovereignty.

Edmund Randolph now rose to speak. Randolph was the one man of real influence still able to join either side. His first speech was eagerly awaited. Randolph acknowledged that ever since Philadelphia he had believed in the necessity of amendments. The only question was whether they would best be adopted previous or subsequent to ratification. "The postponement of this Convention to so late a day has extinguished the probability of the former without inevitable ruin to the proposed Union," he declared. Since he believed the union to be "the anchor of our political salvation," his position now was that the Constitution must be ratified unamended. Those who, like himself, wished amendments must trust to subsequent alterations to improve the system.

After Randolph had spoken, Mason rose to refute the assertion that it was too late to amend the Constitution. It was not too late, nor would it ever be too late. "Its amendment is with me a *sine qua non* of its adoption."

His words could not, however, lessen the devastating blow of Randolph's defection.

On the following day Henry was back on his feet. How could one confine himself to Article I when the people's liberties were endangered by the whole document? History taught all too well the relationship between government and liberty. "I will submit to your recollection," he shouted, "whether liberty has been destroyed most often by the licentiousness of the people, or by the tyranny of rulers."

Henry ranged far and wide, introducing the themes upon which he would play in the weeks to come. He attacked the executive: "If your American chief be a man of ambition and abilities, how easy is it for him to render himself absolute! The army is in his hands." He attacked the House of Representatives: "Virginia is as large as England. Our proportion of representatives [in the national House] is but ten men. In England they have five hundred and fifty-eight." He attacked the Senate: "The Senate, by making treaties, may destroy your liberty and laws." He attacked the national government's authority over the military: "A standing army we shall have, also, to execute the execrable commands of tyranny." He attacked the ability of the federal government to control the state militias: "My great objection to this government is, that it does not leave us the means of defending our rights, or of waging war against tyrants." What resistance could be made? "You will find all the strength of this country in the hands of your enemies; their garrisons will naturally be the strongest places in the country." He attacked the tone of the document: "It has an awful squinting, it squints toward monarchy. . . . There is to be a great and mighty President, with very extensive powers—the powers of a King. He is to be supported in extravagant magnificence; so that the whole of our property may be taken by this American government, by laying what taxes they please, and suspending our laws at their pleasure."

Henry went on for three hours. "I have not said the one hundred thousandth part of what I have on my mind," he commented when he had concluded his speech. In the midst of his voluminous argument, he had uttered in a single simple sentence what to him was the most telling objection of all. "This government," he had declared, "is not a Virginia, but an American government." Henry had succeeded, at least temporarily, in moving the debate onto his turf.

Madison responded by saying that the principal concern expressed by the opposition was "whether it be a federal or consolidated government." If not a confederation, according to the opposition's reasoning, it must be of the feared consolidated type. Madison argued, however, that the proposed government was "unprecedented." It was a new experiment. "In some respects it is a government of a federal nature; in others, it is of a consolidated nature." He tried to explain. "If Virginia was separated from all the states," he said, "her power and authority would extend to all cases: in like manner were all powers vested in the general government, it would be a consolidated government; but the powers of the federal government are enumerated; it can only operate in certain cases, it has legislative powers on defined and limited objects, beyond which it cannot extend its jurisdiction." There was, Madison continued, a second principal difference between the existing Confederation and the proposed government. It lay in the basis of their authority: "The existing system has been derived from the dependent derivative authority of the legislatures of the states; whereas this [Constitution] is derived from the superior power of the people."

Not since the first speech by George Nicholas had anyone spoken directly to Article I. For four days Henry had successfully sidetracked the convention, and he would have his way, choose his topics, and take his time for still another week. Not until Saturday, June 14, would the convention be able to begin the section-by-section analysis it had unanimously chosen almost two weeks before as the order of business.

The Antifederalist leadership was active in another way. If the convention was going to be diverted from ratification by the adoption of prior amendments, a list of suitable amendments had to be prepared and held in readiness for the proper moment of introduction. Near the end of the first week, an informal Antifederalist caucus led by Henry, Mason, and William Grayson began meeting for that purpose. It was not easy to get such a disparate group to agree on a single list of amendments. They finally decided to use Mason's Virginia Declaration of Rights for their model, but they altered much of its wording and dropped two of its provisions. Six additional sections were added to guarantee protection to the individual from "cruel and unusual punishments," "unreasonable searches and seizures," and the quartering of soldiers in homes, as well as to provide "a right peaceably to assemble" and to be a conscientious objector.

By June 11 a list of twenty provisions had been agreed upon and was ready for circulation. Since the adoption of any one amendment would serve Henry's immediate purpose of blocking ratification, he and Grayson had evidently allowed Mason to play the primary role in compiling the list. The entire document was in the nature of a bill of rights for the protection of the individual, but its adoption in this form would not have served Henry's larger purpose of restoring sovereignty to the states.

Latent frustrations ultimately surfaced on Monday, June 23, in a round of rhetoric that was both more intemperate and more personally abusive than any previously aired. The delegates had reached the boiling point. Hot, tired, living and working in close, uncomfortable quarters, equally divided over a momentous matter (if not to themselves, to their posterity), they were now trading barbs, insults, and threats. Fortunately, the last few sections of the Constitution had been read that afternoon. They had fulfilled their resolve to debate every section. Tomorrow would bring a showdown.

The Federalist leadership assessed the situation. The events of the day convinced them that it was time to force a vote on ratification. They had finished their explanations. Further delay would only aid Henry. An escalation of the day's name-calling might offend someone and lose his vote. Madison was of the opinion that "both sides [had by their actions] declared themselves ready for the question." It was time to move for a vote. That would not, however, be a simple matter. Henry and Mason were sure to "bring forward a bill of rights with sundry other amendments as conditions of ratification." "Should these fail or be despaired of," Madison predicted, "an adjournment will I think be attempted." The Federalists' count affirmed that they still held the narrow margin of "3 or 4; or possibly 5 or 6 votes." Madison translated the desperation evidenced by Henry and Mason into a validation of that count. Federalists were very concerned that illness, accident, or personal business might draw delegates away from the convention. With only a vote or two to spare, any kind of unpredictable circumstance could "endanger the result."

Before the June 24 session, Madison predicted the strategy both sides would use. Federalists would introduce a motion to ratify. The opposition would respond with a motion that the document be amended first. Federalists would then be prepared to introduce "a conciliatory declaration of certain fundamental principles in favor of liberty, in a form not affecting the validity & plenitude of the ratification." As a concession, they would recommend "a few amendments" for adoption *after* the Constitution was in operation. This procedure was a compromise within the Federalist ranks, necessitated, said Madison, "to conciliate some individuals who are in general well affected, but have certain scruples drawn from their own reflexions, or from the temper of their Constituents."

George Wythe had been chosen to move adoption. As the session on June 24 opened, the chair immediately recognized the delegate from York County. Wythe briefly reviewed "the defects and inadequacy of the Confederation and the consequent misfortunes suffered by the people." He admitted that the proposed Constitution was not perfect, but he argued that experience would be the best guide to its improvement. As to the choice between previous and subsequent amendments, he contended that "the extreme danger of dissolving the Union rendered it necessary to adopt the latter alternative"; necessary amendments "would be easily obtained *after ratification* in the manner proposed by the Constitution." He thereupon moved the unconditional approval of the Constitution.

Henry was on his feet to reply. One last time he raised the specter of northern domination. "They will search that paper," he warned, "and see if they have power of manumission." Will they not claim it, he insisted, in the "power to provide for the general defence and welfare"? He expressed his distress at the proposal for subsequent amendments. It was altogether a new idea, not to be taken seriously. Wythe must be trying "to amuse the committee." Free men could not seriously be asked to submit to tyranny on the vague promise that it might "be excluded by a subsequent alteration." "Previous amendments, in my opinion, are necessary to procure peace and tranquillity," Henry asserted. Without them the people will refuse obedience to the new government. There will be no government. "When men are free from restraint, how long will you suspend their fury?" he demanded. "But a moment," he answered. In consequence, he declared, "the licentious and wicked of the community will seize with avidity every thing you hold."

Henry asked the clerk to read two sets of amendments. One was the declaration of rights drawn up with Mason during the early days of the convention; the other was a set to amend "the most exceptional parts of the Constitution." The fourteen amendments in the second list were designed to ensure state supremacy in any conflict with national authority. Henry had earlier spoken of the purse, the sword, and the judiciary as the bulwarks of state supremacy. His amendments were directed primarily to those areas. In place of direct taxation, the Congress would have to requisition the states for funds in proportion to their populations. Only if a state refused to pay could Congress "assess and levy such State's Proportion." Federal revenue was expected to come primarily from tariff duties, but tariffs could adversely affect states like Virginia, which imported in quantity. One Antifederalist amendment required two-thirds majorities for passage of commercial legislation or commercial treaties. In time of peace no regular troops were to be raised except by a two-thirds vote, and terms of enlistment were limited to four years. State militias were to remain answerable to state authorities except in "time of War, invasion, or Rebellion." The federal judiciary would be limited to one supreme court and such courts of admiralty as Congress might establish. All cases except those involving a state or a foreign diplomatic representative would thus originate in state courts and be appealable only on the basis of law, not of fact.

After the clerk's reading, Henry launched into a general defense of his resolutions. When he concluded, Randolph attacked each of them in turn. John Dawson, a Spotsylvania lawyer, joined Grayson of Prince William County in Henry's defense. Then Madison received the nod of the chair. It was the crucial moment. Madison swallowed his pride in order to cut his losses. He announced his support for recommending most of Henry's proposals for subsequent adoption, "not because they are necessary, but because they can produce no possible danger." "No possible danger"—though they were as dangerous as a match in a powder magazine. But Madison had to provide assurance to a part of his faction that the convention would propose amendments.

The Virginia Convention: The Final Vote

On Wednesday, June 25, as the nine o'clock hour for convening approached, the galleries filled and all delegates, save two who had been called out of town, took their seats. George Nicholas received the chair's recognition. He bluntly confessed that the Constitution's friends "are convinced that further time will answer no end but to serve the cause of those who wish to destroy the Constitution." He therefore immediately moved for a vote on Mr. Wythe's motion for ratification. John Tyler of Charles City County moved to amend the motion by adding Mr. Henry's lists of amendments. His Charles City colleague, Benjamin Harrison, rose in support of the amendments. He stated that he had heard that Federalists, although promising support of subsequent amendments, were planning to withdraw from the convention immediately after the vote. Madison had sworn himself to keep quiet on this day, but that was too much. He asked for recognition. "If there be any suspicions that, if the ratification be made, the friends of the system will withdraw their concurrence, and much more, their persons," he told the delegates, "it shall never be with my approbation."

The first vote—the all-important vote—was on Henry's resolution that, previous to ratification, a bill of rights and amendments "ought to be referred by this Convention to the other states in the American confederacy for their consideration." The clerk called the roll. Henry's motion went down to defeat, 88 to 80.

Pendleton then directed the calling of the roll on the motion to approve ratification. All those who, with Madison and Randolph, had voted no on Henry's amendments now voted aye for ratification. With one exception, all those who had previously voted aye with Henry and Mason now voted no. The Constitution was ratified, 89 to 79. A shift of just five votes would have defeated it, but Madison, for all his concern, had been the master of his forces. Madison, "Father of the Constitution," present at its conception in Philadelphia, had also presided as attending physician at its birth.

Two committees now had to be appointed. The first, composed exclusively of Federalists, was charged with preparing a formal statement of ratification. The committee was ready to report immediately, since the Constitution's optimistic supporters had drafted their victory statement even before the final vote. Governor Randolph read the proclamation of ratification. "We the delegates of the people of Virginia," it declared, "... *assent to* and *ratify* the Constitution ... hereby announcing to all those whom it may concern, that the said Constitution is binding upon the said people."

The other group, a twenty-man committee, included the prominent spokesmen from both sides. Its task was to report the amendments Virginia would recommend to the new Congress. George Wythe, the committee chairman, presented these recommendations on June 27, the final day of the convention. In addition to the original twenty bill-of-rights provisions, there were now twenty amendments requesting improvements in the new basic law. Antifederalists could thus claim a small victory to salve their wounds.

By its close and hotly contested vote, Virginia had become the tenth, not the ninth, member of the Union. New Hampshire had ratified four days prior to Virginia, although word had not reached Richmond by June 25. It is clear, nonetheless, that the approval of large and influential Virginia cemented the new Union's fate.

The Movement for a Bill of Rights

No sooner had the cement of union set than Virginia turned its own government over to the Antifederalists. Patrick Henry and his followers in the Assembly took their revenge on James Madison by excluding him from the newly formed U.S. Senate. Madison, desiring to be involved in his creation, ran instead for the House of Representatives. His critics portrayed him as an opponent of amending the Constitution. Although successful in defending himself and gaining election, Madison became convinced that the common man favored a federal bill of rights, and he promised to seek one. Once elected, the studious Princetonian felt morally obligated to fulfill his campaign pledges. The people's discontent with the Constitution might seriously weaken the new government, concluded Madison, and the sooner the Constitution contained a listing of protections for citizens against governmental abuse, the sooner the nation could come together in acceptance of the new federal establishment.

There was a compelling need for haste. When the new government formally began operation in March 1789, Lee, Mason, and Henry were encouraging a second national convention movement in hopes of overthrowing the work of the first. Madison felt that if Congress were to propose a set of popular amendments, those who advocated the protection of individual rights would not align with advocates of state sovereignty against the Constitution, and thus this dangerous movement for a second convention could be checked.

Shortly after the first federal Congress convened, Madison raised the issue with his House colleagues. In comparing recommendations submitted by five state ratification conventions, Madison found a common dependence upon George Mason's Virginia Declaration of Rights, whose guarantees did not conflict with the structure of the Constitution. In September 1789 Congress voted to recommend twelve amendments to the states. The states rejected two proposals on apportionment and legislative compensation. The other ten, known today as the Bill of Rights, became a part of the Constitution on December 15, 1791. Fittingly, it was Virginia's vote on that date which put the first ten amendments into effect. The first state to provide legal safeguards for personal liberty became the last of the necessary eleven states to ratify the federal Bill of Rights.

Between 1784 and 1789 James Madison had prodded Virginia into initiating the Philadelphia Convention and had manipulated the convention's Virginia delegates into advocating a radical new departure in American government. He had shepherded the Constitution through the critical Virginia ratifying convention. Finally, he had protected his creation by championing the Bill of Rights. More than any other statesman, Madison could well claim the Constitution as his legacy to the American people.

Virginia: Essay on Sources

For an overview of Virginia's economic, political, and social systems in the Confederation and Early National eras, one should consult Norman K. Risjord, *Chesapeake Politics, 1781–1800* (New York, 1978); Richard R. Beeman, *The Old Dominion and the New Nation, 1788–1801* (Lexington, Ky., 1972); and Rhys Isaac, *The Transformation of Virginia, 1740–1790* (Chapel Hill, 1982). The influences of economic interests on the various regions of Virginia have been examined by Jackson Turner Main, "Sections and Politics in Virginia, 1781–1787," *The William and Mary Quarterly*, 3rd series, 12 (January 1955), 96–112; by Peter Onuf, "Toward Federalism: Virginia, Congress, and the Western Lands," *The William and Mary Quarterly*, 3rd series, 34 (July 1977), 353–374; and by Norman K. Risjord, "Virginians and the Constitution: A Multivariant Analysis," *The William and Mary Quarterly*, 3rd series, 31 (October 1974), 613–632.

Hugh Blair Grigsby, *The History of the Virginia Federal Convention of 1788*, 2 vols. (1890; reprinted New York, 1969) was the definitive source for the study of the ratification process until recently surpassed by John P. Kaminski, Gaspare J. Saladino, and Richard Leffler, eds., *The Documentary History of the Ratification of the Constitution: Virginia*, 3 vols. (Madison, Wis., 1988).

Economic factors influencing delegate voting, particularly the quantities and types of property the delegates owned, have been closely studied by Charles A. Beard, *An Economic Interpretation of the Constitution of the United States* (New York, 1913); Forrest McDonald, *We the People: The Economic Origins of the Constitution* (Chicago, 1958) and *E Pluribus Unum: The Formation of the American Republic, 1776–1790* (Cambridge, Mass.,

1965); and Robert E. Thomas, "The Virginia Convention of 1788: A Criticism of Beard's *An Economic Interpretation of the Constitution*," *The Journal of Southern History*, 19 (February 1953), 63–72. Unlike Beard, historians McDonald and Thomas found little difference in the economic situations of Virginia Federalists and Antifederalists. Currently the best and most readable narrative of the Virginia ratifying convention of 1788 is to be found in David John Mays, *Edmund Pendleton, 1721–1803: A Biography*, 2 vols. (Cambridge, Mass., 1952).

The major figures in Virginia's ratification struggle are the subjects of several important biographies. Madison's definitive biographer, Irving Brant, has explored in depth his subject's contributions at the Philadelphia and the Richmond conventions in his *James Madison: The Nationalist, 1780–1787* (New York, 1948); in his *James Madison: Father of the Constitution, 1787–1800* (New York, 1950); and more briefly in his one-volume *The Fourth President: A Life of James Madison* (Indianapolis, 1970). Also helpful in understanding Madison's actions are Ralph Ketcham, *James Madison: A Biography* (New York, 1971); Lance Banning, "James Madison and the Nationalists, 1780–1783," *The William and Mary Quarterly*, 3rd series, 40 (April 1983), 227–255; and Robert A. Rutland, *James Madison: The Founding Father* (New York, 1987). Although he left few personal papers, Patrick Henry, Madison's great antagonist, has also been the subject of several notable biographies. Among them are Richard R. Beeman, *Patrick Henry: A Biography* (New York, 1974); Henry Mayer, *A Son of Thunder: Patrick Henry and the American Republic* (New York, 1986); Norine Dickson Campbell, *Patrick Henry: Patriot and Statesman* (New York, 1969); and Robert Douthat Meade, *Patrick Henry: Practical Revolutionary* (Philadelphia, 1969). For Edmund Randolph, consult H. J. Eckenrode, *The Randolphs: The Story of a Virginia Family* (Indianapolis, 1946) and John J. Reardon, *Edmund Randolph: A Biography* (New York, 1974).

George Mason receives judicious treatment from Robert A. Rutland in his *George Mason, Reluctant Statesman* (New York, 1961) and from Helen Hill Miller in *George Mason: Gentleman Revolutionary* (Chapel Hill, 1975). Charles Royster, *Light-Horse Harry Lee and the Legacy of the American Revolution* (New York, 1981), William Clarkin, *Serene Patriot: A Life of George Wythe* (Albany, N.Y., 1970), Leonard Baker, *John Marshall: A Life in Law* (New York, 1974), and Albert J. Beveridge, *The Life of John Marshall*, 4 vols. (Boston, 1916–19) provide insight on three of Madison's lieutenants at the Richmond convention.

Neither Thomas Jefferson, Richard Henry Lee, nor George Washington attended the Virginia ratifying convention, but each was intimately involved in the struggle to elect delegates, and each sought to influence the thinking of the delegates elected. The most detailed and respected study of Jefferson's role is Dumas Malone, *Jefferson and the Rights of Man* (Boston, 1951). Lee's contributions are analyzed by Oliver Perry Chitwood in his *Richard Henry Lee: Statesman of the Revolution* (Morgantown, W.Va., 1968). Those interested in Washington's efforts on behalf of the Constitution should consult vol. 6 of Douglas S. Freeman's *George Washington: A Biography*, 7 vols. (New York, 1948–54); Marcus Cunliffe, *George Washington: Man and Monument* (New York, 1960); James Thomas Flexner, *George Washington and the New Nation* (Boston, 1970); or Arthur N. Holcombe, "The Role of George Washington in the Framing of the Constitution," *Huntington Library Quarterly*, 19 (August 1956), 317–334.

A fascinating behind-the-scenes look at Virginia politics during 1787–88 can be obtained by reading James Madison's mail for the period. The editing of Robert A. Rutland and Charles F. Hobson in volumes 10 and 11 of *The Papers of James Madison*, 15 vols. to date (Charlottesville, Va., 1965–) greatly facilitates this process.

Adjusting to Circumstances

New York's Relationship with the Federal Government, 1776–1788

JOHN P. KAMINSKI

Director, The Center for the Study of the American Constitution
University of Wisconsin-Madison

O
N APRIL 20, 1777, the newly declared state of New York adopted its first constitution. Unarguably, it was one of the most conservative forms of government established by any of the thirteen rebellious colonies. Aristocratic New Yorkers looked forward to electing their leader, Philip Schuyler, as the state's first governor in June 1777; but much to their dismay George Clinton, an upstart militia officer from Ulster County, was the people's choice. This election was a harbinger of politics in New York for the next quarter century. Clinton's primary source of support came from the yeoman farmers of the northern counties of Orange, Ulster, Albany, Washington, and Montgomery. His opposition was primarily centered in New York City, the city of Albany, the town of Hudson, and the lower counties of Kings, Queens, Richmond, and Westchester.

This article is adapted from a longer article on New York written by Dr. Kaminski in *The Reluctant Pillar: New York and the Adoption of the Federal Constitution* (Troy, N.Y., 1985).

When George Clinton was first elected governor, the aristocracy thought him unqualified for the position. They looked forward to his defeat in 1780, but, with the military exigencies of the time, Clinton was reelected for a second term. In 1783, with peace restored, Clinton had solidified his position and was easily reelected to his third term. By 1786 the governor's popularity had reached such a level that he was unchallenged in his bid for his fourth consecutive term. Anti-Clintonians continued their opposition to the governor's policies within the state, but by the mid-1780s they had decided to combine their efforts with like-minded men in other states in an effort to strengthen the general government. A stronger central government might be able to limit the radical policies of the state legislatures, such as the New York paper-money issue of 1786. Thus the original intrastate conflict between the middle-class forces of George Clinton and his aristocratic opponents became part of a larger Continental struggle between the supporters of a confederation of sovereign states and the advocates of a strengthened central government with coercive powers over the states and the people.

George Clinton (1739–1812), the son of an Irish immigrant, was an Ulster County lawyer. He fought in the French and Indian War and was a militia brigadier general in the Revolution. He served as a delegate to Congress in 1775 and was elected the state's first governor in 1777. After six consecutive three-year terms from 1777–1795, he chose not to run, partly because defeat seemed inevitable. He was elected president of the state ratifying convention, and as such he did not vote on the final question. In 1800 he was again elected governor and served until 1804, when he became Thomas Jefferson's vice president. He continued in that office until his death, serving his last four years under President James Madison. Drawing by Charles Balthazar Julien Fevret de Saint-Memin, courtesy of the Metropolitan Museum of Art, New York.

The Revolution: A Bond of Necessity

New York suffered more from the Revolution than any other state. Military activity occurred incessantly within its borders, and New York City and the six lower counties were occupied by British troops for much of the war. New York continually sought assistance from Congress—assistance that seldom materialized because of Congress' weakness. Both Clintonians and Anti-Clintonians agreed that the national legislature had to be strengthened in order to deal effectively with the military problems. In early September 1780 Alexander Hamilton called for a national convention that would grant Congress additional powers. On September 7 Governor Clinton addressed the New York legislature and echoed Hamilton's appeal. Later in the month the legislature appointed delegates to attend a convention of states in Hartford that was "to propose and agree to . . . all such Measures as shall appear calculated to give a Vigor to the governing powers, equal to the present Crisis."

The Hartford Convention, composed of delegates from New England and New York, met November 8–22, 1780. It proposed that the army be authorized to collect revenue and that Congress be empowered to levy import duties. Within three months Congress itself asked the states to grant it the power to levy a 5 percent impost (tariff) to help pay the national war debt. With the British occupying New York City and no tariff revenue coming into its coffers, the New York legislature swiftly approved the Continental impost on March 19, 1781, less than three weeks after the new government under the Articles of Confederation had become effective. Eleven other states followed New York's example. Only Rhode Island refused. But because of the unanimity provision of the Articles, Rhode Island's refusal killed the impost.

Two years after the American victory at Yorktown, New York City was still occupied by the British. The American army and the state militias remained unpaid, and public creditors received no interest on their securities. In this atmosphere a special session of the New York legislature met in July 1782 and resolved that Congress be given the power to tax and that a general convention of the states be called to amend the Articles of Confederation accordingly. The resolutions were forwarded to Congress, which took no action on them.

The New Policies of Peace

With the cessation of hostilities and the British evacuation of New York City, the military justification for a strong Union came to an end, and the Clintonians reassessed their state's position within the Union. The governor and his supporters decided that all their efforts should now be directed at making New York as strong as possible within the loose federal alliance that existed under the Articles. Toward this end, the Clintonians devised a new system of revenue composed of three parts: (1) a state tariff, (2) the sale of loyalist estates and unsettled state lands, and (3) a moderate tax on real and personal property. This new system directly pitted the state-oriented Clintonians against their more nationally minded opponents, who wanted a strengthened Congress.

The new Clintonian policy was inaugurated on March 15, 1783, with the repeal of New York's earlier approval of the Impost of 1781. The state tariff was to be the cornerstone of the Clintonian financial system, and as such it could not be surrendered to Congress. Annual income from the state impost during the Confederation years represented one-third to one-half of New York's annual income.

The impost was especially important to the Clintonians because much of it was paid by non-New Yorkers. About half of all foreign goods imported by Connecticut and New Jersey came through the port of New York. The people of these two states, along with those of Vermont, Massachusetts, and (to a lesser degree) the southern states, indirectly contributed to New York's tariff revenue every time they bought European goods imported through New York. Thus out-of-staters reduced the tax burden of New Yorkers. This hidden tax on consumers was collected by merchants—a group not well represented in the ranks of Clintonians. By forcing merchants to pay the impost, albeit through increasing the prices of imported goods, the Clintonians reduced the taxes on real and personal property. In this way the Clintonians championed yeoman farmers, a group who supported the governor's efforts to keep their taxes low.

Besides the tariff, the Clintonians raised almost $4,000,000 from the sale of confiscated loyalist estates. Aristocratic manor lords did not like to see these once glorious estates broken up and sold in small parcels; it was not a good omen for their own future. Nationalists also opposed the Clintonians' confiscation of loyalist property in those areas evacuated by British troops in 1783, because such actions violated the treaty of peace. How could Congress force Britain to obey the treaty if the states violated it with impunity?

New York's unsettled land was also important in the Clintonian financial picture. This vast territory promised huge future revenues, but New Yorkers had fears about this resource. The state's claim to the area known as Vermont was disputed by New Hampshire and Massachusetts and by the Vermonters themselves. New York's delegates to the Confederation Congress pursued its ownership claims with little success, reporting to Governor

Clinton on April 9, 1784, that Congress was determined "not to do any thing about the matter, expecting that in Time we shall be obliged to consent that [Vermont should] . . . become a separate State." In the same letter the delegates warned Clinton about the possible attempts to seize New York's northwestern territory. "Upon the whole Sir it is our opinion that the utmost Vigilence ought to be exercised to prevent any encroachment on our Territory as we are to expect no protection otherwise than from our own arms." On June 4, 1784, another New York delegate warned the legislature to take "every precaution respecting the W. Territory" because "a Plan is formed and perhaps wrought into System to take that Country from us."

Thus the Clintonians clearly saw that any attempt to strengthen Congress would probably result in the loss both of the state impost and of future land sales from confiscated loyalist estates, from Vermont, and from northwestern New York. The Clintonians would not allow Congress to wrest away the state's most productive sources of revenue.

The Hard Times of 1785–1786

The end of the Revolution in New York was accompanied by two years of prosperity followed by a serious economic depression. To relieve the hardships of the depression and to stimulate the economy, a demand arose for the state to create a land bank that would loan paper money on real estate collateral.

Governor Clinton at first opposed such a land bank, but by the spring of 1786 he came to support the proposal as an opportunity to aid distressed debtors while improving his own political standing. A provision added to the paper-money bill provided that $125,000 of the paper money would be used to pay the interest and principal on the entire state debt and on two kinds of federal debt owned by New Yorkers. The federal securities funded by the bill amounted to $1,400,000, owned by about 25 percent of New Yorkers. The remaining $3,600,000 in federal securities, largely owned by several hundred wealthy Anti-Clintonians, was left unfunded. Clinton was therefore able to assist in getting the paper-money bill enacted, cement his strength among state public creditors, and gain new support from the majority of federal public creditors within the state, while not unduly benefiting his opponents.

It was now in the interest of most New York public creditors to support the state's financial interests over those of the Union. Furthermore, the paper money loaned to farmers held its value well and allowed many debtor farmers to avoid bankruptcy and foreclosure proceedings. The paper money, along with revenue from land sales and the state impost, allowed

New York to purchase large quantities of federal securities with its interest-bearing state securities. By 1790 the state of New York owned federal securities worth over $2,880,000 in gold. The interest due New York on these federal securities more than equaled the annual requisitions on the state by Congress. Thus New York had been transformed from a debtor state into one of the wealthiest creditor states in the Union. The interest of most New Yorkers had become connected with the state and its governor rather than with the general government.

Commerce

Although Governor Clinton made a concerted effort to attach farmers to his policies, he also wholeheartedly encouraged foreign commerce. The more trade that came through the port of New York, the greater the tariff revenue. Therefore, when commerce deteriorated in 1785–86, the Clintonians joined their political adversaries in seeking ways to stimulate trade. This explains why New York in April 1785 gave Congress additional commercial powers to restrain trade with countries without commercial treaties with the United States. It also explains why New York appointed five delegates to attend the Annapolis Convention of September 1786, which was called to consider the country's commercial problems. The legislature, however, provided that any proposals emanating from the Annapolis Convention had to be approved by all of the states. Thus New York was willing to consider a national commercial plan, but it reserved the right to reject any plan that might be detrimental to the state.

The Impost of 1783

By the beginning of 1783 the financial condition of Congress was desperate, so during the first four months of the year it debated measures to alleviate the situation. In April a unified program was adopted that included another request for a federal impost. Unlike the Impost of 1781, this new levy did not gain the state's support. Clintonians hoped that some other state would reject Congress' new attempt to seize New York's most lucrative revenue producer. But by spring 1786 all of the other states had adopted the impost in one form or another. New York could no longer avoid the issue.

In order to sway public opinion in their favor, the Clintonians launched a masterful newspaper campaign which emphasized the dangers inherent in giving Congress an independent source of revenue. With its own income guaranteed, Congress would soon swallow up the state legislatures;

and with the disappearance of the states as viable political entities, freemen would lose many of their hard-won rights. Thus, at least in the public debate, the issue was not primarily economic. By rejecting the impost, New York could save the entire country from becoming a centralized despotism.

All attention focused on New York as the legislature debated the impost in May 1786. Clintonians were keenly aware that their motives would be questioned if they simply rejected the impost outright. Consequently the Clintonian-dominated legislature chose a middle ground. New York adopted the duty but refused to give up the right to supervise and remove the collectors of the impost. The state also reserved the right to use the recently issued state paper money to pay the impost revenue to Congress.

As expected, Congress rejected New York's qualified ratification of the impost and asked Governor Clinton to call a special session of the legislature to reconsider the matter. The governor rejected Congress' request because, in his judgment, no emergency existed. Congressional delegates condemned New York for endangering the country and sent a second appeal to Governor Clinton. The governor again refused. The New York legislature reconsidered the impost when it reconvened in regular session; and on February 15, 1787, the Assembly voted 38 to 19 to retain the provisions obnoxious to Congress, despite the eloquent appeal of Alexander Hamilton that it should accept the national formula. Thus revenue from duties collected on imported goods coming through the port of New York would still flow into the state treasury. The Assembly's action had killed the federal impost but preserved the impost of the state. It was evident that New York's interests were not the same as the interests of the United States.

Congress Calls the Constitutional Convention

Only five state delegations attended the commercial convention at Annapolis. Instead of transacting business with such a small representation, the delegates, with New York's Alexander Hamilton in the forefront, called a new general convention of the states to meet in Philadelphia in May 1787 to revise the Articles of Confederation. By the third week in February, when Congress took up the convention issue, several states had already appointed delegates. New York's congressmen proposed that the Annapolis Convention report be ignored, and that Congress consider a resolution agreed to by the New York legislature on February 20, 1787, calling for a general convention to consider "alterations and amendments" to the Articles of Confederation that would "render them adequate to the preservation and support of the Union." Some congressional delegates viewed New York's proposal with skepticism, especially in light of the Assembly's recent defeat of the impost.

Since New York's proposal ignored the Annapolis Convention report and the actions of those states that had already appointed delegates to a general convention, it was believed that New York was attempting to sabotage the entire convention movement by dividing Congress between two different proposals. Other delegates, however, saw the value in the convention proposal originating from a state rather than from an extralegal body such as the Annapolis Convention.

New York's motion was rejected by Congress. Another resolution was proposed and accepted that implicitly acknowledged the Annapolis Convention report and sanctioned the elections of delegates that had already

Alexander Hamilton (1757–1804) was born in the British West Indies. He immigrated to New York in 1772 and entered King's College (Columbia University) the following year. By 1774 he was totally committed to the patriot cause, and he wrote extensively against British policy. He served in the Continental army from 1776 to 1781, much of the time as George Washington's aide-de-camp. In 1782 he resigned from the army, finished his legal studies, and entered Congress (1782–1783). In 1786 he represented New York at the Annapolis Convention, where he drafted its report calling for a constitutional convention to meet in Philadelphia. He served in the state assembly in 1787 and was one of three New York delegates to the Constitutional Convention. He alone signed the Constitution for New York. He was back in Congress in 1788, and during the debate over the ratification of the Constitution, he, along with James Madison and John Jay, wrote The Federalist. *He was one of the Federalist leaders in the state convention that ratified the Constitution. President Washington named him the first secretary of the treasury, an appointment which was the climax of his public career. He was killed in a duel with Vice President Aaron Burr in 1804. Portrait by John Trumbull, courtesy of the Metropolitan Museum of Art, New York.*

taken place. But this resolution limited the power of the proposed convention, which was called "for the sole and express purpose of revising the Articles of Confederation." Any proposals from the convention would have to be approved by Congress and by the states before taking effect.

New York's Delegates to the Constitutional Convention

After a month's debate the New York legislature agreed that three delegates to the Constitutional Convention should be elected by separate balloting in both legislative houses—the same method used to elect the state's delegates to Congress. On March 6 the Assembly voted for its candidates. State Supreme Court justice Robert Yates and Alexander Hamilton were overwhelmingly elected. The final candidate selected, Albany mayor John Lansing, Jr., narrowly defeated New York City mayor James Duane by a vote of 26 to 23. The state Senate nominated the same three candidates, who were thus declared elected. A month later, at Hamilton's behest, the Assembly called for the appointment of two more delegates, but the Senate rejected the enlargement of the delegation.

The three New York delegates to the convention were prominent in state politics. Albany lawyer Robert Yates was forty-nine years old and had served on the state Supreme Court since its establishment in 1777. Thirty-three-year-old John Lansing, Jr., perhaps the wealthiest Clintonian, had studied law with Yates and had been a delegate to Congress in 1785 and a state assemblyman from 1780 to 1784 and again in 1786, when he served as speaker. Alexander Hamilton, a thirty-year-old New York City lawyer, had distinguished himself in the army during the Revolution, and afterwards as a member of Congress in 1782–83, a commissioner to the Annapolis Convention in 1786, and a state assemblyman in 1787. Hamilton's reputation as a strong nationalist was well known. Yates and Lansing, on the other hand, were thought to be opponents of any serious attempt to strengthen the general government, especially if that entailed the loss of the state's impost.

Yates and Hamilton first attended the convention on May 25. Lansing arrived a week later on June 2. During the convention Yates and Lansing aligned with a minority of delegates who favored a revision of the Articles of Confederation that would strengthen Congress without relinquishing the sovereignty of the individual states. They usually voted in tandem against Hamilton, and it was said that Lansing usually followed the lead of and was deferential to Yates. Since voting was by state delegation, New York's vote usually supported state sovereignty.

On June 16 Lansing gave a speech in which he said that the mere consideration of a national government violated the resolution of Congress and the delegates' commissions from their states. New York, he said, "would never have concurred in sending deputies to the convention, if she had supposed the deliberations were to turn on a consolidation of the States, and a National Government." Furthermore, the states would never "adopt & ratify a scheme which they had never authorized us to propose and which so far exceeded what they regarded as sufficient."

Hamilton's stance was diametrically opposed to that of his fellow New Yorkers. On June 18 he delivered an impassioned five-hour oration. Hamilton preferred a bicameral Congress in which the lower house would be elected by the people for three-year terms. The upper house, or Senate, would be selected by electors chosen by the people and would serve for life. The single chief executive was also to be chosen by electors, and he too would have life tenure. This president of the United States would be commander in chief of the armed forces and would have an absolute veto over acts of Congress. The supreme judicial authority was to be lodged in a court of twelve justices with life tenure. Congress could also create inferior courts. All state laws contrary to the national constitution or federal laws would be considered null and void. All state governors would be appointed by the president and would have veto power over their state legislatures. No state was to have an army or navy, and the militias were to be under the exclusive direction of the United States.

Hamilton knew that his ideas were too extreme for the convention or for the public. But he believed that there were "evils operating in the States which must soon cure the people of their fondness for democracies." Once the people tired of democracy, they would endorse his beliefs. Because of his sincerity and his eloquence, Hamilton was "praised by every body" in the convention, but he was "supported by none." Frustrated, he left the gathering at the end of June after being continually outvoted by his two companions.

As the conclave inexorably moved toward a more national government, Yates and Lansing became increasingly more disenchanted. They finally left the convention on July 10 and did not return. New York was thus unrepresented. Hamilton returned after August 6, but under the rules of the convention New York's vote was not counted because only one delegate was present. Hamilton was absent again from August 20 to September 2. On September 8 he was appointed to the Committee of Style that wrote the final version of the Constitution, and nine days later he signed the document as the only delegate for New York.

For some reason Yates and Lansing waited a while before publicly declaring their objections to the proposed Constitution. It was said that

Governor Clinton had a hand in convincing them to write their report. Finally, on December 21, 1787, ten days before the scheduled legislative session, they wrote to Governor Clinton, giving the reasons for their opposition and for not returning to the convention. When a quorum assembled on January 11, 1788, Clinton gave the legislature the letter and the proposed Constitution.

In their letter, Yates and Lansing said that they rejected the Constitution because it created "a system of consolidated Government" which was not "in the remotest degree . . . in contemplation of the Legislature of this State. . . . If it had been the intention of the Legislature to abrogate the

John Jay (1745–1829) was born into a wealthy New York City family. He graduated from King's College in 1764 and was admitted to the bar four years later. He served in the First and Second Continental congresses and in 1776 was a member of the Provincial Congress, where he was the primary author of the new state constitution. He returned to the Continental Congress in 1778 and was elected President in December of that year. He held that position until September 1779, when he was appointed U.S. minister to Spain. His unsuccessful diplomatic service in Madrid (1780–1782) ended when he went as a peace commissioner to Paris, where he helped negotiate the peace treaty with Great Britain that ended the Revolution. Upon his return to America he was appointed Confederation secretary for foreign affairs. He assisted Hamilton and Madison in writing The Federalist *and was a Federalist leader in the New York ratifying convention. President Washington appointed him the first chief justice of the U.S., but Jay resigned in 1794, when he went to Great Britain to negotiate the treaty that bears his name. Returning to New York, he was elected governor for the first of his two consecutive three-year terms. He retired from public life in 1800. Portrait by Cornelius Tiebout after Gilbert Stuart, courtesy of the New York Public Library.*

existing Confederation, they would not, in such pointed terms, have directed the attention of their delegates to the revision and amendment of it, in total exclusion of every other idea." Furthermore, "a general Government," such as the one proposed by the convention, "must unavoidably, in a short time, be productive of the destruction of . . . civil liberty." Although they were not present when the convention signed the Constitution, they were convinced before they left that the Constitution's "principles were so well established . . . that no alteration was to be expected, to conform it to our ideas of expediency and safety. A persuasion that our further attendance would be fruitless and unavailing, rendered us less solicitous to return."

The Public Debate over the Constitution

The public debate over the Constitution in New York was an extension of the debate over strengthening the Articles of Confederation that had been going on since the Revolution. From 1783 to 1787 the debate had in large measure centered on the federal impost. Beginning in February 1787, however, the debate broadened and focused on the type of government best suited for America. During the four months that the Constitutional Convention sat, Federalists used the state's newspapers to prepare the public to receive whatever the convention produced.

The proposed Constitution was first printed in New York City in the *Daily Advertiser* on September 21. Three days later the *Advertiser* published the first New York commentary on the Constitution in the state. The new document, it said, would "render us safe and happy at home, and respected abroad." Adoption of the new form of government would "snatch us from impending ruin" and provide "the substantial basis of liberty, honor and virtue." It was "the duty of all honest, well-disposed men, friends to peace and good government . . . to cultivate and diffuse . . . a spirit of submission" to the Constitution; which, although not perfect, was "much more so than the most friendly and sanguine expected."

In the months of public debate that followed, Antifederalists condemned the Constitutional Convention for violating the Articles of Confederation, the instructions from state legislatures, and the resolution of Congress calling the convention. They predicted that the Constitution would create a national government that would end in either aristocracy or monarchy and would, in time, destroy the state governments. They decried the lack of a bill of rights, especially since the new Constitution and laws and treaties made in pursuance thereof were declared the supreme law of the land. The president and Senate were too powerful, and the Senate held legislative, executive, and judicial authority, thus violating the concept of separation of powers. The House of Representatives was too small to represent all segments of American society, and Congress had dangerous powers, some of which were undefined. Officeholders would surely multiply under the new government, and taxes would consequently rise. Jury trials in civil cases were not guaranteed, and the appellate jurisdiction as to law and fact favored the wealthy. Various provisions in the Constitution recognized, condoned, protected, and even encouraged slavery. Antifederalists believed that the state conventions should not ratify the Constitution but should recommend amendments to another general convention. In this way the people would obtain the best form of government with the least danger to their liberties.

Federalists responded that the new Constitution would create a federal republic with delegated powers divided among legislative, executive, and judicial branches that would check each other. Since the new government would have only delegated powers, it was unnecessary to have a national bill of rights. Federalists stressed the unanimity of the convention in creating a constitution that was an accommodation among thirteen jarring interests. No new convention could hope to produce a more acceptable compromise. The illustrious Washington, the sage Franklin, and other prominent Americans were continually cited as strong supporters of the new government. Opponents were labeled selfish state officeholders, demagogues, debtors, Shaysites, and Tories. If the Constitution were rejected, anarchy would ensue, and in accordance with the commonly accepted circular theory of government, a tyrant would eventually seize power, restore order, and establish a despotism. If the Constitution were adopted, commerce would revive, the economy would flourish, public creditors would be paid, land values would rise, paper money would be abolished, government expenses would decline, taxes would be reduced, immigration would increase, and the prestige of America would rise. Once the new government was functioning, defects in the Constitution could be corrected through the system's own process of amendment.

The public debate over the Constitution in New York began in earnest on September 27 when the *New York Journal* printed the first of seven essays by Cato, said to have been written by Governor Clinton. Cato called on freemen to be prudent and cautious: "Do not, because you admit that something must be done, adopt anything." The Constitution should be adopted if it were found acceptable, but if it were judged to be dangerous, freemen should "reject it with indignation—better to be where you are, for the present, than insecure forever afterwards."

On October 1 Caesar, allegedly Alexander Hamilton, charged Cato with demagoguery. "Shall we now wrangle and find fault with that *excellent whole*," Caesar asked, "because, perhaps, some of its parts *might have been* more perfect?" He then warned Cato and other Antifederalists that it would be wiser to accept George Washington willingly as the first president under the Constitution than to have the former commander in chief lead another army to establish the Constitution by force.

Before October 18, New York newspapers relied heavily on items originally printed outside the state. After that date, however, the New York press became the national center for the public debate over the Constitution. Antifederalist and Federalist propagandists tirelessly produced material. For the most part New York newspapers were Federalist oriented, especially those upstate in Albany, Lansingburgh, Hudson, and Poughkeepsie. New York City had three staunchly Federalists newspapers—the *Daily Advertiser*, the *Independent Journal*, and the *New York Packet*. The *New York Morning Post* was fairly neutral, while the *New York Journal* was rabidly Antifederalist. To assist in disseminating Antifederalist material, a committee of gentlemen was formed in New York City. Led by Collector of Customs John Lamb and his son-in-law Charles Tillinghast, this committee vigorously solicited, edited, published, and distributed Antifederalist literature throughout New York, Connecticut, and, to a lesser extent, the entire country.

The single most important Antifederalist publication in New York, and probably in the entire country, was the forty-page pamphlet by Federal Farmer. Published during the first week in November 1787, it was reprinted in several editions in different states, and several thousand copies were sold.

By far the most admired New York essays were *The Federalist*, written by Alexander Hamilton, James Madison, and John Jay under the pseudonym Publius. A total of eighty-five numbers were published between October 27, 1787, and May 28, 1788, in four New York City newspapers and in book form. The first essays had a fairly extensive nationwide circulation, but as the numbers kept pouring forth from the presses, their circulation diminished. Newspaper republication almost ceased after it was announced that the entire series would be published in a two-volume edition. The first volume, containing thirty-six essays, was published on March 22, 1788. The second volume, containing forty-nine essays, appeared on May 28, 1788. Despite the significant place *The Federalist* has assumed in American political thought, its impact on New York's reception of the Constitution was negligible.

Far more important in the political battle to get the Constitution ratified in New York was John Jay's *An Address to the People of the State of New York*, signed by A Citizen of New-York. In this nineteen-page pamphlet, published on April 15, 1788, Jay asked New Yorkers to unite with the other states "as a *Band of Brothers;* to have confidence in themselves and in one another, . . . to give the proposed Constitution a fair trial, and to mend it as time, occasion and experience may dictate." Jay's pamphlet, according to one contemporary, had a "most astonishing influence in converting Antifederalists, to a knowledge and belief that the New Constitution was their only political Salvation."

The arguments in Jay's pamphlet were ably answered in a twenty-six-page pamphlet entitled *An Address to the People of the State of New-York*, signed by A Plebeian. The pamphlet, perhaps written by Melancton Smith, was published on April 17, 1788. It maintained that "the indefinite powers granted to the general government" endangered the state governments and the liberties of the people "not by express words, but by fair and legitimate construction and inference." Plebeian objected to the idea that the Constitution should be adopted first and then amended. "Why not amend, and then adopt it?" he asked. "Most certainly" this was "more consistent with our ideas of prudence in the ordinary concerns of life."

Melancton Smith (1744–1798) was born in Jamaica, Long Island. Early in life he successfully ran a retail store in Poughkeepsie. He bought land throughout Dutchess County, which he represented in the Provincial Congress in 1775. Early in the Revolution he served as a major in the militia. In 1777 and 1779 he was elected sheriff of Dutchess County. In 1785 he moved to New York City, where he practiced law and ran a prosperous mercantile firm. He served in Congress from 1785 to 1788. Smith probably wrote the influential newspaper series by "Brutus" and perhaps the pamphlet signed by "Plebeian." He masterminded the Antifederalist election campaign for the state convention where he served as manager of the Antifederalist forces, but he lost much of his political power when he abandoned his party in the convention and led a group of Antifederalists who voted to ratify the Constitution. He died of yellow fever in 1798. Drawing in John and Mary L. Jeanneney, Dutchess County: A Pictorial History *(Norfolk, Va., 1983).*

From mid-October 1787 through July 1788, a steady stream of essays, extracts of letters, poems, news items, filler pieces, and convention debates filled the state's newspapers. Nowhere else were the people as well informed about the Constitution as in New York.

Warm Work in Poughkeepsie— The Legislature Calls a Convention

When the legislature met in Poughkeepsie in early January 1788, it was uncertain whether a state convention as prescribed by the framers would be called to consider the Constitution. On January 31 a resolution calling a convention was introduced in the Assembly. Antifederalists wanted to preface the resolution with a statement that the Philadelphia Convention had exceeded its powers by reporting a new Constitution rather than amending the Articles of Confederation. This Constitution would, if adopted, "materially alter" New York's constitution and government "and greatly affect the rights and privileges" of all New Yorkers. After a long, bitter debate, the Antifederalists' preface was defeated 27 to 25. Antifederalists then proposed that the Constitution be submitted to the convention "for their free investigation, discussion, and decision"—an obvious attempt "to introduce the Idea of *Amendment*." This motion was defeated 29 to 23, and the original resolution calling the convention was accepted 27 to 25. On February 1 the state Senate, after a similar debate, approved the Assembly's resolution 11 to 8.

The state convention was to meet at the courthouse in Poughkeepsie on June 17, 1788. The election of delegates was to begin on April 29 and continue until completed, but it was not to exceed five days. For the first time in state history, all free, adult male citizens were eligible to vote by secret ballot, despite the property qualification for voting in the state constitution. Polling places were to be located in every town and precinct—not just in county seats, as was usually the case. Apportionment of convention delegates coincided with Assembly apportionment.

Both parties seem to have favored delaying the meeting of the state convention until mid-June 1788. Federalists, thinking that a majority of the state opposed the Constitution, wanted time to convince the public that the Constitution had to be adopted. They hoped that ratification by nine states would occur before their convention met. This would have two benefits: no state would be adversely influenced by an early New York rejection of the Constitution, and New York might more likely ratify the Constitution if nine states had already adopted it.

Antifederalists had their own reasons for preferring a late convention. Clintonians adopted the same strategy they had used on the Impost of 1783—they hoped that another state, especially a large state such as Massachusetts or Virginia, would reject the Constitution and thus take the onus off New York. Furthermore, although opposition to the new government looked substantial, Antifederalists still were uncertain about their statewide strength. Clintonians also hoped to coordinate interstate activities in an effort to seek amendments to the Constitution through a second constitutional convention. Proposals for such a convention would be made at the New York ratifying convention, but it would take time to communicate with Antifederalists in other states.

In addition, the regular procedure of state government dictated a late convention. The legislature met in January, and the convention election had to be properly announced so that the people were aware when it would take place. Then, according to the election law of 1787, four weeks had to elapse after the elections before the ballots were counted. Once the results were known, delegates had to be given a decent amount of time to ready themselves for the trip to Poughkeepsie, with perhaps a long stay there. Thus, even if an early convention was wanted, it would have been difficult to obtain.

Throughout the last four months of 1787, a great deal of uncertainty prevailed over New York's attitude toward the Constitution. The general (and intuitive) consensus was that New York City warmly supported the new government, Governor Clinton and his party opposed it, and the state as a whole was either hostile or evenly divided. The ambiguity stemmed from the lack of open political activity in all arenas except the newspapers. Elsewhere in the country, state legislatures, towns, counties, associations, and individuals took strong public stances on the Constitution. This, for the most part, was not the case in New York.

Once the legislature set the date for the election of convention delegates, campaigning began with a fury unmatched in any other state. County committees were established to supervise the nomination of candidates; town and county meetings of local political leaders abounded; county committees of correspondence were formed; nomination lists were formulated and published in unprecedented numbers; and writers in newspapers, broadsides, and pamphlets continued their daily appeals to the electorate. "The New Constitution," it was said, was "the Sole Object of all our attention."

By the time of the elections, however, and for a month after, uncertainty still persisted. Since the state election law of 1787 provided that ballots were to be sealed in county ballot boxes for four weeks after the election had begun, the ballots were not counted until May 27, when it was determined that nine of the state's thirteen counties had elected Antifederalists. Only nineteen Federalists had been elected to their opponents' forty-six. Antifederalists had swept to an amazingly one-sided victory much beyond anyone's expectations.

The Convention

The convention opened at noon on June 17. Governor Clinton was unanimously elected president, and the doors of the convention were ordered open to the public. Other procedural matters were handled on that day and the next. The debate on the Constitution began on June 19, when Chancellor Robert R. Livingston delivered an hour-long oration that expounded upon the deficiencies of the Articles of Confederation and condemned New York's inflexible policy on the federal impost. He warned the delegates of the dangers facing New York outside the Union: Staten Island might be seized by New Jersey, and Long Island by Connecticut. Northern New York would be endangered by Canadians and land-grabbing Vermonters, while western New York would be vulnerable to the British and their Indian allies. Livingston urged the delegates to consider the Constitution objectively, not from the point of view of interested state officeholders (which many of the delegates were), but with the open minds of citizens with the best interests of the state and the country at heart. In closing, he moved that the Constitution be discussed by paragraphs and that no votes be taken on the document or any parts of it until the whole had been discussed. Antifederalists agreed to the motion, with the proviso that amendments could be proposed and debated at any time.

Federalists had won the first battle of the convention: they had avoided an immediate adjournment or rejection and had gained a three- or four-week reprieve, during which time they hoped to hear that New Hampshire and Virginia had voted for ratification. Most Antifederalists, however, saw little danger from this delay. With more than a two-to-one majority, they did not wish to give the impression that they were unfair. They would listen to their opponents.

On June 20 Albany delegate John Lansing, Jr., responded to Chancellor Livingston's speech by saying that the problems of the Confederation could be solved if Congress were given the power to raise men and money. Fear of the dissolution of the Union, however, was not a sufficient reason to adopt the new Constitution. Lansing looked upon the abandonment of the Union "with pain," but it was better to break up the Union than to "submit to any measures, which may involve in its consequences the loss of civil liberty." Lansing also attacked Livingston's insinuation that state officeholders opposed the Constitution for selfish reasons.

Dutchess County delegate Melancton Smith "was disposed to make every reasonable concession, and indeed to sacrifice every thing for a Union, except the liberties of his country." The Articles of Confederation, indeed, were defective, but that was no proof "that the proposed Constitution was a good one." Hamilton immediately responded, referring to "the imbecility of our Union" under the Confederation and predicting "that a rejection of the Constitution may involve most fatal consequences." He agreed that "we ought not to be actuated by unreasonable fear, yet we ought to be prudent."

On June 21 Governor Clinton addressed the convention. The United States, he said, was a vast territory and the states were dissimilar—"Their habits, their productions, their resources, and their political and commercial regulations are as different as those of any nation on earth." In response, Hamilton attacked the governor's inference "that no general free government can suit" the states. The governor, in turn, was aghast at the "unjust and

Many of the states celebrated their ratification of the Constitution with processions or parades. States also held processions on the 4th of July 1788, celebrating the adoption of the Constitution along with the anniversary of independence. These parades usually consisted of tradesmen, artisans and professional men who walked (by group) displaying banners, emblems, and the tools of their trade. Often floats represented different professions. The high point of New York's July 23, 1788, "federal procession" was this twenty-seven-foot frigate named The Hamilton *pulled by ten horses on a wagon concealed by canvas waves. The ship was manned by over thirty sailors and marines and carried thirty-two guns that were fired along the way. Engraving by Martha J. Lamb,* History of the City of New York *(New York, 1877).*

unnatural colouring" given to his statements. He declared "that the dissolution of the Union is, of all events, the remotest from my wishes." Hamilton,
the governor said, wished "for a consolidated—I wish for a federal republic.
The object of both of us is a firm energetic government: and we may both
have the good of our country in view; though we disagree as to the means
of procuring it."

On June 24 news arrived in Poughkeepsie that New Hampshire had
become the ninth state to ratify the Constitution. Although the news had
been expected, no one really knew what the event would do to Antifederalist
solidarity. Antifederalists were pleased with the reaction. "The Antis are
Firm," Governor Clinton wrote, "& I hope and believe will remain so to
the End."

A week later an express rider brought word that Virginia too had
ratified. Although Antifederalists remained outwardly confident, claiming that
Virginia's ratification had made "no impressions upon the republican members," signs of disunity began to appear.

On July 7 the convention finished discussing the Constitution, and
a proposed bill of rights that was "to be prefixed to the constitution" was
read by John Lansing. Three days later Lansing submitted a plan with three
kinds of amendments: explanatory, conditional, and recommendatory. The
first included a bill of rights and some explanation of unclear portions of
the Constitution. The conditional amendments provided that until a general
convention considered these matters, Congress should not (1) call the state
militia to serve outside New York for longer than six weeks without the
consent of the state legislature, (2) regulate federal elections within New
York, or (3) collect direct taxes in New York without first requisitioning the
tax from the state legislature, which would then lay state taxes to collect the
federal requisition. The recommendatory amendments, which were "numerous and important," would be submitted to the first federal Congress
under the Constitution.

Federalists attacked Lansing's plan as "a gilded Rejection" that Congress would never accept as a valid ratification. Smith, Clinton, and Lansing
defended the plan as "our *Ultimatum*." In fact, many Antifederalists "thought
they had conceded too much." Debate over the plan continued for almost a
week despite Antifederalist attempts to bring it to a vote. Federalists saw
hope because their opponents were "so evidently deranged and embarrassed"
by their own plan.

Unable to win acceptance of the Antifederalist plan of ratification,
Melancton Smith brought in a new proposal. The convention would declare
that the Constitution was defective; but since ten states had already ratified,
New York would also ratify, reserving the right, however, to withdraw from
the Union if Congress did not call a convention to consider amendments

within four years. In introducing this plan, Smith said that he was convinced that Congress would not accept any conditional ratification, "and as he valued the Union, he was resolved that this State should not be excluded." Therefore, believing that his plan represented an unconditional ratification, Smith announced that he would not vote for any form of conditional ratification.

With Smith's proposal in mind, Alexander Hamilton wrote to James Madison asking whether Congress would accept New York's ratification with a reservation to secede. Before a response came, Antifederalists themselves, in a private caucus, rejected Smith's proposal.

On July 23 the convention considered a proposal by John Lansing for New York to ratify the Constitution "upon condition" that certain amendments be accepted. Queens County delegate Samuel Jones then moved that the words "upon condition" be expunged and replaced with the words "in full confidence." Melancton Smith supported the change. According to the New York *Independent Journal*, Smith said that "he was as thoroughly convinced then as he ever had been, that the Constitution was radically defective, amendments to it had always been the object of his pursuit, and until Virginia came in, he had reason to believe they might have been obtained previous to the operation of the Government. He was now satisfied they could not, and it was equally the dictate of reason and of duty to quit his first ground, and advance so far as that they might be received into the Union. He should hereafter pursue his important and favourite object of amendments with equal zeal as before, but in a practicable way which was only in the mode prescribed by the Constitution." Conditional ratification, said Smith, "must now be abandoned as fallacious, for if persisted in, it would certainly prove in the event, only a dreadful deception to those who were serious for joining the Union." Other Antifederalists agreed with Smith, but Governor Clinton remained unchanged, saying that he "would pursue what he believed to be the sense" of his Ulster County constituents, i.e., conditional ratification. The vote on Jones's motion passed 31 to 29. Antifederalists were stunned. If nothing changed, New York would ratify the Constitution unconditionally.

On July 24 Lansing proposed that the form of ratification include the right of New York to secede from the Union if amendments to the Constitution were not adopted within a certain number of years. Hamilton then read a letter he had received in which James Madison said that "a reservation of a right to withdraw" was "a *conditional* ratification" and, as such, was unacceptable to Congress. The following day Lansing's motion was rejected 31 to 28. The committee of the whole approved the final form of ratification 31 to 28, and it unanimously resolved that a circular letter be sent to the states "pressing in the most earnest manner, the necessity of a general convention to take into their consideration the amendments to the Constitution, proposed by the several State Conventions."

On July 26 the convention approved the committee of the whole's report to ratify the Constitution with recommendatory amendments by a vote of 30 to 27. John Jay then brought in the proposed circular letter, which was unanimously approved. Federalists, according to Philip Schuyler, had with "perserverence, patience and abilities . . . prevailed against numbers and prejudice."

Convinced by Circumstances

Why, then, did the New York convention, with a lopsided Anti-federalist majority, ratify the Constitution? As the debate over ratification progressed, and as one state after another adopted the new form of government, a rising tide of public opinion came to favor adoption. It was felt that all of the ratifying states could not be wrong, and that the Constitution should be given a chance.

Convention Antifederalists were far from being unanimous. From the very beginning only a few of them were willing to hazard such a drastic step as unqualified rejection. Federalist strategy also contributed to the adoption. The ability to keep the convention in session during the first critical weeks ultimately set the stage for ratification. For the most part, Federalist stategists played a waiting game of conciliation. They let John Lansing and Melancton Smith orchestrate the convention. Federalists' perseverance and stamina were much more important than their touted eloquence.

The single most important factor in obtaining ratification, however, was simply the course of events taking place throughout America. As Hamilton observed, "Our arguments confound, but do not convince—Some of the leaders however appear to me to be convinced *by circumstances*." The ratification by New Hampshire and, more important, by Virginia were determining factors. New York could not kill the Constitution by itself. The new government was going into effect with or without New York. Since New Jersey, Pennsylvania, Maryland and Delaware had already ratified the Constitution, New York was isolated, without a chance of establishing a middle confederacy. By staying out of the Union, New York would lose the federal capital and most of the benefit of its lucrative state impost. Furthermore, the threats of civil war within New York and the secession of the southern counties from the state were real and serious possibilities. Finally, the all-important task of amending the Constitution seemed most obtainable if New York was part of the Union. Antifederalists had not been converted to Federalism. For the most part they maintained their objections to the Constitution and viewed ratification as the lesser of two evils.

The most important Antifederalist delegate to moderate his views was Melancton Smith, the self-proclaimed convention manager. While attending the convention, Smith regularly corresponded with Antifederalist friends in New York City, then the nation's capital. On June 28 he wrote Massachusetts congressman Nathan Dane that he wanted "to support the party with whom I am connected as far as is consistent with propriety—But, I know, my great object is to procure . . . good amendments."

On July 3 Dane wrote Smith a lengthy, insightful letter in which he observed that if the Constitution were not ratified, violence would surely occur. The result of such violence would be "at least a system more despotic than the old one we lay aside, or the one we are adopting." Dane told Smith that "our object is to improve the plan proposed: to strengthen and secure its democratic features; to add checks and guards to it; to secure equal liberty by proper Stipulations to prevent any undue exercise of power, and to establish beyond the power of faction to alter, a genuine federal republic. To effect this great and desirable object the peace of the Country must be preserved, candor cherished, information extended and the doors of accommodation constantly kept open."

To accomplish these ends, amendments to the Constitution had to be proposed in the first federal Congress. "For any state now to stand out and oppose" the ratification of the Constitution would be a mistake, said Dane. If New York did not unconditionally ratify, those "men who wish to cement the union of the states on republican principles will be divided and have but a part of their strength in Congress where they ought to have the whole. . . . Men in all the states who wish to establish a free, equal, and efficient government to the exclusion of anarchy, corruption, faction, and oppression ought in my opinion to unite in their exertions in making the best of the Constitution now established."

"I entirely accord with you in Opinion," Melancton Smith responded to Dane. However, Smith knew that he faced a divided Antifederalist party. "Time and patience," he said, "is necessary to bring our party to accord, which I ardently wish." Dutchess County Antifederalist delegate Zephaniah Platt sided with Smith, voting for ratification "not from a conviction that the Constitution was a good one or that the Liberties of men were well Secured. No—I voted for it as a Choice of evils in our own present Situation." The Constitution "Must and would now go into operation," he wrote. "The only Chance remaining was to get a Convention as Soon as possible to take up our Amendments & those of other States while the Spirit of Liberty is yet alive." In sum, Platt said "that we have Endeavoured to consider all Sides of the question & their probable consequence—on the whole [we] decided on what we Supposed was for the Interest and peace of our State under present Circumstances."

The Clintonian goal of a second constitutional convention, of course, failed, but a bill of rights to protect individual liberties from the power of the new national government was promptly championed by James Madison in the first federal Congress. On March 27, 1790, New York gave its assent to eleven of the proposed amendments, becoming the eighth state to approve.

New York: Essay on Sources

The best general sources for New York during the Revolutionary generation are Edward Countryman, *A People in Revolution: The American Revolution and Political Society in New York, 1760–1790* (Baltimore, 1981); Alfred F. Young, *The Democratic-Republicans of New York: The Origins, 1763–1797* (Chapel Hill, 1967); Edmund P. Willis, "Social Origins of Political Leadership in New York from the Revolution to 1815" (doctoral dissertation, University of California, Berkeley, 1967); Jerome J. Gillen, "Political Thought in Revolutionary New York, 1763–1789" (doctoral dissertation, Lehigh University, 1972); Maria T. Eufemia, "The Influence of Republican Ideology on New Yorkers, 1775–1800: An Examination of the British Libertarian Tradition" (doctoral dissertation, Fordham University, 1976); and Edward La Cerra, Jr., "The Role of Aristocracy in New York State Politics during the Period of Confederation, 1783–1788" (doctoral dissertation, New York University, 1969). Several older studies that are very useful include E. Wilder Spaulding, *New York in the Critical Period, 1783–1789* (New York, 1932); Thomas C. Cochran, *New York in the Confederation: An Economic Study* (Philadelphia, 1932); and Alexander C. Flick, ed., *History of the State of New York*, 10 vols. (New York, 1933–37), particularly vols. 3–5. For colonial background, see Carl Becker, *The History of Political Parties in the Province of New York, 1760–1776* (Madison, Wis., 1909) and Michael Kammen, *Colonial New York: A History* (New York, 1975).

The documentary records for New York are voluminous. For the ratification of the Constitution, see John P. Kaminski, Gaspare J. Saladino et al, eds., *Commentaries on the Constitution*, 5 vols. (Madison, Wis., 1981–). For the published papers of New Yorkers or public officials residing in New York, see Harold C. Syrett and Jacob E. Cooke, eds., *The Papers of Alexander Hamilton*, 26 vols. (New York, 1961–79); Robert A. Rutland et al, eds., *The Papers of James Madison*, vols. 8–12 (Chicago and Charlottesville, Va., 1973–79); Henry P. Johnston, ed., *The Correspondence and Public Papers of John Jay*, 4 vols. (New York, 1890–93); W.C. Ford, ed., *Correspondence and Journals of Samuel Blachley Webb*, 3 vols. (New York, 1893–94); and Edmund C. Burnett, ed., *Letters of Members of the Continental Congress*, 8 vols. (Washington, D.C., 1921–36).

Secondary accounts of the ratification of the Constitution are extensive. See Linda Grant DePauw, *The Eleventh Pillar: New York State and the Federal Constitution* (Ithaca, N.Y., 1966); John P. Kaminski, "The Reluctant Pillar," in Stephen L. Schechter, ed., *The Reluctant Pillar: New York and the Adoption of the Federal Constitution* (Troy, N.Y., 1985); Staughton Lynd, *Anti-Federalism in Dutchess County, New York: A Study of Democracy and Class Conflict in the Revolutionary Era* (Chicago, 1962), and "Capitalism, Democracy, and the U.S. Constitution," *Science and Society*, 27 (1963), 365–414; Steven R.

Boyd, "The Impact of the Constitution on State Politics: New York as a Test Case," in James Kirby Martin, ed., *The Human Dimensions of Nation Making: Essays on Colonial and Revolutionary America* (Madison, Wis., 1976), 270–303, and *The Politics of Opposition: Antifederalists and the Acceptance of the Constitution* (Millwood N.Y., 1979); Theophilus Parsons, Jr., "The Old Conviction versus the New Realities: New York Antifederalist Leaders and the Radical Whig Tradition" (doctoral dissertation, Columbia University, 1974); Leonard H. Bernstein, "Alexander Hamilton and Political Factions in New York to 1787" (doctoral dissertation, New York University, 1970); and Richard W. Crosby, "The New York State Ratifying Convention: On Federalism," *Polity*, 9 (1969), 97–116.

For sources dealing with individuals and their roles in the ratification of the Constitution, see Richard B. Morris, "John Jay and the Adoption of the Federal Constitution in New York: A New Reading of Persons and Events," *New York History*, 63 (1982), 132–164, *Witnesses at the Creation: Hamilton, Madison, Jay, and the Constitution* (New York, 1985), and *John Jay, the Nation and the Court* (Boston, 1967); Frank Monaghan, *John Jay* (Indianapolis, 1935); Broadus Mitchell, *Alexander Hamilton: Youth to Maturity, 1755–1788* (New York, 1957); Clinton Rossiter, *Alexander Hamilton and the Constitution* (New York, 1964); Gerald Stourzh, *Alexander Hamilton and the Idea of Republican Government* (Stanford, Calif., 1970); Robin Brooks, "Alexander Hamilton, Melancton Smith, and the Ratification of the Constitution in New York," *William and Mary Quarterly*, 3rd series, 24 (1967), 339–358; George Dangerfield, *Chancellor Robert R. Livingston of New York, 1746–1813* (New York, 1960); and Philip R. Schmidt, "Virginia, Secession, and Alexander Hamilton: New York Ratifies the Constitution" (M.A. thesis, University of Kansas, 1965). Clinton needs a good biography, but until it is written, E. Wilder Spaulding, *His Excellency George Clinton* (New York, 1938) must suffice.

States' Rights and Agrarianism Ascendant

Alan D. Watson

Professor of History

University of North Carolina at Wilmington

S THE YEAR 1776 OPENED, Americans living in the thirteen British colonies along the Atlantic coast were in various stages of rebellion against the mother country. North Carolina, a royal colony since 1729, had deposed its royal governor, Josiah Martin, in 1775. By the end of the year it had erected an elaborate provisional government, raised soldiers, printed money, and offered military aid to neighboring Virginia and South Carolina. Armed confrontation began in North Carolina with the Battle of Moores Creek Bridge in February 1776. Some sixteen hundred loyal Scot Highlanders living in the Upper Cape Fear Valley responded to Governor Martin's call to march to the coast and rendezvous with British troops to retake control of the province. Patriot militia routed the Scots at Moores Creek Bridge to thwart the British design.

The patriot victory at Moores Creek Bridge fueled the demands for independence in North Carolina. On April 12, 1776, delegates to North Carolina's Fourth Provincial Congress at Halifax unanimously approved a resolution instructing North Carolina representatives to the Continental Congress "to concur with the delegates of other colonies in declaring Independency." The Halifax Resolves, as they were called, marked the first official state action for independence among the thirteen states and a significant step toward the creation of a nation. Such action was not surprising in view of North Carolina's colonial past. Settled, in part, by adventuresome migrants from the more prosperous neighboring colonies of South Carolina and Virginia, the "Old North State" was sometimes described as "the vale of humility between two mountains of conceit." With Rhode Island, it shared the reputation of being the most independent-minded of England's North American colonies.

After the Continental Congress declared independence in July, North Carolina held a Fifth Provincial Congress at the end of the year to draft a constitution that would institute a formal state government. The debate over the constitution revealed a dichotomy of views among the patriots, perhaps best described as "conservative" and "radical," that characterized state politics from that point at least through the struggle over the ratification of the federal Constitution. Conservatives, led by Samuel Johnston, James Iredell, and Archibald Maclaine, favored a powerful executive, protection for property, an independent judiciary, and restricted suffrage—an elitist conception of government.

Radicals, led by Willie Jones, Thomas Person, and Griffith Rutherford, envisioned a more "democratic" polity. Approving instructions brought by Thomas Burke from his constituents in the western part of the state, they sought to end aristocratic control of government and to protect the liberties of the people. Practically, the radicals desired a powerful legislature, a weak executive, diminished property requirements for voting and holding office, and a bill of rights. They represented the socioeconomic forces of democracy unleashed by the colonial rebellion against England.

The Provincial Congress compromised by producing an essentially democratic frame of government that recognized the principle of popular sovereignty (though the document was not submitted for ratification in a popular referendum). The executive and judicial departments were distinctly subordinated to a dominant legislature. Voting for members of the lower house of the legislature was extended to all freemen who paid taxes. Despite the religious disqualification of non-Protestants, discrimination in legislative apportionment against the more populous western counties, and the failure to provide for amending the constitution, the new government was decidedly more democratic in spirit, form, and objectives than the colonial structure which it replaced. Not only was a bill of rights attached to the document, but significantly it was adopted before the Congress approved the constitution itself.

North Carolina and the Articles of Confederation

Meanwhile, in 1776–77, the Continental Congress in Philadelphia first proclaimed independence (with Joseph Hewes, William Hooper, and John

Penn signing the Declaration for North Carolina) and then undertook the drafting of a constitution to bind the thirteen states in a formal national union. North Carolina's delegates to Congress in 1777—Cornelius Harnett, John Penn, and Thomas Burke—evidenced extreme concern over the need to protect the rights of the states and the individuals within them. Burke, in particular, seemed almost paranoid about these issues. He was primarily responsible for the inclusion of the second article of the Articles of Confederation, which read: "Each state retains its sovereignty, freedom and independence, and every Power, Jurisdiction and right, which is not by this confederation expressly delegated to the United States, in Congress assembled." It was a restriction later echoed in North Carolina legislative chambers and embodied substantially in the Tenth Amendment to the federal Constitution.

Harnett, justly called "the Samuel Adams of North Carolina" by Josiah Quincy, Jr., of Massachusetts, nicely blended the qualities of nationalism and jealousy of state prerogative. Despite his support for a union of the states and his advocacy of interstate cooperation, Harnett steadfastly worked to protect the interests of his state. He consistently complained that tax quotas assigned North Carolina were too high. In August 1778 Harnett declared that Congress had shamefully neglected the accoutrements for the North Carolina troops of light horse and had failed to promote eligible and deserving men of the state to officer rank in the Continental army.

Still, seconded by a timid John Penn, Harnett approved of the Articles of Confederation that emerged from the Congress in late 1777. Realistically, he viewed the Articles as providing "the best Confederacy that could be formed, especially when we consider the Number of States, their different Interests, Customs, etc." In a November 1777 letter to Burke, who had returned to North Carolina, Harnett remarked that "the child, Congress has been big with, these two years past, is at last brought forth." However, he feared its reception by the various states and thought that Burke would consider it "a monster." He was right.

Despite the inclusion of Article II, Burke remained unreconciled not only to the extent but also to the vagueness of the powers granted to the national government. He was convinced that "unlimited power can not be safely Trusted to any man or set of men on Earth." Presenting his objections in "Notes on the Articles of Confederation," Burke led the opposition to the ratification of the Articles of Confederation in the state legislature and won a temporary victory. However, the General Assembly, responding to constant prodding from Harnett in Philadelphia, reversed its decision and approved the Articles without reservations on April 24, 1778. Nonetheless, the state by no means abandoned Burke's concern for states' rights and the corruptive influence of power.

While realism dictated North Carolina's approval of the Articles, the intra-Whig (i.e., the intra-rebel) struggle between conservatives and radicals continued to beset the state as it tried to cope with the demands of war and civil strife. Though the British turned their attention to the northern and middle Atlantic states, North Carolina had to deal with a Cherokee threat in its western mountains and loyalist conspiracies in the east. Finances proved vexatious. The British invasion by Lord Cornwallis in 1781 and the occupation of the port of Wilmington throughout much of that year were followed by vicious partisan conflict between patriots and loyalists that continued into 1782. The next year, however, Americans celebrated the Treaty of Paris, which formally ended the struggle and granted legal independence to the states.

Throughout the conflict conservatives and radicals clashed over war-related issues. The conservatives preferred lenient treatment of the loyalists, protection of property, and sound money. The radicals, who controlled the legislature during most of the revolutionary years, successfully sought the confiscation of loyalist property, fiat emissions of paper money, and a government more responsive to the wishes of the people.

To a degree the pattern of politics represented a struggle of the elite against the less well-to-do in society. The Revolution not only established independence but also produced great social unrest. As a result, "deferential politics," already under fire before the Revolution, suffered even greater erosion. The conservatives accused their opposition of lacking "virtue," or the capacity to put the commonweal above personal interest. As it turned out, the conservatives were as selfish as the radicals: only their values differed. Each side interpreted "virtue" and the commonweal from its own perspective. Thus conservatives, whose economic interests were often grounded in the Atlantic commercial economy, tended to equate commerce and its attendant small manufacturing and finance with the common good; radicals, more parochial and agrarian-minded, abhorred what they considered the baneful influence of commerce.

The future of the Articles of Confederation remained in abeyance until early 1781, when Maryland finally ratified this constitution and permitted its implementation. The Articles, like the North Carolina constitution, fundamentally represented the American reaction to English rule and reflected the democratic forces unleashed by the Revolution. The document provided a framework in which relatively powerful state governments dominated a weak central structure that lacked the power to tax and regulate commerce. Fear of executive influence and reliance upon colonial assemblies led to a government dominated by Congress, which in turn exercised executive functions. A unicameral legislature in which each state possessed an equal vote reflected the democratic forces at work. As the term *confederation* implied, the Union was a loose alliance of independent states broadly controlled by a national authority.

In North Carolina the Articles soon proved a source of contention between conservatives and radicals. The latter appreciated the democratic aspects of the national government and more particularly the safeguards provided for state autonomy and individual rights. Conservatives deplored the evident ineptitude of the government, the embarrassments suffered in foreign affairs, and the failure to protect property rights and guard against such popular excesses as Shays' Rebellion in Massachusetts in 1786–87.

After the institution of the United States under the Articles in 1781, North Carolina's congressional representatives mirrored the division in state politics. Representing the conservatives, for example, was Richard Dobbs Spaight, a wealthy young resident of the eastern port town of New Bern, who served in Congress from 1781 to 1783. While concerned with protecting the interests of his home state, at the same time Spaight was discomforted by North Carolina's refusal to fulfill its financial obligations to the Confederation by paying its share of the national requisition.

Spaight chafed at the inability of Congress to deal with the demands, both foreign and domestic, that it faced. He castigated the several states, including his own, for not making military preparations to protect the country in the face of a decidedly hostile England. He also criticized the New England states for attempting to weaken the national government in order to enhance their own status. In Spaight's estimation, "There is no man of reflection, who has maturely considered what must and will result from the weakness of our present Federal Government, and the tyrannical and unjust proceedings of most of the State governments, . . . but must sincerely wish for a strong and efficient National Government."

A leader of the radical faction in the state was Timothy Bloodworth, a popular politician of humble origins, jack-of-all-trades, and a man of average means, who served in Congress from 1785 to 1788. Bloodworth worried about national encroachment upon the rights of the states. Writing to Governor Richard Caswell in 1786, when Congress had recently passed an ordinance to regulate Indian affairs, he confided that "after repeated endeavors, we have obliged the Superintendent for the Southern District, to act in conjunction with the Authority of the State in all matters wherein the Legislative Rights of the States may be concerned."

Superseding the controversy over Indian relations was the Jay-Gardoqui treaty negotiations with Spain. Southerners believed that northern commercial interests sought a treaty at the expense of southern agrarianism. More particularly, Bloodworth opposed the negotiations because they might encroach upon the prerogatives of the states. He did not believe Congress could "dispose of any of the privileges [the right of navigation of the Mississippi River] . . . of the individual States, without their consent." Furthermore, the agreement would alienate the loyalties of citizens (including North Carolinians in the present state of Tennessee) living between the Appalachian Mountains and the Mississippi River, and it would depreciate land values in that region.

More broadly, Bloodworth was frightened by Congress' treaty-making power, by which a simple majority of the states was sufficient to approve such a covenant. "If seven States can carry on a treaty," he wrote, "it follows, of course, that the Confederated compact is no more than a rope of sand." Bloodworth and others who voiced reservations about the approval of treaties by Congress were eventually rewarded. Not only was the treaty with Spain shelved, but the federal Constitution contained the stipulation

Richard Dobbs Spaight (1758–1802), the son of an Irish immigrant father, was descended on his mother's side from North Carolina governor Arthur Dobbs. Orphaned at age eight, Spaight was sent by his guardians to Ireland and Scotland for his education. Upon returning to North Carolina in 1778, he launched a successful political career. During the 1780s he served both in the state legislature and in Congress. In 1787, at the age of twenty-nine, Spaight became a member of the North Carolina delegation to the Grand Convention, where he spoke sparingly but attended always. The politically precocious Spaight lost a bid for the governorship that year, and in 1789 he failed in his attempt to become one of his state's first U.S. senators. In 1792 his persistence earned him victory in the race for governor, a position he held until 1795. Thereafter, he served as a Democratic-Republican congressman (1798–1801) at a time when party passions ran high. This rivalry prompted a senseless duel between Spaight and his Federalist successor, in which the forty-four-year-old Spaight met his death. Portrait attributed to James Sharples, Sr., courtesy of Independence National Historical Park.

that a two-thirds majority of the Senate was necessary for the ratification of treaties.

North Carolina and the Constitutional Convention

From the inception of the Confederation government in 1781, efforts had been made to strengthen the national authority. That movement gained momentum in 1785 when commissioners from Virginia and Maryland met at the Mount Vernon home of George Washington to discuss differences between the states arising from their mutual navigation of the Potomac River and Chesapeake Bay. Following that gathering, the Virginia legislature suggested that all the states send representatives to Annapolis, Maryland, the following year to expand the talks and consider other commercial arrangements. North Carolina was not among the five states represented at the Annapolis Convention in September 1786, despite Governor Caswell's appointment of five delegates. Only Hugh Williamson, aligned with the conservatives in the state, attempted the trip, and he arrived after the convention had adjourned.

Although the Annapolis Convention proved unrewarding, its delegates called for a meeting in 1787 to consider amendments to the Articles of Confederation that would augment the power of the national government. Twelve states, excluding Rhode Island, sent representatives to Philadelphia, some not even waiting for Congress to sanction the convention. There, working in self-imposed secrecy, the delegates would wage a "summer's campaign" to formulate plans for a new government, and their exertions would result in the drafting of the federal Constitution.

North Carolina played no significant role in the call for the Constitutional Convention in 1787. In fact, only the energy and skill of a few conservatives during the last two days of the General Assembly in 1786 ensured the state's participation at Philadelphia. The five men who represented North Carolina in the convention—Hugh Williamson, Richard Dobbs Spaight, William Blount, William R. Davie, and Alexander Martin—reflected the respectable, eastern, conservative planter-lawyer-merchant class. In socioeconomic background, profession, education, and cultural attainment, none epitomized the state's great mass of provincial, agrarian radicals.

Despite their overall similarity, the North Carolina delegates exhibited much diversity. They ranged in age from twenty-nine to fifty-seven. Martin boasted an active record in state politics, including a three-year gubernatorial tenure. Spaight, Blount, and Davie were burgeoning politicos, yet to reach the zenith of their distinguished careers. Williamson, to a degree an outsider, came to North Carolina in 1779 from Philadelphia, bringing a medical degree from the University of Utrecht, training in theology, interests in science and writing, and a cosmopolitan, polished character that rendered him well suited to mingle with and influence the representatives at Philadelphia.

Compared to others at the Constitutional Convention, the North Carolina delegation was decidedly mediocre in reputation and ability; it was, for example, quite overshadowed by luminaries from its northern neighbor Virginia. Still, the North Carolinians played a creditable, if not conspicuous, part in framing the Constitution. Williamson was the most distinguished and active. Though not a great orator, he freely entered into the debates, speaking seventy-three times, offering twenty-three motions, and serving on five committees. His good humor and pleasant character, along with a gentlemanly deportment, made a favorable impression upon the members of the convention.

Hugh Williamson (1735–1819), licensed Presbyterian preacher of Scots-Irish ancestry, professor of mathematics, physician, astronomer, merchant, author, and statesman, rivaled his scientific and political colleague Franklin in versatility. During the Revolution, Williamson was surgeon general of the North Carolina militia and participated in the Battle of Camden, the Americans' most bloody defeat. After the cessation of hostilities he served in his state's legislature and in the Confederation Congress (1782–1785, 1788). As a delegate to the Philadelphia Convention, Williamson sat on five committees and played a major role in the debates. He also helped to lead the tough campaign for ratification and wrote an influential essay urging adoption. Williamson was elected U.S. representative to the First and Second Congresses (1789–1793). Thereafter, he moved to New York to devote the remainder of his life to educational, literary, and scientific pursuits. Portrait by John Trumbull, from Cirker, Dictionary of American Portraits *(1967).*

Of the remaining delegates, Spaight made the greatest contribution. Neither Martin nor Blount possessed the oratorical skill to compete in Convention Hall. According to historian Clinton Rossiter, Martin was a "cipher," one of three men at the convention who made no "recorded contribution." Blount spoke but once and failed to participate in committee service. Davie was silent, though in private his opinion was always respected. Behind the scenes he worked to secure the approval of the "Great Compromise" that broke an early convention deadlock and settled the troublesome question of state representation in Congress.

Frequently standing before the convention, Spaight revealed a conservatism that was always tempered by his devotion to his state. He sought to apportion representation in the national legislature on the basis of population, a boon to North Carolina, which had the fourth largest population among the states. Holding an elitist conception of the upper house of the national legislature, he proposed the election of its members by state legislatures for seven-year terms. Spaight also envisioned an authoritative chief executive with a lengthy, though single-term, tenure. All the while, he fought to protect the southern states from northern commercial discrimination. With Williamson, he helped to establish the principle of a requisite two-thirds vote of the Senate for the ratification of treaties, a requirement which was viewed as a safeguard for southern and western economic interests. At the conclusion of the proceedings in Philadelphia, the North Carolina delegates present—Williamson, Spaight, and Blount—signed the Constitution, but they found their state unreceptive to their work.

The Debate over Ratification

North Carolina was the seventh state to call for a ratifying convention, the twelfth to meet in convention, one of two to fail to approve the document, and the twelfth to join the Union. In fact, the August 1787 election for members of the General Assembly, held before the Philadelphia Convention disbanded, portended the adverse climate in the state.

The electorate in North Carolina prepared for the August contest with the assurance that a stronger national government would emerge from the convention. Williamson had written Samuel Johnston in July of the need for "men of understanding" in the legislature, men "who are capable of explaining and promoting such measures as may be recommended by the convention." The election was hotly contested. "No Species of lying has been omitted," claimed one conservative in reference to the radicals' politicking. Another conservative was not only defeated at the polls but suffered two blackened eyes in a fight. Archibald Maclaine evaluated the results from the conservative perspective: "We have a set of fools and knaves in every part of the State, who seem to act as by concert; and are uniformly against any man of abilities and virtue."

Although the election produced an apparent radical majority in the General Assembly, the legislature ignored the strenuous objections of Thomas Person and called for a state ratifying convention. However, elections for members of the convention were slated for March 1788, and the convention would not meet at Hillsborough until July; thus there was sufficient time for opponents of the Constitution to organize and politic. Nonetheless, the conservatives were confident. Maclaine had "little or no doubt of [the approval by] our State . . . the people, if left to themselves, are in favor of a change." But neither side was willing to allow the people to make the decision unassisted.

The proponents of the Constitution, called Federalists, waged a vigorous campaign before the March election to ensure a victory over the opponents of ratification, who were styled Antifederalists. Relying upon their well-educated, articulate leadership of Iredell, Maclaine, and Williamson among others, Federalists approached the public via pamphlets and newspaper essays laudatory of the Constitution. In a calm, dispassionate manner they tried to convince the public of the need for a more powerful national government to cope with foreign and domestic exigencies and thereby prevent the dissolution of the Union.

Antifederalists relied more heavily upon informal discussion and arguments ad hominem. Baptist preacher Lemuel Burkitt frightened his congregation with the declaration that the ten-mile-square area for the proposed seat of the national government would "be walled or fortified. Here an army of fifty thousand, or, perhaps, a hundred thousand men, will be finally embodied, and will sally forth, and enslave the people." Antifederalist leader Willie Jones denied that he had referred to Washington and Davie as scoundrels, but Thomas Person did not retract his denouncement of Washington as a "rascal and traitor to his country for putting his hand to such an infamous paper as the new Constitution."

The Hillsborough Convention

When the first ratifying convention met at Hillsborough on July 21, 1788, Antifederalists, led by Jones, Person, and Samuel Spencer, commanded a substantial majority, allowing them to pacify their opposition by proposing Governor Samuel Johnston, an avowed Federalist, as president of the meeting. Then Jones astonished Federalists by proposing a quick vote, claiming that the delegates were prepared for a decision and that delay would merely waste the public's money. Federalists, led by Iredell and Spaight, demurred, hoping to gain support by delaying a ballot and utilizing their superior debating skills.

During the course of a week-long, relatively one-sided debate, Iredell and Spaight assumed much of the burden of justifying the action of the Philadelphia Convention. Spaight defended the congressional taxing power against the reservations of Spencer, declaring that "Government cannot exist without certain and adequate funds." Spaight also explained the rationale for permitting the continuation of the slave trade for twenty years, allowing Congress to choose the time for selecting presidential electors, and granting the president the command of national military forces. Combating a favorite

Samuel Johnston (1733–1816) came to North Carolina from Scotland as an infant during the gubernatorial tenure of his uncle Gabriel Johnston. After establishing himself as a lawyer in Edenton, he embarked upon a political career that spanned the years from 1759 to 1803. During that long period Johnston held a succession of state and federal offices: after playing a leading role in the break with England, he served in Congress, held the governorship (1787–1789) during the years of constitution-making, became one of his state's first U.S. senators (1789–1793), and rounded out his career as a Superior Court judge (1800–1803). According to his biographer, Johnston—a man of imposing presence and vigorous mental and physical strength—"became a leader of the people, not through their affection, for he did not inspire it, but through his wisdom and force of character." A conservative, Governor Johnston served as president of both state ratifying conventions and worked forcefully with his brother-in-law James Iredell for the Constitution's adoption. Watercolor portrait, courtesy of North Carolina Department of Cultural Resources, Division of Archives and History.

Antifederalist argument, Spaight rejected the possibility of a senatorial-presidential tyranny. When Antifederalists voiced the fear of a national judiciary that might overwhelm the states, Spaight was incredulous, asserting that "no government can exist without a judiciary to enforce its laws."

Toward the conclusion of the convention, Spaight rose to deliver a summary defense of his efforts and the Constitution. First he denied that the Philadelphia delegates had exceeded their authority by proposing a new constitution. Granted full power to amend the Articles, the members of the convention had found it "impossible to improve the old system without changing its very form." Further, pointing out the limited tenure of the executive and legislature and the popular base of political authority, Spaight denied allegations that the Constitution inclined toward aristocracy. Finally he toured a wide range of objections raised by Antifederalists—the Constitution's failure to ensure jury trial in civil cases; absence of a religious test; exclusive governmental jurisdiction over a federal district; the excessive authority of the federal courts; and a system of taxation that would discriminate against the Southern States. Spaight tried to allay the fears of William Lenoir, who spoke for Antifederalists throughout the nation when he called the powers of the government "indefinite." Said Spaight, not anticipating the future Hamiltonian usage of the Constitution, "I am amazed. . . . It is the first time I [have] heard the objection. I will venture to say [that the powers] are better defined than the powers of any government ever heard of."

After Federalists had exerted their best efforts, Antifederalists carried a resolution by a vote of 184 to 84 that neither ratified nor rejected the Constitution. Instead, the Hillsborough Convention countered with a series of amendments designed to check federal power, protect states' rights, and safeguard special interests in North Carolina. The convention also adopted a declaration of rights to secure personal liberties. The refusal to ratify was an audacious move, for by the conclusion of the Hillsborough Convention the Constitution had been ratified by eleven states, more than enough to ensure the inauguration of the new nation without North Carolina's presence. Antifederalists were willing to remain outside the Union in order to exert pressure on the new government to accept their demand for amendment.

What prompted some men to favor the Constitution and others to reject the new document is intriguing. Neither wealth nor political experience greatly distinguished the Federalist from the Antifederalist leadership. However, Federalists, like Spaight, tended to be younger men, perhaps more energetic and more impatient of the status quo than Antifederalists were. Federalists also tended to exhibit a more catholic frame of mind that derived from military service in the Continental army, experience in Congress, or professional contacts beyond state bounds, all of which gave them a broader perspective of America and made them more amenable to a powerful national government.

More fundamentally, Federalists and Antifederalists simply differed in their outlook on life. Federalists, representing the lawyer-merchant-planter elite, exhibited a commercial-urban orientation, as opposed to Antifederalists, who spoke more for the self-sufficient backcountry farmers. And it would not be amiss to observe the conclusion of historian Gordon Wood, who contends that the struggle between Federalists and Antifederalists "represented a broad social division between those who believed in the rights of a natural aristocracy to speak for the people and those who did not." Antifederalist agrarians doubted the wisdom of elitist rule, preferring a government that was more inclusive and more responsive to the people at large.

While Federalists contended that the Constitution nicely blended authority with liberty, establishing the principle of popular sovereignty while checking popular excesses, Antifederalists saw an inordinate concentration of power in the new government. They particularly feared that undue consideration had been given to commerce, which the majoritarian small-farming element in the population viewed as antipathetic to liberty and the common good. Their precapitalistic mentality led them to distrust such "nonproductive" economic pursuits as commerce.

A less prominent strand of opposition thought represented concern for religion. Federalists were associated with the Church of England, the established church in the colony before the Revolution. Antifederalists worried that Congress might impose a state religion, or even that the pope in Rome might somehow gain control of the American government. Though seemingly fanciful, the less educated backcountry Christians of North Carolina saw a state-controlled church as representing the power of the elite whose interests they opposed. Antifederalists did not advocate a secular state, but merely one in which there would be a religious stricture to assure Protestant control of the government—a condition that prevailed in North Carolina under the provisions of its constitution of 1776.

Upon the institution of the new government of the United States in April 1789, North Carolina became a sovereign state. At the behest of Governor Johnston, Hugh Williamson served as the unofficial representative to that government. Williamson remained in the Confederation Congress until it disbanded, and he attempted to portray North Carolina's refusal to ratify in the most favorable light possible. When dealing with the new government, Williamson sought to prevent North Carolina's exclusion from any tariff union erected by the United States and to settle the state's financial accounts with the national government. Williamson's tact helped to turn a rather belligerent national attitude into a conciliatory one of encouraging rather than badgering North Carolina to join the Union.

Subsequent to the Hillsborough Convention a swift and striking change of opinion occurred in North Carolina. The establishment of an orderly government headed by the respected George Washington, plus the promise of amendments to protect personal liberties and states' rights, allayed the fears of many Antifederalists. Federalists, for their part, led by James Iredell, mounted an effective "educational" campaign emphasizing the prospect of discriminatory tariff duties, the need for national protection against the Indians in the West, and the embarrassment of North Carolina's alignment with Rhode Island, a repository of disgusting, if not dangerous, democracy, which had already rejected the Constitution in a statewide refer-

James Iredell (1751–1799), an English-born lawyer and customs official, had been reluctant to support separation from England in 1776. Nonetheless, he was recruited by the rebels because of his fine legal mind and his civic prominence (he had married the sister of Revolutionary leader Samuel Johnston). Elected attorney general in 1779, he served in that office for two years, and in 1788 he was a member of the Council of State. Iredell was not a delegate to the Philadelphia Convention, but he is generally regarded as the leading supporter of North Carolina's ratification. His Federalist essay—"Answers to Mr. Mason's Objections to the New Constitution"—attracted national attention, and in the convention of 1788 he represented Edenton and became floor leader for the Federalists. He and William R. Davie had these debates of 1788 published, and their wide circulation influenced ratification the following year. Iredell's vigorous support of the Constitution led Washington to appoint him an associate justice of the first Supreme Court. In this post he adopted the curious position of a states'-rights Federalist and rode the southern circuit until his death at the age of forty-eight. Painting by M. L. H. Williams, courtesy of North Carolina Department of Cultural Resources, Division of Archives and History.

endum. And, on the whole, the formation of the Union left North Carolina no realistic alternative to joining the nation. As Antifederalist William Lenoir later declared, adoption of the new plan of government was "an alternative less fatal than absolute severance from the adjoining States."

Actually, many Antifederalists agreed in principle that the central government needed to be strengthened. Like Burke in his consideration of the Articles of Confederation, they objected to the indeterminate, nebulous powers of the new federal establishment. Lamented Joseph McDowell in the Hillsborough convention, "I know the necessity of a federal government. I therefore wish this was one in which our liberties and privileges were secure." Once amendments or promised amendments were accepted, the major Antifederalist opposition crumbled.

The Fayetteville Convention

The movement to reverse the decision at Hillsborough began with the General Assembly decision in November 1788 to call for a second ratifying convention to meet at Fayetteville in November 1789. Elections in August produced an overwhelming Federalist majority. With Samuel Johnston again presiding, Federalists in the Fayetteville convention defeated an Antifederalist motion to postpone ratification and to propose more amendments. Instead, on November 21, after three days of unrecorded debates, Federalists carried a motion to adopt the Constitution, offered by William R. Davie, by a vote of 194 to 77. At that juncture, however, the convention instructed North Carolina's future congressmen to attempt to secure the passage of a set of suggested amendments. Next, North Carolina considered and ratified the Bill of Rights. This approval, coming on December 22, 1789, made the Old North State the fourth of the original thirteen to assent to these guarantees of individual liberty.

Federalists in the eastern, mercantile communities of Edenton and New Bern rejoiced at the prospect of joining a government that could protect American interests abroad and property at home, promote a sound currency, and regulate trade throughout the country. On December 1, 1789, Edentonians celebrated ratification. They began by raising the United States flag at dawn, continued with a public dinner at which twelve toasts were drunk, and concluded in the evening with a bonfire. The following day New Bernians harkened to the sound of muskets fired by a local militia company, ate a sumptuous banquet in the early afternoon, and witnessed an "elegantly decorated" float in the shape of a vessel, christened the "ship Federalist," which was pulled through the streets while a salute was fired at each street corner. That night the town was brightly illuminated.

In retrospect, the desire to protect individual and states' rights, tempered by selfish state interests, shaped North Carolina's role in national politics during the Revolutionary era. As evidenced by Harnett and Spaight, even the conservatives were acutely aware of the need to protect the state from an overbearing national government as well as against undue pressure from New England. Still, conservative Federalists sought to replace the Articles of Confederation with a more powerful, active government which would serve to promote their conception of the "good" society, one controlled by an aristocracy and emphasizing commercial endeavor. Antifederalists, representing the radical, majoritarian, rural, farming populace, fought

William R. Davie (1756–1820), English-born and Princeton-educated, compiled an impressive military record during the Revolution, earning a reputation as "a daring and skillful individual fighter and an alert and resourceful commander." When the fighting ended, he married the niece of the future Antifederalist leader Willie Jones and began the practice of law. His imposing appearance and oratorical skills contributed to his political career, which began in 1786 when Davie became a state representative from Halifax. He led the move in the North Carolina legislature to send a contingent to Philadelphia, and though the thirty-one-year-old delegate was not prominent at the Federal Convention and departed early, he was in the vanguard of the battle to secure his state's ratification. A term as North Carolina's Federalist governor (1798), membership on the peace commission to France that ended the quasi-war (1799–1800), and the negotiation of a treaty with the Tuscarora Indians were the most notable of Davie's later political accomplishments. His role in the establishment of the University of North Carolina has prompted many to dub him the father of that renowned institution. Engraving, courtesy of North Carolina Department of Cultural Resources, Division of Archives and History.

just as consistently to protect the people from elitist government and the influence of a mercantile economy.

Ratification of the Constitution failed to crush the radical Antifederalist temperament in North Carolina. The conservative Federalist faction gained only temporary control of the state. Early in the 1790s the Antifederalists' fear of national authority, their parochialism, and their agrarianism reappeared in the form of the Democratic-Republican party. Not only did the Democratic Republicans dominate state affairs thereafter, but they did so by accepting and appropriating the Constitution as their own. James Madison's role in the creation of both that party and the Constitution facilitated this occurrence. As William Dickson wrote in 1790, two years after he had voted against ratification at Hillsborough, "I think [that the Constitution] is formed so as to lay the foundation of one of the greatest Empires in the world." And at a Fourth of July celebration in 1801 in the state capital of Raleigh, Republicans toasted "The Federal Constitution, the sheet-anchor of our peace at home and safety abroad."

North Carolina: Essay on Sources

A survey of North Carolina for the period under consideration can be obtained from standard state histories such as Robert D. W. Connor et al., *History of North Carolina*, 3 vols. (Chicago and New York, 1919) and Samuel A. Ashe, *History of North Carolina*, 2 vols. (Greensboro, N.C., 1908, 1925). More recently, two excellent dissertations update and expand those older treatments: Sheldon F. Koesy, "Continuity and Change in North Carolina, 1775–1789" (doctoral dissertation, Duke University, 1963) and Penelope Susan Smith, "Creation of an American State: Politics in North Carolina, 1765–1789" (doctoral dissertation, Rice University, 1980). J. Edwin Hendricks, "Joining the Federal Union," in *The North Carolina Experience*, edited by Lindley S. Butler and Alan D. Watson (Chapel Hill, 1984), pp. 147–170, provides an excellent brief account. More generally, Gordon Wood, *The Creation of the American Republic, 1776–1787* (Chapel Hill, 1969) is indispensable. An in-depth bibliography for the Revolutionary and Confederation eras may be found in Alan D. Watson, "Revolutionary North Carolina, 1765–1789," in *Writing North Carolina History*, edited by Jeffrey J. Crow and Larry E. Tise (Chapel Hill, 1979), pp. 36–75.

Highly useful for an understanding of particular facets of the Confederation years are John Sayle Watterson, *Thomas Burke: Restless Revolutionary* (Washington, D.C., 1980); C. B. Alexander, "Richard Caswell's Military and Later Services," *North Carolina Historical Review*, 23 (1946), 287–312; James R. Morrill, *The Practice and Politics of Fiat Finance: North Carolina in the Confederation, 1783–1789* (Chapel Hill, 1969); Charles C. Crittenden, *North Carolina Newspapers before 1790* (Chapel Hill, 1928), and *The Commerce of North Carolina, 1763–1789* (New Haven, 1936); Francis G. Morris and Phyllis M. Morris, "Economic Conditions in North Carolina about 1780," pts. 1, 2, *North Carolina Historical Review*, 16 (1939), 107–133, 196–327; Alice B. Keith, "John Gray and Thomas Blount, Merchants, 1783–1800," *North Carolina Historical Review*, 25 (1948), 194–205; William F. Zornow, "North Carolina Tariff Practices, 1775–1789," *North Carolina Historical Review*, 32 (1955), 151–164; Adelaide L. Fries et al., eds., *Records of the Moravians in North Carolina*, 11 vols. (Raleigh, 1922–69); George W. Troxler, "The Homefront in Revolutionary North Carolina" (doctoral dissertation, University of North Carolina, 1970).

North Carolina's role in the Constitutional Convention may be seen broadly in Clinton Rossiter, *1787: The Grand Convention* (New York, 1966) and Max Farrand, ed., *The Records of the Federal Convention of 1787*, 4 vols. (New Haven, reprinted 1966). For the state's representatives to the Philadelphia gathering, consult John W. Neal, "Life and Public Services of Hugh Williamson," Trinity College Historical Society *Papers*, 13 (1919), 62–115; Alexander Andrew, "Richard Dobbs Spaight," *North Carolina Historical Review*, 1 (1924), 93–120; Alan D. Watson, *Richard Dobbs Spaight* (New Bern, N.C., 1987); Alice B. Keith, "William Blount in North Carolina Politics, 1781–1789," in *Studies in Southern History*, edited by J. Carlyle Sitterson (Chapel Hill, 1957), pp. 47–61; William Masterson, *William Blount* (Baton Rouge, 1954); Blackwell P. Robinson, *William R. Davie* (Chapel Hill, 1957).

The ratification debate in North Carolina has been best treated by Louise I. Trenholme, *The Ratification of the Federal Constitution in North Carolina* (New York, 1931) and Albert Ray Newsome, "North Carolina's Ratification of the Federal Constitution," *North Carolina Historical Review*, 17 (1940), 287–301. For Federalist Samuel Johnston, see Robert D. W. Connor, "Governor Samuel Johnston," *North Carolina Booklet*, 9 (1912), 259–285. For leading Antifederalists, consult Blackwell P. Robinson, "Willie Jones of Halifax," pts. 1, 2, *North Carolina Historical Review*, 18 (1941), 1–26, 133–170; Stephen B. Weeks, "Thomas Person," *North Carolina Booklet*, 9 (1909), 16–35; and Jackson Turner Main, *The Antifederalists: Critics of the Constitution, 1781–1788* (Chapel Hill, 1961). Assessing and criticizing Charles Beard's interpretation is William C. Pool, "An Economic Interpretation of the Ratification of the Federal Constitution in North Carolina," pts. 1–3, *North Carolina Historical Review*, 27 (1950), 119–141, 289–313, 437–461. J. Edwin Hendricks, "Joseph Winston: North Carolina Jeffersonian," *North Carolina Historical Review*, 45 (1968), 284–297, and Delbert H. Gilpatrick, *Jeffersonian Democracy in North Carolina, 1789–1816* (New York, 1931) are also helpful. For the proceedings of North Carolina's first ratification convention, see Jonathan Elliot, ed., *The Debates in the Several State Conventions on the Adoption of the Federal Constitution as Recommended by the General Convention at Philadelphia in 1787*, 5 vols. (Philadelphia, 1836–45); for the second convention, consult Walter Clark, ed., *The State Records of North Carolina*, 16 vols., numbered 11–26 (Winston and Goldsboro, N.C., 1895–1907), vol. 22.

13

First in War, Last in Peace

Rhode Island and the Constitution, 1786–1790

PATRICK T. CONLEY
Professor of History
Providence College

OUNDED IN 1636 by Roger Williams and his associates upon the principles of religious liberty and separation of church and state, seventeenth-century Rhode Island became a haven for radical Protestant sects, especially Baptists, Antinomians, and Quakers, and persecuted religious refugees, such as Portuguese Jews and French Huguenots. The colony, dubbed a "moral sewer" by orthodox and intolerant Massachusetts Puritans, developed a dissenting tradition and prided itself on being "the home of the otherwise-minded." During its early years Rhode Island repeatedly fought off attempts by land-grabbing and resentful neighbors to reduce its already diminutive size.

To guarantee its legal right to exist, Dr. John Clarke secured for the colony an extraordinarily liberal charter from King Charles II in 1663. Not only did this document proclaim "full liberty in religious concernments," but it also allowed a self-governing commonwealth wherein all local officials, from the governor and assemblymen to the viewers of fences and corders of wood, were either chosen directly in town meeting by the freemen (i.e., those qualified to vote on the basis of residency, age, sex, religion, and land ownership) or appointed on an annual basis by the elected representatives of the people.

No other English colony possessed such a refreshing combination of religious freedom and local self-government. This condition persisted throughout the colonial era, evoking criticism from English observers. On the eve of the War of Independence, Chief Justice Daniel Horsmanden of New York, investigating the burning of the British revenue ship *Gaspee* by Providence dissidents, disdainfully described Rhode Island as a "downright democracy" whose governmental officials were "entirely controlled by the populace," and conservative Massachusetts governor Thomas Hutchinson lamented to George III that Rhode Island was "the nearest to a democracy of any of your colonies."

Rhode Islanders of the Revolutionary generation and their individualistic forebears were themselves ever mindful that they enjoyed near autonomy within the empire and broad powers of self-government within their colony. They were also keenly aware that their self-determination flowed in large measure from the generous charter of Charles II. Thus they harbored a passionate attachment to that document and stoutly defended it against all comers. They allowed it to weather the Revolutionary upheaval (when eleven colonies discarded their English charters) and retained it as the basic law of the state until 1843, a point far beyond its useful life. Most Rhode Islanders apparently shared the opinion of attorney and educator David Howell, who in 1782, while serving as one of the state's popularly elected delegates to the Confederation Congress, made the following boast: "As you go southward, Government verges towards Aristocracy. In New England alone have we pure and unmixed Democracy and in Rhode Island . . . it is in its perfection."

Revolutionary Rhode Island

Rhode Island was a leader in the American Revolutionary movement. Having the greatest degree of self-rule, it had the most to lose from the efforts of England after 1763 to increase its supervision and control over the American colonies. In addition, Rhode Island had a long tradition of evading the poorly enforced Navigation Acts, and smuggling was commonplace.

Beginning with strong opposition in Newport to the Sugar Act (1764), with its restrictions on the molasses trade, the colony engaged in repeated measures of open defiance, such as the scuttling and torching of the British customs sloop *Liberty* in Newport harbor in July 1769, the burning of the British revenue schooner *Gaspee* on Warwick's Namquit Point in 1772, and Providence's own "Tea Party" in Market Square on March 2, 1775.

On May 17, 1774, after parliamentary passage of the Coercive Acts (Americans called them "Intolerable"), the Providence Town Meeting became the first governmental assemblage to issue a call for a general congress of colonies to resist British policy. A month later, on June 15, the General Assembly made the colony the first to appoint delegates (Samuel Ward and Stephen Hopkins) to the anticipated Continental Congress.

A week after the skirmishes at Lexington and Concord in April 1775, the colonial legislature authorized a fifteen-hundred-man "army of observation" with Nathanael Greene as its commander. Finally, on May 4, 1776, Rhode Island became the first colony to renounce allegiance to King George III when its legislature, sitting at Providence, passed a bold renunciation act. On July 18, meeting at Newport, the Assembly ratified the Declaration of Independence, which had been signed for Rhode Island by Stephen Hopkins and William Ellery.

The Long Struggle to Ratify the Constitution

Surprisingly, Rhode Island's initial response to a plan for a permanent central government was cordial. Such a proposal was advanced by the ad hoc Continental Congress in 1777 and embodied in the instrument known as the Articles of Confederation. The Articles were drafted, debated by the Congress, and placed before the rebellious states in November 1777. Delegate Henry Marchant of Newport bore this first national constitution to Rhode Island and urged its acceptance at a special session of the General Assembly in December. The question of adoption was deferred to the February 1778 session, and at that conclave the state gave the Articles its unanimous assent. Three amendments were suggested, but these were merely recommendations and not prerequisites for ratification.

Rhode Island was so uncharacteristically obliging because several of its towns were under British occupation and because it had incurred enormous military expenditures which might be partially absorbed by the new central government. Rhode Island instructed its delegates to ratify the Articles if eight other states should do so, and in the event that any alterations were advanced, these delegates were empowered to accept whatever changes were approved by nine of the states. Rhode Island further promised that it would be bound by any alterations agreed to in this manner by its delegation. No changes were made in the Articles, however, and the state's representatives unhesitatingly signed the form of ratification in Philadelphia on July 9, 1778, hailing the document as "the Grand Corner Stone" of the new nation.

In the succeeding twelve years Rhode Island would seldom act with such compliance toward the federal union. In fact, Rhode Island exhibited an obstinacy in the national council which proved exasperating to many of its sister states. Its initial contrariness consisted in a flat rejection of the proposed Continental Impost (or tariff) of 1781, despite the efforts of Thomas Paine and other prominent figures to enlist the state's support. Rhode Island's most blatant demonstration of defiance was its repeated refusal to ratify the federal Constitution of 1787.

An acquaintance with the political setting in which Rhode Island's contest over the Constitution took place is essential to an understanding of the ratification controversy. The principal political fact of life was the dominance in state affairs of the so-called Country Party. This faction, led mainly by legislators from the rural and agrarian towns, had swept into power in the annual spring elections of 1786 on a paper-money platform. The victory constituted somewhat of a political revolution because it transformed the legislature from a merchant-dominated body to one in which the interests of the farmer took precedence.

The Country Party made good its campaign pledge and immediately authorized the issuance of £100,000 ($333,000) in paper money. Historians now realize that the primary purpose of the paper emission was to alleviate the tax burden which weighed heavily on the owners of real property, and that the payment of private debts in paper was merely an incidental by-product of this successful program. However, contemporary creditors and many members of the state's mercantile community were not so well informed, and thus paper money was a chief source of controversy in local politics from 1786 through 1791. It engendered the dispute which precipitated the landmark court case of *Trevett* v. *Weeden*, and it served as the bond of union for the dominant Country Party—an organization which opposed the ratification of the Constitution of 1787.

With the exception of its response to the Annapolis Convention of September 1786, Rhode Island exhibited a wariness towards all attempts at forming a stronger central government. Just prior to that Maryland gathering, the state had expressed a desire to secure uniform and centralized regulation of commerce to protect its reexport trade from the tariffs of her neighboring states. Because that important but limited action was the only topic on the proposed agenda at Annapolis, Rhode Island dispatched two delegates. These commissioners, Jabez Bowen and Samuel Ward, Jr., had journeyed as far south as Philadelphia when they received news that the abortive four-day conclave had adjourned.

In the following year, when a call was issued for a more broadly empowered convention to discuss all matters necessary "to render the constitution of the Federal government adequate to the exigencies of the Union," the Country Party was firmly entrenched. Consequently, the state failed to vote on the February 1787 resolution of the Confederation Congress to hold the Philadelphia Convention, and when that momentous assembly convened, Rhode Island was the only state to boycott its proceedings. Three times an attempt to dispatch delegates was rejected by the suspicious General Assembly. Rhode Island's absence was protested both by the deputies (i.e., state representatives) from Providence and Newport and by General James Mitchell Varnum and Peleg Arnold, the state's delegates in Congress, but to no avail.

On September 15, 1787, just prior to the completion of the federal convention, Country Party governor John Collins forwarded to the president of the Confederation Congress the General Assembly's feeble excuse for nonattendance at the Philadelphia sessions. Since the freemen at large had the power of electing delegates to represent them in Congress, the Assembly declared, the legislature could not consistently *appoint* delegates to a convention which might be the means of dissolving that Congress. In view of the broad power which the Rhode Island legislature was accustomed to exercise, these remarks seemed evasive indeed. A spirited rejoinder signed

When the Country Party gained power in 1786, it promptly issued an amount of paper money roughly equivalent to the size of the state debt and implemented an ingenious plan to relieve debtors, most of whom were farmers. Because the new U.S. Constitution banned state issues of paper money (Article I, Section 10), the Country Party opposed ratification, especially until the paper program had been brought to a successful conclusion in 1789. Paper money issue of 1786, from the private collection of Patrick T. Conley.

by the Newport and Providence deputies reminded the General Assembly that it had dispatched delegates to the Continental Congress, ratified the Declaration of Independence, and accepted the Articles of Confederation without a popular referendum. Their arguments, though sound, were fruitless.

When the federal convention completed its labors on September 17, 1787, it transmitted the Constitution to Congress with the recommendation that the document be submitted to the states for ratification by popularly elected conventions. Congress (with Rhode Island absent) complied with this suggestion and gave the states official notice of its action.

The Rhode Island legislature took the new Constitution under advisement at its October 1787 session. It thereupon voted for the distribution of a thousand copies of the proposed document to allow the freemen "an opportunity of forming their sentiments" upon it. This approach was consistent with the Country Party's practice of governing by referendum.

With most of the freemen thus apprised of the federal charter's contents, the February 1788 session assembled. Then, to the consternation of Federalists within the state and without, the Assembly authorized a popular vote on the Constitution and scheduled it for the fourth Monday in March. This ratification procedure was irregular and contrary to the recommendations of the Philadelphia delegates, but the legislature was not deterred by this departure from the norm. In fact, the February session specifically rejected a motion to call a ratifying convention. Over the course of the next twenty-three months, a total of eleven such efforts would be spurned.

The popular referendum on the Constitution was held according to schedule. Although the result was predictable—243 for and 2,711 against—the margin of defeat is deceptive. The Federal port towns of Providence and Newport boycotted the referendum; just one vote was cast in the former community and only eleven were registered in Newport, and these ballots, with one exception (in Newport), were cast by Antifederalists. The only towns in the Federalist column were the bay settlements of Bristol (26–23) and Little Compton (63–57). The critics of the Constitution, however, registered lopsided victories in many rural communities, among them Glocester (228–9), Coventry (180–0), Foster (177–0), and Scituate (156–0).

The total vote in this referendum was 2,954, as compared with the 4,287 who had voted in the well-contested gubernatorial election of 1787. Newport and Providence accounted for most of the abstainers, for these towns, according to fairly reliable estimates, together had between 825 and 900 freemen in 1788. Yet it is obvious that even if these communities had turned out en masse for the Constitution, it would have been rejected by an impressive plurality. Thirteen weeks later New Hampshire became the ninth state to ratify the federal document, but despite the rejoicing over this event

STATE *of* RHODE-ISLAND, *&c.*

In GENERAL ASSEMBLY, *February Session*, A.D. 1788.

An ACT submitting to the Confideration of the Freemen of this State, the Report of the Convention of Delegates for a Conftitution for the United States, as agreed on in Philadelphia, the 17th of September, A. D. 1787.

WHEREAS the Honorable the Continental Congrefs did heretofore recommend to the Legiflatures of the refpective States, to appoint Delegates to meet in Convention, at Philadelphia, in May, A. D. 1787, to make fuch Alterations and Amendments in the prefent Confederation of the United States as would tend to promote the Happinefs, good Government and Welfare of the Federal Union : And whereas the faid Delegates, on the 17th Day of September, 1787, did agree upon, and report to the Congrefs of the United States, a Form of a Conftitution for the United States of America : And whereas the faid United States in Congrefs affembled did, by a Refolution paffed the 28th Day of September, A. D. 1787, tranfmit faid Report to the Legiflature of this State, to be fubmitted to the Confideration of the People thereof : And whereas this Legiflative Body, in General Affembly convened, conceiving themfelves Reprefentatives of the great Body of People at large, and that they cannot make any Innovations in a Conftitution which has been agreed upon, and the Compact fettled between the Governors and Governed, without the exprefs Confent of the Freemen at large, by their own Voices individually taken in Town-Meetings affembled : Wherefore, for the Purpofe aforefaid, and for fubmitting the faid Conftitution for the United States to the Confideration of the Freemen of this State :

B E it Enacted by this General Affembly, and by the Authority thereof it is hereby Enacted, That the Fourth Monday in March inft. be, and the fame is hereby appointed, the Day for all the Freemen and Freeholders within this State, to convene in their refpective Towns, in Town-Meetings affembled, and to deliberate upon, and determine each Individual (who hath a Right by Law to vote for the Choice of General Officers) by himfelf by Poll, whether the faid Conftitution for the United States fhall be adopted or negatived.

AND be it further Enacted by the Authority aforefaid, That the Town-Clerks in the refpective Towns fhall forthwith iffue their Warrants, for the convening of the Freemen and Freeholders to meet, on faid Fourth Monday of March inft. at fuch Place where the Town-Meetings are ufually holden : And the fame fhall be directed to the Town-Serjeants and Conftables of the refpective Towns, who fhall caufe Notifications to be fet up in the moft public Places of Refort within fuch Towns ; and alfo fhall repair to the ufual Place of Abode of the Freemen and Freeholders in fuch Town, and give them Notice of the Meeting aforefaid, for the Purpofe aforefaid. The faid Town-Serjeants and Conftables to have particular Diftricts pointed out to them, to warn the Freemen and Freeholders, fo as not to interfere with each other's Diftrict, that all the Freemen and Freeholders may, if poffible, have Notice and attend accordingly. And upon the Convention of faid Freemen, they fhall appoint a Moderator, who fhall regulate fuch Meeting ; and the Voices of the Freemen and Freeholders fhall be taken by Yeas and Nays, and the Town-Clerk of each Town fhall regifter the Name of each and every Freeman and Freeholder, with the Yea or Nay, as he fhall refpectively give his Voice aloud, in open Town-Meeting, and fhall keep the Original in his Office, and fhall make out a true and fair certified Copy of the Regifter aforefaid, with the Yeas and Nays of each and every Perfon thereon, and carefully feal the fame up, and direct it to the General Affembly, to be holden by Adjournment, at Eaft-Greenwich, in the County of Kent, on the laft Monday of March inft. and deliver the fame to One of the Reprefentatives of fuch Town, or other careful Perfon, who will take Charge of the fame, to be delivered to the faid General Affembly, then and there to be opened, that the Sentiments of the People may be known refpecting the fame.

AND it is further Enacted by the Authority aforefaid, That in Cafe it fhall fo happen that the faid Fourth Monday of March inft. fhall prove to be ftormy or boifterous Weather, fo that the Freemen and Freeholders in general cannot conveniently attend, the faid Town-Meeting may adjourn, from Day to Day, not exceeding three Days, fo that the Voices of the People may be taken.

AND it is further Enacted by the Authority aforefaid, That the Secretary fhall forthwith tranfmit to each Town-Clerk of the refpective Towns within this State a Copy of this Act.

A true Copy :

Witnefs, HENRY WARD, *Secretary.*

[PROVIDENCE : Printed by BENNETT WHEELER.]

When the completed Constitution was sent to the states to be ratified by specially called conventions, the Country Party defied the instructions of the framers and authorized a popular referendum instead. In that March 24, 1788, balloting, which most supporters of the Constitution boycotted, Rhode Island rejected the handiwork of the Founding Fathers by the lopsided margin of 2,711 to 243 (historians' tabulations vary slightly). Rhode Island was the only state to hold a referendum on the new Constitution, thereby incurring the wrath of Federalists. Broadside published by Bennett Wheeler for the referendum of 1788, courtesy of the Rhode Island Historical Society.

in Providence, the chances that Rhode Island would follow the lead of her more amenable brethren seemed extremely remote. Antifederal sentiment ran high. On the Fourth of July 1788, some Antifederalists even formed a mob to prevent Providence Federalists from merely celebrating the progress of ratification.

During the early summer of 1788 the crucial states of Virginia and New York also fell in line, but Rhode Island was unrelenting. In March 1789, as the new federal government prepared to convene, the General Assembly for a fifth time rejected a motion to call a ratifying convention. In May the issue was sidestepped, and in the June and October sessions it was rejected again.

The only other holdout at this late date was North Carolina, a state which, like Rhode Island, was settled by outcasts and was noted for its individualism and separatist tendencies. On November 21, 1789, the Carolinians at last capitulated and left Rhode Island alone and, in effect, an independent republic.

As the year 1790 dawned, the pressures on Antifederalists increased, and the prospects for at least a convention grew brighter. The opponents of the Constitution had shown signs of wavering in the early October session when they voted to print and distribute among the towns 150 copies of the twelve amendments to the Constitution which had been recommended by the new Congress of the United States. Ten of these would become the Bill of Rights.

In the January session the Federalist minority was further encouraged when the legislature, after two unsuccessful efforts, narrowly passed a bill, introduced by Henry Marchant, authorizing a ratification convention to meet on March 1, 1790, at South Kingstown. Four-term governor John Collins, who was always cool towards Antifederalism, courageously incurred the wrath of his own Country Party when he cast the deciding vote on Marchant's measure and broke a 4–4 Senate deadlock. He was not renominated by his political associates. The tie that led to Collins' political demise was created when Antifederalist assistant (i.e., senator) John Williams missed the Sunday legislative session at which the crucial vote was taken to attend his religious duties as a Baptist preacher.

The election of delegates for the long-delayed ratifying convention went unfavorably in the view of Marchant, a Newport Federalist. Two weeks before the session convened, he prophesied its outcome: "The Anti's are about ten majority. I have hopes however they will not totally reject the Constitution, but I think they may adjourn it over our Genl. Election," which was to be held in April.

Marchant's intuition was correct. The convention met and considered both the Constitution and the twelve amendments thereto proposed by

Congress. In addition, it adopted an eighteen-clause "declaration of rights" and advanced eighteen other constitutional amendments. These were sent to the freemen for consideration.

The major points of discussion during the six-day March session were the allocation of representatives, direct taxation, the slave trade, the method of adopting future amendments, the ratification of the congressionally proposed Bill of Rights, and the power of the convention to adopt the Constitution. Although some Antifederalists had mellowed, a majority of them were resolved to resist the Constitution to the bitter end. Merchant-prince John Innes Clark, one of the four Federalist delegates from Providence, observed that "we have as determined a set of men to oppose it as ever were combined together." On Saturday, March 6, over the protests of Federalists, the gathering adjourned to meet in Newport on May 24 by a vote of 41–28, a margin which was a fairly accurate indication of the relative strength of the anti- and pro-Constitution factions.

Henry Marchant (1741–1796) was a well-educated Newport intellectual of French Huguenot ancestry and a protégé of Ezra Stiles, president of Yale University. Marchant was an ardent Son of Liberty during the Stamp Act protest, and when war came, he served as a Rhode Island delegate to Congress (1777–1779) and signed the Articles of Confederation. After the war he entered the General Assembly as a vigorous spokesman for the state's commercial interest (1784–1790). In January 1790, as a strong supporter of the new federal Constitution, Marchant introduced the successful bill for the call of a ratifying convention, at which he played a leading role. His efforts on behalf of Federalism were rewarded when George Washington appointed him Rhode Island's first federal judge, a post in which Marchant served from July 1790 until his death in August 1796. Etching by Max Rosenthal, courtesy of the Rhode Island Historical Society.

277

During the interim between sessions the spring elections were conducted, and the Country Party (minus Governor Collins) scored its fifth consecutive victory. At the head of its ticket was Arthur Fenner of the distinguished Providence clan. So formidable and prominent was Fenner and so potent was his party that Federalists endorsed him rather than arouse the ire of the Country majority on the eve of the ratification convention.

Despite this success and the Antifederal majority of approximately a dozen in the seventy-member convention, several critics of the Constitution were beginning to find their position no longer tenable in the face of increasing pressure from within and without the state. When the ratifying body reconvened, the Constitution's adherents, led by Marchant, Benjamin Bourne of Providence, and William Bradford from the port town of Bristol, pushed vigorously for its acceptance. Finally, after five days of political jousting, Bourne moved (in the words of convention secretary Daniel Updike) "for the grand question of adopting or rejecting the federal government." At 5:20 p.m. on Saturday, May 29, the motion squeaked through by a vote of 34–32.

The contest was so close that a full convention might have reversed the decision. The three absent delegates—Edward Hill and Ray Sands, representing remote New Shoreham (Block Island), and Job Durfee of Portsmouth—appear to have been Antifederal, while Country Party chieftain Daniel Owen of Glocester was prevented from voting, except to break a tie, by virtue of his position as convention chairman. The margin of acceptance was narrower than that of any other state, and Rhode Island was one of only three states in which the delegates voting for ratification represented fewer people than those voting against it. But an inch was as good as a mile.

Soon after this momentous action, the formal bill ratifying and adopting the Constitution was approved by the convention. This measure also gave assent to eleven of the twelve amendments to the Constitution proposed by Congress and boldly offered twenty-one additional amendments, many of which had been previously proposed by the Virginia and New York conventions.

At its June session the General Assembly gave its necessary approval to the Bill of Rights (making Rhode Island the ninth state to take such action), established procedures for the election of federal senators and representatives, and chose Theodore Foster, a moderate Providence Federalist who had kept the minutes of the South Kingstown convention, and Joseph Stanton, Jr., an Antifederal leader from Charlestown, as Rhode Island's first United States senators. Foster was the brother-in-law of Governor Fenner, a fact which helped him gain the support of the Country Party. When Benjamin Bourne, a champion of the Constitution, won the August contest for the state's lone seat in the House of Representatives, Rhode Island at last became a full participant in the new federal union.

The Reasons for Rhode Island's Antifederalism

Although the principal events of this turbulent period are fairly discernible, the motives behind Rhode Island's long-term opposition and then grudging acceptance of the Constitution are multiple and complex. Certainly, the paper-money controversy contributed to the state's rejection of the new federal instrument. The Country Party came to power on a pro-paper platform in 1786, and this agrarian faction, led by Jonathan J. Hazard, Joseph Stanton, Jr., John Collins, Job Comstock, and Daniel Owen, firmly held the reins of political power from May 1786 until well after the reluctant ratifi-

The final session of Rhode Island's ratifying convention was held at the Newport Colony House. Built in 1739 from the designs of architect Richard Munday, the Colony House, or Old State House, stands at the head of Newport's Washington Square. It was the site of the General Assembly's annual organizational meeting until 1900, when Providence became the state's only capital. This Newport landmark is the oldest of Rhode Island's "state houses," as the old county courthouses were called. The General Assembly rotated its sessions among the five counties until 1854, giving the smallest state five capitals. Newport Colony House. Photo by John Rujen (ca. 1915), courtesy of the Rhode Island Historical Society.

cation of the national document by Rhode Island in mid-1790. Although the party was not monolithic, it was dominant and cohesive, and the major opposition to the Constitution emanated from its ranks. In Rhode Island the Country Party served as an effective and organized vehicle of Antifederalism.

When the ratification process began, Rhode Island was too deeply enmeshed in the paper-money program to back out, and Article I, Section 10, of the federal document, forbidding states from making anything but gold and silver coin a tender in payment of debts, might have forced her to do so. The financial chaos that would have resulted from the abandonment of the paper program before it had run its course would have made the existing financial situation seem peaceful and orderly by comparison.

Speculating on the possibilities of ratification, William Ellery, Continental loan officer in Newport, several times expressed the view that the Country Party would "wait till they shall have completely extinguished the State debt" before accepting the Constitution. It was Ellery's contention that ratification would not take place before the "accursed paper money system" had achieved its intended purpose.

In Rhode Island there was a definite correlation between the pro-paper towns and those which opposed the Constitution, but Antifederalism and advocacy of paper money were not synonymous. Such an equation admits of too many exceptions and incongruities. Although the same towns and the same individuals who favored the paper money also opposed the Constitution, a comparison of the vote on the constitutional referendum with the votes for the Country Party candidates in 1786 and 1787 seems to indicate that the sentiment against the Constitution was noticeably greater than the normal strength of the Country Party.

In the light of these considerations, we must identify other factors in addition to the currency controversy to adequately understand the intensity of Rhode Island's Antifederalism. Additional economic motives for the state's resistance are strongly in evidence. The most important of these was the fear that exorbitant taxes on land and polls would be levied by the new national government to pay the public debt and the allegedly high salaries of federal officials. Unprecedented and burdensome state taxes on land were in large measure responsible for the paper-money emission, and the land-holders' dread of similar federal taxes was to a considerable extent responsible for Rhode Island's opposition to the new federal union.

This apprehension was evidenced by the serious attention given to the question of direct taxes on land and polls in the March 1790 ratifying convention. It was further exhibited in three constitutional amendments (VII, VIII, and IX) proposed and approved by that convention. In suggested amendment VII, Rhode Island joined New York in urging that "no capitation or poll tax shall ever be laid by Congress"; in amendment VIII, she joined six sister states in requesting a prohibition on the laying of direct taxes except after the failure of a federal requisition upon the states; and in proposed amendment IX (one of five that were unique to Rhode Island), the state, as an insurance measure, recommended that "Congress shall lay no direct taxes, without the assent of the legislatures of three fourths of the states in the Union."

Of the economic reasons for Rhode Island's reluctance to adopt the Constitution, it would appear that a fear of heavy taxes on land and polls probably influenced more voters than any other single factor. Perhaps former deputy governor Jabez Bowen, a leading Federalist, summed up the situation as well as any contemporary in a letter to George Washington:

> The Towns of Newport, Providence, Bristol etc. with the whole Mercantile interest in the other Towns in the State are Federal, while the Farmers in general are against it. Their opposition arises principally from their being much in Debt, from the Insinuations of wicked and designing Men that they will lose their Liberty in adopting it; that the Salaries of the National Officers are so very high that it will take the whole of the Money Collected by the Impost to pay them, that the Interest & principle of the General Debt must be raised by Dry Taxation on Real Estates, etc.

As Bowen's observation indicates, there were ingredients in Rhode Island's Antifederalism in addition to those of an economic nature. Bowen spoke of the loss of liberty, which seemed to many a necessary consequence of ratification. A consideration of this pervasive belief brings us into the sphere of what might be termed political, philosophic, or ideological motivations for Rhode Island's suspicion of the proposed federal union, and these motives were of great and, perhaps, transcendent importance.

Rhode Island had a strong tradition of individualism, separatism, democracy, and liberty, both civil and religious. It harbored a long-standing distrust of government too far removed from the people, together with an attachment to popular control of government, that one historian has termed "democratic localism." These principles were not endangered by the Articles of Confederation, to which the state readily assented. The Articles gave the people of a state—or, more precisely, their legislature—close control over delegates to Congress. Under the Confederation, members of Congress were annually appointed in a manner prescribed by the state legislature, they were subject to recall, and they were paid by their respective states. Under the Articles, as in Rhode Island, supreme governmental power was vested in the legislature.

In addition to these features, the Articles, of course, exalted state sovereignty. In all important civil matters Congress was dependent upon the voluntary compliance of the state legislatures to carry out its recommendations, and the approval of all states was necessary to amend our inflexible first frame of government.

This system was rejected by the Constitution in ways too familiar to enumerate, and Rhode Island disapproved of the change. Some of her specific objections were contained in the eighteen amendments to the new federal document offered by the Rhode Island ratifying convention of March 1790. These amendments revealed a deep suspicion of the new central establishment, a suspicion that had been increased by the failure of the proposed Constitution to contain a bill of rights.

Rhode Island's first suggested amendment requested a guarantee to each state of its sovereignty and of every power not expressly delegated to the United States by the Constitution; amendment II attempted to limit federal interference in a state's conduct of congressional elections; amendment XII prohibited as "dangerous to liberty" standing armies in time of peace; amendments XIII and XIV called for a two-thirds vote of those present in each house to borrow money on the credit of the United States or to declare war; amendment XVIII subjected senators to recall and replacement by their state legislature. Rhode Island was so fearful that the newly created federal system would develop beyond control that it offered a unique amendment (IV) which would have required all changes in the Constitution after 1793 to receive the consent of eleven of the thirteen original states. Those congressionally advanced amendments which eventually became the Bill of Rights, of course, won the state's support.

In an official communication to Congress in September 1789, the General Assembly quite adequately and accurately expressed the ideological basis of the state's Antifederalism:

> The people of this State from its first settlement, have been accustomed and strongly attached to a democratic form of government. They have viewed in the new Constitution an approach, though perhaps but small, toward that form of government from which we have lately dissolved our connection at so much hazard and expense of life and treasure. . . . We are sensible of the extremes to which democratic governments are sometimes liable, something of which we have lately experienced, but we esteem them temporary and partial evils compared with the loss of liberty and the rights of a free people.

This was not mere rhetoric. Just as Rhode Islanders were quick to protest an alleged abridgement by England of their individual and collective freedom, so also did they resist an anticipated curtailment of their liberty and autonomy by the Founding Fathers. Self-determination in late eighteenth-century Rhode Island was a way of life, and no portion of it would be easily surrendered, as the contest over ratification dramatically revealed.

Another formidable factor contributing to the strength of the state's Antifederalism was a strong hostility toward slavery, a hostility that pervaded the state. This attitude was intense among Rhode Island's sizable Quaker community, but it was shared by others as well, perhaps to atone for past sins. Opponents of slavery realized that the Philadelphia Convention had compromised on this issue, and they were aware that the Constitution thrice gave implied assent to the institution through the clauses on representation, fugitives, and the slave trade. In particular, the twenty-year prohibition on federal legislation banning the foreign slave trade was a concession too great for many Rhode Islanders to accept.

Only five weeks after the adjournment of the Philadelphia conclave, the General Assembly passed an act, initiated by the influential and irrepressible Quakers, prohibiting any Rhode Island citizen from engaging in the slave trade. In vigorous language, this statute termed the nefarious traffic "inconsistent with justice, and the principles of humanity, as well as the laws of nature, and that more enlightened and civilized sense of freedom which has of late prevailed." A constitution which gave temporary protection to this trade was not an instrument to be warmly embraced.

Thus the state's antislavery contingent took refuge in Antifederalism, and during the critical year 1790 this connection nearly thwarted ratification. Fortunately, however, there were some abolitionist leaders who began to see the difficulties inherent in Rhode Island's continued rejection of the Constitution. One such man was the influential Quaker Moses Brown of the famous mercantile family. Despite some initial misgivings, he embraced the Federalist cause by 1790. Early in that fateful year Brown toured the state, talking with Friends at the various monthly meetings in an attempt to overcome their opposition. His campaign seems to have met with limited success, but the antislavery objections to the Constitution were by no means dispelled when the March session of the ratifying convention assembled.

Slavery engendered much discussion and debate at this South Kingstown meeting. In fact, the slave-trade provision of the Constitution provoked such opposition that an amendment (XVII) was specifically proposed and approved exhorting Congress to ban the traffic immediately. Rhode Island was the only state to suggest such an amendment to the federal Constitution during the ratification struggle.

Some local opponents of slavery doggedly maintained their Antifederalism until the end. When the Providence Abolition Society, founded in February 1789, received its charter from the state in June 1790, the list of incorporators revealed that ten of its signers were members of the May ratifying convention. The antislaveryites included President Daniel Owen and Antifederal floor leaders Joseph Stanton, Jr., and Job Comstock. Only three of these ten abolitionist delegates voted to accept the federal document on May 29.

Finally, Rhode Island's hostility toward the Union was conditioned in part by the Union's hostility to Rhode Island. Since the days of Roger Williams, when Rhode Island was dubbed a "moral sewer" by her haughty Puritan neighbors, the state had been subjected to the slings and arrows of outraged "foreigners." In the decade of the 1780s, however, this abuse from without reached unprecedented proportions. Beginning with Rhode Island's initial rejection of the Impost of 1781 and continuing through the paper-money era, the state and its citizens were subjected to an endless stream of invective. Rhode Island newspapers of the day were replete with verbal barbs reprinted from distant presses. The Confederation Congress attempted to unseat Rhode Island delegate David Howell for his strenuous opposition to the impost; later, after the paper-money issue, the state was caricatured as the "Quintessence of Villany" and as an example of "democracy run rampant." Such harsh actions and words of condescending foreign critics were most distressing to Rhode Islanders.

During the Constitution-making process Federalists took Rhode Island to task. For them the state symbolized the danger to order posed by popularly controlled state legislatures. From the outset, when the *Massachusetts Centinel* described Rhode Island's absence from the Grand Convention as a "joyous rather than a grievous" circumstance, to the end of the ratification struggle, when some proposed the state's dismemberment and absorption by the surrounding states, Rhode Island endured repeated insult. Even the temperate James Madison found Rhode Island exasperating. "Nothing can exceed the wickedness and folly which continue to rule there," he exclaimed. "All sense of character as well as of right have been obliterated."

The most eloquent censure of all came from Connecticut, from the pens of a foursome who later joined a group of literati known as the Connecticut Wits. Their contribution to Rhode Island's litany of shame was a long poetical satire entitled "Anarchiad, 1786–1787."

> Hail! realm of rogues, renown'd for fraud and guile,
> All hail; ye knav'ries of yon little isle.
> There prowls the rascal, cloth'd with legal pow'r,
> To snare the orphan, and the poor devour;
> The crafty knave his creditor besets,
> And advertising paper pays his debts;
> Bankrupts their creditors, with rage pursue,
> No stop, no mercy from the debtor crew.
> Arm'd with new tests, the licens'd villain bold,
> Presents his bills, and robs them of their gold;
> Their ears, though rogues and counterfeiters lose,

No legal robber fears the gallows noose.

....

Each weekly print new lists of cheats proclaims,
Proud to enroll their knav'ries and their names;
The wiser race, the snares of law to shun,
Like Lot from Sodom, from Rhode Island run.

Such derision caused anger and resentment in Rhode Island, and it
produced a banding together of the citizenry, especially in the country towns,
against the outside agitators. Federalists won few friends in Rhode Island
with their abusive tirades.

The Reasons for Rhode Island's Federalism

As the foregoing discussion reveals, Rhode Island's opposition to
the Constitution stemmed primarily from an adherence to the paper-money
program, aversion to direct taxation, attachment to liberty and the principles
of direct democracy, detestation of slavery, and adverse reaction to "foreign"
criticism. These obstacles for a time seemed insuperable. However, there
were countervailing forces at work in this era which eventually produced a
tenuous triumph for the cause of Federalism.

Several of these forces were operative from the inception of the
controversy; others developed gradually as the tides of change left Rhode
Island high and dry outside the Union. From the outset, the existence within
the state of Continental Loan Office certificates (i.e., U.S. government bonds)
in the face amount of $524,000 provided an important source of support for
a new, more stable and fiscally responsible national government that could
honor its debts. The major repositories for these securities, Providence and
Newport, were also the major strongholds of Federalism.

Ratification would benefit not only those private creditors of the
national government who held these certificates but a number of the coastal
towns as well. Exposed communities such as Newport, Middletown, Portsmouth, Jamestown, Tiverton, Little Compton, Bristol, and Warren held substantial compensation claims against the United States for war damages. Newport, Middletown, and Portsmouth, in fact, had audited claims amounting
to $719,280 out of a state total of $899,100. The establishment of a government
with effective taxing power would enhance their chances for compensation,
but it appears from the slow conversion of these communities (Newport and
Bristol, of course, excepted) that the claims were a peripheral rather than a
decisive consideration.

The mercantile community favored ratification because it had come
to realize the importance of unified national control over interstate and for-

eign commerce. The proliferation of interstate tariffs and the failure of the Confederation diplomats to secure commercial treaties with such important nations as England and Spain as a result of the Articles' weakness in the area of commercial regulation would be remedied by the new Constitution. Effective central direction and encouragement of commerce, the merchants felt, would enhance the state's economy and their personal fortunes as well.

Finally, ratification presented the prospect of a protective tariff to the small but growing and influential class of mechanics and incipient industrialists who were concentrated mainly in Providence. In the spring of 1789 the newly created Providence Association of Mechanics and Manufacturers appointed a committee of correspondence to dispatch circular letters to similar groups in other states lamenting Rhode Island's obstructionism and expressing an "anxious desire and fervent prayer that this State may speedily take measures to be reunited under the Federal Head and thereby enjoy the benefits [presumably in the form of a protective tariff] of that Government."

As of March 1788, these economic factors notwithstanding, the only Federalist communities were Providence, Newport, and Bristol, the state's principal seaports, plus the coastal town of Little Compton. Certain developments in 1789 and 1790, however, gradually swung the bay towns of Portsmouth, Middletown, Tiverton, Jamestown, Warren, and Barrington into the Federal camp. These were joined by Westerly, a minor port and shipbuilding town on the southwestern coast.

Surprisingly, Hopkinton, Westerly's adjacent but interior neighbor to the north, made a last-minute switch to Federalism, as did inland but shipbuilding Cumberland on the Blackstone River in the state's northeastern corner. The four delegates from Warwick, an agrarian town on the upper bay, split evenly in the May 1790 convention.

Among the factors accounting for the slow attrition in the Antifederal ranks were the incessant labors of the Federalist press, which dramatized the need for union. Notable propagandists for adoption were John Carter's *Providence Gazette* and Peter Edes's *Newport Herald*. Even the pro-paper and antislavery *United States Chronicle*, published in Providence by Bennett Wheeler, embraced ratification by late 1789.

In addition, Rhode Island felt increasingly isolated as the inexorable ratification movement toppled the opposition in state after state. George Washington's snub of Rhode Island during his triumphal New England tour in the fall of 1789 emphasized its ostracism. The state's isolation was further accentuated, and Rhode Island wavered markedly, after North Carolina ratified in November 1789.

The proposal by Congress of a bill of rights, coupled with the state's submission of its own amendments, gave the Federalist cause a perceptible lift and deprived the "Antis" of a formidable objection, while the prestige and integrity of the new federal officials, especially President Washington, lessened the fears and suspicions Antifederalists harbored toward the new governmental system. Moses Brown, for example, persuasively argued that the nature of the government would depend more upon the caliber of the men who were sent to administer it than on the Constitution itself.

A severe jolt was delivered to Antifederalists when Providence threatened to secede from the state unless Rhode Island joined the Union. This drastic but well-considered step was proposed in the Providence Town Meeting on May 24, 1790, and embodied in instructions to that town's convention delegates. If the Constitution was rejected or a decision thereon unduly delayed, the Providence delegates were empowered to meet with those from Newport and other interested towns to discuss means by which the pro-Constitution communities could apply to Congress "for the same privileges and protection which are afforded to the towns under their jurisdiction."

The principal proximate cause for Rhode Island ratification was the economic coercion exerted upon the state by the new federal government. Within weeks after the first Congress set to work, William Ellery of Newport began his campaign to persuade the national legislature to lower the economic boom on Rhode Island. Ellery, a staunch Federalist, was commissioner of the Continental Loan Office and a signer of the Declaration of Independence. He was in frequent contact with Connecticut congressman Benjamin Huntington and Connecticut senator Oliver Ellsworth, urging them to abandon "a policy of leniency" toward Rhode Island. Repeatedly he advised them that Antifederalists "must be made to feel before they will ever consent to call a convention," and that they could be made "to feel ... by subjecting the goods, wares, and manufactures of this state" to the same high duties "as foreign States not in alliance with the United States."

Although such duties would hurt Federalists in the port towns, the result would be worth the sacrifice, claimed Ellery. As time went on, he suggested ways to hit Antifederalists more directly. Place duties on the produce of the country folk, he advised; stop their "lime, flaxseed, and barley" from entering the neighboring states duty-free, and "the Antis will ... be compelled by a sense of interest to adopt the Constitution." Further, "Congress should require an immediate payment of a sum of money from the State with an assurance that if [it is] not collected an equivalent will be distrained." The sum to which Ellery referred was Rhode Island's share of the Revolutionary debt. A call for immediate payment would necessitate the reinstitution of high taxes on land.

Prodded by Ellery's shrewd observations, Congress began to move. In July 1789 it enacted a tariff program which subjected "all goods, wares, and merchandise" which Rhode Island exported to other states to foreign duties if such merchandise were not of Rhode Island "growth or manufacture." The state immediately petitioned for a suspension of these duties, and Congress, to Ellery's dismay, relented. In mid-September an act was passed holding the discriminatory levies in abeyance until January 15, 1790.

Just as this period of grace expired, the Rhode Island General Assembly approved, not by coincidence, the act calling a ratifying convention. Immediately Governor Collins informed the president and Congress and requested a further suspension. The patient Congress again complied. On February 8, 1790, Rhode Island's privilege was extended "until the first day of April next, and no longer."

At this juncture Vice President John Adams, the Senate's presiding officer, began to show signs of exasperation. Just prior to the South Kingstown convention, he confided to Providence merchants John Brown and John Francis that he was "really much affected at the obstinate infatuation of so great a part of the People of Rhode Island." Then he admonished, "If the Convention should reject the Constitution or adjourn without adopting it, Congress will probably find it necessary to treat them as they are, as Foreigners, and extend all the laws to them as such. . . . If the lime, the barley and other articles, whether of foreign or domestic growth or manufacture, should be subjected to a Duty, it would soon show your People that their interests are in the power of their neighbors."

When the March ratifying convention adjourned without issue and the Country Party swept the April elections, more drastic pressures, such as those of which Adams warned, appeared necessary. On April 28, 1790, a five-man Senate committee was created "to consider what provisions will be proper for Congress to make in the present session, respecting the State of Rhode Island." Among the membership of this group were Ellsworth and Caleb Strong of Massachusetts. Ellery now reiterated his bold plans to coerce the Antifederal majority, and he urged prompt action. "It is my opinion," he stated, "that the Convention will adjourn again unless you do something which will touch the interest of the Antis before the Convention meets."

With Senator Ellsworth in the lead, the committee heeded Ellery's admonition. On May 11 it reported a two-point program imposing a prohibition on all commercial intercourse between the United States and Rhode Island, effective July 1, and demanding an immediate payment, eventually set at $25,000, on the state's Revolutionary debt. A bill encompassing those recommendations was drawn, and on May 18, after long debate, it passed by a vote of 13 to 8. Noncompliance with the requisition could, perhaps, offer sufficient pretext for a resort to military force by the United States.

According to Senator William Maclay of Pennsylvania, a vigorous opponent of the measure, some were induced to support it "to get two Senators more into the House on whose votes they can reckon on the question of residence." He was referring, of course, to the current controversy over the permanent location of the national capital. This consideration, however, was of secondary importance. As it headed for the House, Maclay observed that the bill "was meant to be used in the same way that a robber does a dagger or a highwayman a pistol, and to obtain the end desired by putting the party in fear."

Rumors regarding the measure appeared in the press in Providence just prior to the convention. This community had long been apprehensive that the federal duty act would become operative against Rhode Island. Now, in view of the Senate's even more drastic action, Providence decided to

William Ellery (1727–1820) was the son of a wealthy Newport merchant. After graduating from Harvard and trying several occupations, he eventually settled upon the practice of law. When Rhode Island political leader Samuel Ward died early in 1776, Ellery replaced him in Congress and signed the Declaration of Independence. Ellery's long but twice-interrupted service in the national Congress was ended in 1786 by the victory of the Country Party. However, his congressional colleagues appointed him commissioner of the Continental Loan Office for Rhode Island (1786–1790). In this post he worked with nationalists such as U.S. Representative Huntington of Connecticut and Vice President John Adams to undermine Antifederalism in Rhode Island. For Ellery's efforts on behalf of the new nation, George Washington appointed him customs collector for the district of Newport, a lucrative position he held for three decades (1790–1820) until his death. Etching, courtesy of the Rhode Island Historical Society.

employ that long-contemplated resort—secession—if ratification were not forthcoming.

Unquestionably, some of the reluctant bay towns, such as Portsmouth, were also moved by the sustained politico-economic pressure of the federal government. There is no doubt that it was a decisive factor in Rhode Island's ratification on May 29. The strategist Ellery, who was animated by a not uncommon blend of principle and patronage, was later rewarded by the new central government for his efforts on its behalf when he received the prized appointment of collector of customs for Newport.

This analysis of Rhode Island's ratification struggle reveals that the commercial interest (including some farmers who produced crops for export, but excluding many Quakers) generally supported the Constitution, while the agrarian elements opposed it. As one historian has stated, "The Federal tide in Rhode Island rose slowly from Providence and Newport to engulf the other bay towns."

The greater fervor for paper money in the interior towns and the stronger fear of direct taxes on land fueled the farmer's Antifederalism, while the relatively large amount of Continental securities held in the mercantile towns, the war damage claims of the Narragansett Bay communities, and the commercial coercion of Congress induced the merchant and his economic allies to support the new federal establishment.

A final factor, attitudinal in nature, was perhaps more significant than any other in explaining Rhode Island's response to the handiwork of the Philadelphia Convention. The rural folk in the country towns held provincial, localistic, and democratic beliefs. Their outlook rendered them slow in grasping or accepting the full significance of the momentous events transpiring on the national stage. Most of the inhabitants of these communities were agrarian-minded. Their remote environment and their often inferior social status had shaped their ideology, and that ideology predisposed them to distrust the power of government, especially a government far removed from local and popular supervision and control.

The mercantile interests, on the other hand, were more cosmopolitan and politically sophisticated. Their mode of life brought them into contact with people of other states, making them less suspicious, broader in outlook, more inclined to realize the necessity of change and less disposed to fear it. The commercial-minded Federalists believed that the government must be strong and centralized if it were to function creatively in advancing the general welfare and dispensing justice. Moreover, they felt that it must have both positive powers to enlarge opportunities and coercive powers to prevent groups or sections from indulging their own interests, passions, and errors at the expense of the commonwealth. Theirs was the idea of nationalism which found ever-increasing expression under the Constitution of 1787.

When the members of the commercial community of merchants, shipbuilders, monied men, artisans, mechanics, and exporting farmers saw their enterprises deprived of the protection of the United States and shorn of the benefits of her commercial treaties, and when their commerce was faced with heavy duties laid upon it not only by Europe but by the United States as well, they grew more determined in their Federalism.

These Federalists—men like William Ellery, Henry Marchant, Jabez Bowen, William Bradford, Benjamin Bourne, and John, Nicholas, and Moses Brown—worked both for private gain and the public good. They regarded their advancement and their endeavors as essential to the nation's prosperity and growth. Time and the Founding Fathers were on their side. Thanks to their exertions, Rhode Island rejoined the Union which had left it behind and embarked with the nation upon a new era of political and economic development.

Together at Last

Great festivity occurred in Rhode Island's seaport towns in the aftermath of ratification, and "the Father of His Country"—George Washington—gave the new state a greeting similar to that accorded the Bible's prodigal son. To atone for his rebuff of 1789, when he avoided Rhode Island during his fall tour of New England, the president decided to make a special visit to the state in August 1790, while Congress was adjourned.

Washington arrived in Newport on Tuesday, August 17, accompanied by a small but politically balanced entourage that included Secretary of State Thomas Jefferson and Governor George Clinton of New York, a former Antifederalist. The much esteemed chief executive received an emotional welcome and spent a day touring the seaport town, which was still attempting to recover from the ravages of war.

Touro Synagogue became Washington's most remembered visitation in Newport. In a grateful response to his warm welcome from the Jewish community, the president later wrote the congregation a now famous letter which prophesied that the new nation would provide the world with a model society where all people would enjoy liberty and the natural right to respect from their fellows. Washington also assured his Jewish audience that "happily the Government of the United States, which gives to bigotry no sanction, to persecution no assistance, requires only that they who live under its protection should demean themselves as good citizens."

291

On Wednesday, August 18, the president sailed by packet for Providence, bypassing the staunch Federal strongholds of Bristol and Warren en route. Here his reception was more exuberant. Governor Arthur Fenner was so zealous in offering his respects that he jumped aboard the ship even before it came to rest at the Providence wharf. After two days of touring and toasts, Washington and his entourage reboarded the packet and returned to New York City, the temporary national capital.

Indeed the president's visit and the adulation with which he was received helped to cement relations between Rhode Island and the Union. Washington's benign presence also seemed to dispel most of the state's lingering doubts concerning the new federal experiment.

A final ironic episode in this constitutional drama occurred in the immediate aftermath of ratification. In February 1791 the General Assembly granted the petition of merchant Silas Casey by giving this prominent Warwick debtor a three-year exemption "from all arrests and attachments" arising from his substantial indebtedness. Two of Casey's English creditors—Alexander Champion and Thomas Dickason—filed suit in federal circuit court to set aside this state interference with the obligation of contracts, asserting that the Assembly's action was a violation of Article 1, section 10, of the new Constitution.

In June 1792 a three-judge panel, consisting of Supreme Court chief justice John Jay, Associate Justice William Cushing, and federal district judge Henry Marchant, ruled for the Englishmen. Though no written opinion was filed, the local papers provided ample insight into the court's rationale. According to the *Providence Gazette*, the federal justices unanimously determined "that the legislature of a state have no right to make a law to exempt an individual from arrests and his estates from attachments, for his private debts, for any term of time, it being clearly a law impairing the obligation of contracts and, therefore, contrary to the Constitution of the United States."

In November another circuit tribunal, consisting of Marchant and Supreme Court associate justices James Wilson and James Iredell, heard rearguments in *Champion and Dickason* v. *Casey*. They reaffirmed the earlier decision—an opinion that ranks as the first instance in American history where a federal court struck down a state statute for violating the Constitution of the United States. In this ruling the fears of the agrarian debtors were realized, yet they acquiesced in the bold decision without serious protest or complaint. Those defending merchant Casey in this landmark legal contest were attorneys Benjamin Bourne, the incumbent U.S. congressman, and William Bradford, two of Rhode Island's most zealous Federalists!

Such a reversal of form again suggests that the so-called ebb and flow of politics is merely the eternal contest between the surge of principle and the undercurrent of expediency. Each will, inevitably, take its turn directing the ship of state.

Rhode Island: Essay on Sources

The best general survey of this crucial period in Rhode Island history is Irwin H. Polishook, *Rhode Island and the Union, 1774-1795* (Evanston, Ill., 1969), which analyzes the state's internal politics in depth. Also useful is Florence Parker Simister, *The Fire's Center: Rhode Island in the Revolutionary Era, 1763-1790* (Providence, 1979), a popularly written, illustrated account. Detailed background is provided in Sydney V. James, *Colonial Rhode Island: A History* (New York, 1975). David S. Lovejoy, *Rhode Island Politics and the American Revolution, 1760-1776* (Providence, 1963) is excellent on the first party system and the movement toward independence.

Patrick T. Conley, *Democracy in Decline: Rhode Island's Constitutional Development, 1776-1841* (Providence, 1977) views the ratification controversy against the backdrop of the state's constitutional history, while Conley's "Rhode Island's Paper Money Issue and *Trevett v. Weeden* (1786)," *Rhode Island History*, 30 (August 1971), 95-108, and "Rhode Island in Disunion, 1787-1790," *Rhode Island History*, 31 (November 1972), 99-115, explore those issues in depth. Hillman Metcalf Bishop, *Why Rhode Island Opposed the Federal Constitution* (Providence, 1950) is a reprint of four well-written articles that appeared serially in *Rhode Island History*, vol. 8 (1949). Forrest McDonald, *We the People: Economic Origins of the Constitution* (Chicago, 1958) enumerates in detail the economic factors influencing Rhode Island's course but errs in tying ratification to the assumption of state debts.

The most important published contemporary sources are William R. Staples, ed., *Rhode Island in the Continental Congress, with the Journal of the Convention that Adopted the Constitution, 1765-1790* (Providence, 1870); John Russell Bartlett, ed., *Records of the Colony of Rhode Island and Providence Plantations, 1636-1792*, 10 vols. (Providence, 1856-1865), vols. 9 and 10; Robert C. Cotner, ed., *Theodore Foster's Minutes of the Convention Held at South Kingstown, Rhode Island, in March 1790, Which Failed to Adopt the Constitution of the United States* (Providence, 1929); and Irwin H. Polishook, ed., "Peter Edes' Report of the Rhode Island General Assembly, 1787-1790," *Rhode Island History*, 25 (April, July, October 1966), 33-42, 87-97, 117-129, and 26 (January 1967), 15-31.

Dated but still useful are J. Franklin Jameson, "The Adjustment of Rhode Island into the Union in 1790," *Rhode Island Historical Society Publications*, 7 (July 1900), 104-135; Frank Greene Bates, *Rhode Island and the Formation of the Union* (New York, 1898); and Sidney S. Rider, "How the United States Senate Forced Rhode Island to Ratify the United States Constitution," *Book Notes*, 11 (1894), 73-75, 85-86.

Of the few biographical works on the participants in the constitutional drama, the best are James B. Hedges, *The Browns of Providence Plantations*, 2 vols. (Providence, 1952, 1968); Mack Thompson, *Moses Brown: Reluctant Reformer* (Chapel Hill, N.C., 1962); Susan B. Franklin, "William Ellery: Signer of the Declaration of Independence," *Rhode Island History*, 12 (October 1953), 110-119, and 13 (January, April 1954), 11-17, 44-52; William Fowler, Jr., *William Ellery: A Rhode Island Politico and Lord of the Admiralty* (Metuchen, N.J., 1973); James M. Varnum, *A Sketch of the Life and Public Services of James Mitchell*

Varnum ... (Boston 1906); and William E. Foster, "Sketch of the Life and Services of Theodore Foster," *Collections of the Rhode Island Historical Society,* 7 (1885), 111–134.

Other important references include Joseph M. Norton, "The Rhode Island Federalist Party, 1785–1815" (doctoral dissertation, St. John's University, 1975); John P. Kaminski, "Democracy Run Rampant: Rhode Island in the Confederation," in James Kirby Martin, ed., *The Human Dimensions of Nation Making* (Madison, Wis., 1976), pp. 243–269, and "Political Sacrifice and Demise—John Collins and Jonathan J. Hazard, 1786–1790," *Rhode Island History,* 35 (August 1976), 91–98; Elizabeth Donnan, "Agitation against the Slave Trade in Rhode Island, 1784–1790," in *Persecution and Liberty: Essays in Honor of George Lincoln Burr* (New York, 1931); James F. Reilly, "The Providence Abolition Society," *Rhode Island History,* 21 (April 1962), 33–48; and Abe C. Ravitz, "Anarch in Rhode Island," *Rhode Island History,* 11 (October 1952), 117–124. On the *Champion* case, see Patrick T. Conley, Jr., "The First Judicial Review of State Legislation: An Analysis of the Rhode Island Case of *Champion and Dickason* v. *Casey,*" *Rhode Island Bar Journal,* 36 (October 1987), 5–9.

Posterity Views the Founding:

General Published Works Pertaining to the Creation of the Constitution; A Bibliographic Essay

PATRICK T. CONLEY

Q UITE RIGHTLY, the literature on the framing and adoption of the Constitution is voluminous, for the 1787 document is our greatest political creation. This essay seeks to identify the most useful and pertinent general works dealing directly with the Constitution-making process. Remote influences upon our basic law from ancient Israel, Greece, Rome, the Teutonic tribes, Switzerland, the Italian city-states, the Netherlands, Enlightenment France, and early modern England are beyond the scope of this essay (though historians of ideology have done much recent work on seventeenth- and eighteenth-century British constitutional theory). Also excluded are doctoral dissertations and studies tracing the evolution of the Constitution from the date of its implementation in 1789 onward, because this book does not progress beyond that year except for its notice of reluctant Rhode Island. State contributions and biographies or ideological analyses of individual framers have been cited in the state essays, which may be used as supplements to this general historiographical commentary.

Key to Abbreviations

AHR   *American Historical Review*
Annals   *Annals of the American Academy of Political and Social Science*
APSR   *American Political Science Review*
JAH   *Journal of American History*
PSQ   *Political Science Quarterly*
WMQ   *The William and Mary Quarterly*

Interpretive Accounts: From Bancroft to Beard to Babel

Despite abolitionist criticism of the Constitution, which gave assent to slavery, as a "bloody compromise" and a "covenant with death"—a view epitomized by Wendell Phillips' *The Constitution: A Pro-Slavery Compact* (New York, 1844)—most nineteenth-century writers who aspired to the title "historian" and wrote in depth on the decade of the 1780s viewed the Constitution and its authors in a heroic light (Richard Hildreth, Henry Wilson, Hermann von Holst, and Henry B. Dawson were notable exceptions to this filiopietistic appraisal). Reflecting the romantic and chauvinistic spirit of their era, most early students of the founding years saw the framers as selfless and public-spirited nationalists, whose political efforts and concern saved a troubled nation from dissolution.

Prominent examples of this perspective, which later historians have called the traditional, patriotic, or nationalist interpretation, are George Bancroft, *History of the Formation of the Constitution of the United States of America*, 2 vols. (New York, 1882), which is included in the author's last revision of his famous *History of the United States from the Discovery of the Continent*, 6 vols. (New York, 1883–86); George Ticknor Curtis, *History of the Origin, Formation and Adoption of the Constitution of the United States with Notices of Its Principal Framers*, 2 vols. (New York, 1854–58; revised and enlarged, New York, 1889); and John Fiske, *The Critical Period of American History, 1783–1789* (Boston, 1888), a popularly written work that emphasized the inadequacy of the Articles and the crisis the nation faced because of their weakness—what Merrill Jensen later called the "chaos and patriots to the rescue" approach.

During the early years of the twentieth century, this favorable estimate of the founders was repeated, but with less romantic ardor, by several prominent constitutional scholars, most notably Andrew C. McLaughlin, *The Confederation and Constitution, 1783–1789* (New York, 1905), a volume in the original American Nation Series; Max Farrand, *The Framing of the Constitution of the United States* (New Haven, 1913) and *The Fathers of the Constitution: A Chronicle of the Establishment of the Union* (New Haven, 1921); Robert L. Schuyler, *The Constitution of the United States: An Historical Survey of Its Formation* (New York, 1923); and Charles Warren, *The Making of the Constitution* (Cambridge, Mass., 1928).

Early in this century, however, during a wave of reform known as Progressivism, a new, less idealistic, and much more controversial view of the framers and their motives was advanced by Columbia University professor Charles A. Beard (1874–1948). Beard's "hypothesis" (for he claimed it was nothing more) was embodied in a book entitled *An Economic Interpretation of the Constitution of the United States* (New York, 1913; reprinted with an explanatory introduction by Beard in 1935). Expanding upon the research and suggestions of several earlier writers—most notably Orin G. Libby, *The Geographical Distribution of the Vote of the Thirteen States on the Federal Constitution, 1787–1788* (Madison, Wis., 1894); J. Allen Smith, *The Spirit of American Government: A Study of the Constitution, Its Origin, Influence, and Relation to Democracy* (New York, 1907); and Algie M. Simons, *Social Forces in American History* (New York, 1911)—Beard advanced the hypothesis that the Founding Fathers were motivated by economic self-interest when they drafted and ratified the Constitution. Actually, in the preface to his 1935 reprint Beard denied that he had "accused the members of working merely for their own pockets." Citing page 73 of his original text, he contended that the basic question that he considered was this: "Did they [the framers] represent distinct groups whose economic interests they understood and felt in concrete, definite form through their own personal experience with identical property rights, or were they working merely under the guidance of abstract principles of political science?" Despite Beard's disclaimer, this subtle difference between class consciousness and personal interest was abandoned in practice as his story unfolded.

Beard's analysis led to several conclusions: (1) that the Constitution was spearheaded by an active and small minority group whose personal property would be safeguarded and enhanced by the outcome of their efforts; (2) that the Founding Fathers, with few exceptions, derived economic benefit from their handiwork; and (3) that those in the ratifying conventions who supported the Constitution represented the same economic groups as the Philadelphia delegates and were also directly and personally interested in the establishment of the new and fiscally stable government. For Beard, the animating surge behind the Constitution came from the holders of depreciated Continental securities who hoped to see their certificates paid at face value and from conservative elements throughout the country who wanted a national bulwark against the agrarian-debtor radicalism that affected many state legislatures. Beard believed that the Constitution differed in spirit from the Declaration of Independence and that the Founding Fathers were counter-revolutionary conservatives who were attempting to overthrow the Articles and check the democratic impulses of the Revolution.

Beard's hypothesis had a huge effect on the scholarly (if not the popular) view of the Founding Fathers. By 1936, according to Richard Hofstadter, thirty-seven of forty-two leading college texts had substantially adopted Beard's views. So had some distinguished treatises on American constitutional development, including Homer Carey Hockett, *The Constitutional History of the United States, 1776–1826* (New York, 1939) and a Pulitzer Prize-winning survey of American literature and ideology, Vernon Louis Parrington's *Main Currents in American Thought*, 3 vols. (New York, 1927–30), vol. 1, *1620–1800, The Colonial Mind*.

Although Beard's interpretation came under attack in the 1940s and 1950s, it was buttressed by the detailed and original research of Merrill Jensen, who wrote *The Articles of Confederation: An Interpretation of the Social-Constitutional History of the American Revolution, 1774–1781* (Madison, Wis., 1940); *The New Nation: A History of the United States during the Confederation, 1781–1789* (New York, 1950); "The Idea of a National Government during the American Revolution," *PSQ*, 58 (1943), 356–379; *Making of the American Constitution* (Princeton, N.J., 1964); and *The American Revolution within America* (New York, 1974). Jensen's work enlarged and supplemented the Beardian hypothesis. However, the University of Wisconsin scholar was more attentive to the Founding Fathers' political ideology than their security holdings, and unlike Beard he denied that the Confederation era was a critical period. Nonetheless, the points of similarity between the two men's views gave rise to an interpretation that historians labeled "the Beard-Jensen thesis."

Jensen had more admiration for the Articles than earlier scholars, for he saw the loose arrangement of states thereunder as conducive to democratic self-rule. He believed that this system, which gave free rein to local democracy by placing primary authority in the state legislatures, was the true end and goal of the Revolution. Those who opposed the Articles were a small, tightly organized group of conservatives who were "by temperament or economic interest believers in executive and judicial rather than legislative control of state and central governments, in the rigorous collection of taxes, and, as creditors, in strict payment of private and public debts." Further, said Jensen, these conservatives "deplored the fact that there was no check upon the actions of majorities in state legislatures; that there was no central government to which minorities could appeal from the decisions of such majorities, as they had done before the Revolution." These "counterrevolutionary conservatives" undermined the Articles by hyperbolic rhetoric alleging their inadequacy and then masterminded the framing and adoption of the Constitution. Such an iconoclastic view of the Founding Fathers as propounded by Beard and Jensen would have made Bancroft and Fiske apoplectic, and it was certain, eventually, to invite a harsh rebuttal.

In the relatively conservative ideological milieu of the post-World War II generation, a reaction to Progressive history was launched by certain members of the American historical profession. These writers attempted to replace the conflict theme of the Progressives with a consensus interpretation that stressed continuity and concord as the major features of America's political and constitutional past. These writers emphasized the beliefs that Americans shared rather than the distinctions that divided them. As the quintessential socioeconomic historian, Beard became the principal target of the new revisionism, called by some the neoconservative interpretation of the Constitution.

By the mid-1950s many studies of individual states had cast serious doubt on the validity of Beard's two major premises: that the society which produced the Constitution was undemocratic, making that document the result of a minority coup, and that the contest over the Constitution was one that pitted real property interests (the Antifederalists) against personal property holders (the Federalists).

At that point a frontal assault against Beard's hypothesis was launched by Robert E. Brown in an essay entitled "Economic Democracy before the Constitution," *American Quarterly*, 7 (1955), 257–274. Brown followed this brief rebuke with *Charles Beard and the Constitution* (Princeton, N.J., 1956), a harsh and pugnacious rebuttal, and a work entitled *Reinterpretation of the Formation of the Constitution* (Boston, 1963). In these general accounts and in local studies of Massachusetts and Virginia, Brown attempted to reduce Beard to stubble, using the now deceased historian's own framework to refute him. According to Brown, Beard manipulated evidence, took the framers out of context, committed logical fallacies, inadequately tested his generalizations, selected the facts to fit his preconceived notions, and used invalid historical methodology.

Employing a similar approach, Forrest McDonald conducted a state-by-state economic analysis to test the accuracy of Beard's sweeping generalizations and also found them to be invalid. His refutation effort, presented in *We the People: The Economic Origins of the Constitution* (Chicago, 1958) was followed by two original attempts to advance an alternative economic theory to explain the founders' motivation: "The Anti-Federalists, 1781–1789," *Wisconsin Magazine of History*, 46 (1963), 206–214, and *E Pluribus Unum:*

The Formation of the American Republic, 1776–1790 (Boston, 1965). McDonald's views were endorsed by the aged Robert L. Schuyler (who had resisted the seductions of the Progressives when he wrote his account of the convention in 1923) in a review essay entitled "Forrest McDonald's Critique of the Beard Thesis," *Journal of Southern History*, 27 (1961), 73–80.

Meanwhile, Henry Steele Commager, addressing the question "The Constitution: Was It an Economic Document?" *American Heritage*, 10 (1958), 58–61, 100–103, had answered, "Not primarily." Richard B. Morris, "The Confederation Period and the American Historian," *WMQ*, 13 (1956), 139–156, revived Fiske's view of the "critical period," taking Beard and Jensen to task in the process, while Stanley Elkins and Eric McKitrick, "The Founding Fathers: Young Men of the Revolution," *PSQ*, 76 (1961), 181–216, saw the energy and drive of the Federalists as key ingredients in their success and the Constitution as a consummation, rather than a repudiation, of the Revolution. Elisha P. Douglass, *Rebels and Democrats: The Struggle for Equal Political Rights and Majority Rule during the American Revolution* (Chapel Hill, N.C., 1955) challenged the Beard-Jensen claim that the Revolutionary state governments were democratic, asserting that they were often controlled by politicians fearful of unchecked majority control.

Other postwar historians (sometimes called the democratic, idealist, or intellectual school) undermined the Beard-Jensen thesis indirectly by emphasizing the importance of ideas and democratic theory in the Constitution-making process and stressing the consistency between the ideology of the American Revolution, the Declaration of Independence, and the Constitution. This consensus approach, which depicted the Founding Fathers as patriotic theorists, has been advanced by several major students of late eighteenth-century America, including Douglas Adair, "The Tenth Federalist Revisited," *WMQ*, 8 (1951), 48–67, "The Federalist Papers," *WMQ* 22 (1965), 131–139, and "Fame and the Founding Fathers," in Trevor Colburn, ed., *Fame and the Founding Fathers: Essays by Douglas Adair* (New York, 1974). These essays refurbished the framers' image by asserting that their concern for "liberty, justice, and stability" far outweighed any selfish economic concerns. Similar conclusions were reached by Cecelia Kenyon, "Men of Little Faith: The Anti-Federalists on the Nature of Representative Government," *WMQ*, 12 (1955), 3–43, *The Anti-Federalists* (Indianapolis, 1966), and "Republicanism and Radicalism in the American Revolution: An Old-Fashioned Interpretation," *WMQ*, 19 (1962), 153–182; Benjamin Fletcher Wright, *Consensus and Continuity, 1776–1787* (Boston, 1958); David G. Smith, *The Convention and the Constitution: The Political Ideas of the Founding Fathers* (New York, 1965); Clinton Rossiter, *1787: The Grand Convention* (New York, 1966); and Martin Diamond, "The Declaration and the Constitution: Liberty, Democracy, and the Founders," *The Public Interest*, 41 (1975), 39–55, and *The Founding of the*

Democratic Republic (Itasca, Ill., 1981), a book which is the capstone of Diamond's years of inquiry into the thought of the framers (his previous essays on constitutional theory, all stressing the democratic theme, will be cited subsequently in conjunction with the discussion of the ideology of *The Federalist*).

Edmund S. Morgan, *The Birth of the Republic, 1763–1789* (Chicago, 1956; revised edition 1981); and Esmond Wright, *Fabric of Freedom, 1763–1800* (New York, 1961; revised edition 1978)—the two best brief surveys of the era—also stress the theme of continuity and downplay conflict and socioeconomic rivalries. The general studies by Robert R. Palmer, *The Age of the Democratic Revolution*, vol. 1: *The Challenge* (New York, 1959), and Hannah Arendt, *On Revolution* (New York, 1963), likewise adhere to the theme of ideological continuity. So does the foremost living authority on the Confederation era, Richard B. Morris, in *The American Revolution Reconsidered* (New York, 1967) and *The Forging of the Union, 1781–1789* (New York, 1987). The latter book, a volume in the New American Nation Series, is the culmination of a lifetime of research and writing on the founding period. Most recently, William E. Nelson, "Reason and Compromise in the Establishment of the Federal Constitution, 1787–1801," *WMQ*, 44 (1987), 458–484, downplays the view that the Constitution grew out of "interest-group conflict" and that it was designed to enable some groups to advance their interests at the expense of others, emphasizing instead "the role of compromise and the importance of instrumental reason in the creation of the federal government."

Not all historians, however, thought that Beard's view was both dead and buried. Merrill Jensen continued to espouse the conflict theme through the decade of the 1970s, and newer writers (called by historians the neo-Progressives) continued to see value in Beard's general approach, if not in his specific premises and conclusions. These historians still emphasized social and/or ideological divergence or the clash between socioeconomic interest groups as essential to an understanding of the Constitution-making process and criticized the consensus historians for overreacting to Beard and for incorrectly "homogenizing" our history. The subtlety of the neo-Progressive approach has won it many converts.

Jackson Turner Main, "Charles Beard and the Constitution: A Critical Review of Forrest McDonald's *We the People*, with a Rebuttal by Forrest McDonald," *WMQ*, 17 (1960), 86–110, led the attempt to salvage what was still valid or useful in the Beard-Jensen interpretation. In a volume entitled *The Anti-Federalists: Critics of the Constitution, 1781–1788* (Chapel Hill, N.C., 1961), Main persuasively advanced the thesis that the "commercial folk" (including exporting farmers) generally supported the Constitution while the "non-navigating folk" were most often Antifederal. Main followed this effort with several works suggesting a social, geographical, and ideological division within late eighteenth-century American politics: "Government by the People: The American Revolution and the Democratization of the State Legislatures," *WMQ*, 23 (1966), 391–407; *The Upper House in Revolutionary America, 1763–88* (Madison, Wis., 1967); and *Political Parties before the Constitution* (Chapel Hill, N.C., 1973).

Main's view of the ratification struggle was anticipated by Orin G. Libby, *The Geographical Distribution of the Vote of the Thirteen States on the Federal Constitution, 1787–1788* (Madison, Wis., 1894), a work that also influenced Beard. On Libby, consult Robert P. Wilkins, "Orin G. Libby: His Place in the Historiography of the Constitution," *North Dakota Quarterly*, 37 (1969), 5–20.

Lee Benson, *Turner and Beard: American Historical Writing Reconsidered* (Glencoe, Ill., 1960), 93–233, reaches conclusions similar to Main's by contending that the struggle over the Constitution pitted localistic "agrarian-minded" opponents against more cosmopolitan "commercial-minded" supporters; Curtis P. Nettels, in *The Emergence of a National Economy, 1775–1815* (New York, 1962), paints the socioeconomic conflict on a broader canvas, as he did in his study of the colonial era, *The Roots of American Civilization* (New York, 1938; revised edition 1963). Nettels is much influenced by Beard's economic interpretation, though he does not accept Beard's conclusions concerning the self-interestedness of the framers. See also Nettels, "The American Merchant and the Constitution," Colonial Society of Massachusetts, *Publications*, 34 (1943).

E. James Ferguson, *The Power of the Purse: A History of American Public Finance, 1776–1790* (Chapel Hill, N.C., 1961), analyzes the relationship between the framers' alarm about public indebtedness and their desire for governmental reform. Ferguson stresses the connection between the framers' desire for general economic growth and their political nationalism in his "Review of *E Pluribus Unum: The Formation of the American Republic, 1776–1790*, with a Rebuttal by Forrest McDonald," *WMQ*, 23 (1966), 148–155, his "Political Economy, Public Liberty, and the Formation of the Constitution," *WMQ*, 40 (1983), 389–412, and his "The Nationalists of 1781–1783 and the Economic Interpretation of the Constitution," *JAH*, 56 (1969), 241–261. As a motive, says Ferguson, "the profit of speculators was incidental." Ferguson's continuing emphasis on economic influences (though much less personal than Beard's) prompted an exchange with Stuart Bruchey: "The Forces behind the Constitution: A Critical Review of the Framework of E. James Ferguson's *The Power of the Purse* with a Rebuttal by E. James Ferguson," *WMQ*, 19 (1962), 429–438. Ferguson synthesizes and refines his views in *The American Revolution: A General History, 1763–1790* (2nd edition, Homewood, Ill., 1979).

Other works emphasizing socioeconomic or ideological conflict between Federalists and Antifederalists include Robert A. Rutland, *The Ordeal of the Constitution: The Antifederalists and the Ratification Struggle of 1787–1788* (Norman, Okla., 1966), which posits a democratic-versus-elitist cleavage; Paul Eidelberg, *The Philosophy of the American Constitution: A Reinterpretation of the Intention of the Founding Fathers* (New York, 1968), which sees the Constitution as a Federalist attempt to check the "leveling spirit" of the Revolution by introducing the "aristocratic principle" to restrain rampant democracy; Christopher Wolfe, "On Understanding the Constitutional Convention of 1787," *The Journal of Politics*, 39 (1977), 97–118, which takes sharp issue with the democratic interpretation, especially as advanced by Martin Diamond; James H. Hutson, "Country, Court, and Constitution: Antifederalism and the Historians," *WMQ*, 38 (1981), 337–368, which sees the Federalist-Antifederalist rivalry as analogous to the country versus court battles that occurred in the wake of the Glorious Revolution; James A. Henretta, "Society and Republicanism: America in 1787," *this Constitution*, No. 15 (1987), 20–26, which emphasizes socioeconomic divisions accompanied by racial and gender-based discrimination; Michael Lienesch, "The Constitutional Tradition: History, Political Action, and Progress in American Political Thought, 1787–1793," *The Journal of Politics*, 42 (1980), 2–30, and "Historical Theory and Political Reform: Two Perspectives on Confederation Politics," *Review of Politics*, 45 (1983), 94–115, which sees the contest as the struggle between radical "revolutionaries" and "counterrevolutionary" conservatives, but regards the Constitution as a "triumph for balance"; Joyce Appleby, "The American Heritage: The Heirs and the Disinherited," *JAH*, 74 (1987), 799–813, which regards the Founding Fathers as a conservative elite whose Constitution "closed the door on simple majoritarian government in the United States"; and, most notably, Gordon Wood, *The Creation of the American Republic, 1776–1787* (Chapel Hill, N.C., 1969).

Professor Wood's detailed and imposing study sees the Federalists as an emergent national elite who supported a stronger central government to check the democratic and parochial excesses of state governments. Simply put, said Wood, "both the proponents and opponents of the Constitution focused throughout the debates on an essential point of political sociology that ultimately must be used to distinguish a Federalist from an Antifederalist. The quarrel was fundamentally one between aristocracy and democracy." Four years later, however, in his introduction to an anthology of conflicting interpretations of the Constitution, Wood modified this dualism, asserting that "American society in 1787–88 does not appear to have been sharply divided into two coherent classes." Rather, the contest over the Constitution was a manifestation of "antagonism between elites."

Wood's deemphasis of the influence of the Lockean political tradition upon the framers and his stress, instead, on the centrality of the English republican tradition has prompted Gary J. Schmitt and Robert H. Webking to reaffirm Locke's significance in "Revolutionaries, Antifederalists, and Federalists: Comments on Gordon Wood's Understanding of the American Founding," *The Political Science Reviewer*, 9 (1979), 195–229. In addition, Wood has been criticized by Jensen and Main for introducing "a conservative bias" into the debate over the origins of the Constitution. For the current scholarly assessment of Wood's contribution, see "Forum, *The Creation of the American Republic, 1776–1787:* A Symposium of Views and Reviews," *WMQ*, 44 (1987), 549–640, in which twelve specialists offer their reactions to Wood's learned volume.

A final contemporary interpretation (called by historians the "neo-abolitionist" view) has been advanced by New Left writer Staughton Lynd in *Class Conflict, Slavery, and the United States Constitution* (Indianapolis, 1967) and "The Compromise of 1787," *PSQ*, 81 (1966), 225–250. Lynd has revived the mid-nineteenth-century abolitionist charge of William Lloyd Garrison, Wendell Phillips, and Richard Hildreth that an unholy alliance between northern merchants and southern planters made slavery and the compromises over that institution central to an understanding of the framing of the Constitution. Whatever the validity of Lynd's thesis, it has, at least, the merit of restoring the slavery question to the prominence it had for the framers.

The controversy over the motives of the Founding Fathers and the influences upon them is far from resolved, and after more than four decades of refutation and modification, Charles Beard remains a central figure in the historiography of the Constitution, as the following assessments indicate: Eugene C. Barker, "Economic Interpretation of the Constitution," *Texas Law Review*, 22 (1944), 373–391; Robert E. Thomas, "A Re-Appraisal of Charles A. Beard's *An Economic Interpretation of the Constitution of the United States*," *AHR*, 57 (1952), 370–375; Eric Goldman, "The Origins of Beard's *Economic Interpretation of the Constitution*," *Journal of the History of Ideas*, 13 (1952), 234–249; Howard K. Beale, ed., *Charles A. Beard: An Appraisal* (Lexington, Ky., 1954); Cushing Strout, *The Pragmatic Revolt in American History: Carl Becker and Charles Beard* (New Haven, 1958); Harvey Wish, "Charles A. Beard and the Economic Interpretation of History," in Wish, *The American Historian* (New York, 1960), 265–292; David F. Trask, "Historians, the Constitution, and Objectivity: A Case Study," *Antioch Review*, 20 (1960), 65–78, which makes a plea for increased use of the social sciences to resolve the problems posed by Beard's hypothesis; Peter J. Coleman, "Beard, McDonald, and Economic Determinism in American Historiography," *Business History Review*, 34 (1960), 113–121; Bernard C. Borning, *The Political and Social Thought of Charles A. Beard* (Seattle, Wash., 1962); Cecelia Kenyon, *"An Economic Interpretation of the Constitution* after Fifty Years," *The Centennial Review,* 7 (1963), 327–352; D. W. Brogan, "The Quarrel over Charles Austin Beard and the American Constitution," *Economic History Review,* 2nd series, 18 (1965), 199–223; Richard Hofstadter, *The Progressive Historians* (New York, 1968), 165–346, and "Beard and the Constitution: The History of an Idea," *American Quarterly,* 2 (1950), 195–213; Forrest McDonald, "Charles A. Beard," in *Pastmasters: Some Essays on American Historians,* edited by Marcus Cunliffe and Robin Winks (New York, 1969), 110–141; James P. O'Brien, "The Legacy of Beardian History," *Radical America,* 4 (1970), 67–80; Marvin C. Swanson, ed., *Charles A. Beard* (Greencastle, Ind., 1976), the proceedings of a centennial symposium with essays by Eugene D. Genovese, John Braeman, and Henry Steele Commager; John Patrick Diggins, "Power and Authority in American History: The Case of Charles A. Beard and His Critics," *AHR,* 86 (1981), 701–730, an analysis sympathetic to Beard and reinforced by Diggins' *The Lost Soul of American Politics* (New York, 1985), a general study that sees self-interest and property as the driving forces behind the Constitution; Pope McCorkle, "The Historian as Intellectual: Charles Beard and the Constitution Reconsidered," *American Journal of Legal History,* 28 (1984), 314–363; Robert A. McGuire and Robert L. Ohsfeldt, "Economic Interests and the American Constitution: A Quantitative Rehabilitation of Charles A. Beard," *Journal of Economic History,* 44 (1984), 509–519; and Ellen Nore, *Charles A. Beard: An Intellectual Biography* (Carbondale, Ill., 1983) and "Charles A. Beard's Economic Interpretation of the Origins of the Constitution," *this Constitution,* No. 17 (1987), 39–44.

One of Beard's earliest and most effective critics is also still at work. In *Novus Ordo Seclorum: The Intellectual Origins of the Constitution* (Lawrence, Kan., 1985), Forrest McDonald has made the most impressive attempt at a general synthesis since Gordon Wood's effort in 1969. Though the framers brought a variety of ideological and philosophical positions to bear upon their task of building a "new order of the ages," concludes McDonald, they were guided primarily by their own experience, their wisdom, and their common sense.

James H. Hutson, "The Creation of the Constitution: Scholarship at a Standstill," *Reviews in American History,* 12 (1984), 463–477, assessed the muddled state of scholarship on the eve of the Constitution's bicentennial by lamenting that "the energy invested in writing about the Constitution in the 1950s and 60s has flagged, perhaps because the complexity of the subject and the brief life expectancy of everything written about it have intimidated prospective students." According to Hutson, "What has happened is not surprising: in any discipline the discrediting of a dominant model like the Beard thesis is followed by a period of trial and error, perplexity and muddle.

For disarray to prevail now is peculiarly unfortunate, however, since the Bicentennial of the Constitution is approaching and the public will expect enlightenment from historians about the creation of the document. Their reply—we are uncertain, or theories abound, take your pick—will not satisfy those seeking simple answers and may confirm the prejudices of those who decry the alleged irrelevancy of history."

Beard himself and his learned colleague Carl Becker were acutely aware of the elusiveness of objective truth in the study of history. In his 1933 presidential address before the American Historical Association, Beard termed written history "an act of faith" that is "merely relative to time and circumstance" because "any selection or arrangement of facts ... is controlled inexorably by the frame of reference in the mind of the selector or arranger," i.e., the historian. Two years earlier, in an essay entitled "Everyman His Own Historian," Becker attested to the relativism of historical writing by speaking of two very different histories: "the actual series of events that once occurred; and the ideal series that we affirm and hold in memory."

Despite the best efforts of historians to view and depict the American founding "as it really happened," it has been the relativity that troubled Beard and Becker, rather than the irrelevancy feared by Dr. Hutson, that has been the specter which continues to haunt that momentous event.

Compacts, Covenants, Charters, and State Constitutions: Colonial and Revolutionary Antecedents

Sydney George Fisher, *Evolution of the Constitution of the United States* (Philadelphia, 1897) is an early and learned attempt to show how the Constitution developed from the colonial charters and plans of union, as well as from English practice. Other works analyzing the colonial origins of American constitutionalism include James Harvey Robinson, "The Original and Derived Features of the Constitution," *Annals*, 1 (1890), 203–243; Archibald C. Coolidge, *Theoretical and Foreign Elements in the Formation of the American Constitution* (Freiburg, Germany, 1892); Andrew C. McLaughlin, *The Foundations of American Constitutionalism* (New York, 1932); Charles H. McIlwain, *Constitutionalism: Ancient and Modern* (Ithaca, N.Y., 1940) and "The Historical Background of the Federal Government," in *Federalism as a Democratic Process* (New Brunswick, N.J., 1942); Arthur E. Sutherland, *Constitutionalism in America: Origins and Evolution of Its Fundamental Ideas* (New York, 1965); Bernard Bailyn, *Ideological Origins of the*

306

American Revolution (Cambridge, Mass., 1967); Stanley N. Katz, "The Origins of American Constitutional Thought," *Perspectives in American History*, 1st series, 3 (1969), 474–490; A. E. Dick Howard, *Road from Runnemeade: Magna Carta and Constitutionalism in America* (Charlottesville, Va., 1968); George Dargo, *Roots of the Republic: A New Perspective on Early American Constitutionalism* (New York, 1974); Jack P. Greene, "Values and Society in Revolutionary America," *Annals*, 426 (1976), 53–69, which contends that the original principles and values of the American republic were rooted primarily in the colonial American experience; Jack P. Greene, *Peripheries and Center: Constitutional Development in the Extended Politics of the British Empire and the United States, 1607–1788* (Athens, Ga., 1986); Gordon S. Wood, "Eighteenth-Century American Constitutionalism," *this Constitution*, No. 1 (1983), 9–13, which examines the indigenous influences on American constitutional thought; Donald S. Lutz, "From Covenant to Constitution in American Political Thought," *Publius*, 10 (1980), 101–134, which shows that written church covenants conditioned Americans to seek written basic laws in the political sphere; Rozann Rothman, "The Impact of Covenant and Contract Theories on Conceptions of the U.S. Constitution," *Publius*, 10 (1980), 149–163; and Peter C. Hoffer, "The Constitutional Crisis and the Rise of a Nationalistic View of History in America, 1786–1788," *New York History*, 52 (1971), 305–323, which emphasizes the indigenous (i.e., earlier American) influences upon the Constitution.

The Native American contribution to constitutionalism is presented by Bruce E. Johansen, *Forgotten Founders: How the American Indian Helped Shape Democracy* (Boston, 1982). Johansen argues that American Indians (principally Iroquois) influenced Franklin and other founders in the formulation of such concepts as "federal union, public opinion in governance, political liberty, and the government's role in guaranteeing citizens' well-being—'happiness' in the eighteenth century sense."

Early state constitution-making and its influence upon the framers is seen in the contemporary work of John Adams, *A Defence of the Constitutions of Government of the United States of America . . .*, 3 vols. (London, 1786–87), an apologetic treatise written to refute the contention of Baron Turgot of France that the early state constitutions exhibited "an unreasonable imitation of the usages of England" and a "want of centralization." Primarily through this book and his efforts in Massachusetts, Adams exerted as much influence on the early written constitutions as any other American.

Modern scholarly examinations of this topic include William C. Morey, "The First State Constitutions," *Annals*, 4 (1893), 201–232, and "The Genesis of a Written Constitution," *Annals*, 1 (1891), 529–557; William C. Webster, "Comparative Study of the State Constitutions of the American Revolution," *Annals*, 9 (1897), 380–420; Walter F. Dodd, "The First State

Constitutional Conventions, 1776–1783," *APSR*, 2 (1908), 545–561; Edward S. Corwin, "The Progress of Constitutional Theory between the Declaration of Independence and the Meeting of the Philadelphia Convention," *AHR*, 30 (1925), 511–536; Benjamin F. Wright, "The Early History of Written Constitutions," in *Essays ... in Honor of Charles Howard McIlwain*, edited by Carl Wittke (Cambridge, Mass., 1936), 344–371; and Carl J. Friedrich and Robert G. McCloskey, eds., *From the Declaration of Independence to the Constitution: The Roots of American Constitutionalism* (Indianapolis, 1954). Donald S. Lutz, *Popular Consent and Popular Control: Whig Theory in the Early State Constitutions* (Baton Rouge, La., 1980), shows that colonial covenants and compacts influenced constitutional practice in the Revolutionary era; and in "The United States Constitution as an Incomplete Text," *Intergovernmental Perspective*, 13 (1987), 14–17, Lutz contends that "anyone attempting to do a close textual analysis of the document is driven time and again to the state constitutions to determine what is meant or implied by the national Constitution." Willi Paul Adams, *The First American Constitutions: Republican Ideology and the Making of State Constitutions in the Revolutionary Era* (Chapel Hill, N.C., 1980) emphasizes the diverse influences that affected the draftsmen of early state constitutions.

Studies of particular aspects of the Confederation era that provide background information essential to a full understanding of the conditions that led to the Philadelphia Convention include Allan Nevins, *The American States during and after the Revolution, 1775–1789* (New York, 1924); Edmund Cody Burnett, *The Continental Congress* (New York, 1941), long the standard account of its subject; and Jack N. Rakove, *The Beginnings of National Politics: An Interpretive History of the Continental Congress* (New York, 1979), now the best account of the politics leading to the call of the convention. H. James Henderson, *Party Politics in the Continental Congress* (New York, 1974) argues that sectionalism was a divisive element during the Confederation era, a thesis echoed by Joseph L. Davis, *Sectionalism in American Politics, 1774–1787* (Madison, Wis., 1977). Peter S. Onuf, *The Origins of the Federal Republic: Jurisdictional Controversies in the United States, 1775–1787* (Philadelphia, 1983) shows how western land issues and mutual state needs to adjust boundaries contributed to the movement to strengthen the national government. Onuf expands this view in "Liberty, Development, and Union: Visions of the West in the 1780s," *WMQ*, 43 (1986), 179–213, and in Cathy Matson and Peter Onuf, "Toward a Republican Empire: Interest and Ideology in Revolutionary America," *American Quarterly*, 37 (1985), 496–531.

Albion W. Small, *The Beginnings of American Nationality: The Constitutional Relations between the Continental Congress and the Colonies and States from 1774 to 1789* (Baltimore, 1890) is a pioneering study of its subject. Other useful, specialized accounts of Confederation politics are Lance Banning, "James Madison and the Nationalists, 1780–1783," *WMQ*, 40 (1983), 227–255, which traces the evolution of the nationalist faction in Congress and shows that Madison emerged as a member of this group in 1783 because he felt that the Union was threatened by Congressional reliance on the states for revenue, and Gordon S. Wood, "The Origins of the Constitution," *this Constitution*, No. 15 (1987), 4–11, which sees the abuses of power by the state legislatures, more than the defects of the Articles, as the real source of the crisis of the 1780s which led to the Philadelphia Convention. Other informative accounts include Lance Banning, "From Confederation to Constitution: The Revolutionary Context of the Great Convention," *this Constitution*, No. 6 (1985), 12–18; Edgar E. Hume, "The Role of the Cincinnati in the Birth of the Constitution of the United States," *Pennsylvania History*, 5 (1938), 101–107, which studies the influence of former Continental army officers who were members of the Society of the Cincinnati; and Jack Rakove, "The Gamble at Annapolis," *this Constitution*, No. 12 (1986), 4–10. Ronald Hoffman and Peter Albert, eds., *Sovereign States in an Age of Uncertainty* (Charlottesville, Va., 1981) contains several original essays on state politics in the period from 1776 to 1789, with Massachusetts, South Carolina, Pennsylvania, Maryland, New York, and Virginia spotlighted.

The Drafters and Their Document

Several collective biographies or analyses of the Founding Fathers have been written. The most useful of these are Wesley Frank Craven, *The Legend of the Founding Fathers* (New York, 1956); Nathan Schachner, *The Founding Fathers* (New York, 1954); David C. Whitney, *Founders of Freedom in America: Lives of the Men Who Signed the Constitution . . .* (Chicago, 1965); Dorothy H. McGee, *Framers of the Constitution* (New York, 1968); Vincent Wilson, Jr., *The Book of the Founding Fathers* (Brookeville, Md., 1985); Richard B. Morris, *Seven Who Shaped Our Destiny* (New York, 1973), which contains biographical vignettes of Washington, Adams, Jefferson, Hamilton, Franklin, Madison, and Jay; M. E. Bradford, *A Worthy Company: Brief Lives of the Framers of the Constitution* (Marlborough, Mass., 1983); Albert Furtwangler, *American Silhouettes: Rhetorical Identities of the Founders* (New Haven, 1987); Richard D. Brown, "The Founding Fathers of 1776 and 1787: A Collective View," *WMQ*, 33 (1976), 465–480; and James H. Charleton, Robert G. Ferris, and Mary C. Ryan, eds., *Framers of the Constitution* (Washington, D.C., 1986, a revised version of *Signers of the Constitution* (1976). Biographical sketches of all Philadelphia attendees, as well as profiles of many leaders in the state ratification contests, are contained in Allen Johnson, ed., *Dictionary of American Biography*, 20 vols. plus supplements (New York, 1928–).

The sesquicentennial observance in 1937 inspired several popular accounts of the Grand Convention, none of which were much affected by the controversy over the framers' motivation. Examples of this popular history are Walter Hastings Lyon, *The Constitution and the Men Who Made It: The Story of the Constitutional Convention, 1787* (Boston and New York, 1936); Fred Rodell, *55 Men: Story of the Constitution Based on the Day-by-Day Notes of James Madison* (New York, 1936); and Sol Bloom, *The Story of the Constitution* (Washington, D.C., 1937). Sol Bloom, comp., *History of the Formation of the Union under the Constitution . . .* (Washington, D.C., 1940) is the report of the U.S. Constitution Sesquicentennial Commission by its director; though poorly organized, it contains much useful information.

Postwar accounts of the Philadelphia conclave, all written when Beard was under attack and all avoiding his economic emphasis, include Carl Van Doren, *The Great Rehearsal: The Story of the Making and Ratifying of the Constitution of the United States* (New York, 1948); Broadus Mitchell and Louise P. Mitchell, *A Biography of the Constitution of the United States: Its Origins, Formation, Adoption, Interpretation* (New York, 1964); and Catherine Drinker Bowen, *Miracle at Philadelphia: The Story of the Constitutional Convention, May to September, 1787* (Boston, 1966).

The current bicentennial observance has produced a relative outpouring of these general accounts, all written to appeal to the nonspecialist. The best of these new studies are Christopher Collier and James Lincoln Collier, *Decision in Philadelphia: The Constitutional Convention of 1787* (New York, 1986); Charles L. Mee, Jr., *The Genius of the People: The Constitutional Convention of 1787* (New York, 1987), a lively account of day-by-day developments emphasizing (perhaps too much) the divergent views and interests of the delegates; William Peters, *A More Perfect Union* (New York, 1987); Elizabeth McCaughey, *Government by Choice: Inventing the United States Constitution* (New York, 1987); Walter Berns, *Taking the Constitution Seriously* (New York, 1987); Walter B. Mead, *The United States Constitution: Personalities, Principles, and Issues* (Columbia, S.C., 1987); and Robert A. Rutland, *The American Solution: Origins of the United States Constitution* (Washington, D.C., 1987). Both Richard B. Morris, *The Framing of the Federal Constitution* (Washington, D.C., 1986) and Richard S. Bernstein with Kym S. Rice, *Are We to Be a Nation: The Making of the Constitution* (Cambridge, Mass., 1987) are authoritative and well illustrated. Jeffrey St. John, *Constitutional Journal: A Correspondent's Report from the Convention of 1787* (Ottawa, Ill., 1987) and Bill Moyers, *Moyers: Report from Philadelphia; The Constitutional Convention of 1787* (New York, 1987) are creative, accurate day-by-day accounts using modern reportorial techniques.

Detailed analyses of the internal mechanisms of the convention and the process of constitutional drafting are William M. Meigs, *Growth of the*

Constitution in the Federal Convention of 1787 (Philadelphia, 1900), which traces the development of each clause from its earliest appearance in the debates to its final form in the completed Constitution; John Alexander Jameson, *A Treatise on the Principles of American Constitutional Law and Legislation: The Constitutional Convention, Its History, Power, and Modes of Proceeding* (New York, 1867), still one of the most valuable studies of the convention process, which contains detailed information on the Philadelphia gathering and its influence on state constitutional development; Hamilton P. Richardson, *The Journal of the Federal Convention of 1787 Analyzed; the Acts and Proceedings Thereof Compared...* (San Francisco, 1899); Arthur Taylor Prescott, *Drafting the Federal Constitution* (Baton Rouge, La., 1941); and Saul K. Padover, ed., *To Secure These Blessings* (New York, 1962), which arranges the convention debates topically, with editorial commentary. Wilbourn E. Benton, ed., *1787: Drafting the U.S. Constitution*, 2 vols. (College Station, Tex., 1986) is the most recent and detailed attempt to organize the convention debates sequentially according to article and section, rather than chronologically. The editor develops each provision of the original document from the notes of those delegates who kept such journals.

Richard S. Kay, "The Illegality of the Constitution," *Constitutional Commentary*, 4 (1987), 57–80, discusses the legal impact of the framers' decision to ignore their mandate to merely revise the Articles. John P. Roche, "The Founding Fathers: A Reform Caucus in Action," *APSR*, 55 (1961), 799–816, analyzes the processes of compromise while deemphasizing ideology and stressing the pragmatic political influences upon the framers. Roche's view is firmly rejected by Morton J. Frisch, "The Constitutional Convention and the Study of the American Founding," *Benchmark,* 3 (1987), 101–108.

Other glimpses into the workings of the convention are Margaret A. Banks, "Drafting the American Constitution—Attitudes in the Philadelphia Convention towards the British System of Government," *American Journal of Legal History*, 10 (1966), 15–33; Pauline Maier, "The Philadelphia Convention and the Development of American Government: From the Virginia Plan to the Constitution," *this Constitution*, No. 15 (1987), 12–19; Christopher Wolfe, "On Understanding the Constitutional Convention of 1787," *Journal of Politics*, 39 (1977), 97–118, an essay that discusses the theoretical cleavage between the advocates of a small republic and those who favored an extended one; Rozann Rothman, *Acts and Enactments: The Constitutional Convention of 1787* (Philadelphia, 1974), which emphasizes the founders' political ideology and constitutional theories; Charles F. Hobson, "The Virginia Plan of 1787: A Note on the Original Text," *Quarterly Journal of the Library of Congress*, 37 (1980), 210–214; Robert A. Rutland, "The Virginia Plan of 1787: James Madison's Outline of a Model Constitution," *this Constitution*, No. 4 (1984), 23–30; James H. Hutson, "Writing the Constitution: The Report of the Committee of Detail, August 6, 1787," *this Constitution*, No. 3 (1984), 23–30; and Walter Berns, *The Writing of the Constitution of the United States* (Washington, D.C., 1983), an offprint from an American Enterprise Institute symposium, which contends that the Constitution was an ordinance of the people rather than a compact of the states. James H. Hutson, "Riddles of the Constitutional Convention," *WMQ*, 44 (1987), 411–423, and "Creation of the Constitution: The Integrity of the Documentary Record," *Texas Law Review*, 65 (1986), 1–39, deal with the authenticiy and availability of the surviving convention records.

Statistical studies by political scientists include S. Sidney Ulmer, "Sub-group Formation in the Constitutional Convention," *Midwest Journal of Political Science*, 10 (1966), 288–303; Gerald M. Pomper, "Conflict and Coalitions at the Constitutional Convention," in *The Study of Coalition Behavior*, edited by S.O. Groennings et al. (New York, 1970); Calvin C. Jillson, "Constitution-Making: Alignment and Realignment in the Federal Convention of 1787," *APSR*, 75 (1981), 598–612; and Calvin C. Jillson and Cecil L. Eubanks, "The Political Structure of Constitution Making: The Federal Convention of 1787," *American Journal of Political Science*, 28 (1984), 435–458, the last of which contends that ideological issues dominated the early debates while materialistic and economic concerns become prominent in the convention's final stages. Jane Butzner, comp., *Constitutional Chaff—Rejected Suggestions of the Constitutional Convention of 1787 with Explanatory Argument* (New York, 1941) offers an interesting and novel approach.

The manner in which the framers shaped specific portions of the Constitution has attracted considerable interest, principally in the form of scholarly articles. Such microscopic examinations include the following (listed according to the order in which the topic appears in the Constitution): Mortimer J. Adler and William Gorman, "A Commentary on the Preamble to the Constitution of the United States," *Center Magazine*, 9 (1976), 38–65; Michael J. Malbin, "Framing a Congress to Channel Ambition," *this Constitution*, No. 5 (1984), 4–12; Jean Yarbrough, "Representation and Republicanism: Two Views," *Publius*, 9 (1979), 77–98, which contrasts the positions of Federalists and Antifederalists on these concepts; Calvin Jillson, "The Representation Question in the Federal Convention of 1787: Madison's Virginia Plan and Its Opponents," *Congressional Studies*, 81 (1981), 21–41; Calvin Jillson and Thornton Anderson, "Voting Bloc Analysis in the Constitutional Convention: Implications for an Interpretation of the Connecticut Compromise," *Western Political Quarterly*, 31 (1978), 535–547; Jack N. Rakove, "The Great Compromise: Ideas, Interests, and the Politics of Constitution Making," *WMQ*, 44 (1987), 424–457; Bernard Donahoe and Marshall Smelser, "The Congressional Power to Raise Armies: The Constitutional and Ratifying Conventions, 1787–1788," *Review of Politics*, 33 (1971), 202–211; and Reginald C. Stuart, "War Powers of the Constitution in Historical Perspective," *Parameters*, 10 (1980), 65–71.

On Article II, consult Charles C. Thatch, Jr., *The Creation of the Presidency, 1775–1789: A Study in Constitutional History* (Baltimore, 1922); Gene W. Boyett, "Developing the Concept of the Republican Presidency, 1787–1788," *Presidential Studies Quarterly*, 7 (1977), 199–208; Richard Loss, "Presidential Power: The Founders' Intention as a Problem of Knowledge," *Presidential Studies Quarterly*, 9 (1979), 379–386; Calvin C. Jillson, "Presidential Power: The Executive in Republican Government: The Case of the American Founding," *Presidential Studies Quarterly*, 9 (1979), 386–402; William H. Riker, "The Heresthetics of Constitution-Making: The Presidency in 1787, with Comments on Determinism and Rational Choice," *APSR*, 78 (1984), 1–16; R. Gordon Hoxie, "The Presidency in the Constitutional Convention," *Presidential Studies Quarterly*, 15 (1985), 25–32; Donald L. Robinson, "The Inventors of the Presidency," *Presidential Studies Quarterly*, 13 (1983), 8–25; Kirby W. Patterson, "The Making of a President: The Thinking in 1787," *American Bar Association Journal*, 60 (1974), 1357–1362; Richard B. Morris, "The Origins of the Presidency," *Presidential Studies Quarterly*, 17 (1987), 673–687; Stephen J. Wilhelm, "The Origins of the Office of the Vice Presidency," *Presidential Studies Quarterly*, 7 (1977), 208–214; Judith A. Best, "Legislative Tyranny and the Liberation of the Executive: A View from the Founding," *Presidential Studies Quarterly*, 17 (1987), 697–709; Paul L. Simon, "The Appointing Powers of the President," *Cithara*, 3 (1963), 41–55, which analyzes the influence of the executive on the judiciary in the thought of the Founding Fathers; Jeffrey Leigh Sedgwick, "Executive Leadership and Administration: Founding Versus Progressive Views," *Administration & Society*, 17 (1986), 411–432; Judith A. Best, "The Item Veto: Would the Founders Approve?" *Presidential Studies Quarterly*, 14 (1984), 183–188, which suggests that they would; John J. Turner, Jr., "The Revolution, the Founding Fathers, and the Electoral College," *West Georgia College Studies in the Social Sciences*, 15 (1976), 31–42; John T. Feerick, "The Electoral College: Why It Was Created," *American Bar Association Journal*, 54 (1968), 249–255; Shlomo Slonim, "The Electoral College at Philadelphia: The Evolution of an Ad Hoc Congress for the Selection of a President," *JAH*, 73 (1986), 35–58; Jack N. Rakove, "Solving a Constitutional Puzzle: The Treatymaking Clause as a Case Study," *Perspectives in American History*, new series, 1 (1984), 233–281; Arthur Bestor, "Respective Roles of the Senate and President in the Making and Abrogation of Treaties: The Original Intent of the Framers Historically Examined," *Washington Law Review*, 55 (1979), 1–135; James H. Hutson, "Intellectual Foundations of Early American Diplomacy," *Diplomatic History*, 1 (1977), 1–19; Charles A. Lofgren, "Compulsory Military Service under the Constitution: The Original Understanding," *WMQ*, 33 (1976), 61–88; W. Taylor Reveley

III, "War Powers of the President and Congress: Who Decides Whether America Fights?" *this Constitution*, No. 8 (1985), 19–24; Charles A. Lofgren, *"Government from Reflection and Choice": Constitutional Essays on War, Foreign Relations, and Federalism* (New York, 1986); Abraham D. Soafer, *War, Foreign Affairs and Constitutional Power: The Origins* (Cambridge, Mass., 1976); and Michael P. Riccards, "The Presidency and the Ratification Controversy," *Presidential Studies Quarterly*, 7 (1977), 37–46.

Concerning the judicial branch, Charles A. Beard, *The Supreme Court and the Constitution* (New York, 1912) persuasively argued against the charge that judicial review was a "usurpation," as claimed by Louis Boudin in a 1911 article that Boudin subsequently expanded into a lengthy treatise—*Government by Judiciary*, 2 vols. (New York, 1932). Beard showed that a majority of the framers believed the Supreme Court should exercise such power even though they neglected to state it specifically in the Constitution. Recently Bruce A. Ackerman has used *The Federalist* to defend the legitimacy of judicial review while denying that the doctrine is "counter-majoritarian" in "Discovering the Constitution," *Yale Law Journal*, 93 (1984), 1013–1072. Other detailed treatments of the convention and the judiciary are William W. Crosskey and William Jeffrey, Jr., *Politics and the Constitution in the History of the United States*, 3 vols. (Chicago, 1953 and 1980), especially vol. 3: *The Political Background of the Federal Convention*, and Julius Goebel, Jr., *Antecedents and Beginnings to 1801*, vol. 1 of Paul Freund, ed., *The Oliver Wendell Holmes Devise History of the Supreme Court of the United States* (New York, 1971).

Brief studies of this topic include William F. Swindler, "Of Revolution, Law and Order," *Supreme Court Historical Society Yearbook* (1976), 16–24, which describes the debate from 1775 to 1789 that shaped the federal judicial system; George W. Carey, "The Supreme Court, Judicial Review and the Federalist Seventy-Eight," *Modern Age*, 18 (1974), 356–369; and John Ferling, "The Senate and Federal Judges: The Intent of the Founding Fathers," *Capitol Studies*, 2 (1974), 57–70.

Further studies of the Constitution's specific clauses include James Stasny, "The Constitutional Convention Provision of Article V: Historical Perspective," *Cooley Law Review*, 1 (1982), 73–108; Ann Stuart Diamond, "A Convention for Proposing Amendments: The Constitution's Other Method," *Publius*, 11 (1981), 113–146; Philip L. Martin, "The Application Clause of Article Five," *PSQ*, 85 (1970), 616–628; Bill Gaugush, "Principles Governing the Interpretation and Exercise of Article 5 Powers," *Western Political Quarterly*, 35 (1982), 212–221; and Robert H. Birkly, "Politics of Accommodation: The Origin of the Supremacy Clause," *Western Political Quarterly*, 19 (1966), 123–135.

The modern civil rights revolution has caused historians to give great attention to the way in which the Constitution dealt with slavery. Studies focusing specifically on this question include William W. Freehling, "The Founding Fathers and Slavery," *AHR*, 77 (1972), 81–93; Joseph C. Burke, "Max Farrand Revisited: A New Look at Southern Sectionalism and Slavery in the Federal Convention," *Duquesne Review*, 12 (1967), 1–21; Calvin Jillson and Thornton Anderson, "Realignment in the Convention of 1787: The Slave Trade Compromise," *Journal of Politics*, 39 (1977), 712–729; Jay H. Sigler, "Rise and Fall of the Three-Fifths Clause," *Mid-America*, 48 (1966), 271–277; and Howard A. Ohline, "Republicanism and Slavery: Origins of the Three-Fifths Clause in the United States Constitution, *WMQ*, 28 (1971), 563–584. Examinations of the problem in a broader context include Winthrop D. Jordan, *White over Black: American Attitudes Toward the Negro, 1550–1812* (Chapel Hill, N.C., 1968); Donald L. Robinson, *Slavery in the Structure of American Politics, 1765–1820* (New York, 1971); Duncan J. MacLeod, *Slavery, Race, and the American Revolution* (Cambridge, Mass., 1974); David Brion Davis, *The Problem of Slavery in the Age of Revolution, 1770–1823* (Ithaca, N.Y., 1975); William M. Wiecek, *The Sources of Antislavery Constitutionalism in America, 1760–1848* (Ithaca, N.Y., 1977); and Ira Berlin and Ronald Hoffman, eds., *Slavery and Freedom in the Age of the American Revolution* (Charlottesville, Va., 1983).

An increasingly important constitutional issue is dealt with in William Anderson, "The Intention of the Framers: A Note on Constitutional Interpretation," *APSR*, 49 (1955) 340–352; Donald O. Dewey, "James Madison Helps Clio Interpret the Constitution," *American Journal of Legal History*, 15 (1971), 38–55; Earl Maltz, "Some New Thoughts on an Old Problem—The Role of the Intent of the Framers in Constitutional Theory," *Boston University Law Review*, 63 (1983), 811–851; Raoul Berger, " 'Original Intention' in Historical Perspective," *George Washington Law Review*, 54 (1986), 296–337; H. Jefferson Powell, "The Original Understanding of Original Intent," *Harvard Law Review*, 98 (1985), 885–948; and Charles A. Loftgren, "The Original Understanding of Original Intent?" *Constitutional Commentary*, 5 (1988), 77–113, which is a critique of Powell's essay.

Two previously overlooked influences upon the framers have recently engaged the attention of historians. Edmund S. Morgan, "The Witch and We, the People," *American Heritage*, 34 (1983), 6–11, looks at the mob murder of an alleged witch in Philadelphia while the convention was in session to illustrate the difficult task faced by the founders in a country still beset by old superstitions and mob violence. Thomas Wendel, "America's Rising Sun: The Humanities and Arts in the Framing of the Constitutional Liberty," *San Jose Studies*, 10 (1984), 4–13, reviews the role of the arts and humanities in 1787, highlighting the humanistic interests of the signers.

Esmond Wright, "The Revolution and the Constitution: Models of What and for Whom?" *Annals*, 428 (1976), 1–21, states that the American founding was a unique occurrence with limited value as a model for other nations, a position at variance with Albert P. Blaustein, "Our Most Important Export," *The World & I*, (September 1987), 95–99. Milton M. Klein, "The Constitution as Myth and Symbol," *this Constitution*, No. 16 (1987), 15–21, discusses the emergence of a "cult of the Constitution," by which the document became the national symbol and an "object of civil worship." Michael Kammen brilliantly explores the symbolic function of the Constitution in depth, especially its place in the minds of ordinary Americans, in *A Machine That Would Go of Itself: The Constitution in American Culture* (New York, 1986). For an earlier statement of this theme, see Frank I. Schechter, "The Early History of the Tradition of the Constitution," *APSR*, 9 (1915), 707–734. Seymour Martin Lipset's *The First New Nation: The United States in Historical and Comparative Perspective* (New York, 1963) is an innovative attempt to examine the American experience, especially constitutional government, within the context of developing nationhood.

Fundamental Principles: Federalists versus Antifederalists

Basic constitutional concepts such as natural rights, separation of powers, democracy, popular sovereignty, republicanism, property, suffrage, citizenship, liberty, union, nationalism, and federalism have received extensive analysis by historians, philosophers, and political scientists, not only because of their enduring significance but also because of their centrality in the ratification struggle. Good general discussions of these concepts include Adrienne Koch, *Power, Morals and the Founding Fathers: Essays in the Interpretation of the American Enlightenment* (Ithaca, N.Y., 1961); Morton White, *The Philosophy of the American Revolution* (New York, 1978), which stresses the influence of the liberal Lockean political tradition upon the founders; James T. Kloppenberg, "The Virtues of Liberalism: Christianity, Republicanism, and Ethics in Early American Political Discourse," *JAH*, 74 (1987), 9–33; Ralph Lerner, *The Thinking Revolutionary: Principle and Practice in the New Republic* (Ithaca, N.Y., 1987), which contends that the former determined the latter among the leading founders; and Paul K. Conkin, *Self Evident Truths: Being a Discourse on the Origins and Development of the First Principles of American Government—Popular Sovereignty, Natural Rights, and Balance and Separation of Powers* (Bloomington, Ind., 1974).

On specific "first principles," consult Benjamin F. Wright, *American Interpretations of Natural Law* (Cambridge, Mass., 1931); Edward S. Corwin,

"The 'Higher Law' Background of American Constitutional Law," *Harvard Law Review*, 42 (1928–29), 149–185, 365–409 (published separately by Cornell University Press, 1955); Charles H. McIlwain, "The Fundamental Law behind the Constitution of the United States," in McIlwain, *Constitutionalism and the Changing World* (Cambridge, England, 1939); Thomas C. Grey, "Origins of the Unwritten Constitution: Fundamental Law in American Revolutionary Thought," *Stanford Law Review*, 30 (1978), 843–893; Arthur O. Lovejoy, "The Theory of Human Nature in the American Constitution and the Method of Counterpoise," in *Reflections on Human Nature* (Baltimore, 1961), 37–65, which examines the framers' views of human nature; and Thad W. Tate, "The Social Contract in America, 1774–1787: Revolutionary Theory as a Conservative Instrument," *WMQ*, 22 (1965), 375–391, which contends that the "one substantial monument of the social contract theory was the development of procedures "for drafting, ratifying, and amending constitutions."

Much has been written on the principle of separation of powers. The most valuable discussions are Benjamin F. Wright, Jr., "The Origins of the Separation of Powers in America," *Economica*, 13 (1933), 169–185; William Seal Carpenter, "The Separation of Powers in the Eighteenth Century," *APSR*, 22 (1928), 32–44; Francis G. Wilson, "The Mixed Constitution and the Separation of Powers," *Southwestern Social Science Quarterly*, 15 (1934), 14–28; Malcom P. Sharp, "The Classical American Doctrine of the Separation of Powers," *University of Chicago Law Review*, 2 (1935), 385–436; W. B. Gwyn, *The Meaning of the Separation of Powers: An Analysis of the Doctrine from Its Origin to the Adoption of the United States Constitution* (New Orleans, 1965); Maurice J. C. Vile, *Constitutionalism and the Separation of Powers* (New York, 1967); Murray Dry, "The Separation of Powers and Republican Government," *Political Science Reviewer*, 3 (1973), 43–83; Louis Fisher, "The Efficiency Side of Separated Powers," *Journal of American Studies*, 5 (1971), 113–131, which shows that the framers supported separation of powers to obtain greater administrative efficiency; Martin Diamond, "The Separation of Powers and the Mixed Regime," *Publius*, 8 (1978), 33–43; and George W. Carey, "Separation of Powers and the Madisonian Model: A Reply to the Critics," *APSR*, 72 (1978), 151–164, which denies the notion that Madison advocated separation of powers to thwart majority rule, contending instead that Madison's real purpose was to protect against governmental tyranny and to guarantee popular control of government. Ann Stuart Diamond, "The Zenith of Separation of Powers Theory: The Federal Convention of 1787," *Publius*, 8 (1978), 45–70, contends that the purpose of checks and balances was to prevent deadlocks and to entrust vast powers to popular government without threatening liberty; Ferdinand A. Hermens, "The Choice of the Framers," *Presidential Studies Quarterly*, 11 (1981), 9–27, asserts that the Founding Fathers formed two political systems—a representative republic that has worked and a system of divided or separated powers that has caused many political failures; and Arthur Bestor, "Separation of Powers in the Domain of Foreign Affairs: The Intent of the Constitution Historically Considered," *Seton Hall Law Review*, 5 (1974), 527–665, discusses the issue with special reference to the Constitution's war and treaty powers.

On democratic theory, consult Martin Diamond, "Democracy and *The Federalist*: A Reconsideration of the Framers' Intent," *APSR*, 53 (1959), 52–68; William R. Brock, *The Evolution of American Democracy* (New York, 1970); Douglas Adair, "Experience Must Be Our Only Guide: History, Democratic Theory, and the United States Constitution," in *The Reinterpretation of Early American History: Essays in Honor of John Edwin Pomfret*, edited by Ray A. Billington (San Marino, Calif., 1966); and Robert W. Shoemaker, " 'Democracy' and 'Republic' as Understood in Late 18th Century America," *American Speech*, 41 (1966), 83–95, a revealing analysis contending that concentration of power in the legislature versus separation of powers was the acid test between a "democracy" (concentration) and a "republic" (separation).

J. R. Pole, *Political Representation in England and the Origins of the American Republic* (New York, 1966) and "Historians and the Problem of Early American Democracy," *American Historical Review*, 67 (1962), 626–646, deal with the development of popular choice and popular participation in government, while Pole's *The Pursuit of Equality in American History* (Berkeley, Calif., 1973) assesses the impact of the Constitution on that concept. The theme of equality and the founders is also developed by Marvin Myers, "Liberty, Equality, and Constitutional Self-Government," in *Liberty and Equality under the Constitution*, edited by John Agresto (Washington, D.C., 1983), 1–43. Richard Hofstadter, "The Founding Fathers: An Age of Realism," in Hofstadter's *The American Political Tradition and the Men Who Made It* (New York, 1948), 3–17, emphasizes the antidemocratic sentiments of many framers.

On the principle of republicanism, see John T. Agresto, "Liberty, Virtue and Republicanism, 1776–1787," *Review of Politics*, 39 (1977), 473–504, and " 'A System Without Precedent'—James Madison and the Revolution in Republican Liberty," *South Atlantic Quarterly*, 82 (1983), 129–144; George M. Dutcher, "The Rise of Republican Government in the United States," *PSQ*, 55 (1940), 199–216; James Conniff, "On the Obsolescence of the General Will: Rousseau, Madison, and the Evolution of Republican Political Thought," *Western Political Quarterly*, 28 (1975), 32–58; and Marcus Cunliffe, "Republicanism and the Founding of America," *The World & I* (September 1987), 37–45.

Two recent articles dealing with the complex meaning that the term "republicanism" had for both the Founding Fathers and historians are Robert

Shalhope, "Republicanism and Early American Historiography," *WMQ* (1982), 334–356, and Linda K. Kerber, "The Republican Ideology of the Revolutionary Generation," *American Quarterly*, 37 (1985), 474–495.

Chilton Williamson, *American Suffrage: From Property to Democracy, 1760–1860* (Princeton, 1960) and Jack P. Greene, *All Men Are Created Equal: Some Reflections on the Character of the American Revolution* (Oxford, 1976) treat the development of theory and practice pertaining to voting, while James H. Kettner, *The Development of American Citizenship, 1608–1870* (Chapel Hill, N.C., 1978) is a masterful survey of the status of citizenship and the way it was influenced by the Constitution. Richard Hofstadter, "A Constitution against Parties," *Government and Opposition*, 4 (1969), 345–366, discusses the pluralistic, antiparty attitudes of Madison, Washington, and other founders. William B. Scott, *In Pursuit of Happiness: American Conceptions of Property from the Seventeenth to the Twentieth Century* (Bloomington, Ind., 1977), is the best analysis of that basic principle.

J. R. Pole, *The Idea of Union* (Alexandria, Va., 1977) says of the "public men whose duties brought them together in Congress and in the Constitutional Convention of 1787" that the "great and central truth was that all their interests did gravitate toward unity." Conversely, Kenneth M. Stampp, "The Concept of a Perpetual Union," *JAH*, 65 (1978), 5–33, makes the interesting case that the Convention of 1787 invalidated the historical argument for an enduring Union by replacing the existing "perpetual Union" created by the Articles and by failing to resolve the question of whether or not a state could secede from the new Union. The Founding Fathers, says Stampp, "left the dilemma of perpetuity to posterity." Paul C. Nagel, *One Nation Indivisible: The Union in American Thought, 1776–1861* (New York, 1964) is an excellent general treatment.

William P. Murphy, *The Triumph of Nationalism: State Sovereignty, the Founding Fathers, and the Making of the Constitution* (Chicago, 1967) is a persuasive study which argues that the passing of "dual federalism" in this century was in accord with the intent of the framers, "historically legitimate," and "part of the founders' grand design." Charles F. Hobson, "The Negative on State Laws: James Madison, the Constitution, and the Crisis of Republican Government," *WMQ*, 36 (1979), 215–235, shows Madison's support for a national legislative veto over state laws. Yehoshua Arieli, *Individualism and Nationalism in American Ideology* (Cambridge, Mass., 1964) is the classic study of the relationship between those concepts, and it gives the Constitution's influence on both extensive treatment. Also valuable is Hans Kohn, *American Nationalism: an Interpretative Essay* (New York, 1957).

Much attention has been given to the system of Federalism, a theme which has not lost its constitutional vitality. Notable analyses include Andrew C. McLaughlin, "The Background of American Federalism," *APSR*, 12 (1918),

215–240; Claude H. Van Tyne, "Sovereignty in the American Revolution: An Historical Study," *AHR*, 12 (1907), 529–545, an analysis of the division of sovereignty between Congress and the state governments prior to 1787; John C. Ranney, "The Bases of American Federalism," *WMQ*, 3 (1946), 1–35; William T. Hutchinson, "Unite to Divide; Divide to Unite: The Shaping of American Federalism," *Mississippi Valley Historical Review*, 46 (1959), 3–18, which analyzes the acceptance of the practice that new states were to be added on the basis of equality; M. J. C. Vial, *The Structure of American Federalism* (New York, 1961); Martin Diamond, *"The Federalist's* View of Federalism," in George C. S. Benson et al., eds., *Essays in Federalism* (Claremont, Calif., 1961), 21–64, and "What the Framers Meant by Federalism," in Robert Goldwin, ed., *A Nation of States: Essays on the American Federal System* (Chicago, 1963), 24–41; Herbert Johnson, "Toward a Reappraisal of the 'Federal' Government: 1783–1789," *American Journal of Legal History*, 8 (1964), 314–325; Walter Hartwell Bennett, *American Theories of Federalism* (University, Ala., 1964); Jean Yarbrough, "Federalism in the Foundation and Preservation of the American Republic," *Publius*, 6 (1976), 43–60; Jonathan Clark, "The Myth of Consolidating Federalists," *Historical Reflections*, 4 (1977), 111–135; Rozann Rothman, "The Ambiguity of American Federal Theory," *Publius*, 8 (1978), 103–122; S. Rufus Davis, *The Federal Principle: A Journey through Time in Quest of Meaning* (Berkeley, Calif., 1978); Harry N. Scheiber, "Federalism and the Constitution: The Original Understanding," in *American Law and Constitutional Order: Historical Perspectives* edited by Lawrence M. Friedman and Harry N. Scheiber (Cambridge, Mass., 1978), 85–98; Daniel J. Elazar, "Confederation and Federal Liberty," *Publius*, 12 (1982), 1–14; Jack P. Greene, "The Imperial Roots of American Federalism," *this Constitution*, No. 6 (1985), 4–11; Raoul Berger, *Federalism: The Founders' Design* (Norman, Okla., 1987); and Murray Dry, "Federalism and the Constitution: The Founders' Design and Contemporary Constitutional Law," *Constitutional Commentary*, 4 (1987), 233–250. Roy Lechtreck, "Who Created Whom? The Myth of State Sovereignty," *Midwest Quarterly*, 24 (1983), 182–187, is an unconvincing attempt to dispel "the myth."

The best contemporary statement of American constitutional theory is found in the Federalist essays of Hamilton, Madison, and Jay. Three excellent editions of this classic work are Jacob E. Cooke, ed., *The Federalist* (Middletown, Conn., 1961); Clinton Rossiter, ed., *The Federalist Papers* (New York, 1986); and Benjamin Fletcher Wright, ed., *The Federalist* (Cambridge, Mass., 1961).

On the authorship and meaning of the various Federalist essays, consult Frederick Mosteller and David L. Wallare, *Inference and Disputed Authorship: "The Federalist"* (Reading, Mass., 1964), which uses a statistical approach to examine the authors' verbal habits; Thomas E. Engeman et al., eds., *The Federalist Concordance* (Middletown, Conn., 1980), a guide to political vocabulary and usage; and Irving Brant, "Settling the Authorship of *The Federalist*," *AHR*, 67 (1961), 71–75.

General studies of this constitutional classic include Gottfried Dietze, *The Federalist: A Classic on Federalism and Free Government* (Baltimore, 1960); William F. Swindler, "The Letters of Publius," *American Heritage*, 12 (1961), 4–7, 92–97; David F. Epstein, *The Political Theory of the Federalist* (Chicago, 1984); Albert Furtwangler, *The Authority of Publius: A Reading of the Federalist Papers* (Ithaca, N.Y., 1984); Morton Gabriel White, *Philosophy, The Federalist and the Constitution* (New York, 1986); Daniel W. Howe, "The Political Psychology of *The Federalist*," *WMQ*, 44 (1987), 485–509; Jean Yarbrough, "The Federalist," *this Constitution*, No. 16 (1987), 4–9; James B. Williams and George W. Carey, "The Founding Fathers and *The Federalist*," *Modern Age*, 26 (1982), 315–317; William F. Campbell, "The Spirit of the Founding Fathers," *Modern Age*, 23 (1979), 246–250, a textual analysis of *The Federalist*; Richard B. Morris, *Witnesses at the Creation: Hamilton, Madison, Jay and the Constitution* (New York, 1985), which deals with the authors of the Federalist essays; and Charles R. Kesler, ed., *Saving the Revolution: The Federalist Papers and the American Founding* (New York, 1987), an anthology of scholarly essays by leading historians and political scientists.

Garry Wills, *Explaining America: The Federalist* (New York, 1981) stresses the influence of David Hume and the Scottish Enlightenment on Madison and Hamilton, a view rejected by George W. Carey, "On Inventing and Explaining America," *Modern Age*, 26 (1982), 122–135. Paul Peterson, "Republican Virtue and *The Federalist*: A Consideration of the Wills Thesis," *Benchmark*, 3 (1987), 87–95, criticizes Wills's notion of the role of public virtue.

Alpheus T. Mason, "*The Federalist*—A Split Personality," *AHR*, 57 (1952), 625–643, alleges an ideological divergence between Hamilton and Madison, a topic also analyzed by George W. Carey, "Publius—A Split Personality?" *Review of Politics*, 46 (1984), 5–22, which denies such a dualism.

Perhaps the leading student of *The Federalist* is Martin Diamond. Like the writings of Bancroft, Beard, and Jensen, his efforts have evoked praise and criticism. For a distillation of Diamond's views, see his "Democracy and *The Federalist*: A Reconsideration of the Framers' Intent," *APSR*, 52 (1959), 52–68; and "*The Federalist*," in Leo Strauss and Joseph Cropsey, eds., *History of Political Philosophy*, 2nd edition (Chicago, 1972), 631–651. Commentaries on Diamond's interpretations include Vincent Ostrom, "The Meaning of Federalism in *The Federalist*: A Critical Examination of the Diamond Theses," *Publius*, 15 (1986), 1–21; Paul Peterson, "Federalism at the American Founding: In Defense of the Diamond Theses," *Publius*, 15 (1986), 23–30; Patrick Riley, "Martin Diamond's View of *The Federalist*," *Publius*,

8 (1978), 71–101; William A. Schambra, "Martin Diamond's Doctrine of the American Regime," *Publius*, 8 (1978), 213–218; Jeane J. Kirkpatrick, "Martin Diamond and the American Idea of Democracy," *Publius*, 8 (1978), 7–31; and Herbert Garfinkel, "Martin Diamond: Teacher-Scholar of the Democratic Republic," *Publius*, 8 (1978), 123–127.

More specific examinations of Federalist theory include Benjamin F. Wright, "*The Federalist* on the Nature of Political Man," *Ethics*, 59 (1949), 1–31; James P. Scanlan, "*The Federalist* and Human Nature," *Review of Politics*, 21 (1959), 657–677; Edward J. Erler, "The Problem of Public Good in *The Federalist*," *Polity*, 13 (1981), 649–667; Thomas L. Pangle, "Federalists and the Idea of 'Virtue,' " *this Constitution*, No. 5 (1984), 19–25; B. Ramesh Babu, "The Ephemeral and the Eternal in *The Federalist*," *Indian Journal of American Studies*, 9 (1979), 3–14; Paul Peterson, "The Meaning of Republicanism in *The Federalist*," *Publius*, 9 (1979), 43–75; Jean Yarbrough, "Thoughts on *The Federalist*'s View of Representation," *Polity*, 12 (1979), 65–82; Heinz Eulau, "Polarity in Representational Federalism: A Neglected Theme of Political Theory," *Publius*, 3 (1973), 153–171; Robert J. Morgan, "Madison's Analysis of the Sources of Political Authority," *APSR*, 75 (1981), 613–625; and Albert Furtwangler, "Strategies of Candor in *The Federalist*," *Early American Literature*, 14 (1979), 91–109.

Federalist essay Number 10, dealing with such issues as factions, interest groups, majority rule, republicanism, and representation, has attracted more scholarly scrutiny than any of the other eighty-four essays. The most perceptive commentaries are Douglas Adair, "That Politics May Be Reduced to a Science: David Hume, James Madison, and the Tenth *Federalist*," *Huntington Library Quarterly*, 20 (1957), 343–360; Theodore Draper, "Hume & Madison: The Secrets of Federalist Paper No. 10," *Encounter* [Great Britain], 58 (1982), 34–47; James Conniff, "The Enlightenment and American Political Thought: A Study of the Origins of Madison's Federalist Number 10," *Political Theory*, 8 (1980), 381–402; Robert J. Morgan, "Madison's Theory of Representation in the Tenth Federalist," *Journal of Politics*, 36 (1974), 852–885; and Paul F. Bourke, "The Pluralist Reading of James Madison's Tenth Federalist," *Perspectives in American History*, 9 (1975), 271–295.

On Antifederalist thought and writing, consult Herbert J. Storing and Murray Dry, eds., *The Complete Anti-Federalist*, 7 vols. (Chicago, 1981) and its one-volume abridgment, *The Anti-Federalist* (Chicago, 1985). Storing's *What the Anti-Federalists Were For* (which is volume 1 of *The Complete Anti-Federalist*) is especially helpful. See also Murray Dry's brief but illuminating article "The Constitutional Thought of the Anti-Federalists," *this Constitution*, No. 16 (1987), 10–14.

The omissions of the "complete" Anti-Federalist are revealed by John P. Kaminski, "Antifederalism and the Perils of Homogenized History:

A Review Essay," *Rhode Island History*, 42 (1983), 30–37, and James H. Hutson, "The Incomplete Antifederalist," *Reviews in American History*, 11 (1983), 204–207. Both reviews point to several shortcomings in Storing and Dry's compilation and interpretation.

Briefer representative anthologies with useful editorial commentary are Morton Borden, ed., *The Anti-Federalist Papers* (East Lansing, Mich., 1965); John D. Lewis, ed., *Anti-Federalists versus Federalists: Selected Documents* (San Francisco, 1967); Alpheus T. Mason, *The States Rights Debate: Anti-Federalism and the Constitution*, 2nd edition (Englewood Cliffs, N.J., 1972); and W. B. Allen and Gordon Lloyd, eds., *The Essential Antifederalist* (Lanham, Md., 1985). In *Federalists and Antifederalists* (Madison, Wis., 1988), editors John P. Kaminski and Richard Leffler organize a selection of documents topically. Michael Lienesch, "In Defence of the Antifederalists," *History of Political Thought* [Great Britain], 4 (1983), 65–87, is a recent rehabilitation, while Charles F. Hobson, "The Tenth Amendment and the New Federalism of 1789," *Virginia Cavalcade*, 35 (1986), 110–121, and Steven R. Boyd, *The Politics of Opposition: Antifederalists and the Acceptance of the Constitution* (Millwood, N.Y., 1979) show how Antifederalists became reconciled to the new political system. For a longer perspective on the process of adjustment, consult Richard Buel, *Securing the Revolution: Ideology in American Politics* (Ithaca, N.Y., 1972).

Important aspects of the ratification effort are dealt with by William F. Swindler, "The Selling of the Constitution," *Supreme Court Historical Society Yearbook* (1980), 49–54, a brief survey of the pamphlet war and the battle in the press between Federalists and Antifederalists; Marvin Meyers, "Revolution and Founding: On Publius—Madison and the American Genesis," *Quarterly Journal of the Library of Congress*, 37 (1980), 192–200, which shows how Madison defended the Convention of 1787 against charges that it was a counterrevolutionary coup to overthrow the system established by the Revolution; Frederick R. Black, "The American Revolution as 'Yardstick' in the Debates on the Constitution, 1787–1788," *Proceedings of the American Philosophical Society*, 117 (1973), 162–185, which contends that both the supporters and the opponents of the Constitution claimed to be heirs of the American Revolution; and Thomas P. Slaughter, "The Tax Man Cometh: Ideological Opposition to Internal Taxes, 1760–1790," *WMQ*, 41 (1984), 566–591, and "Liberty and Taxes: The Early National Contest," *this Constitution*, No., 7 (1985), 11–16, which link the pre-Revolutionary American opposition to internal taxes to the "localists" or Antifederalists of 1787.

Frederick W. Marks III, "Foreign Affairs: A Winning Issue in the Campaign for Ratification of the United States Constitution, *PSQ*, 86 (1971), 444–469, and "American Pride, European Prejudice and the Constitution," *Historian*, 34 (1972), 579–595, emphasize national pride as a factor in the framers' efforts to forge a stronger union, a thesis stated more fully by Marks in *Independence on Trial: Foreign Affairs and the Making of the Constitution* (Baton Rouge, La., 1973). Jonathan Marshall, "Empire or Liberty: The Anti-federalists and Foreign Policy, 1787–1788," *Journal of Libertarian Studies*, 4 (1980), 233–254, also deals with this theme. Michael Lienesch, "Interpreting Experience: History, Philosophy, and Science in the American Constitutional Debates," *American Political Quarterly*, 11 (1983), 379–401, analyzes the intellectual conflicts between Federalists and Antifederalists; Isaac Kramnick, "The 'Great National Discussion': The Discourse of Politics in 1787," *WMQ*, 45 (1988), 3–32, examines their "modes of discourse"; Morton Borden, "Federalists, Antifederalists and Religious Freedom," *Journal of Church and State*, 21 (1979), 469–482, comments upon their differing positions in this sensitive sphere; Linda Grant De Pauw, "The Anticlimax of Antifederalism: The Abortive Second Convention Movement, 1788–89," *Prologue*, 2 (1970), 98–114, deals with a last-ditch plan by opponents to derail the Constitution; and Charles W. Roll, Jr., "We, Some of the People: Apportionment in the Thirteen State Conventions Ratifying the Constitution," *Journal of American History*, 56 (1969), 21–40, concludes that malapportionment benefited Federalists.

Staughton Lynd, "Abraham Yates's History of the Movement for the United States Constitution," *WMQ*, 20 (1963), 223–245, analyzes and reprints a 1789 Antifederalist tract that combined the allegation of counterrevolutionary conspiracy with the characterization of Federalists as an aristocracy in its explanation of the movement to adopt the Constitution. In Lynd's judgment, Yates's manuscript anticipated the Beard-Jensen interpretation.

On the genesis of the Bill of Rights from the ratification contest, consult Robert A. Rutland, *Birth of the Bill of Rights, 1776–1791* (Chapel Hill, N.C., 1955), by the biographer of George Mason; Irving Brant, *The Bill of Rights: Its Origin and Meaning* (Indianapolis, 1965), by the authoritative biographer of James Madison; Zechariah Chafee, Jr., *How Human Rights Got into the Constitution* (Boston, 1952); Richard L. Perry and John C. Cooper, eds., *Sources of Our Liberties: Documentary Origins of Individual Liberties in the United States Constitution and Bill of Rights* (Chicago, 1959); Rene de Visme Williamson, "Political Process or Judicial Process: The Bill of Rights and the Framers of the Constitution," *Journal of Politics*, 23 (1961), 199–211; and the appropriate sections of Bernard Schwartz, *The Bill of Rights: A Documentary History*, 2 vols. (Chicago, 1959) and *The Great Rights of Mankind: A History of the American Bill of Rights* (New York, 1977). Jon Kukla has compiled a set of essays on the Bill of Rights entitled *The Bill of Rights: A Lively Heritage* (Richmond, Va., 1987).

Anthologies

There are several valuable anthologies of constitutional essays. Some collections contain original pieces, while others reprint excerpts from longer, previously published works together with an introduction or evaluation by the editor. In the former category are John Franklin Jameson, ed., *Essays in the Constitutional History of the United States in the Formative Period, 1775–89* (Boston, 1889), which contains five well-researched essays, the most enduring of which has been Edward P. Smith's analysis of the movement towards a second constitutional convention; Conyers Read, ed., *The Constitution Reconsidered* (New York, 1938), which treats both the framing and the evolution of the document; Ralph A. Rossum and Gary L. McDowell, eds., *The American Founding: Politics, Statesmanship, and the Constitution* (Port Washington, N.Y., 1981); Richard Beeman, Stephen Botein, and Edward C. Carter II, eds., *Beyond Confederation: Origins of the Constitution and American National Identity* (Chapel Hill, N.C., 1987), a collection of learned essays on the founding by leading contemporary scholars; Leonard W. Levy and Dennis J. Mahoney, eds., *The Framing and Ratification of the Constitution* (New York, 1987), containing twenty-one original pieces; J. Jackson Barlow, Leonard W. Levy, and Ken Masugi, eds., *The American Founding: Essays on the Formation of the Constitution* (Westport, Conn., 1988); and Patrick T. Conley and John P. Kaminski, eds., *The Constitution and the States: The Role of the Original Thirteen in the Framing and Adoption of the Federal Constitution* (Madison, Wisc., 1988), which systematically explores an obvious but neglected topic.

Examples of excerpt anthologies include Jack P. Greene, ed., *The Reinterpretation of the American Revolution, 1763–1789* (New York, 1968), a collection that contains an excellent historiographical essay by Greene; Leonard W. Levy, ed., *Essays on the Making of the Constitution*, 2nd edition (New York, 1987); James Morton Smith, ed., *The Constitution* (New York, 1971); Robert F. Jones, ed., *The Formation of the Constitution* (New York, 1971); Gordon Wood, ed., *The Confederation and the Constitution: The Critical Issues* (Boston, 1973); and Earl Latham, ed., *The Declaration of Independence and the Constitution*, 3rd edition (Lexington, Mass., 1976). Kermit L. Hall, comp., *[Collected Essays on] United States Constitutional and Legal History*, 20 vols. (New York, 1987) is a massive reprint series of major scholarly articles; see especially vol. 2, *Formation and Ratification of the Constitution*.

Other worthwhile anthologies include Leonard W. Levy, Kenneth L. Karst, and Dennis J. Mahoney, eds., *Encyclopedia of the American Constitution*, 4 vols. (New York, 1986); Jack P. Greene, ed., *Encyclopedia of American Political History*, 3 vols. (New York, 1984); and Robert J. Janosik, ed., *Encyclopedia of the American Judicial System*, 3 vols. (New York, 1987). These volumes contain original essays by recognized scholars on such topics as "The Articles of Confederation," "Framing the Constitution," "Federalism," "The Commerce Clause," and the "Bill of Rights."

The American Historical Society and the American Political Science Association have joined to celebrate the bicentennial of the Constitution by forming Project '87 and publishing a quarterly journal entitled *this Constitution* (1983–), which has printed brief, popularly written articles on American constitutional development by major historians and political scientists. The most noteworthy and original of these essays have been cited separately in this bibliography.

Other journals and magazines have also published brief articles to swell this current outpouring of constitutional scholarship, and several have devoted special issues to the Constitution. Among those commemorative issues that contain important essays on the founding era are *National Forum*, 64 (Fall 1984); *Benchmark*, 3 (January-April 1987); *American History Illustrated*, 22 (Summer 1987); *The World & I*, (September 1987); *The Journal of American History*, 74 (December 1987); *Presidential Studies Quarterly*, 17 (Fall 1987); and *The William and Mary Quarterly*, 44 (July 1987).

The Constitution of the United States of America: Analysis and Interpretation (Washington, D.C., 1987) is the latest edition of a government publication that serves as the best one-volume legal treatise on its subject. Also excellent is Edward S. Corwin's *The Constitution and What It Means Today*, revised by Harold W. Chase and Craig R. Ducat (Princeton, N.J., 1978), a volume that has been revised thirteen times since its original edition in 1920 and is presently being updated in annual supplements. Alfred Kelly, Winifred Harbison, and Herman Betz, *The American Constitution: Its Origins and Development*, 6th edition (New York, 1983) is the best one-volume historical text.

Primary Sources

Published primary materials, general in scope, include Worthington C. Ford et al., eds., *Journals of the Continental Congress, 1774–1789*, 34 vols. (Washington, D.C., 1904–37); Edmund C. Burnett, ed., *Letters of Members of the Continental Congress*, 8 vols. (Washington, D.C., 1921–36), now in the process of being updated and enlarged in Paul H. Smith et al., eds., *Letters of Delegates to Congress, 1774–1789*, 12 vols. to date (Washington, D.C., 1976–); Francis Newton Thorpe, comp., *The Federal and State Constitutions, Colonial Charters, and Other Organic Laws of the States, Territories, and Colonies Now or Heretofore Forming the United States of America*, 7 vols. (Washington, D.C., 1909); Department of State, comp., *Documentary History of the Con-*

stitution of the United States of America, 5 vols. (Washington, D.C., 1894–1905); and Charles C. Tansill, ed., *Documents Illustrative of the Formation of the Union* (Washington, D.C., 1927), still the best one-volume compendium.

The standard source book on the convention itself is Max Farrand, ed., *The Records of the Federal Convention of 1787*, 4 vols., revised edition (New Haven, 1937) and James H. Hutson, ed., *Supplement to Max Farrand's "The Records of the Federal Convention of 1787"* (New Haven, 1987).

Several delegates took notes on the proceedings of this secret conclave. By far the most revealing are those in James Madison, *Notes of Debates in the Federal Convention of 1787*. The best of the many editions of this source were prepared by Galliard Hunt and James Brown Scott (Washington, D.C., 1920), Charles Tansill in *Documents Illustrative of the Formation of the Union of American States* (Washington, D.C., 1927), and Adrienne Koch (Athens, Ohio, 1966). For a comparison of these texts and allusions to others, see the review of the Koch edition by Patrick T. Conley, *The Catholic Historical Review*, 55 (1969), 536–537.

Other delegate accounts include James H. Hutson, "Robert Yates' Notes on the Constitutional Convention of 1787: Citizen Genet's Edition," *Quarterly Journal of the Library of Congress*, 35 (1978), 173–182; Joseph R. Strayer, ed., *The Delegate from New York; or, Proceedings of the Federal Convention of 1787, from the Notes of John Lansing, Jr.* (Princeton, N.J., 1939); James H. Hutson, "Pierce Butler's Records of the Federal Constitutional Convention," *Quarterly Journal of the Library of Congress*, 37 (1980), 64–73; and James H. Hutson, "John Dickinson at the Federal Constitutional Convention," *WMQ*, 60 (1983), 256–262. For a comparison of the Madison and Yates accounts, consult Arnold A. Rogow, "The Federal Convention: Madison and Yates," *AHR*, 60 (1955), 323–335.

The best brief general documentary collections are Page Smith, *The Constitution: A Documentary and Narrative History* (New York, 1978), which also contains extensive interpretation and editorial commentary; Samuel Eliot Morison, ed., *Sources and Documents Illustrating the American Revolution, 1764–1788* (Oxford, England, 1929); Winton U. Solberg, ed., *The Federal Convention and the Formation of the Union of the American States* (Indianapolis, 1958); Alfred Young, ed., *The Debate over the Constitution, 1787–1789* (Chicago, 1965); Jack P. Greene, ed., *Colonies to Nation, 1763–1789: A Documentary History of the American Revolution* (New York, 1967); Richard B. Morris, ed., *Basic Documents on the Confederation and Constitution* (Princeton, N.J., 1970); Charles S. Hyneman and Donald S. Lutz, comps., *American Political Writing during the Founding Era, 1760–1805*, 2 vols. (Indianapolis, 1983), which collects and reprints numerous political tracts, public letters, and pamphlets illustrative of American political thought; J. R. Pole, ed., *The Revolution in America, 1754–1788: Documents and Commentaries* (Stanford, Calif., 1970);

Michael Kammen, ed., *The Origins of the American Constitution: A Documentary History* (New York, 1986); and J. R. Pole, ed., *The American Constitution, For and Against: The Federalist and Anti-Federalist Papers* (New York, 1987). Philip B. Kurland and Ralph Lerner, eds., *The Founders' Constitution*, 5 vols. (Chicago, 1987) is a large, impressive compilation of contemporary documents and writings by the founders that explicate each provision of the original Constitution and the twelve amendments proposed as the Bill of Rights.

Collections of primary materials pertaining to ratification, other than Herbert J. Storing's seven-volume *The Complete Anti-Federalist* (cited above), are both dated and incomplete. The standard sources have been Jonathan Elliott, ed., *The Debates, Resolutions, and Other Proceedings in Convention on the Adoption of the Federal Constitution*, 5 vols. (Washington, D. C., 1836); Paul Leicester Ford, ed., *Essays on the Constitution of the United States Published during Its Discussion by the People, 1787–1788* (Brooklyn, N.Y., 1892); and *Pamphlets on the Constitution of the United States Published during Its Discussion by the People, 1787–1788* (Brooklyn, N.Y., 1888). Merrill Jensen, John P. Kaminski, and Gaspare J. Saladino, eds., *The Documentary History of the Ratification of the Constitution*, 20 vols. projected (Madison, Wis., 1976–) will supersede all previous collections when it is completed by the Center for the Study of the American Constitution. Ten volumes have been released to date.

Bibliographies: Listings and Essays

Detailed bibliographical guides pertaining to the Constitution-making process are Kermit L. Hall, comp., *A Comprehensive Bibliography of American Constitutional and Legal History*, 5 vols. (Milwood, N.Y., 1984), whose listings cover the whole range of American constitutional development, and Dwight T. Smith, ed., *Era of the American Revolution: A Bibliography* (Santa Barbara, Calif., 1975) and Suzanne Robitaille Ontiveros, ed., *The Dynamic Constitution: A Historical Bibliography* (Santa Barbara, Calif., 1986), reference volumes that reprint the descriptions of scholarly articles that appeared in *America: History and Life*. Ronald M. Gephart, comp., *Revolutionary America, 1763–1789: A Bibliography*, 2 vols. (Washington, D.C., 1984), Alpheus T. Mason and D. Grier Stephenson, Jr., comps., *American Constitutional Development* (Arlington Heights, Ill., 1977), and E. James Ferguson, comp., *Confederation, Constitution, and Early National Period, 1781–1815* (Northbrook, Ill., 1975) are mere listings by category. The Gephart compilation is a guide to the more important printed primary and secondary works in the Library of Congress' collections listed in Library of Congress catalog form. Chapters 9 and 10, on the Confederation and the Constitution respectively, contain 1,016 entries.

Jack P. Greene, *A Bicentennial Bookshelf: Historians Analyze the Constitutional Era* (Philadelphia, 1986) is the most useful bibliographic essay yet written on its topic, while Richard B. Bernstein, "Charting the Bicentennial," *Columbia Law Review*, 87 (1987), 1565–1624, is a learned and provocative assessment of very recently published works, including documentary collections.

Jack P. Greene, *The Intellectual Heritage of the Constitutional Era— The Delegates' Library* (Philadelphia, 1986) inventories the works upon which the founders themselves relied in developing their political and constitutional theories and analyzes the intellectual world of the framers through a discussion of the books they read. This essay also contains a survey of British theoretical influences upon the framers' thought—the Lockean liberal tradition, Coke's jurisprudential tradition, the literature of political economy and improvement represented by Daniel Defoe, the civic humanist tradition of the Whig libertarians, the literature of the Enlightenment, and the Scottish moral and historical tradition epitomized by David Hume. This topic is beyond the scope of this bibliographical essay. Robert A. Rutland, *"Well Acquainted with Books": The Founding Framers of 1787* (Washington, D.C., 1987) employs an approach similar to Greene's impressive survey.

INDEX

Illustrations are enumerated in this index. Short biographical sketches of individuals accompany each illustration in the text.

NOTES ON CONTRIBUTORS

DR. ALAN VANCE BRICELAND grew up in Towson, Maryland, and Sparta, New Jersey, and received his A.B. from the College of William and Mary and his Ph.D. from Duke University. He is an associate professor in the Department of History and Geography of Virginia Commonwealth University. Dr. Briceland is the author of *Westward from Virginia: The Exploration of the Virginia-Carolina Frontier, 1650–1710* (1987), and his articles on political controversies during the Early National period have appeared in the *Journal of American Legal History*, the *Journal of Church and State*, the *Journal of Presbyterian History*, the *Alabama Review*, *Vermont History*, and the *Pennsylvania Magazine of History and Biography*.

DR. CHRISTOPHER COLLIER is professor of history at the University of Connecticut and Connecticut state historian. He has published many scholarly and popular articles on the Revolutionary and Early National eras in the field of Connecticut history. He has been editor of the Public Records of the State of Connecticut and is the author of *Roger Sherman's Connecticut: Yankee Politics and the American Revolution* (1971). With his brother, James L. Collier, he is the author also of *Decision in Philadelphia* (1986), the story of the Constitutional Convention of 1787.

DR. PATRICK T. CONLEY holds an A.B. from Providence College, an M.A. and Ph.D. from the University of Notre Dame, and a J.D. from Suffolk University Law School. He has published eight books, including *Democracy in Decline: Rhode Island's Constitutional Development, 1775–1841* (1977) and *An Album of Rhode Island History, 1636–1986* (1986), and more than a dozen scholarly articles for history, law, and political science journals. The youngest person ever elevated to the rank of full professor at Providence College, Dr. Conley also practices law, runs a used and rare book firm, and manages a real estate development business. He has served as chairman of the Rhode Island Bicentennial Commission (ri76), chairman and founder of the Providence Heritage Commission, chairman and founder of the Rhode Island Publications Society, and general editor of the Rhode Island Ethnic Heritage

Pamphlet Series. In 1977 he founded the Rhode Island Heritage Commission as a successor organization to ri76. Presently Dr. Conley is chairman of the Rhode Island Bicentennial [of the Constitution] Foundation and vice chairman of the U.S. Constitution Council.

DR. JERE DANIELL is professor of history at Dartmouth College. He has published two books on early New Hampshire, *Experiment in Republicanism* (1970) and *Colonial New Hampshire* (1981). A former trustee of the New Hampshire Historical Society, he serves on the state Bicentennial Commission on the United States Constitution. Professor Daniell, who comes from an old New Hampshire family, was raised in Millinocket, Maine. He graduated from the local high school, Phillips Exeter Academy, and Dartmouth College; and he received his Ph.D. from Harvard in 1964. Daniell lectures throughout New England on a variety of regional topics, including ratification of the Constitution.

DR. PAUL DOUTRICH earned a B.A. and a Ph.D. at the University of Kentucky and an M.A. at the Pennsylvania State University. He is currently employed as an associate historian at the Pennsylvania Historical and Museum Commission, where he is responsible for coordinating numerous statewide history projects as well as serving as an expert on colonial and Revolutionary Pennsylvania. In addition, Dr. Doutrich teaches history at Franklin and Marshall College and at the Harrisburg campus of the Pennsylvania State University. Dr. Doutrich has published several pieces about Pennsylvania's role in the making and ratification of the Constitution and regularly speaks about the topic throughout the state.

JOHN J. FOX graduated from Pittsfield (Massachusetts) High School in 1949. After service during the Korean War, he entered North Adams State Teachers College, from which he graduated in 1959. In 1964, upon completing graduate work at Lehigh University, he joined the history faculty of Salem State College. Founder and past president of the New England Association of Oral History, he currently is on the executive board of the national Oral History Association. He has served two terms on the board of trustees of the Essex Institute and is a past vice president of the Bay State Historical League. He is the director of Salem State College Summer Institute for the Study of Local History.

DR. HAROLD HANCOCK, late emeritus professor of history at Otterbein College in Ohio, earned his A.B. at Wesleyan University (1936), his M.A. at Harvard (1938), and his Ph.D. at the Ohio State University (1955). He wrote on a variety of areas in Delaware history, including such eighteenth-century topics as the American Revolution and the role of the loyalists in that conflict. Dr. Hancock also prepared for publication introductory material for two volumes of the proceedings of the Delaware Assembly from 1770 to 1792. He was writing a book on social and cultural life in Confederation-era Delaware at the time of his death in July 1987.

DR. JOHN P. KAMINSKI is the director of The Center for the Study of the American Constitution at the University of Wisconsin–Madison. He is the editor of *The Documentary History of the Ratification of the Constitution* and has written and spoken widely on the Constitution. Dr. Kaminski earned his B.A. and M.A. at Illinois State University and his Ph.D. at the University of Wisconsin in 1972. He serves on the Wisconsin and the Dane County Bicentennial commissions. In 1986–87 he was president of the Association for Documentary Editing.

MARY R. MURRIN is a research associate at the New Jersey Historical Commission, an agency in the Department of State. Murrin holds a B.A. and an M.A. in American history from Washington University in St. Louis. She is the author of *To Save This State from Ruin: New Jersey and the Creation of the United States Constitution, 1776–1789* and *New Jersey Historical Manuscripts: A Guide to Collections in the State*, both published by the commission in 1987. She has also edited a number of publications for the agency, including *Religion in New Jersey Life before the Civil War* (1985) and *Women in New Jersey History* (1985), and she has coedited *Conflict at Monmouth Court House* (1983).

DR. JEROME NADELHAFT is professor of history at the University of Maine-Orono. He received his B.A. from Queens College (New York) in 1959 and his M.A. and Ph.D. from the University of Wisconsin–Madison in 1961 and 1965. He taught three years at the State University of New York–Geneseo before moving to Maine in 1967. Professor Nadelhaft is the author of *The Disorders of War: The Revolution in South Carolina* (Orono, Maine, 1981).

DR. ALBERT BERRY SAYE, a native of Georgia, is the emeritus Richard B. Russell professor of political science at the University of Georgia, where he taught history and political science from 1934 to 1936 and from 1939 to 1980. Dr. Saye graduated from Emory University (B.A., 1932), the University of Georgia (M.A., 1934), the University of Dijon, France (diplôme de français, degrè supèrieur, 1938), and Harvard University (Ph.D., 1941). He is the author of twelve books, including *A Constitutional History of Georgia* (1970), *Georgia: Government and History* (3rd ed., 1981), and two widely used and highly acclaimed textbooks: *American Constitutional Law* (3rd ed., 1979) and *Principles of American Government* (10th ed., 1986). In 1982 he was awarded a Fulbright professorship to lecture in India on the American governmental system. Presently Dr. Saye is a Georgia trustee of the U.S. Constitution Council.

DR. PAUL J. SCUDIERE, who serves as the immediate past president of the United States Constitution Council, is the state historian of New York, administrative officer of the New York State Commission on the Bicentennial of the United States Constitution, director of science and historical research and collections at the New York State Museum in Albany, New York, and adjunct professor of historical agency administration at the State University of New York at Albany, from which he received his doctorate. As state historian, Dr. Scudiere administers programs for over 1,400 local government historians and 1,500 museums, historical societies, and related cultural institutions in New York State. He has written and spoken extensively on issues related to New York history and cultural agency management.

DR. GREGORY STIVERSON is a native of Washington State. He did his undergraduate work at the University of Washington, where he graduated Phi Beta Kappa, and his graduate work at the Johns Hopkins University, where he was a Ford Foundation fellow and a Woodrow Wilson fellow. He received his Ph.D. in American history in 1973. Dr. Stiverson has been employed as a research associate for the Colonial Williamsburg Foundation and since 1975 has been the assistant state archivist of Maryland at the state archives. Since 1985 he has also served as director of the Maryland Office of the Bicentennial of the U.S. Constitution. He is the author or coauthor of numerous books and articles on Maryland history, agricultural history, and literary culture in early America, including *William Paca: A Biography* (1976), *Poverty in a Land of Plenty: Tenancy in Eighteenth Century Maryland* (1977), and *A Biographical Dictionary of the Maryland Legislature, 1635–1789* (1979–85). He is a coauthor of the Maryland history high school textbook, *Maryland: A History of Its People* (1986). Dr. Stiverson is a Maryland trustee of the U.S. Constitution Council.

DR. ALAN D. WATSON, a native North Carolinian, is currently professor of history at the University of North Carolina at Wilmington, where he has been teaching since 1971. In addition to editorial service for the *North Carolina Historical Review*, the North Carolina Bicentennial Commission, and the American Quadricentennial Commission, he has published widely in such journals as *The William and Mary Quarterly*, *North Carolina Historical Review*, *South Carolina Historical Magazine*, *Journal of Negro History*, and *South Atlantic Quarterly*. His monographs include several North Carolina county histories, *Society in Colonial North Carolina* (1975), and *The North Carolina Experience* (1984), coedited with Lindley S. Butler.